Baseball's Union Asso

Baseball's Union Association

The Short, Strange Life
of a 19th-Century Major League

JUSTIN MCKINNEY

McFarland & Company, Inc., Publishers

Jefferson, North Carolina

This book has undergone peer review.

ISBN (print) 978-1-4766-8060-6
ISBN (ebook) 978-1-4766-4736-4

LIBRARY OF CONGRESS AND BRITISH LIBRARY
CATALOGUING DATA ARE AVAILABLE

Library of Congress Control Number 2022049942

Front cover: The 1883 Washington Nationals team,
whose players appeared in the Union Association the following year
(photograph courtesy of the DC History Center, with digital restoration by Carson Lorey).

Printed in the United States of America

*McFarland & Company, Inc., Publishers
Box 611, Jefferson, North Carolina 28640
www.mcfarlandpub.com*

For Fiona, who enabled this strange adventure,
and Carroll, who inspired it.

Acknowledgments

This book could not have been completed without the steadfast patience, love, and support of my wonderful wife, Fiona. I am grateful for her kindness and encouragement.

Thank you to my mom and dad, and my brothers David and Mike, each of whom inspired and encouraged my curiosity and the value of pursuing my interests. To Bac Bac and the Mak family for being supportive and encouraging my writing.

This book would not be possible without all the marvelous work done by SABR and its members. By getting involved with the gracious and encouraging Mark Fimoff and Bill Hickman of the SABR Pictorial History Research Committee, I became obsessed with the obscure figures of 19th-century baseball. As I located photos and woodcuts, I also began uncovering the players' lives, leading to friendships with Peter Morris and Bill Carle of the SABR Biographical Research Committee. Peter and Bill have been incredibly generous with their time and insight.

The support of all of these folks has been a tremendous encouragement.

By uncovering the stories of the forgotten figures that litter the Union Association, I soon discovered I was building enough research materials and knowledge to work on this book. Thank you, SABR, for being such a great organization.

Thank you to Richard Hershberger for his tremendous collection of 19th-century newspaper clippings, which made this work much richer and more manageable to pull off than it might have been otherwise. Immense gratitude to John Thorn for being willing to provide feedback and answer emails (imagine that: John Thorn answering my emails). Thanks to Jeffrey Kittel, the veritable expert on nineteenth-century baseball in St. Louis, who answered some of my questions. Thank you to Peter Mancuso and the folks in the SABR 19th Century Committee as well. Thank you to Carson Lorey and Craig Brown as well for help with image procurement and research.

Thank you to the National Baseball Hall of Fame librarians, who fielded my questions and digitized player files. A final thank you to the folks at newspapers.com and genealogybank.com, who put out so much great content and made this work possible.

Table of Contents

Preface

What do you think of when you hear the name "the Union Association"? If you are like most baseball fans, you have probably never heard the words. If you know a little about baseball history, you might have encountered the otherworldly batting line compiled by Fred Dunlap while searching on baseball-reference.com or flipping through an old baseball encyclopedia. Dunlap's 1884 truly stands out; after all, he hit .412 while leading the Union Association in virtually every offensive category. If Dunlap's line piqued your interest, maybe you dug a little deeper and found out about his team that year, the St. Louis Maroons, who ran away with the pennant thanks to a 94–19 record. You might have done some more searching and encountered the story of Henry V. Lucas, the Maroons owner and president of the league, who built a team of stars to dominate the circuit. Maybe you came across the short-lived Altoona Mountain Citys or the St. Paul Saints. The point of all this is to say that the Union Association is virtually unknown to all but the most intrepid of baseball nerds.

A full-length book exists on virtually every aspect of baseball and its history. Therefore, it came as a great surprise to me that no one had written a complete account of the Union Association, the short-tenured major league that lasted for exactly one season 136 years ago. To anyone curious about the league, there is a paucity of information. You can consult the immeasurably valuable site baseball-reference.com and see league standings and player records, but that will not tell you the whole story. There have been published histories of the league dating back to Al Spink's description of the league in his seminal book *The National Game*, published in 1910. Harold and Dorothy Seymour's account of the league in 1960's *Baseball: The Early Years* revisited the league and provided the first detailed reporting on the behind-the-scenes machinations that brought the league into existence. Historians such as Preston Orem compiled notes on the league using contemporary sources. At the same time, intrepid researchers like Lee Allen, Tom Shea, and Bill Haber sought out biographical details of some of the obscure figures who populated Union Association box scores nearly 100 years before.

The creation of the Society for American Baseball Research in 1971 opened the door to further scholarship. Bill James, perhaps the most important thinker and researcher in baseball history, wrote an incisive deconstruction of the Union Association's major league credentials that appears in his indispensable work *The New Bill James Historical Baseball Abstract*. This likely remains the best-known written work on the league, a meticulous and forceful dismissal claiming that the Union Association's classification as a major league was a mistake. Through his extensive research on nineteenth-century baseball's deepest and darkest corners, David Nemec has provided invaluable insight into the Union Association and its many participants. Others have contributed essays to various journals on the topic. Accounts of the league have also appeared in books focused on other subjects. Surprisingly, to date, no one has taken on the task of writing a complete account focused entirely upon the tumultuous single-year existence of the Union Association. This book is my humble attempt to do just that.

The goal of this book is to convince you that the Union Association is more than just Fred Dunlap, Henry Lucas, and a debate about league quality. It is about the spiteful magnates, disgruntled superstars, hungry youngsters, drunks, screw-ups, castoffs, anonymities, future stars, never-weres, hangers-on, and fanatics who did battle with the baseball establishment. It is the story of men who loved baseball and liberty and fought to make a dream happen. It is the story of 12 teams in 13 cities and one of the most bizarre seasons in baseball history.

A few notes on this book:

1. All statistics are from baseball-reference.com. I used wins, losses, and ERA, even though those stats were not used in the 1880s, to provide context for readers. I also use advanced stats like OPS+ (on-base percentage + slugging percentage), ERA+, and WAR (wins about replacement) to place player performance in the context of the rest of the league.

2. Team names. The team nicknames provided by most sources for nineteenth-century baseball clubs are often fabricated and completely inaccurate. Many clubs of the era did not adhere to the current terminology, which typically includes a club's home city and official nickname (i.e., Boston Red Sox, Los Angeles Dodgers). For the duration of the 1880s, clubs were most commonly associated with their city. The Boston National League club of the era might be referred to alternatively as "the Bostons," as "the Boston Nationals," or officially as "the Boston Baseball Association," but seldom as "the Beaneaters."

    In some cases, mainly where the club had ties to a social or an athletic club, a team would adopt what to modern eyes would be a nickname. The Philadelphia club of the American Association bore the name the Athletics in partial homage to the famed amateur and professional clubs that had borne the name from 1860 to 1876. The club was commonly listed as the Athletics in the box scores and media. Of the 12 clubs in the Union Association, only the Philadelphia Keystones and the Washington Nationals featured an official nickname. All other clubs in the circuit were almost exclusively referred to by their city (i.e., the Wilmingtons, the Altoonas) or with the sobriquet the Unions (i.e., Boston Unions, St. Louis Unions) to differentiate themselves from rival clubs in the National League and the American Association. For this book, I am using the terminology used to discuss the teams at the time.

3. Personal names. I use the spelling provided on baseball-reference.com. This

decision is not ideal, as many people featured in the book used different spellings of their names than what is currently listed on baseball-reference. com. For example, Ed and Emory Hengel went by the spelling Hengle, and Ed even signed his name with that spelling. Pat Deasley, the Brown Stockings catcher, was usually referred to in contemporary sources as Tom, but now is listed as Pat. For the sake of consistency, I will use the modern standard since it will help you in case you want to research these men. When quoting contemporary sources, I will use the spelling featured in the source.

4. What is a Major League? In 1968, the Special Baseball Records Committee met to decide on a host of issues related to baseball's historical recordkeeping. A key issue discussed was what leagues in the game's history could be considered major. With the publication of the first comprehensive baseball encyclopedia slated for release in 1969, this was a pivotal matter to decide. The goal was to standardize the record book and eliminate inconsistencies where possible. The committee was co-chaired by Robert Holbrook, executive assistant to the president of the American League, and David Grote, director of public relations for the National League. Other members included Lee Allen, historian of the Baseball Hall of Fame, Joseph Reichler, director of public relations of the office of the Commissioner of Baseball, and Jack Lang, secretary-treasurer of the Baseball Writers Association of America.[1] After much deliberation, the committee determined that for the purposes of baseball's record book, the following leagues would be considered major: the National League (1876–present); the American League (1901–present); the American Association (1882–91); the Union Association (1884); the Players' League (1890); and the Federal League (1914–15). Somewhat controversially, the National Association, 1871–1875, was kept off of the list "due to its erratic schedule and procedures" despite its historical significance as the first professional baseball league.[2]

In the decades since, there has been much debate about this decision to recognize the Union Association as a major league. The single season of the Union Association also featured an erratic schedule and was undeniably the weakest league of those added. This conversation has been reignited by the December 2020 decision by Major League Baseball to add seven twentieth-century Negro Leagues to the list of officially designated Major Leagues: the Negro National League (I) (1920–1931); the Eastern Colored League (1923–1928); the American Negro League (1929); the East-West League (1932); the Negro Southern League (1932); the Negro National League (II) (1933–1948); and the Negro American League (1937–1948).[3] This laudable act cannot amend the historical wrongs of the past, but hopefully it will bring more light to a significant and overlooked part of baseball's history. With these seven new leagues added to the official Major League record book, it is worth discussing why the Union Association was granted major league status in 1969.

The primary reason would seem to lie with two men, Al Spink and Ernest Lanigan. Spink was the St. Louis–born founder of *The Sporting News* and later claimed to have started his career in baseball working for the St. Louis Unions as a secretary for owner Henry V. Lucas. Spink's 1910 book, *The National Game*, devoted several pages to the famed Union nine, who won the first and only UA pennant. His book also featured portrait photos of several players from the club. Spink was one of the most respected journalists in baseball, and his aggrandizing of the exploits of the St. Louis Unions helped preserve their legacy.

Ernest Lanigan was a nephew of Spink and began working for his uncle as a teenager. Given that he grew up in St. Louis, it seems very likely that he shared his uncle's admiration for the St. Louis Unions. Lanigan became a highly respected sportswriter and statistician, credited with inventing RBI (runs batted in) and CS (caught stealing) as official statistics. He published the first attempt at a baseball encyclopedia in 1922, *The Baseball Cyclopedia*, which attempted to document every major league player of the 20th century to that point. In his write-up of the history of baseball, like his uncle before him, Lanigan devoted time to discussing the St. Louis club and the UA, positioning the league as a threat to the National League and American Association. Lanigan would later become the curator and historian of the National Baseball Hall of Fame and Museum. In 1959, Lanigan was replaced by Lee Allen, a sportswriter and gifted researcher and historian who later served on the Special Baseball Rules Committee in 1968–69. This lineage of Spink brothers to Lanigan to Allen would seem to be the primary source of advocacy for the UA's major league status.

I believe that both the Union Association and the 1871–1875 version of the National Association should be considered major leagues. I will not spend much time refuting Bill James's arguments that the Union Association should not be classified as a major league. He is Bill James, after all. I will say that I recognize the standard argument against the Union Association as having validity. There is no question that the quality of play in the Union was lower than any other major league, aside from perhaps the earliest seasons of the National Association. The league was top heavy, with the best players confined primarily to the champion St. Louis and second-place Cincinnati clubs. The league was unstable, and numerous teams did not complete their schedules. These are each demonstrable facts.

What makes the Union Association classification as a major league valid is intent. The intent of the Union Association in its formation and execution is what makes it a major league. The new league formed in the fall of 1883. The league's organizers intended to put clubs in major league cities and compete with them. Club owners tried to sign away major league players to build the strongest teams possible. More tellingly, the response of the two established major leagues, the National League and the American Association, was to attempt to stop the new league from succeeding. They achieved this through hastily expanding to potential UA markets, blocking the new league from putting teams there, and weaponizing the reserve rule to prevent their star players from jumping. The established major leagues saw it as a threat and tried to stop it. This fact alone makes the Union Association a major league.

"As we turned to take our places, Carroll, who was a big fellow, paralyzed Capt. Phil [Baker],
by innocently inquiring:
"'Where is left field, Mr. Baker?'
"He had never played a game in his life! Mike Scanlon had given him a whole big one hun-
dred instead of dismissing him with a blessing. Mike turned him away to:
"'Go back to Pennsylvania and shovel coal the rest of your life.'"

Former Washington Nationals pitcher Alex Voss recounting an event during the
Washington Nationals pre-season in April 1884 (*The Sporting News*, February 2,
1889).

1

◇◇◇◇◇◇◇◇◇◇◇◇◇

Al Pratt's Association

"The new Base Ball Association organized in this city may or may not be a success, but in its competition with the older associations it will have right and popularity on its side. By declaring in favor of the abolition of the arbitrary eleven men reserve rule, it has secured the good will of every manly base ball player or patron of the National game in the United States."—*Pittsburgh Times* upon the formation of the Union Association on September 12, 1883

As the 1883 season came to a close, professional baseball was booming like never before. Economic depression had stalled the game's professional growth at the end of the previous decade.[1] As the economy rebounded, so did professional baseball. Attendance was at an all-time high. The pennant races in the established National League (NL) and the upstart American Association were hard fought with multiple teams in a dogfight for glory. The ugliness of 1882 was seemingly over. The American Association (AA) had begun play that year as the bawdy rival to the stodgy National League. The AA vowed to play games on Sundays and sell beer at their games. They charged 25 cents admission rather than the standard 50 cents required to attend NL games. These tactics opened the game up to lower-class fans. The AA put clubs in previously disgraced National League cities: Cincinnati, Philadelphia, Louisville, and St. Louis. Cincinnati was excommunicated from the NL following the 1880 season for selling alcohol at games and opposing the newly formed reserve rule. The Philadelphia club, representing the nation's second-largest city, was kicked out after the NL's inaugural season in 1876 when they failed to complete a costly late-season western road trip. Louisville and St. Louis were removed from the NL after their clubs became embroiled in gambling and game-fixing scandals that marred the 1877 season.

The AA debuted on May 2, 1882, as a six-team circuit. The inaugural rosters were composed primarily of castoffs from the National League and the Eastern Championship Association, another six-team circuit containing virtually every top eastern player outside of the National League. No players who NL clubs had reserved appeared on AA rosters. For the better part of the season, the two leagues authored an uneasy coexistence. This unspoken peace came to a crashing halt in September of that year. At the National League meeting on September 22, the Detroit club's president and owner, William G. Thompson, who also happened to be the city's mayor, provided some alarming news. He informed the league directors that the AA was

7

after their players and that the rival league could pay out higher salaries since they had clubs in large markets. Thompson claimed the NL was bogged down by struggling clubs in Worcester, Massachusetts, and Troy, New York, who simply could not afford a professional nine. He noted that a number of the NL's top players had agreed to jump to the new league in 1883. This list included his star catcher, Charlie Bennett, and first baseman Lon Knight, who had already signed contracts for 1883 with the Allegheny club of Pittsburgh. Other NL stars such as Buck Ewing, Mickey Welch, Jim Whitney, Ed Williamson, Charles "Old Hoss" Radbourn, and Jerry Denny had also reportedly signed with AA clubs. Thompson suggested that the five-man reserve rule had done nothing to prevent the signings.

The NL established the reserve rule after the 1879 season.[2] The initial iteration of the reserve rule would allow NL clubs to list up to five players on their rosters that other teams could not sign. Thompson rightfully noted that since the American Association was ignoring the rule entirely, any power it had was moot. The disgruntled owner also voiced a surprisingly pro-player stance, arguing that the rule was unjust, since unscrupulous managers used it to prevent players from improving their prospects.[3]

This flagrant opposition to the reserve rule meant that any player on a National League roster and even those blacklisted by the NL were fair game for the embryonic AA. The motivations of the new rival were clear. They planned to sign the best available talent and establish their brand of baseball in markets that had been neglected for years by the NL.

Sensing the threat to the status quo, NL clubs soon responded in kind. Boston signed catcher Pat Deasley from St. Louis and outfielder Lewis Dickerson from Pittsburgh while the League threatened NL contract jumpers with a blacklist. The blacklist had proven to be a powerful tool to enforce codes of behavior amongst players. Owners wielded power to ban players for infractions ranging from drunkenness, fixing ball games, contract jumping, or even holding out for more money. Despite the presence of the AA, the blacklist still held power and caused a number of the would-be contract jumpers to renege on their deals. In one case, Charlie Bennett's return to Detroit resulted in a lawsuit by the Allegheny club, which the catcher won. The American Association held its annual convention on December 13 and 14, 1882. A key point of discussion was what to do about the blacklist and the contract jumpers. The Association decided to create its own blacklist. This blacklist would include any NL players who had signed AA contracts and then reneged on them.

The threat of legal trouble and raising player salaries had disrupted the stability of the NL while also taxing the resources of the AA. It was also untenable from a financial perspective to wage war for players, since it would increase salaries at a rapid rate. It was equally problematic for club managers, who did not know if their players' contracts would be respected or disregarded.

After several months of discussion and negotiation between the warring leagues, peace was reached at the Fifth Avenue Hotel in New York City on February 17, 1883, just a couple of months before the start of the coming baseball season. On this date, the heads of the two major leagues, along with members of the newly formed Northwestern League (NWES), signed what came to be known as the

National Agreement, also known as the Tripartite Agreement. The agreement laid down five ground rules that the directors of each of the 24 clubs across the three leagues would adhere to regarding player contracts. First, players would remain under contract to their current teams until November 1, unless otherwise expelled or released. Second, any player contracts would have to be forwarded to the secretary of each league, who would then notify the other league secretaries. Third, any player expelled or blacklisted by one of the 24 clubs in the agreement would not be eligible to sign a contract unless reinstated by their respective association. Fourth, the reserve list would be expanded to 11 for each club, with a minimum salary of $1,000, to be submitted on September 20. Fifth, the launch of an Arbitration Committee consisting of three members of each association. The committee would oversee any dispute over contracts or players.

As a show of conciliation, the decision was also made to reinstate all blacklisted players who were currently signed to a contract by any of the clubs in the agreement. All of the attempted contract jumpers were reinstated, restoring them to their original clubs. This decision also paved the way for a number of blacklisted National League players to be fully reinstated. Among those reinstated was Charley Jones, a hard-hitting outfielder, who the NL had banned following a dispute over back pay that he was rightfully owed in 1880. The National Agreement also had the dual benefit of increasing roster stability and controlling players' salaries. Disgruntled players could no longer jump from team to team, and impetuous owners would be less likely to engage in salary wars.

The National Agreement created a peaceable path forward for both the National League and the American Association in terms of players and contracts. That did not mean that the war was over. In many ways, it was just starting. The 1882 season was a bonafide success for the AA, with all six clubs completing their schedules while attendance was strong in most markets. Recognizing the existential threat posed by their new rival, the NL directors jettisoned the circuit's two weakest franchises and markets in Troy and Worcester.

The NL had been structured for the past few years with a focus on lowering travel expenses rather than maximizing profits.[4] This fact alone was what had kept the minuscule markets of Troy and Worcester in the league. It had also prevented expansion to the south and the west. This structure had been necessitated by a series of failed clubs in locales such as Hartford, Milwaukee, Indianapolis, and Cincinnati. The success of the AA, an improving economy, and the promised security of the Tripartite Agreement meant that the NL could take a risk and look towards increasing revenues. Troy and Worcester were removed despite not breaking any League regulations and were replaced by clubs in New York and Philadelphia. Undoubtedly, the NL was prompted by the success of the AA's Philadelphia franchise and understood the financial benefits of having a club in the City of Brotherly Love. Both leagues also saw the importance of cracking the New York market. John B. Day, a New York cigarette manufacturer, had been one of the initial organizers of the American Association but held his Metropolitan club out of the initial AA season. This was likely a result of NL president William Hulbert's influence, who by some accounts had promised Day a spot in the NL in 1883 if he didn't field a New York club in the AA in 1882.[5] Day was granted entry into the NL, but in a strange situation, also cast his lot with the AA for 1883. Both clubs would play at the Polo Grounds in Harlem, acting ostensibly as rivals, though Day would end up shuffling players back and forth between the two clubs on a fairly regular basis. The AA also placed a club in Columbus, Ohio, in an attempt to continue its domination of the west, a region ignored in large part by the NL, with Chicago, Detroit, and Cleveland being their westernmost locales.

By late August 1883, it could unequivocally be stated that both the National League and American Association were having their most successful seasons to date in terms of attendance. The AA pennant race between St. Louis and Philadelphia had proven just how large the audience for baseball could be, with contests regularly drawing over 10,000 fans. The tenuous peace had been established, allowing clubs to control costs and stabilize rosters, and the nation's largest eastern and western markets are now home to major league clubs. It was under these circumstances on August 31, 1883, that an unusual missive appeared in the *Pittsburgh Daily Post*, like a voice in the wilderness calling forth what it is to come:

> Al. Pratt, late manager of the Allegheny club, has on foot a scheme for the organization of an independent baseball association which shall embrace St. Louis, Chicago, Indianapolis, Pittsburgh, New York, Philadelphia, Brooklyn and Hartford. He has been corresponding with parties in all these cities, and says the outlook for the scheme is rosy. The association will have no affiliation with the others, and will take players wherever it can get them, without regard to the eleven men reserve rule. The probabilities are that it will not amount to anything.[6]

Little did anyone realize at the time, but the seeds were being sown for the fledgling Union Association. This new organization would upend the world of professional baseball for the next year and a half. At this moment, however, the fledgling league was just a gleam in Al Pratt's eye.

Al Pratt began his baseball career as a pitcher for the Cleveland Forest Citys in the early days of the National Association. He had been one of the key figures in bringing major league baseball to his native Pittsburgh. Pratt founded the Alleghenys as a semi-pro club in 1880 and was the club's first manager when they joined the American Association in 1882. In their inaugural season, he guided the club to a respectable 39 and 39 record, though he was involved in an unusual scandal involving his star outfielder Ed Swartwood. In August 1882, while on the road in Louisville, Pratt went out for a night on the town and brought a prostitute back to the team hotel. To provide cover for his unprofessional activities, he registered the woman in a separate room and informed the hotel clerk that the woman was the sister of one of his players. He entered her name on the hotel register as Miss Swartwood. After an intrusive hotel detective caught on to the situation, the woman was questioned and insisted that she was the sister of Swartwood and that Pratt was her lover. Pratt was a married man, and when news of the incident reached Swartwood's family in Cleveland, his father wrote an angry editorial to the *Cleveland Herald* defending the virtue and honor of his actual daughter.[7]

The incident seems to have blown over without consequence for Pratt but provides an insight into the carefree personality of the man and points to his questionable leadership skills. It also gives a glimpse of what life was like for a ball team on the road in the 1880s. It was a lifestyle filled with baseball, booze, and women, and not necessarily in that order. When Pratt's club got off to a dismal 12 and 20 start in 1883, he was relieved of his duties by Ormond Butler. His departure was reportedly amicable, as he left "with the warm friendship of all the team."[8] Pratt was immediately enlisted to join the umpire corps of the AA thanks to his reputation as a "well-known, tried umpire."[9] He served as umpire until late July, when he asked for his release, shortly after a game on July 21 in Cincinnati where "abuse of the foulest sort was heaped"[10] upon him. In August, Pratt was umpiring in the Western Interstate League, a minor circuit with teams in Pittsburgh and various mining towns in western Pennsylvania and Ohio. Pratt was a widely respected man in the baseball world and had a wide range of connections. His relationships allowed him to transition from player to manager to umpire to fledgling organizer of a new baseball league. Pratt's motivations for starting this new venture remain unknown. His departure from the Allegheny club was reportedly amicable, and he left his umpiring position with the AA of his own volition. One can imagine an embittered baseball man looking to get payback on his former club by starting a rival, but it does not seem to be the case here.

The initial announcement attracted minimal attention despite Pratt's threat to ignore the 11-man reserve rule and encroach on major league markets such as St. Louis, Chicago, Pittsburgh, New York, and Philadelphia. Undoubtedly, this indifference can be attributed to Pratt's relative lack of standing as a power broker. After all, he had gone from managing in the big leagues to umpiring in the Western Interstate League within two months. There was little reason to believe Pratt's plan would come to fruition. Nevertheless, he did have some important connections.

On September 2, it was reported that Pratt had hired Charles "Chick" Fulmer, the veteran shortstop of the AA's Cincinnati club, to become the manager of Pratt's Pittsburgh franchise.[11] Pratt had some other Cincinnati connections, including a relationship with Justus Thorner, the disgruntled former founder of the Cincinnati club and a key figure in the formation of the AA. In 1881, the indescribably energetic organizer "Hustling" Horace Phillips had put out a call for men interested in forming a new baseball league to come to

This woodcut of Al Pratt appeared in the August 25, 1883, *New York Clipper*. Less than one week later, the former Pittsburgh manager announced his plans to form a new league that would challenge the reserve rule (courtesy Illinois Digital Newspaper Collections).

Pittsburgh. Phillips fell ill and could not make the voyage, and the trio of Thorner, *Cincinnati Commercial* sportswriter O.P. Caylor, and sportswriter Frank B. Wright were the only people to show up. Not wanting the trip to be a waste, the men visited Pratt, figuring he could get the ball rolling. Pratt put the men in touch with H.D. "Denny" McKnight, and soon after that, a league was born with McKnight taking on the role of league president and the key financier of the Pittsburgh franchise.

On September 3, Pratt's venture, newly christened the American League of Professional Base Ball Clubs, announced its first meeting to be held in Pittsburgh. The list of clubs in the league included New York, Brooklyn, Philadelphia, Baltimore, Washington, Pittsburgh, Chicago, and Indianapolis, with St. Louis and Cincinnati also expected to join. Pratt's name was not mentioned in the announcement, which introduced a new and mysterious figure, James Jackson of New York, described as "the projector of the new association."[12]

The term projector was commonly ascribed to entrepreneurial characters in the baseball world in the 1880s. They were the kind of folks that would swoop into town, start a ball club from nothing, and promise the world. The aforementioned "Hustling" Horace Phillips was the prototype. James Jackson wanted to follow in his footsteps. His involvement in the newly formed league proved short-lived, but it is worth spending some time detailing some of his more outlandish exploits. Jackson was the 31-year-old New York press agent for the weekly sporting newspaper *Sporting Life*, based out of Philadelphia. Before the 1883 season, Jackson unsuccessfully applied for an umpiring position with the American Association.[13] Before his job with *Sporting Life*, he had reportedly sold scorecards at the Polo Grounds.[14] Jackson's involvement as the projector of the new league was roundly met with derision. *Sporting Life* immediately announced that Jackson was no longer associated with them. They also mocked his character, stating, "our business relations with him were extremely unsatisfactory, and if he doesn't display any more ability in managing the proposed new League than he did in managing our business in New York … he will make a sad mess of it."[15] The sensationalist weekly *National Police Gazette*, a colorful purveyor of societal scandals, lurid crimes, and baseball gossip in the era, was equally skeptical. The New York–based paper referred to Jackson as a "mushroom," claiming that he had tried to bribe the National League president $100 for an umpiring position before suggesting his involvement would amount to nothing but "surplus air."[16]

The mark of the projector was to make bold promises and speak in hyperbole. Jackson immediately put his foot in his mouth, promising the involvement of Charles H. Byrne, owner of the Brooklyn club in the minor league Interstate Association, claiming he would helm a club in the City of Churches. Byrne offered a quick rebuttal in the *New York Daily Tribune,* noting, "That he had been approached by a young man named Jackson about some such project, but that he had refused to have anything to do with it."[17] Byrne would soon enter his Brooklyn nine in the American Association. Jackson was prone to exaggeration and repeatedly demonstrated that his bluster and self-promotional abilities outstripped his organizational skills. As a result, his involvement with the new league quickly ended. By early October, Jackson's relationship with the venture was non-extant, a victim of his bluster and likely due to his failure to bring a New York franchise into the fold. Jackson applied to be an umpire in the same league he had organized but was rejected once again. His next venture was the publication of a general baseball guide for the 1884 season, though no copies are known to exist.

Jackson's spent the ensuing years as something of a nomad in the baseball world, organizing clubs and leagues at a remarkable rate. In 1885, he organized the New York State League and ran the Rochester, New York, team. His tenure was cut short over a dispute of the team's finances that resulted in him being punched in the eye by his second baseman Grace Pearce.[18] He launched another failed club in Troy, New York, in 1886. In 1887, he organized a club in Springfield, Massachusetts, and promptly moved it to Lockport, New York. The negative coverage of the incident with the Lockport club had Jackson threatening to file a libel suit against *Sporting Life*, his old employer.[19] At the same time, rumors had him on the verge of managing a myriad of major and minor league clubs. Undoubtedly, he was acting as his own press agent, sending in tidbits about his exploits and trying to keep his name in the papers. In 1888, he founded the Hudson River Baseball League and managed its club in Kingston, New York. He tarnished his already dubious reputation by absconding with $200 in gate receipts while abandoning his club on a road trip, accompanied by former National Association star Jim Holdsworth. This appears to have been his last job in baseball, as he soon entered the literary profession. His name would appear periodically over the next few years, primarily thanks to his work as a press agent, but after 1894, he seems to have vanished into thin air.

With Jackson out of the picture, the business of forming the league commenced in earnest on September 12, 1883. On that day, a group of erstwhile baseball men met at the lavish Monongahela House in Pittsburgh, Pennsylvania, then considered one of the finest hotels in the country. The order of business was the creation of a new major baseball league to rival the National League and the American Association. Representatives from Chicago, Baltimore, Philadelphia, Washington, D.C., Richmond, St. Louis, and Pittsburgh were at the Monongahela House that day. Each group seemed eager to take a step towards grabbing a piece of the expanding baseball pie.

The primary outcome of the meeting was the formation of the Union Association of Base Ball Clubs, a new major baseball league with its sights set on competing with the rival National League, established in 1876, and the American Association, established in 1882. The newly formed Union Association (UA), as it would become known, would challenge the establishment for baseball supremacy in two ways. First, they would put clubs in cities with major league clubs, and second, they would ignore the so-called "11-man reserve rule" in their search for suitable talent. The official resolution of the meeting read:

> Resolved. That while we recognize the validity of all contracts made by the League and American Association, we cannot recognize any agreement whereby any number of ball-players may be reserved for any club for any time placed beyond the terms of their contracts with such club.[20]

This resolution was designed to upend the stability of the two rival major leagues. Curiously, the resolution omitted the third party of the Tripartite Agreement, the

Northwestern League. Whether intentional or not, the circuit was the strongest in the country outside of the two majors and was home to a wealth of talent, who would most certainly be of interest to the newly formed UA clubs.

The newly formed league announced its organizational structure with Henry B. Bennett, organizer of the league's Washington franchise and a veteran presence in the city's baseball community, named its first president. Thomas J. Pratt, a hard-throwing pitcher for the Atlantic club in Brooklyn in the 1860s, was named the league's vice president. Warren William White, a Civil War veteran whose professional baseball career dated to 1871, was named the league's treasurer. The 40-year-old White would end up being the UA's jack of all trades, serving as a media spokesperson, statistician, and ambassador. He was involved in the day-to-day management of the Washington franchise and would even end up playing four games at third base. All this while holding down a position at the Treasury Department. The board of directors was announced with Albert H. Henderson of Chicago, Michael B. Scanlon of Washington, organizer Al G. Pratt of Pittsburgh, and the aforementioned Thomas J. Pratt of Philadelphia.

The generally accepted history of the Union Association has Henry V. Lucas, a St. Louis–based baseball fanatic from a wealthy family, as the league's creator, driving force, and financier. However, the evidence suggests that he was not the league's creator. Lucas's involvement with the league was formally confirmed in late October, with the announcement that he would put a club in St. Louis.[21] At the league's inaugural meeting, Timothy P. "Ted" Sullivan was on hand to represent the city of St. Louis, while Lucas's name was nowhere to be found.[22] Sullivan was the former manager of the St. Louis club in the American Association and one of baseball's greatest organizers. Lucas's absence suggests that he was not involved in the initial formation of the league or, more likely, that he kept his name out of the mix until the venture proved more concrete.

Before Lucas became involved, Al G. Pratt was the Union Association's John the Baptist, the voice calling in the wilderness announcing the coming Messiah, soon to get his head cut off. Pratt was heavily involved in the inception of the league. In the weeks following the meeting, his name was frequently connected with the league, with several notices describing the new venture as "Al Pratt's Association."[23] Pratt attended the league's second meeting on October 20, 1883, representing his hometown. Once Henry Lucas's involvement with the league was officially announced on October 24, the St. Louis magnate quickly took over leadership of the new league and garnered the majority of the media's attention. Meanwhile, Pratt's role as the league's initial organizer was forgotten. Much like James Jackson, Pratt's influence was quickly obscured and erased from the narrative of the Union Association, as it became universally understood to be Henry Lucas's league.

Another crucial figure in the foundation of the Union Association was Albert H. Henderson. While Pratt and Jackson may have been the league's imaginative inventors and Lucas its eventual figurehead, Henderson was the source of the league's initial capital. Henderson was born in Canada in June 1847, but his family relocated to the United States, eventually settling in Baltimore around 1854. Henderson had a long history of organizing baseball teams, dating back to his role as an official with the Maryland club in 1867. He joined the management of Pastimes, Baltimore's top amateur club. From 1872 to 1874, Henderson served as the leading officer and business manager of the Lord Baltimores (also known as the Canaries) franchise in the National Association.[24] He formed another pro club called the Baltimores in 1878, eventually transferring the right to the club to "Hustling" Horace Phillips. In a precursor to his later endeavors, Henderson made his first trip west to Cincinnati to generate funding for a club back east. His organizational proclivities and passion for baseball belied his seemingly modest status as a post office clerk, which he held until 1880. The man had an entrepreneurial bent and the creativity of an inventor. He was soon the head of a local mattress manufacturer, which appears to have been his primary source of income.

Henderson's entry into the league is something of a mystery. He had formed the Unions of Chicago as an independent club in early June 1883. Henderson was the president, and the club started with $20,000 in capital stock, a significant sum for an independent club.[25] Several Baltimore business owners, including his younger brother William C. Henderson and a Civil War veteran named Captain Benjamin F. Matthews, were also invested. They would become the directors of the UA's Baltimore club the following year. The Unions also contracted a plot of land on Chicago's south side for five years, intending to build a ballpark that would hold between 3,000 and 7,000 people.[26] These plans were announced three months before the announcement of the Union Association.

The Unions played throughout the summer of 1883 as an independent club, taking on various challengers. The club's goal was to make a strong enough reputation to earn entry into the American Association. The club played 30 games from June 26 to August 26, winning 16 contests while losing 14. The club took on the Brown Stockings of St. Louis, one of the top AA clubs. They also took on top clubs in the Northwestern League and several other top traveling independent nines, such as the Union Pacifics of Omaha, the Blues of Leadville, Colorado, and local Chicago amateur clubs. Henderson's unit fared well against the NWES teams, putting up a 4–3 record. They lost their one contest against St. Louis by a score of 12–4. James F. McKee was the team's manager. He would go on to manage Milwaukee's Northwestern League club in 1884. The team featured multiple future major leaguers, including Ed McKean, Emmett Seery, Abner Powell, and Chris Fulmer. By late July, it was reported that the Chicago Unions planned to apply for membership in the American Association. O.P. Caylor, the *Cincinnati Commercial* sportswriter, was skeptical of Henderson's chances. He placed the odds at 12 to 1, noting that the current eight-team circuit would not be able to expand by only two teams, which would make the schedule unworkable.[27] Caylor's words carried weight because he was also the secretary of the Red Stockings, Cincinnati's AA club, and frequently used his column as a mouthpiece for the circuit's directors.

In early August, McKee was let go as the club manager. After their game on August 26, the team disbanded for the season. Henderson hired Ed S. Hengel, a 28-year-old from Chicago, who had served as a Northwestern League umpire that year. Hengel would manage the club going forward and was given the task of acquiring players for the coming 1884 season. Hengel's role as an umpire gave him a close-up view of the most talented players in the Northwestern League, and not surprisingly, he began to recruit players from that circuit for the coming season. With Hengel as the manager, Henderson made his formal application to the American Association in August and was confident of his chances. A series of correspondence between Hengel and a talented young player for the East Saginaw, Michigan, club named William "Yank" Robinson reveals that Henderson viewed its acceptance to the AA as a formality. In one letter, Hengel claimed unequivocally: "there is no doubt but that we will enter the American Association in '84."[28]

The allure of Chicago for Henderson was simple. It was the fourth-largest city in the country behind New York, Philadelphia, and Brooklyn. It also had a well-earned reputation as a great baseball town thanks to the success of the National League's White Stockings, arguably the premier franchise in all of baseball. This fact also represented a significant obstacle to success in the Windy City. One of the most powerful men in baseball, Albert G. Spalding, headed the club, and he was not afraid to wield his influence to serve his own needs and those of the National League. For reasons unknown, the AA rejected Henderson's application. It can be speculated that the AA's directors had little interest in upsetting a figure like Spalding and breaking the still-fragile peace between the leagues. This is evidenced by the fact that the AA never placed a rival franchise in the city in the nine years of their existence from 1882 to 1891, despite the city's large population and evident capability of supporting two major league clubs. Another possibility is that Henderson withdrew his application upon joining the fledgling UA. The Hengel letter to Robinson boasting of his club's imminent admission to the AA was dated August 29, 1883. Yet, two days later, when Pratt made his announcement, Henderson's club was linked to the rebel organization.

A.H. Henderson's investment in the league extended beyond the Chicago franchise and into his native Baltimore. He bankrolled a UA franchise in his hometown and ceded day-to-day management to his younger brother, William C. Henderson. The Henderson syndicate treated the franchises as one entity, with players being signed by one club and often transferred to the other in the pre-season. Several pieces of correspondence from this period reveal the fluidity of the two organizations. In one letter to Yank Robinson dated December 4, 1883, A.H. Henderson promised the recently signed player that he would not have to play for Chicago manager Ed Hengel and could easily be transferred to the Baltimore club.[29] The document in question featured the letterhead of the "Chicago Union Base Ball Club," with the word Chicago scratched out and Baltimore written in its place.

Henderson's decision to fund two clubs was unusual since it meant that he was now taking on significant financial risk. It would also pose questions about how the teams would compete. The syndicate ownership of New York Giants and New York Metropolitans by John B. Day was already causing problems with ongoing pressure to merge the two nines into the strongest team possible. One club would then thrive, and the other would be left to perish, an issue that came to be a reality just a few years later when Day gutted the AA's Metropolitan club to strengthen the city's NL club. Would Henderson face the same temptation if one of his clubs struggled to win or turn a profit? On the plus side, Henderson seemed to have had sound financial

backing from a group of prominent Baltimore business owners.
There were also rumors that a large
brewing consortium was contrib-
uting to the venture.

The decision by Henderson
and other owners to join the new
venture seems to have been motivated by three factors. First, the
incredible success of the American Association created a sort of
blueprint for how a new league
could form and rival the National
League. Second, the improving
economy led to the increasing popularity of professional baseball
and was transforming the sport
into big business. Third, there
were growing concerns about the
11-man reserve rule put in place
when the AA and the NL signed
the Tripartite Agreement before
the 1883 season. The reserve rule
was put in place to limit contract
jumping, but it also stifled player
freedom. The directors of the new
league seemed to side with the
player. However, the league's opposition to the reserve rule was also

The versatile William "Yank" Robinson was a key
cog for the Baltimore Unions in 1884 before going
on to national stardom as an eagle-eyed utility man
for the pennant-winning St. Louis Brown Stockings
later in the decade (courtesy Southern Illinois University Press).

in their self-interest since ignoring it was the likeliest path to building a competitive
club. The baseball world had changed significantly since the American Association
had formed in late 1881. The AA had started by placing clubs primarily in western markets that were unopposed by the NL. The Association had a huge strategic
advantage since they ostensibly had first dibs on those markets and could build a fan
base from the ground up. The signing of the Tripartite Agreement had also ensured
that the two leagues were now in sync and would fend off any would-be usurpers.
While the AA took on the NL in a head-to-head battle, the UA would be taking on
a two-headed monster. Since almost every worthwhile baseball market now had a
major league team, that meant that the new circuit would be running in direct opposition to other clubs. The UA was at a considerable disadvantage compared to the relatively straightforward path the AA had forged to success in 1882.

The response to the Union Association's first meeting was mixed. Some sources
were supportive of the UA's intention to ignore the 11-man reserve rule. The *Pittsburgh Times* championed this vision, noting that the new league had "secured the
good will of every manly base ball player or patron of the National game in the

United States."[30] A *Sporting Life* editorial presented a more skeptical opinion on the potential of the league:

> [In 1882] there was but one organization in the field and a number of large cities unprovided for. The new body might well realize from the start that it will have a hard, unequal fight, and prepare itself accordingly. The American Association found the field ripe for it, and but little cultivation was required. With the new organization thing will be different because it has in its ranks too many cities where strong clubs are already located, and it is just possible that the base ball business may be overdose.[31]

Of the seven cities represented at the initial Union Association meeting: Chicago, Baltimore, Philadelphia, Washington, D.C., Richmond, St. Louis, and Pittsburgh, five were already home to major league clubs, while Philadelphia was home to two clubs. Richmond and Washington were each home to independent clubs. Three other rumored locales, Hartford, Brooklyn, and Indianapolis, were also without major league clubs. However, Brooklyn had fielded an Interstate Association club in 1883, while Indianapolis had fielded one of the top independent clubs in the country.

The stark contrast between the two leagues' starting situations is clear. The American Association was formed with access to a wide-open field of large markets ripe for professional baseball. The Union Association formed after both major leagues had expanded, with nearly every major eastern market now fielding clubs and the two established leagues now in cahoots. After placing clubs in New York and Philadelphia in 1883, the NL stood pat for the coming 1884 season. The AA responded to the UA threat by adding four clubs for the 1884 season, Toledo, Brooklyn, Washington, and Indianapolis. Not coincidentally, three of the four cities had been projected to join the Union Association at their inaugural meeting. The Brooklyn and Indianapolis clubs had played in 1883, while the Washington AA franchise would be created from scratch. It was clear from this move that a war was brewing, and the American Association's rapid expansion was intended to cut off the new league at the knees and freeze them out of key locations. The moves marked a massive shift from O.P. Caylor's July proclamation that the AA had no plans to expand: "The only increase [of teams] allowable or possible, would be twelve, and it is safe to say that the Association do not hanker after an increase to this number. Granted, then, that the next year's number will be eight."[32]

2

✧✧✧✧✧✧✧✧✧✧✧✧

The Very Best
of Ball Players

"Will Al Pratt's new base ball association amount to anything? Is the leading question just now with a number of players who have not yet affixed their signatures to contracts for next season."—*Cincinnati Enquirer*, September 16, 1883

"We are organizing a club for '84 that will be of the very best of ball players that we can engage."—Chicago Unions manager Ed S. Hengel, letter to William "Yank" Robinson, August 30, 1883

Al Pratt and Albert Henderson had created the Union Association, but it was Henry V. Lucas who would become its dominating figure. The diminutive, driven, and determined young man's lavish spending and aggressive pursuit of baseball glory would come to be the defining marks of the Union Association. His story is closely intertwined with virtually every facet of the league's history. To understand the Union Association, you must first understand Henry Lucas.

Henry Van Noye Lucas was born in St. Louis on September 5, 1857.[1] He was the youngest of twelve children of James H. Lucas and Marie Emile (Desruisseaux) Lucas. The Lucas family was one of the wealthiest in the state of Missouri, their fortune earned through massive land holdings, first accumulated by his French-born paternal grandfather, John Baptiste Charles Lucas, a Federal Territory Judge appointed by President Thomas Jefferson. Young Henry was well bred and attended St. Louis University. In 1873, after his father James passed away, he inherited $2 million of his $9 million estate. The Lucas family was reputed to be one of the wealthiest families in St. Louis, while also being one of the city's two largest landholders. The family belonged to the elite of the elite. This fact would prove to be the driving motivation for Henry Lucas and his entry into the world of professional baseball.

Henry's older brother John B.C. Lucas II loved baseball and was a member of one of St. Louis's first baseball teams, The Union Club, in the years following the Civil War. The club was formed of young gentlemen, primarily from the upper class, and served as an influential force in the development of baseball in St. Louis.[2] The club had built the first enclosed ballpark in the city. It was likely the first to start paying their players in an era where baseball was very much clinging to its origins as a form of amateur leisure dominated by young members of the well-to-do class. John

19

B.C. Lucas was a central part of baseball's development in Mound City. He was one of the organizers of the original St. Louis Brown Stockings, the city's first major league team that appeared in the National Association in 1875. The club would be one of eight teams to enter the National League for their inaugural season in 1876. The Brown Stockings would finish in third place with an excellent 45–19 record but failed to make money. In 1877, the Brown Stockings fell to fourth place with a 28–32 record while again failing to turn a profit. The club's struggles at the gate were exacerbated by the erosion of public trust in professional baseball that resulted from the gambling and game-fixing scandals that marred the 1877 season.

In the wake of the highly publicized scandal that saw four Louisville players suspended for their role in fixing games during the 1877 National League pennant race, Billy Spink, a sportswriter for the *St. Louis Globe-Democrat,* began an investigation into an alleged fixed game between the Brown Stockings and the visiting Chicago White Stockings on August 24.[3] Spink alleged that third baseman Joe Battin, pitcher Joe Blong, and possibly shortstop Davy Force had all taken part in throwing the contest, which resulted in a 4–3 Chicago victory.[4] Blong was the starting pitcher and was suspected of easing up at critical moments, while Battin made a crucial error at third base that broke up a tie game.

The men were believed to have conspired with a Chicago gambler named Mike McDonald to throw the games on August 24 and 25. Team captain Mike McGeary had reportedly grown suspicious of the plot in the game that took place on August 25. He quickly removed starting pitcher Blong from the box in the second inning, denying the pitcher the opportunity to fix that day's result. The Brown Stockings prevailed by a score of 12–8. Despite the bold actions of McGeary, he was implicated in the scandal, based primarily on the fact that he had also been the subject of his own gambling allegations dating back to 1875.[5] Spink speculated that Battin's poor performance on the season, which saw him hit just .199 in 1877 after batting .300 in 1876, could have resulted from his regular fixing of games.

The case against the four St. Louis players was never formally investigated by the National League as the Louisville scandal overshadowed the allegations. Despite the lack of formal punishment for St. Louis players, the future of the Brown Stockings was in doubt for 1878. First, the club had signed two players implicated in the Louisville fix. Before the scandal broke, star pitcher Jim Devlin and outfielder George Hall signed with St. Louis for the following season.[6] The pair was expected to bolster the team's 1878 pennant chances. When the NL formally blacklisted them, the hopes of St. Louis fans and investors, including club president John B.C. Lucas II, were dashed for good. The scandal and lack of profitability spelled the end of the Brown Stockings in the NL. The club had lost significant amounts of money in 1876 and 1877. Their combined attendance for their two National League seasons was less than their single season in the National Association. With the poor attendance and their potential drawing cards excommunicated, the confidence of the St. Louis public, investors, and local media in the potential for professional baseball in the city was virtually nil. In December 1877, the club formally withdrew from the National League.

The club reformed as a semi-professional outfit in 1878 under Ned Cuthbert, a veteran ballplayer from Philadelphia, who had appeared for the Brown Stockings in 1875–1876. The Spink brothers, Al and the aforementioned Billy, two of the city's leading sportswriters, were also behind the club's reorganization. The Spinks had hoped the club would garner re-entry into the National League and galvanize St. Louis's fans, but the club mainly played to empty stands. Baseball had entered something of a depression in the late 1870s, with the National League struggling for stability, and a decline in profitability for traveling clubs, resulting in a general lack of interest from paying fans. Cuthbert's Brown Stockings were just as unprofitable as the Lucas version, equally lacking in decent opponents and fan interest. Professional baseball had proven a tough sell in St. Louis in those early days, and it would be several years before a pro club would finally succeed in St. Louis.

Much to the chagrin of John B.C. Lucas and his younger brother Henry, that success came not from their family's efforts or even that of other members of St. Louis's upper class, who had done so much to shape baseball in the city. Instead, it came from the creative mind of an outsider, Chris von der Ahe. The Prussia-born von der Ahe was 30 years old in 1881 and gifted with a keen mind for a business opportunity. He ran a saloon on the western edge of the city that bordered a lot that had been a popular spot for baseball games since the 1860s.[7] The grounds were known as the Grand Avenue Ball Grounds and had been home to both Lucas's and Cuthbert's Brown Stockings. During the 1880 season, Cuthbert was a frequent visitor to von der Ahe's saloon. There, the immigrant learned the intricacies of baseball and took an interest in the National Game and the money-making opportunities that came with it. For the 1881 season, von der Ahe purchased the Brown Stockings from Cuthbert and set out to revitalize the decaying park that was the Grand Avenue Ball Grounds. Von der Ahe sunk his life savings of $1,800 into the scheme and, with some other investors, founded the Sportsman's Park and Club Association.[8] The ambitious saloon owner was now a burgeoning baseball magnate. He turned the grounds into the first iteration of Sportsman's Park, complete with cricket field, ball diamond, running track, handball court while adding a fine grandstand that would allow fans to experience the game in the finest comfort.[9]

Von der Ahe's innovation paid off, with the help of the Spinks and Cuthbert, and the St. Louis Brown Stockings operated as an independent club in 1881, playing contests against all comers, including several of the teams that would join the American Association the following season. Von der Ahe ran his new club on the same principles that would later define the American Association of which he was one of the founders and central figures: 25-cent tickets, Sunday games, and beer. These three factors appealed greatly to the working-class crowds who flocked to the games and were a marked break from the stodginess of the National League. The NL charged 50 cents a ticket, banned contests on the Sabbath, and prohibited alcohol sales at their games. Von der Ahe's Brown Stockings succeeded in capturing the imaginations of St. Louis's working-class fans, and the result was a hugely profitable enterprise. With all their wealth and status, the Lucas family had failed to make baseball work as a business. Yet, von der Ahe had succeeded. The Lucas family was old money and truly American (never mind that they were of French ancestry), representing the upper class of St. Louis and the values of high society. Von der Ahe was an outsider, an immigrant, a saloon owner for God's sake, and he had done what John B.C. Lucas and all of his familial wealth and status could not: make professional baseball work in St. Louis.

This slight at the hands of an uncouth tavern owner motivated Henry Lucas to found a professional baseball team. He wanted to beat von der Ahe and avenge the besmirched honor of his family and his class. He would do anything it took to make his club the premier club in the city, but first, he needed to find a league to play in. Lucas officially announced his desire to form a professional team on October 25, 1883. Prior to the initial announcement, it was noted that Lucas and Ellis Wainwright, a St. Louis brewery owner, purchased a tract of land and raised a stock company of $15,000.[10] The money would go towards building a ballpark and forming a new professional team in St. Louis.

It was coyly suggested that Lucas had not decided what league to play in, noting the unlikeliness of his club's admittance into the American Association because of the presence of von der Ahe's team. There were concerns about joining the National League since they prohibited Sunday contests and demanded 50-cent admissions. Lucas was an intelligent man and knew that his best chance to compete with von der Ahe was to employ the same tactics. His partnership with a brewing magnate also showed a willingness to sell beer at contests. It is almost certain that Lucas had already agreed to join the Union Association at this point. Still, a curious note had appeared a few days earlier in the *National Police Gazette*: "Efforts are being made to locate a league club in St. Louis, with bright prospects of its being a success. St. Louis is a first-class baseball city, and as the Cleveland people have not been supporting their team very well this season there is a possibility of the Cleveland club being transferred bodily to St. Louis."[11]

This Cleveland connection was interesting since there were rumors that Cleveland might not have a ballpark to play in for the coming year and would be forced to disperse their

Chris von der Ahe was the owner of the St. Louis Brown Stockings. He was one of the driving forces behind the American Association and the man who made professional baseball a success in St. Louis, much to the chagrin of Henry Lucas (Library of Congress).

talent.[12] The club had played at the Kennard Street Grounds since 1879, but without a lease for the 1884 season, the club would be homeless. Local antipathy towards the club's plight had created a sense of uncertainty going into the off-season. The city's landowners were unwilling to cut a deal to provide suitable grounds. Lucas knew his path into the National League would require one of its weaker clubs to be taken out of the picture. With the reserve rule in place, there would be no viable way to form a competitive club from scratch to join the circuit. Buying an existing club and moving it to his home would be the only viable strategy. This proved a moot point, as any efforts to purchase the Cleveland franchise in 1883 were quickly snuffed out. Lucas's new club was soon announced as the Union Association's newest entrant. For Lucas, it does not appear to have mattered what league he was in, simply that he had a chance to compete with von der Ahe. The Union Association could provide him with that opportunity, and he took full advantage. In his first interview after announcing his involvement, Lucas outlined his position: "I am a business man and would do no such foolish thing as to meddle with a player under contract elsewhere or with other parties. In regard to the reserve rule, that is an entirely different matter and it will not stand in my way."[13]

Lucas recognized his limitations as a baseball man, despite having organized a semi-professional club, the Lucas Reds, during the 1883 season. The Reds featured St. Louis semi-pros and amateurs, and Lucas even appeared with the club at third base and right field. The club played their contests on his massive Normandy estate. Games were often followed by luncheons organized by his lovely wife, Mrs. H.V. Lucas, the former Louise Espenschied, the youngest daughter of Louis Espenschied, a wealthy owner of a wagon factory.[14] Lucas's brother-in-law Fred F. Espenschied also became a prominent investor in the new franchise, purchasing 350 of the 600 shares offered at $25 each.[15] The savvy young owner found allies in Ted Sullivan and Ned Cuthbert, both well-connected baseball men in St. Louis, who could leverage their considerable experience, knowledge, and interpersonal relationships to construct a competitive nine for Lucas.

Timothy P. "Ted" Sullivan had attended the first Union meeting in September, possibly on behalf of Lucas or possibly in his own interests. The feisty native of Clare, Ireland, had earned a reputation as a fantastic organizer of teams and leagues. He was reputed as one of the finest identifiers of baseball talent in the country. He had risen to fame in the 1870s, managing the famed Red Stockings from Dubuque while organizing the Northwestern League, the first ever pro league west of the Mississippi River. The 1879 iteration of the club won the Northwestern League pennant. It was generally regarded as one of the finest clubs outside of the National League, posting a 19–5 record before the circuit disbanded on July 17.[16] Including non-league contests, the club won 34 of 50 games. The Red Stockings featured a star-studded lineup comprising virtually every top player in the west, all signed, sealed, and delivered by the astute Sullivan. The lineup featured seven future major leaguers, including two Hall of Famers, Charlie Comiskey and Charles Radbourn. The club also featured several men who would anchor the St. Louis Unions, no doubt signed under the advice of Sullivan, third baseman Jack Gleason, catcher Tom "Sleeper" Sullivan, and utility man Billy Taylor. Radbourn famously "Chicagoed" (early baseball parlance for a shutout) the Chicago White Stockings, 1–0 on August 4, striking out eight men and allowing just four hits.

Ted Sullivan's managerial bona fides were confirmed on the major league level in 1883. He helmed the St. Louis Brown Stockings, guiding the club to a 53–26 record and first place in the standings before a dispute with owner Chris von der Ahe led to his departure. On August 29, with his club hanging on to first place by one game, Sullivan quit as manager midway through the club's contest in New York after enduring a humiliating browbeating by von der Ahe, who had demanded a pitching change. Sullivan responded by throwing his $300 watch at his domineering boss. The watch was a pre-season gift from the owner and bore the inscription: "C. Vonderahe to T.P. Sullivan, April 4th, 1883." His replacement was his old protégé, team captain Charlie Comiskey.[17] The Brown Stockings eventually lost the pennant race after Sullivan's resignation, though they would eventually become the dynasty of the decade under Comiskey's leadership. Sullivan later recalled a reconciliation with his boss, who presented him with the watch once again: "I can pay the highest compliment to the grand old Teuton who recognized my merit when he first met me and presented me with the watch, as a token of his esteem. He put the watch in his pocket and in two months afterward, at Sportsman Park, placed it back in my hand and told me not to be so high strung."[18] Perhaps Lucas also found in Sullivan an ally who also shared animosity towards von der Ahe. Despite his issues with von der Ahe, Sullivan seemed to remain amicable with his one-time charges on the Brown Stockings. He even appeared in a fascinating exhibition contest on November 4 that pitted the Brown Stockings against a crew headed by world heavyweight boxing champion John L. Sullivan (no relation). Ted Sullivan shared the pitching and shortstop duties on the pugilist's nine that featured a mixture of local St. Louis players and some of the stray members of the Brown Stockings. The boxing champion's pitching abilities failed to match his boxing prowess, and his club lost by a score of 15–3, allowing 13 runs in seven innings of work. The *St. Louis Republican* summed up his performance on the day: "John L. Sullivan, he of the hitting propensities, has the satisfaction of knowing he has at last been knocked out. It took nine ballplayers, however, to accomplish the heretofore impossible feat."[19]

With the Union Association's stated opposition to the reserve rule, the members went about the most essential task of all if the league was going to see the playing field in 1884, finding players. A ball team is nothing without its players, after all. Filling out a roster of 11 men or more was the primary task that the various clubs who had pledged allegiance to the Union Association faced heading into the offseason of 1883. The hunt for talent had begun in earnest for the Chicago Unions, who had actively reached out to talent as early as July 1883, with letters and telegrams sent to players of interest. The mere fact that Albert H. Henderson's franchise was already formed was a considerable advantage. He had the infrastructure in place and a knowledgeable manager in Ed Hengel. In the search for talent, being first was often the difference-maker.

The Union Association had scheduled its second meeting for October 20, 1883, at the Bingham House in Philadelphia. It was hoped that the meeting would further solidify what franchises would represent the league in its inaugural season.

Confusion had arisen as another organization, calling itself the Union League, announced its intentions to form as a minor-league circuit in the east. They would also operate in compliance with the National Agreement. After several weeks of being mixed up unfavorably with the Union Association, they rebranded as the Eastern League (EL). The formation of another league meant more competition for players and crowded markets, which now might be expected to support two or even three teams. The squeeze for players was exacerbated by the reserve lists provided by each of the three circuits in the National Agreement, with most teams opting to reserve the full 11 men allowed. The eight National League clubs reserved 85 players; the eight American Association teams also reserved 85 men, while the eight clubs of the Northwestern League reserved 65 players. Two hundred thirty-five of the top players in the country were bound by the rules of the National Agreement, though being reserved did not mean that the player was legally under contract. It simply meant that the reserving team had the sole right to sign the player for the coming season. For the Union Association, this technicality was important and would be a crucial point in their player negotiations throughout the offseason. The Union had vowed not to sign any player under contract but would ignore the reserve rule that bound a player to a team.

The first rumors of players being approached by the fledgling circuit appeared in the weeks leading up to the second Union Association meeting. The *Cleveland Leader* reported that "several managers of the new [Association] have been following the League clubs around the country, trying to get the players to sign with them."[20] Al G. Pratt was reported to have offered Buffalo's star pitcher, James "Pud" Galvin, and first baseman big Dan Brouthers salaries of $3,500 each to jump to his Pittsburgh club for the coming season.[21] Both men were tremendous players in the midst of Hall of Fame careers and were under reserve to Buffalo. Targeting star players was expected to be a key strategy for the new league. Signing star players would materially strengthen the circuit's quality and hopefully draw media attention and fans to the ballpark. The downside of such a strategy was that it was costly. It was also likely to draw the ire of the two major leagues, who were committed to protecting their assets at all costs.

Albert H. Henderson, motivated partly by the fact that he was, in essence, eating for two in having to fill out credible lineups for two nines, took a different approach to roster construction. Aided by his lieutenant, Ed Hengel, the former Northwestern League umpire, he set his sights on signing players en masse from that minor league. This strategy was clever since it would enable him to build his clubs featuring the best available talent outside of the major leagues at considerably less cost while also drawing less attention in doing so. The Northwestern League was without question the strongest baseball league outside of the majors in 1883. Such promising prospects as future 300 game-winner and Hall of Famer John Clarkson, up and coming pitching aces Dave Foutz, Bob Caruthers, Charles "Pretzels" Getzien, Bill Hutchison, and Henry Porter, as well as two future cogs in the St. Louis Brown Stockings dynasty, Curt Welch and Yank Robinson appeared that season.

The primary target for Henderson's approach was the Peoria, Illinois, club. Peoria was coming off a third-place finish in the Northwestern League in 1883. The club went 49–35 and featured several players with major league experience, including pitcher Bill Sweeney, third baseman John "Trick" McSorley, and catcher Eddie Fusselback. The Illinois club reserved ten players for the coming 1884 season: Sweeney, McSorley, and Fusselback, as well as Charles Levis, Ed Burch, Bill Schwartz, James "Dick" Phelan, Chris Fulmer, Ed Kent, and George Pinkney. Every player except for Burch would end up signing with the Unions during the coming months. Late in September 1883, a fascinating notice was published in the *Port Huron Daily Times* that listed the salary requests made by the reserved members of the Peoria club: "The following proposals from the players desirous of playing with the Peorias were received: Fusselback, $1,000, $200 to be paid in advance; Sweeney, $1,000, $200 to be paid in advance; Levis, $900; Phelan, $125, per month; Swartz, $150 and board, Fulmer, $150; Kent, $150; Pinckney, $125."[22] The salary requests give great insight into what a typical minor league player was making in that era. They also demonstrated what a club would need to offer a player to induce him to jump.

Rumors began to swirl that Henderson's Chicago Unions had signed Sweeney, Fusselback, and Phelan to contracts, though each of the men denied signing.[23] The case of Charles Levis provides some details about the timeframe of Henderson and Hengel's raid and the salaries that Henderson paid out to his Northwestern League recruits. Levis was a 23-year-old first baseman from St. Louis who had just completed his first season in professional baseball. He had asked Peoria for a $900 salary for the 1884 season, a modest sum but not extravagant for a player with minimal professional experience. Henderson and Hengel signed Levis to a contract with the Chicago Union Base Ball Association on October 23, 1883. Levis' contract, which remains the only extant Union Association contract, would pay $200 per month for a six-month season stretching from April to October.[24] The amount was $300 more than he had requested from Peoria, and apparently, it was enough of a raise to mitigate the threat of being blacklisted. It was also a salary that was on par with many major league salaries.

Henderson and Hengel also targeted the Springfield, Illinois, club in much the same manner. The duo signed up Tom Gunning, Charles Householder, Fleury Sullivan, Billy Colgan, Joe Ellick, and Emory "Moxie" Hengel, younger brother of the Unions' manager. Could the young Hengel have been a mole on the inside, suggesting players to his older brother? Catcher Tom Gunning soon got cold feet and broke his Union Association contract, with one commentator later stating that he had become the first man to sign a Union contract and the first man to break one. By December, Henderson and Hengel had signed eight of Peoria's reserved players to contracts. The signees were divvied up between the Baltimore and Chicago rosters, along with the six Springfield players.

The second UA meeting took place on October 20, just a few days before Henry Lucas formally announced his membership. Delegates from Philadelphia, Pittsburgh, Chicago, St. Louis, Washington, and Baltimore were in attendance. Washington owner Henry B. Bennett, named president at the first meeting in September, also presided over this meeting. Bennett was a native of Fall River, Massachusetts, who had earned his wealth through real estate while also working for the Federal Government in Washington. Bennett was a lover of baseball and had been one of the backers of the Washington nine that had entered the minor league iteration of the National Association in 1880. He would be involved financially with various professional clubs in his adopted home throughout the decade. The meeting also saw applications submitted from Kingston, New York, Lancaster, Pennsylvania, and New York City. No action was taken on the Lancaster and Kingston applications, though a committee was appointed to investigate the status of the New York City applicants. The most noteworthy event of the meeting was the reading of a letter written by Pittsburgh Allegheny and American Association president H.D. McKnight. The letter was addressed to a player who had signed a Union Association contract, attempting to convince the player to violate his contract. The delegates responded with outrage to the letter. The outcome was a forceful resolution to battle any club who dared poach one of their players: "any attempt on the part of any base ball organization to induce players who have signed contracts with this Association to violate said contracts, must be considered as a declaration of war, and will be met by all the means at our command."[25] Secretary Warren White commented further on the meeting, noting that all clubs represented in the Union Association were financially sound while boasting that 27 players had already signed with the circuit. The majority of these were signed by Henderson, while Pittsburgh and Washington had also signed several unnamed players.

While Henderson was scouring the Northwestern League, Lucas and Sullivan set their sights on targets in the American Association and National League. After weeks of rumors that saw virtually every top player in the major leagues being offered large sums of cash to join the new league, Lucas fired the first salvo on November 6. On that day, Lucas signed Tony Mullane, the star hurler of von der Ahe's Brown Stockings, for a contract worth $2,500 with an advance of $500. The dashing Irishman had established himself as one of the game's most extraordinary young pitchers, winning 65 contests over his first two full seasons and at age 24, seemingly primed for even greater success. Signing Mullane was intended to be a great coup for the new Lucas club since it would give the club a workhorse pitcher to build around while also weakening the rival Brown Stockings. In the 1880s, team success was primarily driven by the quality of the team's battery, with one pitcher expected to carry the bulk of the innings on the season. In his career thus far, Mullane was up to the task. He had pitched over 460 innings in each of the past two seasons. He had paced the American Association in winning percentage (.700) and ERA+ (160) in 1883. In reward for his efforts, von der Ahe reportedly offered him $1,900 to pitch in 1884, $600 less than Lucas offered.

Lucas's subsequent signing occurred on the following day when he enlisted Jack Gleason, the current third baseman for Louisville. Gleason was a St. Louis native and alumnus of the St. Louis Brown Stockings, where he played alongside his brother Bill. Jack had been let go by the Brown Stockings and signed with Louisville, where he hit .299/.345/.369 in 84 games for the Kentucky club. He wasn't a star, but he was a good solid ballplayer with deep ties to the city. His willingness to sign was likely due to the meager $1,000 salary he was offered for the coming season. The paltry figure was the minimum amount a club needed to offer a reserved player. The signings of Mullane and Gleason, both reserved players, started a panic amongst moguls in the established major leagues. Lucas's increasingly aggressive pursuit of talent further exacerbated the situation.

Lucas and Sullivan's targeting of players was not indiscriminate. They were undoubtedly avid readers of the sporting weeklies that tracked the triumphs and travails of the various clubs across the country. Their awareness led them to target dissatisfied players on clubs in weakened financial states. One of those clubs was the Pittsburgh Alleghenys. Al Pratt's old club had endured a rocky 1883 season that saw the club finish in seventh place with a 31–67 record, under three different managers, Pratt, Ormond Butler, and Joe Battin. The club featured Ed Swartwood, the league's best hitter, and hard-hitting outfielders Mike Mansell and Lewis "Buttercup" Dickerson. Another key contributor was the versatile "Bollicky" Billy Taylor, a stout and remarkably versatile utility man who possessed the ability to play all nine positions effectively and could hit a little too. The club's downfall was the tendency of a number of its best players to imbibe like there was no tomorrow. The American Association had a number of hard drinkers, but the Alleghenys took the cake, earning the club the derisive nickname "the Brewery Nine."[26] Taylor and Dickerson, in particular, had a well-earned reputation as "elbow-benders," and the National League had banned Dickerson for his failure to keep his personal habits in check.

To make matters worse, the club had lost money and, at the end of the season, still owed $2,027.61 in back pay to the members of its roster.[27] Despite the presence of league president H.D. McKnight as the club's overseer, there was reason for concern about the club's long-term health. The club wasn't very good, and their best players could not be counted on to give their best performance. Now McKnight owed some of them back pay.

On November 9, the *St. Louis Globe-Democrat* broke the news that Lucas had signed six more players from the rival leagues.[28] Two were former members of the Alleghenys, Billy Taylor and Buttercup Dickerson. Pittsburgh had initially reserved the men but released the pair in early November. Their release was in recognition of their considerable drinking abilities and concerns about their sobriety, particularly in tandem with the other hard drinkers on the club. Mike Mansell, another of the club's outfielders, was also reported to have signed, though his status was the source of conjecture over the coming weeks. The club's best player, Ed Swartwood, was also recruited by Lucas. He was offered $2,500, but he turned down the offer since he had signed an 1884 contract with Pittsburgh. Taylor and Dickerson signed contracts with Lucas for $2,000 per annum, with each man receiving a coveted advance of $300.

The other three signings were Emil Gross, a talented but hard-drinking catcher and the Rowe brothers, Dave and Jack. The pair signed lavish contracts for reported sums of $2,600 each. Dave was coming off a fine campaign in Baltimore that saw him hit .313 and post a 129 OPS+ while brother Jack was the star catcher for Buffalo and became the first backstop in major league history to lead the league in triples when he hit 11 in 1881. The reported signings by Lucas ended up being a mixture of fact and fiction, as neither Jack Rowe nor Emil Gross appeared for Lucas's club.

Until the story broke, there had been many rumors of Union contract offers. At the October 20 meeting, it was reported that 27 men had signed Union contracts, with Henderson's tactic of raiding the Northwestern League accounting for most of the signings. The signings drew ire in Peoria and Springfield but received little notice in the major league cities. Lucas's raid of both the established major leagues was the shock wave that demonstrated the threat to the National Agreement was real.

Lucas's next big coup was a member of the Cleveland National League club, their star second baseman, Fred Dunlap. The second baseman was 24 years old at the end of the 1883 season. The budding superstar had just completed a remarkable year in Cleveland. Dunlap batted .326 while playing stellar defense and was among the very best players in baseball. The hardscrabble second baseman was feisty, belligerent, and brilliant. "Dunnie," as he was often called, had fought and clawed his way to the big leagues. He had grown up in the rural pastures just outside of Philadelphia and was orphaned as a child.[29] He grew up poor, and he could not read or write. Nevertheless, he found a home on the ball field, and by the time he was 18, he was making his mark in professional baseball, first starring for the club in Auburn, New York, in the 1877 League Alliance. By 1880, he was in the majors as the 21-year-old second baseman for Cleveland. He was an instant star, leading the league in doubles with 27 while posting a solid .276/.289/.429 batting line and a 142 OPS+. He excelled in the field, posting a 1.0 defensive WAR and leading all second baseman in assists and double plays. He became well known for his incredibly accurate throwing arm, which earned him the sobriquet "Sure Shot" and his refusal to back down from a fight. At just 5'8" and 165 pounds in his best playing condition, Dunlap took on all comers and proved adept at fisticuffs. On one occasion, "one of his teammates had abused him in the clubhouse after a game and threatened to beat him to death for an error on the field, to which Dunlap responded that would do little good, as neither would be able to play the next day." He then gave his much-bigger opponent "the worst beating a man ever received."[30] Dunlap was a bit of an egotist and believed highly in his own abilities, but he was a tremendous player on the field. He had begun his career with four consecutive top-ten finishes in WAR and established himself as the best second baseman in all of baseball.

In 1883, Cleveland remained in contention late into the season, despite the league's worst offense, thanks to Dunlap's sterling play and the pitching duo of Jim McCormick and the mercurial Hugh "One Arm" Daily. The club also boasted a star shortstop in 25-year-old "Pebbly" Jack Glasscock who was making his name as a hard-nosed and heady infielder who could hold his own at the plate. With this core of four stars, the future of the Blues was looking bright, and with a little more offense, they would have won the pennant. After several bumpy years, Cleveland was home to a winning club, though the fans were still not coming out to the park, and there were some signs of dissension in the ranks. The final month of the Cleveland season had seen frustrations boil to the service, highlighted by a fight between Daily and rookie pitcher named Robert Lemuel Hunter aboard a train in early September: "All is not lovely in the camp of the Cleveland club, as is evidenced by the fact that last Saturday in a sleeping car [Daily] and Hunter, the pitchers had a violent war of words. Fred Dunlap and Glasscock, who never had any love for each other, next quarreled and came to blows, Glasscock getting decidedly the worst of it."[31]

The club was riddled with dissension but could not afford to lose Dunlap. His presence at second base gave the club the best chance at success in 1884, even if he could pose a disruption to team harmony. Reserving him was the club's only option. In the added event that the Blues did not take the field the coming year, the Cleveland owners could also potentially sell the rights to their reserved players to the highest bidder. Recognizing the uncertainty that was besieging the Cleveland franchise and identifying the dissatisfaction of their stars, Henry Lucas saw an opportunity to poach a player like Dunlap for his squad. If Cleveland lost their stars to Lucas, it would have the dual effect of strengthening Lucas's club and the Union Association. It would also weaken one of the National League's most perilous franchises and potentially the League itself.

It seems likely that Dunlap was recruited in late October 1883, when his Cleveland Blues were in St. Louis playing a weeklong exhibition series against the St. Louis Brown Stockings. On November 3, reports out of Cleveland suggested he was on the verge of signing a pact for the coming year when mysteriously, he left town to attend to business.[32] As it turns out, the second baseman went to meet Henry Lucas to sign a contract with his St. Louis club. Lucas later noted that he signed Dunlap in New York City. The signing occurred on an eastern trip during which he also signed Mike Mansell in Buffalo, Dave Rowe in Baltimore, and agreed to verbal terms with Buffalo's hard-hitting outfielder George "Orator" Shafer.[33] That would place Dunlap's contract signing in early November since the Mansell and Rowe signings were announced on November 9, though Mansell later claimed not to have signed any agreement. A detailed account of Dunlap's signing was given in a 1919 syndicated column, 35 years after the transaction took place, portraying Lucas as larger than life tycoon approaching a shy and illiterate ballplayer:

> "I want you to captain, and play second base for my St. Louis Club." said Lucas to Dunlap. "I'll pay you any salary that you think you can earn."
>
> "What's that?" asked the startled Dunlap.
>
> "How much are you getting now?" countered Lucas.
>
> "$1,750 a season, was the answer." And Dunlap's salary it can be said, represented the pay of the starriest of stars 25 years ago.
>
> Lucas extracted a huge roll of bills from his pocket tore off $1,750 pushed it toward Dunlap and said: "There's $1,750. Now, look over the rest of this money and decide how much more of it you want to play for me. There's $50,000 in the bundle."
>
> Lucas nonchalantly separated the bills from the roll … the sight of the money so bewildered Dunlap that he couldn't talk for a few minutes and taking advantage of Dunlap's silence Lucas said: "How would $5,000 a year and a contract for two years strike you?" asked Lucas.
>
> A gulp—in the affirmative was Dunlap's only reply.
>
> "All right—that's settled." responded Lucas. "Now there's one more detail. Some folks are skeptical about how long the new league will last. Perhaps you feel the same way. So…"—and Lucas reached down to the table, picked up ten bills of $1,000 denomination, handed them to Dunlap—"I'll pay you in advance. Here's your $10,000. Here's the contract. Sign it."[34]

Most contemporary accounts have Dunlap signing for a salary of $3,500 rather than $5,000; nonetheless, the account demonstrates the tactics of Lucas, flashing his considerable wealth to tempt players to jump. His approach was to show upfront that he had the money to pay out the salaries, since any established major league player would risk a great deal by jumping to his club. Flaunting his wealth in such a provocative manner was a way of securing a player's trust and confidence in the new organization.

In the case of Dunlap, the tactic worked. On November 21, Lucas was in Boston continuing his talent search and in his possession was the contract signed by Dunlap.[35] The star second sacker had jumped ship and would become the crown jewel of Lucas's club and the league. He was a legitimate and certifiable star in his prime. Lucas certainly hoped that Dunlap's bold leap to the new circuit would encourage other stars to consider following in his footsteps. With Dunlap in hand, the St. Louis owner remained aggressive in pursuit of star players. Rumors swirled that he had signed players such as New York's star pitcher/shortstop John Ward and slugging first baseman and future all-time home run king, Roger Connor, as well as Chicago White Stockings star third baseman Ed Williamson. Sadly for Lucas, none of these signings came to fruition. Dunlap would prove to be the single top-shelf player that Lucas would successfully obtain. The question now was how the other clubs in the Union Association would respond?

3

✓

Enter Henry V. Lucas

Henry V. Lucas had made headlines and went from being a virtual unknown in the baseball world to its most compelling and controversial figure within the span of a month. Lucas's presence loomed large over everyone involved in the fledgling circuit in the days leading up to the third Union Association meeting scheduled for December 18–19, 1883, in Philadelphia at the Bingham House. Would other clubs adopt Lucas's tactics? Could they even afford to?

For Al Pratt, the arrival of Lucas and his free-spending ways spelled trouble for his proposed franchise in Pittsburgh. While Pratt was indisputably the league's originator, he never established that he had the financial resources to bankroll a team, especially one featuring high-priced stars. Despite the rumors that he was offering large salaries to several established major league stars, no player was confirmed to have signed with his franchise. It was not clear if Pratt had secured a park, nor were there any details about the necessary stock company to fund the new nine. Considering that Pratt had organized clubs in the past, the absence of information or updates was surprising and suggested that he could not secure funding. By November, Pratt's franchise was reported to have "fizzled out of want for capital."[1]

For Albert Henderson, Lucas's strategy ran in direct contrast to his own. Henderson had strategically signed players from the Northwestern League at salaries in the range of $1,200 per man. Conversely, Lucas was spending double and even triple that amount for the members of his nine. Amid his major league raids, Lucas had even signed two semi-professionals, Jack Brennan and Jimmy Woulfe, from New Orleans at salaries reported to be near $2,000 each. Lucas would also sign Joe Quinn, a semi-pro first baseman, for a reported $2,000 in December.[2] Quinn was born in Australia and emigrated to Iowa when he was ten.[3] Quinn's family settled in Dubuque, the old stomping grounds of Ted Sullivan, where he was an understudy to the great Charlie Comiskey.[4] In response to the large sums of money being thrown about, Henderson made a splash of his own by going after one of the best pitchers in baseball.

The diminutive Larry Corcoran had been the anchor of the Chicago White Stockings pitching staff for several years. The 23-year-old Corcoran had won 135 games in his four-year career. The mighty White Stockings led by stars like Cap Anson and Ed Williamson were arguably the most famous team in the country, having won three consecutive pennants from 1880 to 1882. Recognizing his bargaining power as the ace of the White Stockings, Corcoran asked his bosses for a

✓

The Australian-born Joe Quinn began his long major league career as the starting first baseman for the St. Louis Unions. He was one of the last active Union Association alumni when he appeared for Washington in the inaugural season of the American League in 1901 (courtesy Southern Illinois University Press).

salary of $4,000 for the coming season. When his demands went unmet, he countered by signing with Henderson's Chicago Unions at a staggering salary of $4,100 per annum on December 9.[5] The figure that would make him the highest-paid player in baseball. Pitchers in the 1880s did not have long shelf lives, and a $4,100 salary would provide much-needed relief from the immense pain and exhaustion that came from hurling four hundred or more innings a season. At just 5'3" and 127 pounds, the slightly built Corcoran must have felt this burden even more than most, every pitch sapping a little bit of strength from his tiny frame. Since Corcoran had been reserved for the coming season, the White Stockings threatened to blacklist their star pitcher if he did not return to the club. For the time being, Henderson had his ace.

Tom Pratt, the founder of the Union's Philadelphia Keystones, had been relatively quiet in the City of Brotherly Love. Perhaps he was biding his time, waiting to see how the league unfolded. The divergent paths of Henderson and Lucas could prove instructive about where the league was heading. One could target solid minor league talent and focus on fielding a solid but unspectacular club while keeping costs manageable. Alternatively, one could try and open up the purse strings and chase the big fish. Pratt decided to follow a third path: nostalgia. Pratt was a respected fixture in Philadelphia baseball, whose singular major league appearance in 1871 in the National Association belies the fact that he had starred as a hard-throwing pitcher for the famed Brooklyn Atlantics in the mid–1860s and was one of the most well-known players in the country. After his career, Pratt remained active in the baseball scene in his adopted home of Philadelphia, frequently umpiring contests and occasionally getting involved in discussions to formulate new clubs in the city. Outside of baseball, he was reportedly making good money as a paint manufacturer. His money was in paint, but his heart remained in baseball, and he was one of a group of investors who founded the Philadelphia National League franchise in November 1882. For unknown reasons, he decided to leave the NL behind and launch his own franchise in the Union Association.

The City of Brotherly Love was home to more baseball players per capita than any city in the country and had a long history of amateur, semi-pro, and professional nines, who had built their reputation in the city. Pratt's approach to team construction was to tap into this rich baseball history by targeting famous names from Philadelphia's baseball past and putting them on the field for 1884. For an old-time player like Pratt, he must have held a tremendous reverence and sense of loyalty to the players he had played alongside. Pratt's first signings were a pair of cagey veterans, Fergy Malone and Levi Meyerle. The 39-year-old Malone had been a star catcher in the National Association but had not played major league baseball since 1876, nor professionally since 1879. The lanky Meyerle, now 34 years old, was once a great star. "Long Levi," as he was called, was arguably the greatest hitter in the National Association and baseball's first-ever batting champion, hitting .492 for the Philadelphia Athletics in 1871. He would add another batting title in 1874 when he hit .394 for Chicago. He had last played major league baseball in 1877 and professionally in 1880. Pratt was also rumored to have signed Mike McGeary, another old-time National Association star, along with several other ancients. Say what you will about Pratt's approach, but it was truly unique, and the unengaged vets would come cheap and might have something left in the tank.

Pratt would finally waver from his commitment to the decrepit former stars when he signed Louisville's Sam "Buck" Weaver on November 27. The 28-year-old hurler was a two-time 20 game-winner and Philadelphia native. Weaver had been on Louisville's reserve list but had balked at taking a $600 pay cut from $1,800 to $1,200 for the coming season. When Pratt offered him a reported salary of $1,500 with a $500 advance, he must have been happy to cast his lot with the usurpers, who were offering a chance to play in his hometown.[6] Another Philadelphian, third baseman Jerry McCormick, signed with the club after being reserved by the Baltimore Orioles. Baltimore released him in November, likely at his own request, so there was no risk of a blacklist on his part. McCormick had been the Baltimore Orioles starting third baseman and posted a respectable 91 OPS+ as a 21-year-old while handling the hot corner adequately. In that era, third base was arguably the most challenging infield position to defend, as the lack of gloves made line drives hard to handle while bunting had started to come into vogue. McCormick wasn't bound to be a star, but he was a major league regular and was still in his early 20s, with the potential to improve. Several other local players signed, including Bill Kienzle. The outfielder had a sizzling cup of coffee with the Philadelphia Athletics in September 1882, batting .333 in nine games but had labored in the Interstate Association in 1883. Buster Hoover, a 21-year-old outfielder who had also spent time in the Interstate Association, was joined on the roster by veteran outfielders and partners in crime, Henry Luff and Billy Geer. Pratt's fixation on local talent came to be a defining factor of the roster. This strategy could be viewed as an intelligent attempt to leverage the vast resources of Philadelphia's baseball community. It could also be interpreted as a myopic and lazy sign that Pratt was utterly out of touch with modern baseball and unwilling to turn his eyes to the world outside his window.

Pratt's Keystone club would face stiff local competition for fandom against the AA's Athletics, coming off their dramatic pennant victory over the Brown Stockings. Pratt's former charge, the dismal but rapidly improving Philadelphia National League club, would also be an obstacle. The club had hired the legendary Harry Wright to take over management duties. Wright had managed the 1869 Cincinnati

Red Stockings and the Boston Red Stockings dynasty of the previous decade. There were big expectations that he would employ his proven managerial genius and help Philadelphia improve upon their dreadful 17–81 record and last-place finish in the previous year. Pratt appears to have sought to gain an edge and win fans by featuring a roster of exclusively hometown players. Only time would tell.

In the nation's capital, precious little had been revealed about the club's plans for the coming season. No rumors about player signings or front office goings-on were coming to light, though nothing negative was in the air either. The club had existed as a semi-professional nine in 1883, featuring almost exclusively local players, who also happened to hold government jobs. It was unclear what the path forward for the club would be, but manager Mike Scanlon had been a driving force in the Washington baseball scene as an organizer since the 1870s. He was the proprietor of the Art Billiard Palace, which served as the city's baseball headquarters and stomping grounds for fans and players alike. Scanlon knew every ballplayer in town, and it seemed probable that the Nationals of 1884 would draw heavily from local talent.

In the lead-up to the circuit's December meeting, the question about Al Pratt's Pittsburgh franchise was finally answered. A few days before the December 18 meeting, several Pittsburgh newspapers reported that Pratt had resigned management of the city's UA franchise.[7] The rumors of Al Pratt's departure became a reality at the meeting when he failed to show, leaving Pittsburgh with no representatives. Fortunately for the rest of the Union Association, another city was ready to take the leap and join the adventure. A group from Cincinnati headed by Justus Thorner, a local brewery manager, with financial backing from his employer, George Gerke of Gerke Breweries, and the *Cincinnati Enquirer* newspaper, was accepted at the meeting.[8] Henry Lucas had recruited Thorner to join the circuit earlier in the month, and Thorner was more than happy to get involved with the rogue organization.[9] Thorner's history in professional baseball had been a rocky one.

By the time of his entry into the Union Association, Thorner was a 36-year-old Jewish brewery manager, opera singer, and the founder of two major league baseball teams in Cincinnati. Thorner first came to prominence in public life in the 1870s as an avid participant and supporter of Cincinnati's artistic community. As a young man, Thorner wrote and published several songs, was an active member of the Young Men's Hebrew Association, and regularly gave singing performances as a tenor.[10] He was well connected in both the Jewish and German communities. Like the Brown Stockings' Chris von der Ahe, Thorner was a German immigrant. In October 1879, the incumbent Cincinnati Red Stockings, one of the National League's inaugural members, withdrew from the circuit. Thorner, the president of the independent Cincinnati Star Base Ball Club, applied for membership and was accepted, aided by the city's premier sportswriter, O.P. Caylor. His Star club made a rough transition to the National League, hindered by a dispute with league president William Hulbert over the rights to third baseman Mike "King" Kelly. The 21-year-old had put forth a magnificent campaign for the Red Stockings, which saw him hit .348/.363/493 for a league-leading OPS+ of 182. When the Red Stockings withdrew, Hulbert's Chicago White Stockings quickly signed Kelly while Thorner fought valiantly to keep the prodigious talent for his Star club. Unsurprisingly, Hulbert ruled in his own favor, and Kelly went on to superstardom for the White Stockings while the Stars finished in last place with a 21–59 record. Thorner complained bitterly about the reserve rule, which had prevented him from having access to suitable talent to compete. The 1879–80 iteration of the rule ensured that NL clubs could reserve five players on their roster for the coming season. For a new club such as the Stars, they could only construct a club from non-reserved players, which limited their options and hindered the quality of the team. Thorner filled out his club with a mixture of unproven locals and over-the-hill vets, though the brother duo of pitcher Will and outfielder James "Deacon" White each gave commendable performances for the club. Thorner drew the ire of the National League by having the gall to sell alcohol at his games. He claimed it was the only way his club could make a profit since he could not sign worthwhile talent because of the reserve rule.[11] The Stars beleaguered owner also drew animosity from his own directors, who ousted him as club president in September of that year. The Stars were not long for the National League and would be replaced in 1881 by Detroit.

Thorner's unpleasant National League tenure inspired him to form another independent club in 1881, which would face off against all comers. By the fall, Thorner had entered his club into the new American Association. The club was financed in part by George Herancourt, the head of a brewery, for whom Thorner had once been employed. Thorner would act as a surrogate for Herancourt in lieu of providing his own money, and in case of any profits on the season, Thorner would receive part of Herancourt's share. Another key source of capital was David R. McLean, the owner of the *Cincinnati Enquirer*. O.P. Caylor, the acerbic scribe working for the rival *Cincinnati Commercial*, was also involved in getting the association up and club running as team secretary. On the field, the newly incorporated Cincinnati Red Stockings were a smash hit. After years of dismal results in the National League, the new AA squad took the inaugural pennant with a record of 55–25. The pennant restored the Red Stockings' name to the glory of the famed 1869 squad, which had gone undefeated and helped turn baseball into America's pastime with their cross-country tour. For Thorner, who had been instrumental in forming the new nine and the new league, the experience turned bitter once again. When the season started badly for the new club due to rainy weather and poor play, Thorner became increasingly impatient. Never afraid to speak his mind, he found himself quarreling with his fellow shareholders and withdrew from the organization before the season had ended.[12] In the aftermath of the pennant victory, Thorner filed suit against the club's shareholders, claiming he was due a quarter share of the $15,000 profit the club had made.[13] His old friend, Caylor, was claimed to have fooled Thorner into thinking the club's financial outlook was worse than it was, causing Thorner to depart.[14] The court ruled that since Thorner had signed the contract for shares in the club, but only as a representative of Herancourt, who had put up the money, he was not due any of the club's proceeds. Thorner was not entitled to the profits and would have to take up the issue with Herancourt. Thorner would file suit against Herancourt, but all records show that he once again lost his case. Thorner made a last-ditch effort to have the Red Stockings expelled from the American Association after they played forbidden postseason exhibitions against NL clubs in hopes that he could regain ownership, but this effort failed too.[15]

Having founded and later been ousted from two different major league franchises, Thorner must have harbored some bitterness towards the establishment. He felt that his time in the National League was ruined by the reserve rule, which denied him the opportunity to compete. His time in the American Association was undermined by his partners in the Cincinnati Red Stockings, who forced him out of the club and withheld what he viewed as his rightful share. Joining the Union Association gave him the chance to fight against the hated reserve rule and also to go to war with his former friends in the American Association. Thorner was the kind of man who would not back down and was not afraid to speak his mind. One account described him as "a blunt, jolly gentleman, ready alike for a joke or a discussion, and very emphatic in the expression of his opinions."[16] Like Lucas, he seemed to possess an unshakeable zeal and pulsating energy. His old partner Caylor once described

Thorner in the following words: "I never met a man so full of hope and energy, so ripe with a spirit of undertaking."[17] His undying hope, undiminished by two failed experiences, would be a key force in the formation of his new club.

With his entry into the new league confirmed, he quickly went to work in building his roster. Aided by the presence of a number of Philadelphia ballplayers who were lingering in the hallways of the meeting, Thorner quickly signed up three local players. His biggest signing was undoubtedly George "Grin" Bradley, coming off a fine bounce-back season as the change pitcher for the Philadelphia Athletics, winning 16 games with a 110 ERA+ in 214.1 innings. Bradley had once been the greatest pitcher in baseball back in 1876 but had spent most of the 1880s injured or ineffective. He was now a 30-year-old grizzled veteran whose right arm could give out at any moment. This fact meant that Thorner's offer of a two-year contract at $2,500 a year and $1,000 advance money was too good to pass up.[18] Bill Harbridge, a 28-year-old outfielder, fresh off a dismal .221/.283/.286 line

Henry V. Lucas as he appeared in the late 1890s when he was an investor in a St. Louis cycling track. In 1884, he was the Union Association's guiding light as league president and owner of the circuit's best club, the St. Louis Unions (Missouri Historical Society).

for last-place Philadelphia was signed for $1,400, a modest salary for a player with eight years of major league experience.[19] Thorner also signed Charles Barber, a 30-year-old veteran infielder of Philadelphia semi-professional ranks, without major league experience to a $1,400 deal.[20] Barber reportedly made just $300 the previous season toiling in the Interstate Association, so the nearly 500 percent increase in salary was impossible to resist.

Along with the addition of Thorner and the departure of Al Pratt, the Union Association's December meeting saw perhaps the most critical change in the makeup of the league. Henry V. Lucas, the millionaire, was elected president, replacing the sitting leader, Washington Nationals director Henry B. Bennett. There appears to have been no animus on the part of Bennett in the decision, even though Lucas's determined pursuit of high-priced players ran in direct contrast to the inactivity of Bennett's club. Installing Lucas as president signaled a complete changing of the guard. The outspoken millionaire from St. Louis would guide every decision made by the circuit going forward. He would be aided every step along the way by Justus Thorner, who shared a similar distaste for the reserve rule and desire to undermine his city's established franchise. As 1883 ended, the Union Association was inching ever closer to becoming a living, breathing organization, with six solidly financed clubs slated for play in 1884.

4

◇◇◇◇◇◇◇◇◇◇◇◇◇◇

The War Begins

The inaugural season of the American Association included seven teams and an 80 game schedule. A six-team circuit was seen as unsustainable since it created scheduling difficulties, with the belief that "any number [of teams] not divisible by four, made a schedule exceedingly awkward."[1] With this understanding in mind, the directors of the Union Association were determined to find two more clubs to join their venture, bringing the number of clubs to eight. Locating two more teams had become an increasingly challenging task due to the simple fact that, as the year 1884 began, there were more professional baseball teams and leagues in existence than ever before. By season's end, a record 17 different professional leagues and over 90 teams would see play.[2] By contrast, the 1883 season had seen seven professional leagues in operation and 48 teams.[3] The only prospects for new entrants would be from an existing club deciding to jump to the Unions or the addition of a new club formed from scratch.

The first month of 1884 saw the first cracks in the Union Association's plans for the coming season. The organizations in the National Agreement set out to push back against their new threat. At the National League meeting in November 1883, New York president John B. Day put forth a resolution that would blacklist any reserved player who jumped his contract. The intention of the plan was not only to punish the deserters but also to limit "the temptation to lure him back with a higher salary, which amount to rewarding instead of punishing him for leaving."[4] As a further consequence, "it meant extending the reserve far beyond its original intent by converting it into a weapon for fending off outside competition."[5] The National League did not immediately adopt the proposal. Day, who was also the owner of the New York Metropolitans, also proposed it at the December 1883 meeting of the AA, where the Association's owners passed the measure. The "Day resolution," as it came to known, gave contract jumpers the option of returning to their respective clubs without penalty as long as they had not appeared in a game for a rival organization. At the National League's December 1883 meeting, the League tried to put further pressure on both deserters and those considering jumping to the Union Association by threatening to blacklist any players "who did not sign contracts within thirty days of receiving them."[6] The NL eventually passed the Day resolution at their spring meeting in March 1884.

Most of the players signed thus far by UA clubs had been reserved by one of the clubs in the National Agreement. The list of signees included stars like Larry

Corcoran, Tony Mullane, and Fred Dunlap. It also included the cadre of Northwestern Leaguers accumulated by the Henderson syndicate. With the Day resolution and the weaponization of the reserve rule, the established leagues now had a tremendous amount of leverage over the contract jumpers in the form of a blacklist. The heads of each respective league were perfectly willing to impose the threat of a blacklist over the jumpers, which would cut off all professional opportunities in the case of the Union Association's failure. National League president A.G. Mills vowed that the loss of players to the Union would be "positively beneficial, as they could be made an example of for the benefit of the great mass of players."[7]

For a player like George Bradley, there was little to fear from jumping to the Union. He had achieved National League stardom but was now worn down, injury addled, and at the tail end of his career. There was a very reasonable chance his career would be over after 1884. However, for young stars like 23-year-old Corcoran and 24-year-old Mullane, there was a significant risk. Both were aces in the middle of their primes and would be in high demand. Elite pitchers, both in 1884 and in 2021, were the most valuable commodity in baseball. With their whole careers seemingly ahead of them, these youngsters viewed the blacklist as a potential career-ender. With their careers at stake and blacklist looming, the pair soon reneged on their Union contracts.

Corcoran was the first to waffle on his commitment with the usurpers. White Stockings head Al Spalding offered Corcoran a contract for 1884 and gave the pitcher thirty days to accept the offer, wielding the threat of banishment. The pitcher agreed to terms with his former club in early January. Thanks to the reserve rule and the blacklist, the White Stockings had all the negotiating power over Corcoran. Spalding re-signed the pitcher for a salary of $2,100 with a $400 advance.[8] This amount was a full $2,000 less than the contract he had signed with Henderson and the Chicago Unions. Spalding summed up Corcoran's choice: "Larry had no fault to find with or treatment of him, and he knows that $2,100 in cash goes further than $200,000 in promises … he has not been bulldozed, bribed, coaxed or frightened."[9] In hindsight, this proved to be a mistake on Corcoran's part. Eighteen eighty-four would be his last full season in the majors, his arm thoroughly wrecked by 516.2 innings of work for the fifth place White Stockings. Corcoran began to prove ineffective and unreliable was let go by the White Stockings early in 1885. He would pitch just seven more contests in the majors and was washed up at age 27. At some point, the hurler developed a drinking habit. After unsuccessful stints in the minors, highlighted by a frightening incident in which he nearly bit the finger off of teammate John "Shorty" Howe, he would return to his native Newark, where he passed away at age 32 from Bright's Disease in 1891.[10]

The departure of Corcoran was a blow for Henderson and Hengel, who now had to find another top-flight pitcher to lead the Windy City club. They would soon find their man in the tempestuous Hugh "One-Arm" Daily, a 35-year-old Baltimorean. The remarkable Daily had experienced a tumultuous road to the major leagues. The Irish-born hurler had grown up in Baltimore, where he had lost his hand around age 13 after being "shot through the left wrist with a loaded musket in backstage horseplay at Baltimore's Front Street Theater, a Union armory during the Civil War."[11]

OLD JUDGE Cigarettes

INDIANAPOLIS

CORCORAN, P. Indianapolis
COPYRIGHTED BY GOODWIN & CO. 1887.
GOODWIN & CO. New York.

The diminutive Larry Corcoran stood just 5'3", but he was one of the most feared pitchers of the 1880s. As the ace of the Chicago White Stockings, he hurled three no-hitters and won 170 games from 1880 to 1884. He nearly jumped to the Union Association before reneging on his contract after he was threatened with blacklisting (Library of Congress).

He had toiled in the amateur leagues in Maryland throughout the 1870s. He came to national prominence while pitching for Rochester in the National Association in 1880 and the independent New York Metropolitans in 1881. A staggering 1.57 ERA in 614 innings and 73 starts that year finally earned him a shot in the National League. He debuted for Buffalo in 1882, going 15–14 in 29 starts with a 2.99 ERA but failed to show the remarkable durability of the previous season. Daily joined Cleveland in 1883 and burst to stardom, winning 23 games and throwing a no-hitter on September 13, 1883. Nevertheless, he was deeply unhappy with his handling by club manager Frank Bancroft. In late August, his pitching partner Jim McCormick was placed out of commission for the season with an ailing right arm. With the club hanging on to first place by a thread, Bancroft leaned heavily on Daily, who started 11 of the club's final 22 games without McCormick. The Blues won just seven of their final 22 games and finished in fourth place. Daily's late-season performance drew the ire of local scribes, who noted that he appeared to be "out of condition."[12] Daily was disgruntled and bristled at being placed on Cleveland's reserve list after the season. At such an advanced age and unhappy in his current situation, Daily was more than willing to jump for a big payday. Henderson and Hengel needed a workhorse and signed Daily in January for a reported salary of $3,000.[13] Daily's signing was a reunion of sorts, as he and Henderson had been important contributors to Baltimore's baseball fraternity for many years.

In early February, Henry V. Lucas's prospective nine was dealt a significant blow by the news that Tony Mullane, like Corcoran, was breaking his Union contract. Unlike Corcoran, he would not be returning to his original club. Instead, he joined the Toledo franchise, which had recently been admitted to the American Association after winning the 1883 Northwestern League pennant. Mullane was free to sign with the Ohio club since Toledo's management had worked out an

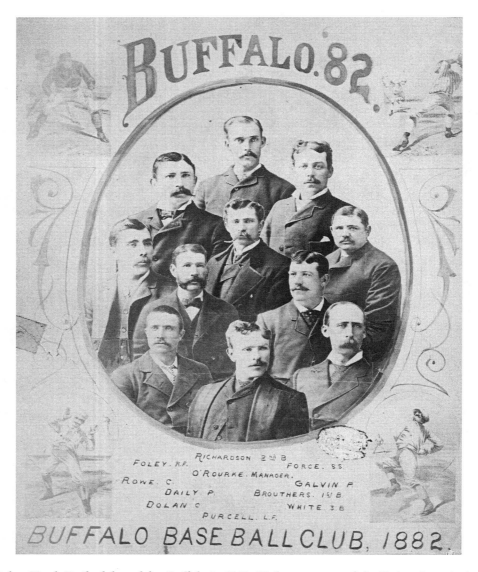

Pitcher Hugh Daily debuted for Buffalo in 1882. He became one of the Union Association's top performers in 1884, winning 28 games with a 2.43 ERA, while striking out 483 batters in 500.2 innings. The taciturn hurler had lost his left hand in an accident during his youth and was universally known as "One Arm." Working from the outside, clockwise from top: Hardy Richardson, second baseman; Davy Force, shortstop; Pud Galvin, pitcher; Deacon White, third baseman; Blondie Purcell, left fielder; Tom Dolan, catcher; Jack Rowe, catcher; and Will Foley, right fielder. Inside, clockwise from top: James O'Rourke, manager; Dan Brouthers, first baseman; and Hugh "One Arm" Daily, pitcher (Boston Public Library).

agreement with Chris von der Ahe that would see the Brown Stockings release Mullane on the condition that Mullane reneged on his Union Association contract.[14] Mullane's Toledo contract would match the terms of the Lucas contract, $2,500 including $500 advance, and the pitcher would return his original advance money to Lucas. The pitcher's signing was a significant victory for the clubs in the National

Agreement, even if it went against the spirit of on-field competition. After all, the Brown Stockings held Mullane in reserve, and letting him go to a direct competitor would weaken their club while improving their rival. However, von der Ahe, with a vision larger than just that of his own club's success, seemed to see letting Mullane go to Toledo as a case of losing the battle but winning the war. Agreeing to release Mullane to Toledo would prevent the pitcher from playing for Lucas. This would weaken the Union Association and Lucas's club while also strengthening one of the American Association's new teams and making the league stronger as a whole. Henderson had willingly let Corcoran return to the National League, not pursuing any legal recourse.[15] Lucas was upset with losing Mullane and enraged by the backroom dealings between St. Louis and Toledo that enabled the transaction. The president of the Union Association planned to sue Mullane for breach of contract, and the resulting legal proceedings would last well into the season.

One of baseball's most polarizing figures, the handsome and talented pitcher Tony Mullane made enemies everywhere he went. His penchant for contract jumping led to numerous suspensions and likely cost him a chance at 300 career wins. He pitched for Toledo in 1884 after breaking his Union Association contract (Library of Congress).

The losses of two prospective stars in Corcoran and Mullane overshadowed the lower profile departures of a number of the Northwestern League players that Henderson had signed for his two rosters. Three of Henderson's Peoria signees, John "Trick" McSorley, Ed Kent, and George Pinkney, broke their Union contracts after taking advance money from Henderson to return to their previous club under threat of blacklist by Peoria. The Springfield battery of pitcher Fleury Sullivan and catcher Billy Colgan broke their Chicago Unions bond and signed with the Pittsburgh Alleghenys. Another Springfield signee, catcher Tom Gunning, had been the first Union player to renege on his contract and ended up signing with Boston's National League club. Since the Springfield, Illinois, franchise had recently disbanded, Sullivan, Colgan, and Gunning were no longer bound by the reserve rule and could freely sign with another club.

The circuits in the National Agreement were not only looking to prevent the Union Association from having access to their players but, through the expansion of the American Association, were also looking to cut off potential markets. At their December 1883 meeting, the American Association decided to admit four new clubs, going from eight teams to twelve. The aforementioned Toledo nine was admitted from the Northwestern League. They were joined by the Interstate Association champion Brooklyn club, Dan O'Leary's strong independent team in Indianapolis, and a new nine to be formed from scratch in Washington, D.C. The hasty expansion of the AA was done to undermine the Union Association. Toledo, Brooklyn, and Indianapolis had each been pursued as potential markets for the Union, while the Nationals in Washington were one of the original clubs to join the circuit. The National League stood pat, content to let the AA take on the considerable risk of the expansion. Adding four teams so quickly would weaken the overall quality of play, create competitive imbalance while increasing travel costs and overall expenses. If it kept the Union Association from succeeding, then the risk would be worth it.

The eight-team Northwestern League also announced plans to play as a 12-team circuit in 1884. The league had lost two teams, with league champion Toledo jumping to the American Association and Springfield disbanding. At their January meeting, the circuit added six new teams. The 1884 season would feature six original league members, Bay City, Saginaw, Fort Wayne, Grand Rapids, Peoria, and Quincy, joined by new nines in Milwaukee, St. Paul, Minneapolis, Terre Haute, Stillwater, and Muskegon.[16] The expansion of the circuit would provide "the League with two good circuits east and west," with the Michigan and Indiana teams comprising the eastern loop and the Minnesota, Illinois, and Wisconsin clubs making up the western loop.[17] Whether the league's decision was made to spite the Union Association or simply happenstance, the addition of six new markets meant that the Unions would have even fewer places to look for new markets.

The expansion of two of the three leagues in the National Agreement would mean an increased fight for players since there were now eight more teams who would be on the field in 1884. Many National League and American Association teams also formed so-called "reserve teams" in response to the increased demand for players. These clubs would contain promising players who could not be kept on the main rosters, which typically fielded 11 men. In essence, these were the first farm teams in baseball history. The practice started at least as early as 1883, with the Cincinnati Red Stockings using the local Shamrock nine as their reserve team.[18] In 1884, these clubs were hastily created en masse by teams in all three major leagues to hang on to promising young talent and deny rival clubs of potential diamonds in the rough. The strongest reserve club was likely the Boston Reserves, the reserve club of the National League's Boston franchise. The club was stable and talented enough to compete in the Massachusetts State League for the 1884 season while providing several players to the parent club. In other instances, such as the Baltimore Union reserve club, it was little more than a short-lived and financially wasteful extravagance that was quickly brought to a halt once the economic realities of operating a professional baseball club became clear. Henry Lucas, who had fielded a team in 1883 from a pool of St. Louis semi-pros, would field a reserve team in the coming season under the name of the Lucas Amateurs.

The practice of reserve clubs put a further strain on talent hungry clubs already thinned by the mass expansion of major league clubs from 16 in 1883 to 28 in 1884. This was in addition to the proliferation of new minor leagues for the coming season. For the Union Association, the combination of the Day resolution, league expansion, and now reserve clubs put further pressure on Union clubs to acquire players. Every player with a pulse was either under contract or the subject of a bidding war. Under this unusual pressure, Lucas and company had to find two more clubs willing to join the league.

The seventh club to claim a spot in the Union Association came from Altoona, Pennsylvania. The town of Altoona was a railroad town that boasted an 1880 population of 19,710, a figure that placed it just outside of the 100 largest urban places in the country, with former Northwestern League locale, Springfield, Illinois, edging it out for the 100 spot.[19] That would make the club the smallest in the league by far. The next smallest population in the Union Association was Washington, D.C., which ranked 14th largest in 1880 with a population of 147,293, nearly eight times as large as Altoona. To their credit, the town had fielded a strong club in the Western Interstate League in 1883. Including exhibition contests, the club had posted a record of 51–22–1 in 74 games, including a victory over the Pittsburgh Alleghenys. A late-season report noted that the club had spent nearly $2,000 to improve their ballpark and, after all, obligations, posted a positive balance, further noting that the "financial condition of the association has been healthy, contributed largely to by able management."[20] The club was slated for play in 1884 in the Interstate Association, a proposed six-team circuit. Altoona's principal directors were W.W. Ritz, a local pharmacist, and Edward R. Curtis, a bookseller, who would manage the club. Curtis was also elected president of the Interstate Association in January.[21] Ritz and Curtis had begun signing players in December 1884. The initial roster focused primarily on attracting Pennsylvania amateurs and resigning some of the players who appeared for the Altoona club in 1883.[22] The club's sole player with major league experience was the troubled Jack Leary, a well-traveled pitcher-infielder with significant ability and prone to going on drinking binges. He had appeared with Louisville in 1883. While out of the lineup with a hand injury, he was banned for drunkenness by the club and finished the season pitching for a club in Carlisle, Pennsylvania. Leary's dubious personal habits were the primary reason he was available to the Altoonas. Despite Leary's presence, the Altoonas were strictly a low-level minor league outfit.

By early February, the proposed Interstate Association was in peril, and a last-ditch meeting failed to yield a promising result.[23] Altoona was at risk of having no league to call home and was open to any offers. The Union Association's directors had expressed a preference for larger markets and were avidly pursuing a situation in Boston. However, since that situation was unfolding too slowly, Lucas turned his attention towards Altoona. The market in Altoona was problematic but had some strategic advantages. Altoona was a railroad hub and a common stop for travelers going from east to west and vice versa. Eastern clubs could stop in Altoona on their way to western road trips while the western clubs would begin their eastern trips the same way. Lucas and the Altoona backers saw this factor as a solid justification for their inclusion in the new league. This fact did not remove the significant risks associated with putting a franchise in a tiny locale, particularly when that club was to be composed of players signed to compete in a lower minor league. From Altoona's perspective, the club had performed well in 1883 and drawn strong crowds for its various exhibition games against major league clubs. The promise of 56 home games against top-flight professional clubs was bound to attract fans and generate revenue. These potential revenues would be compounded by the low salaries that the club would pay out. While salary figures for the club are not known to exist, the club's formation as a low-level minor league nine would have likely kept salary demands modest, likely below $1,000 a year per man.

With seven clubs in tow, the Unions were almost ready to start their season. The long-rumored Boston Union club came together incredibly quickly, considering the circumstances. A Boston group headed by George Wright and Tim Murnane had applied to the Union Association back in January.[24] This group was reported to have dragged their feet in lining up specific logistical details, and thus their application remained in a state of limbo for several months.[25] Boston was finally awarded a franchise on March 17, 1884, at the Union Association's final pre-season meeting in Cincinnati, having beat out applica-tions from Kansas City, Rock Island, Illinois, Evansville, Indiana, Wheeling, West Virginia, and Johnstown, Penn-sylvania. Boston was selected as the league's fourth eastern club, ensuring a scheduling balance with the four west-ern clubs. Their admission on March 17 gave the Boston directors precisely one month to construct a roster and be ready to hit the field for the season opener on April 17 in Philadelphia.

The new franchise would be backed by $10,000 in capital stock, which included an investment from Lucas. George Wright, only a couple of years removed from superstar career highlighted by his role as the all-world shortstop for his brother Harry's 1869 Cincinnati Red Stockings and the Bos-ton Red Stockings dynasty of the 1870s, would be the director. Wright was now a partner in the Wright & Ditson sport-ing goods company. He was following in the footsteps of his old teammate Al Spalding and another former ball-player, Al Reach, who had become very successful in that industry. Despite rumors that Wright would be taking

Baseball's first superstar, George Wright, had become a household name as the shortstop for the famed 1869 Cincinnati Red Stockings. He founded his own sporting goods com-pany, Wright & Ditson, and became one of the founders of the Boston Unions in March 1884. His company supplied the league's official baseball, as well as its annual guide (courtesy Southern Illinois University Press).

the field, the former superstar stayed behind the scenes with the club. He handed over managerial and player acquisition reigns to another former teammate, Tim Murnane. The 33-year-old Murnane was a veteran of the National Association and the National League but had not played professionally since 1880. Murnane would later become the nation's leading sportswriter and was one of the most respected people in baseball. Murnane installed himself as the club's first baseman and quickly set about constructing a roster out of thin air in less than a month.

Philadelphia's Murnane took a two-pronged approach by signing available locals with major league experience and scouring the local sandlots for diamonds in the rough. Tommy Bond had been baseball's most outstanding pitcher in the second half of the 1870s before arm troubles caused by overwork had diminished his ability to get batters out. Murnane signed his old teammate for a reported salary of $1,300.[26] Lew Brown was a lovable but unreliable drunkard who had been the best catcher in baseball, equally adept at handling pitchers and at-bat. Brown

Tim Murnane, shown here in 1874, starred in the National Association. After a long hiatus from professional baseball, he assumed the reins of the Boston Unions in March 1884. The 32-year-old acted as player-manager of the hastily-formed club. After his playing career, he became one of the leading sportswriters in the country (New York Public Library).

had been banned for life by the National League for his erratic behavior. By 1884 he was suffering from a sore shoulder. He consulted with a local physician named Dr. Blodgett, who treated his ailing shoulder in the months preceding the season.[27] The treatments were successful enough for Brown to sign with Murnane's rapidly forming nine, though one observer suggested that he "ought to put his 'elbow' under the care of a total abstinence society."[28] Murnane supplemented his high risk-high reward battery with a heaping helping of local sandlotters and unsigned minor leaguers from the area. Walter Hackett and John Irwin, the younger brothers of National League stars Mert Hackett and Arthur Irwin, were two of Murnane's recruits. Ed Crane and a 17-year-old outfielder named Michael Slattery were enlisted from the sandlots. Like Tom Pratt in Philadelphia, who had constructed a roster filled with Philadelphians, old and young alike, Murnane too filled his roster with local talent. Every member of the club's preseason roster was from the Boston area, which, thanks to a rich baseball community, was not necessarily the handicap it might have been. The roster came cheap with virtually every player making between $75 a month to $200 a month, with Bond's $1,300 salary being the highest on the team, a veritable steal for a number one pitcher, but also a sign of how little was expected of the former great.[29]

Perhaps more daunting than finding a playable roster for opening day was the task of locating suitable grounds to build a viable ballpark to play in. The club's home debut was scheduled for the end of April, which meant that the directors had less than six weeks to make something happen. The Boston Union Athletic Exhibition Company, the baseball club's official stock company, was tasked with accomplishing this seemingly impossible task. The company's president, Frank E. Winslow, who was the owner of several roller skating rinks, set out to build the park as a joint baseball grounds, cycling park, and track and field facility, as a means to utilize the field when the Unions were out of town and in the offseason.[30] Winslow located a 134,000 square foot tract of land at Dartmouth Street and Huntington Avenue.[31] Construction commenced in early April, and amazingly, a fully-fledged ballpark, with the capacity to seat 4,575 fans, was ready for the club's home debut on April 30. Miracle of miracles, the hastily formed Boston Unions had managed to build a team and a ballpark from scratch in under a month.

With eight teams now lined up, the Union Association was now on the verge of actually taking the field. A 112 game schedule was drawn up, and the season would officially start on April 17. This starting date was a full two weeks before either the American Association or the National League seasons would commence. For two weeks, all eyes in the baseball world would be looking towards Henry Lucas, Justus Thorner, Albert Henderson, and the rest of the Union Association clubs to see what they had to offer. A strong showing could win over skeptics and entice fans to the ballpark. A dismal showing might cause others to write off the venture entirely. The old adage is that you never get a second chance to make a first impression, and April 17 would be the first the world would see of this new league, and every single owner and player wanted desperately to make good. Their baseball lives depended on it.

5

The Union Association
Takes the Stage

April 17, 1884

As President Lucas made his way to his seat at Union Athletic Park in Cincinnati to witness the inaugural game of the Union Association, he must have felt a tremendous sense of pride and relief. After months of exhaustive effort to get the fledgling circuit from idea to reality, the Union Association season was about to start. The upstarts from Altoona had made the voyage to the Queen City to begin play. Because Lucas's own St. Louis nine was not scheduled to play for a couple more days, the league president made the journey to Cincinnati to witness the historic event.

Opening day was equally crucial to Cincinnati's owner, Justus Thorner, as well. Thorner had been angling for sweet vengeance after his contentious departure from the leadership of the Cincinnati Red Stockings and the American Association, the same league he had helped to start. Thorner boasted significant political connections in the Queen City, including his employer, George Gerke, who would run for mayor of Cincinnati in 1885.[1] He also had the financial backing of David R. McLean, the owner of the *Cincinnati Enquirer*. With McLean's immense resources, Thorner made a strategic move to lease the Red Stockings' ball grounds at Bank Street, hoping to force the established club out of the city by leaving them without a place to play.[2] The plan worked somewhat, as the Red Stockings were forced out of their home park and had to scramble to find suitable grounds to play the coming season.[3]

McLean's *Cincinnati Enquirer* would serve as a pro–Union newspaper and provide excellent but relatively even-handed coverage of the entire league throughout the year while providing thorough coverage of both the National League and the American Association. In contrast to the favorable *Cincinnati Enquirer* coverage was the deeply critical coverage in the *Cincinnati Commercial*. Thorner's ally turned rival O.P. Caylor was now the most vociferous critic of the rival league as the acid-tongued writer of the *Commercial*'s sports section. Some believed he had double crossed Thorner to become a key figure in the management of the Red Stockings. Caylor's negativity towards the Union may have stemmed from a personal rivalry with Thorner. His acerbic and bitter commentary on the rival association was a stark contrast to the generally positive spin put forth by McLean's *Enquirer*.

Newspaper coverage of the Union Association could often be interpreted as either pro–Union or anti–Union propaganda. In St. Louis, the *St. Louis Republican* and the *St. Louis Critic* were unabashedly mouthpieces for Lucas and his priorities. The *St. Louis Globe-Democrat* provided thorough but even-handed coverage. Conversely, the *St. Louis Post-Dispatch* was generally critical, though not to the level of Caylor's paper. The Philadelphia papers, now tasked covering three teams, typically paid little attention to the Keystones. However, the *Philadelphia City Item* was often vicious in their takedowns of the new league in general. They were kinder to Tom Pratt's nine, thanks to his well-regarded reputation in the city. In Boston, media coverage was even-handed and supportive of the new venture. This was undoubtedly a result of the immense respect local Boston scribes held towards George Wright, who was the face of the venture early in the season. In non–Union cities like Cleveland, where the loss of Dunlap and Daily was viewed as theft, the coverage of the new league was almost universally negative.

Cincinnati Commercial **sportswriter O.P. Caylor was the Union Association's most vociferous critic. The clever scribe was involved in the management of the rival Cincinnati Red Stockings and used his paper to launch regular attacks on the rebel league (courtesy Southern Illinois University Press).**

The national weeklies also took sides. The *New York Clipper* had been the country's leading source of sporting news since its inception in 1853. The paper had been hugely influential in the popularization of baseball across the nation.[4] The periodical employed English sportswriter Henry Chadwick who provided indefatigable coverage of the game's development. For his efforts, he was bestowed with the nickname "the Father of Baseball." He is credited with the creation of batting average and earned run average as statistics for evaluating players.[5] The *Clipper*, which had reported on the formation of the National Association, the National League, and the American Association, was generally dismissive of the upstarts in the Union Association. Their skepticism was undoubtedly influenced by the close relationships the paper had with virtually every important figure in the baseball world, including the magnates of the NL and the AA.

In converse to the cynicism of the *Clipper*, Francis Richter's Philadelphia-based *Sporting Life* often provided positive coverage, though depending on the commentator, it also offered valuable critiques. Richter founded his sporting weekly in April 1883, and it soon became a rival to the *Clipper* as the nation's premier baseball resource. Richter had started the country's first-ever sports section for the

Philadelphia Evening Ledger in 1880 and had been instrumental in the formation of the Philadelphia Athletics in 1882, the entrance of Philadelphia into the National League in 1883, and had even drafted the National Agreement. Despite his ties to the baseball establishment, he oversaw his paper with an evenhandedness that was reflected by the paper's eventual motto, "Devoted to the Baseball Men and Measures, with Malice Toward None and Charity for All."[6] Richter's paper provided thorough coverage of the upstart league. It often championed the rebels as beneficial for players since having more options would allow men to improve their lots in life and potentially earn more money.

Thorner and Lucas would develop a unique relationship while emerging as the guiding forces of the Union Association season. Each man was driven by a desire to get even with the baseball establishment. Lucas sought to restore his family's baseball legacy by establishing the premier club in his hometown and hopefully beating out Chris von der Ahe in the process. Thorner had been forced out of both the National League and American Association and denied his rightful share of the profits by the Red Stockings management. They were determined to make good and show their rivals that they were serious threats. Both men also enjoyed a friendly rivalry, with each man attempting to outdo the other with the energy and resources they spent on their respective ball clubs. The pair seemed to possess similar personalities, incredibly driven, energetic, and outspoken to the point of brashness. However, both desired for the Union Association to succeed and were willing to dig deep into their pocketbooks to make it a reality.

For all the anticipation, it must have come as something as a disappointment to both men when a meager attendance of just over 500 fans filed through the turnstiles to witness the debut matchup.[7] The *Cincinnati Enquirer* posited that the modest attendance resulted from the fact that the ball game had to contend with "Robinson's Circus and other similar attractions."[8] Attendance was also diminished by an exhibition game played in direct opposition between the Red Stockings and Muskegon of the Northwestern League. Caylor's paper noted that the Unions expected to outdraw their rival three to one for their debut but had failed to do so, as the Red Stockings game drew 462 fans.[9] If the circus and an established rival were not enough to keep fans from the Unions' first game, it seems that the virtually unknown Altoona squad had done little to rouse the interests of the locals. The club had been billed as "the Famous Altoonas" in anticipation of their arrival, but the *Cincinnati Commercial* questioned their legitimacy: "Will somebody please tell us for what they are famous as a team or as players."[10]

Despite the modest attendance and the relative anonymity of the visitors, the inaugural UA contest was a tense one, enjoyed enthusiastically by the crowd. Cincinnati lost the coin toss and batted first with "Yaller" Bill Harbridge the club's veteran outfielder and noted dandy, stepping into the batter's box against Altoona's pitcher John Murphy. Murphy retired Harbridge, as well as right fielder Bill Hawes and first baseman Martin Powell in order. George "Grin" Bradley entered the pitcher's box in the bottom of the first, with a storied reputation. Grin had helped the Athletics to the pennant the previous season and was the highest salaried player for Cincinnati. After signing his Union contract, the Athletics, who had previously low-balled him, made multiple bids to resign him once he had jumped.[11] Bradley remained loyal to Thorner and Cincinnati and chose to take his chances in the new league. Thorner and player-manager Dan O'Leary had hoped that a rejuvenated Bradley would serve as the cornerstone of Cincinnati's pennant hopes. It had been eight long years since he had authored one of the greatest seasons in major league history while pitching for the St. Louis Brown Stockings. In 1876, the 23-year-old Bradley was the toast of baseball, winning 45 games against 19 losses, with a microscopic 1.23 ERA in 573 innings. He also set a record with 16 shutouts while completing 63 of 64 starts. His 170 ERA+, 0.887 WHIP, and 7.4 hits per nine innings also paced the circuit. Bradley had struggled in the following years with bouts of ineffectiveness and injury. He was ostensibly washed up until his standout performance for the Athletics in the heat of the 1883 AA pennant race.

Bradley's long journey had brought him to Cincinnati and a new adventure in a new league. Now facing off against Altoona in the league's debut, he was determined to show that his right arm still had something left to offer the baseball world and that he could still get batters out. Bradley retired Altoona's first two batters, Jack Leary and shortstop Germany Smith, before pitcher John Murphy reached base on an error by second baseman Fred Robinson. Catcher Lou Meyers allowed a passed ball after splitting his finger on Bradley's swift curveball, allowing Murphy to reach second. Meyers was unable to continue in the game and was replaced by John Kelly. The newly installed catcher allowed another passed ball and then threw wildly trying to nab Murphy, and the Altoonas had scored their first run. The lead would hold until the top of the fourth inning when Martin Powell reached base on an error. He quickly stole second and then was driven home on a hit by shortstop Frank McLaughlin. Cincinnati scored the go-ahead run in the seventh on a sac fly by Harbridge. The contest stood 2–1 at the end of seven. In the top of the eighth, Altoona collapsed in a manner that would become all too familiar as the season wore on. Murphy walked Powell, who promptly scored on a double by McLaughlin. Cincinnati scored four more runs in the inning on back-to-back hits and two Altoona errors. Down 7–1 in the bottom of the ninth, Altoona catcher Jerry Moore hit a long drive to right field that enabled him to score for a home run, to make the score 7–2.[12] Bradley finished the inning without additional damage, and Cincinnati had won their first contest.

Despite the 7–2 final score, the game had been a close contest most of the way. The *Enquirer* was laudatory of Altoona's performance noting that "anybody who witnessed the contest yesterday … will not hesitate to compare them favorably with most of the League or American Association teams."[13] The cynical *Cincinnati Commercial* was less charitable in their appraisal of the Altoona's performance: "After classing the railway meal station club 'Famous Altoonas,' it is but proper to let up on the supposed weakness of the Moxley Washington Club … and the Washington Nine could have a 'festival' with such a team as the Altoonas."[14] They also noted that the visiting Muskegon club of the Northwestern League was in every way superior to Altoona and warned, "wait til the Lucas Club gets a chance at that Altoona crowd."[15]

Opening day for the Union Association also featured two additional contests. In Baltimore, the Maryland nine faced off against the Washington Nationals at Union Park. While the fans of Cincinnati had yet to warm to the UA's brand of baseball, nearly 5,000 fans showed up for the debut of the Baltimore Unions.[16] Baltimore was one of the critical markets for the Union Association since the city was the seventh-largest market in the country with an 1880 population of 332,313.[17] The city was also in close proximity to the circuit's eastern teams. The rival American Association club had performed poorly on the field in 1883, which meant there was an opportunity to win over the city's baseball fans with solid play. Baltimore was represented in the inaugural American Association season as a hasty and last-minute addition in March 1882, after a planned Brooklyn franchise managed by Billy Barnie fell through.[18] The new club's performance was so poor, and the public response so tepid, that the franchise folded at the end of the year. A new franchise headed by Barnie was awarded to the city and would see play in 1883.[19] The club now had stable ownership and saw improved attendance, though their on-field performance was still lacking. The Orioles had developed a reputation similar to the Pittsburgh Alleghenys, as a team full of drinking men who did not keep in condition. Men such as Hardie Henderson, Lou Say, Rooney Sweeney, Jack Leary, and Frank "Gid" Gardner had deserved reputations as drinkers. As part of Barnie's commitment to improving his club's fortunes, a number of his players were either suspended or released by the club in an effort to change team culture. The cast-offs from Barnie's 1883 squad proved to be fruitful acquisitions for the Union Association. Nine men from Barnie's club would become regulars in the Union Association, which is either a nod to the untapped potential of the team, which had just posted a brutal 28–68 record, or a comment on the quality of the Union Association.

The struggles of Barnie's crew meant the Unions had an opportunity to become the preeminent club in the hearts of the city's fans. Two members of the 1883 club would become key contributors for the new Baltimore Unions. Lou Say would play shortstop for the Unions. He was a hard-drinking infielder and a fixture in Baltimore dating back to the 1870s. John "Rooney" Sweeney, a weak-hitting but formidable backstop, was banned by the American Association for his drinking and would be picked up by the Unions, who had little interest in adhering to the National Agreement's blacklist.[20] Sweeney's post-baseball career included countless drunken incidents in his native Manhattan before reinventing himself as a heroic dock master on Blackwell's Island (now Roosevelt Island). He was credited with saving at least twelve people from drowning in the East River over the course of 15 years. Sweeney was awarded gold medals by the United States Congress, the United States Volunteers, and the United States Benevolent Association before disappearing from view, his final resting place unknown.[21]

William C. Henderson must have been ecstatic to see the large crowd on opening day. Henderson was entrusted with the day-to-day management of the Unions while his older brother Albert provided financial backing. The elder Henderson was turning his efforts towards the circuit's Chicago franchise. The younger Henderson had spent a great deal of time and energy securing the club's grounds at Belair Lot and constructing a beautiful park. Henderson had overseen the construction of the park during the final weeks of March, and a proposal was even put forth in the Baltimore City Council to construct electric lights along the streets surrounding the park to enable the club to "experiment with night games."[22] The proposed night games never came to fruition. Still, it sheds light on the fact that the Henderson brothers had significant connections in the city and were not facing the uphill battle for credibility that some of the other UA clubs were.

The *Cincinnati Enquirer* offered a somewhat embellished account of the scene in Baltimore:

> The opening of Union Park ... which took place to-day was an important event in the annals of the national sport. The managers of the clubs this morning paraded their men in carriages through the principal streets, headed by a band of music. Their appearance was quite attractive and made a favorable impression. There are few base-ball grounds in the country that are fitted up more elaborately or handsomely than Union Park. Aside from its nine and eligible situation it had few advantages to recommend it as a baseball field, but by the exercise of good judgment and a liberal expenditure of money, the hilly, sandy ground has been made level as the surface of a lake and transformed into a beautiful greensward, the attractiveness of which is further enhanced by the erection of substantial and handsome buildings. The grand stand, of beautiful architectural design, and complete in all its appointments, is 180 feet long and 30 feet deep, twelve tiers of seats high, and had a seating capacity of 1,700 ... the open stands, of which there are two, will seat 1,800 each.[23]

The park also boasted two large clubhouses and a restaurant. There was nothing second rate about the Baltimore Unions' ballpark.

The visiting Nationals, managed by the frugal Mike Scanlon, were hoping to be a worthy rival to their next-door neighbors. Scanlon had formed the nucleus of his club from beloved and experienced local players, who had starred for the semi-professional iterations of the Nationals, including team captain Phil Baker, pitcher Bill Wise, and second baseman Tom Evers. The rest of the team was composed of promising youngsters from all parts of the country. This included California exports, shortstop Henry Moore and catcher Mark Creegan. First baseman Alec Voss and pitcher Milo Lockwood came to the club from Ohio.[24] While most of the clubs in the Union Association had signed high-priced aces with major league track records, Scanlon had signed the hard-throwing Lockwood from the Johnstown, Pennsylvania, club where he had starred the previous year. It was hoped that the rookie would anchor the club's pitching staff and form a duo with the more experienced Bill Wise. Creegan had come from out west as part of the large crew of 16 Californian ball-tossers that had departed from the Golden State in mid–March.[25] The youngster arrived in Washington along with the more experienced Jerry Denny and Charlie Sweeney at the end of March. The trio was exhausted and looking worse for wear from their cross-country trip. The *Boston Daily Globe* described their arrival: "they were tired and dirty. In short, they were rather a hard-looking trio, and their appearance aroused the suspicions of a detective at the depot. He shadowed them to Mike Scanlon's."[26] The Nationals manager informed the detective that the three bedraggled travelers were professional ballplayers, and the incident resulted in a memorable story for everyone involved. The 19-year-old Creegan was reputed to be a defensive wizard behind the plate and was expected to support Lockwood and raise him to greatness.[27] The importance of a good catcher in the 1880s cannot be overstated, as it could mean the difference between success and unmitigated disaster.

A pitcher was only as good as his catcher's ability to handle his pitching. In 1884, catchers were still gloveless, and though masks were now a common sight, the chest protector was still such an anomaly that it drew notice in the press. Later in the year, the Nationals' diminutive catcher and utility man Ed McKenna was singled out for being the first player to wear a chest protector in the history of baseball in Cincinnati.[28] The increasing number of hurlers throwing overhand heightened the importance of finding an able and durable catcher. Though the Union Association prohibited overhand pitching, the rule was difficult to enforce, and pitchers continued to push the envelope.[29] The result was increased velocity and movement on breaking pitches, both of which made the catcher's job even harder and heightened the risk of injury. A secondary factor that was unique to the Union Association was the type of baseball used by the league. The league's official ball was provided by George Wright's firm Wright & Ditson. The official ball reportedly contained more rubber, which made the ball extra hard. In June, it was reported that the Wright & Ditson ball had ensured that "nearly all the Union Association players are more or less crippled ... to stop a square hit made on one of these balls at close range is like tacking a cannon ball."[30]

Creegan and Lockwood would face off against the Baltimore battery of Bill Sweeney and Ed Fusselback. Both Sweeney and Fusselback were Philadelphia natives who had appeared in the American Association in 1882. The pair formed the battery for the Northwestern League's Peoria Reds in 1883. The duo had been among the first players signed by the Henderson syndicate. Despite reports throughout the offseason that Sweeney was on the verge of jumping his Union contract to rejoin Peoria, he was in the box for Baltimore to face the Nationals.[31] The Nationals came to bat in the top of the first and were quickly sent down in order, with Baker, Wise, and Moore each being retired. Baltimore opened the scoring thanks to the sloppy Nationals defense, netting two unearned runs in the bottom of the first. Sweeney sent the Nationals down in order again in the second. In the bottom of the second, William Robinson made league history. The Baltimore third baseman hit the first-ever Union Association home run off Lockwood. Robinson later earned the moniker "Yank" or "Yankee" as a member of the St. Louis Brown Stockings due to his northern upbringing in Natick, Massachusetts. Baltimore scored another three runs in the third and added one more in the fourth. The Nationals were now down 7–0 and held out little hope for a comeback. The duo of Sweeney and Fusselback performed masterfully, coasting the rest of the way to a 7–3 finale. Lockwood's delivery proved hard to hit, allowing only Fusselback and Robinson to reach base via hit, with the pair delivering two and three hits, respectively. Despite this, he struck out just three hitters, and the catching of Creegan was a disappointment as he allowed three passed balls.[32]

The league's third opening day game took place in Philadelphia, where the local Keystones would take on the visiting Boston Unions. The Keystones were expected to be one of the stronger clubs in the circuit, as eight of their nine opening day starters had previous major league experience. Only Buster Hoover, the club's baby-faced 21-year-old left fielder, had never appeared in the majors. At least one observer had placed the club in the running for the pennant, noting that the club was filled with "heavy batting material and promises to make it decidedly warm for the gilt-edged St. Louis and Cincinnati Unions."[33] Owner Tom Pratt and the aged catcher and field manager Fergy Malone had built their squad using almost exclusively Philadelphia players, a matter that was a point of pride for Pratt.[34] It was hoped that veterans like Malone, Levi Meyerle, Billy Geer, and Henry Luff would drink from the fountain of youth and bring the club to success.

Conversely, the Boston Unions hastily formed as the eighth and final Union Association club in late March 1884. Remarkably, owner George Wright and player-manager Tim Murnane, who were both old stars for the Boston Red Stockings the previous decade, had been able to sign a roster and field a team within the span of three weeks. Murnane drew upon the rich reservoir of Boston-based ballplayers, including veterans such as himself, Tommy Bond, and Lew Brown, and unproven and raw youngsters like Ed Crane, Mike Slattery, and John Irwin. Every member of their opening day squad was from New England.

Pratt's Keystones had hoped to find a niche in the city of Brotherly Love, which boasted a vast baseball-loving public. The rival Athletics had set attendance records in 1883, with a reported 305,000 fans attending their 51 home games, for an average of 6,000 fans per contest.[35] The dismal Phillies, the club he had helped found, had drawn over 55,000 fans.[36] Pratt certainly must have believed that he could siphon off a portion of that audience, particularly if his club got off to a good start. His hopes that Philadelphians would take an interest in the new circuit and the Keystones were not immediately evident by the crowd that turned out to Keystone Park at Broad Street and Moore to witness their debut contest.

The contest took place under chilly conditions, with the park still under construction and under 500 fans showing up to the game.[37] The small crowd witnessed a dismal performance by the local club. Fergy Malone, who was now 39 years old and had not played in the majors since 1876 nor professionally since a brief three-game stint with a club in Holyoke, Massachusetts, in 1879, took his position behind the plate to catch. It proved a colossal mistake, as the geriatric and exceedingly rusty catcher proved ill equipped to handle the delivery of the starting pitcher Buck Weaver. Before the first inning was completed, Weaver had allowed six runs to put the game out of hand. The *Philadelphia Inquirer* noted that Weaver had to slow his delivery to help his struggling catcher, who allowed five passed balls on the day.[38] Weaver's performance did not escape scrutiny; however, as the *Philadelphia Times* noted, "it was very evident that he was not doing his best."[39] The surprisingly effective nine from Boston took full advantage of the Keystones' battery woes and scored 14 runs on 15 hits. Tommy Bond looked like his old self, striking out 10 Keystones hitters while allowing just two runs. The local nine did garner 11 hits, suggesting that reports of their hitting ability were not overstated, but the club was in desperate need of a catcher. Malone's dreadful performance would be his last professional game, and he retreated to a role as club's manager.

The opening day of the Union Association season was now in the books and had revealed several truths about what to expect in the coming season. First, the league could not count solely on the curiosity of baseball fans to draw a crowd. In both Cincinnati and Philadelphia, opening day attendance was under 500, which had to have been a concern for the league's directors. If fans were not going to show up for novelty purposes in those markets, then it meant that the teams of the circuit would have to stand out by the quality of their play. Second, the disparity in quality between the clubs was going to be an issue going forward. All three opening day contests could easily be described as blowouts. It was apparent to most observers that the Nationals and the Altoonas, in particular, were not of the same caliber as the rest of the league's clubs. The Altoona situation was of particular concern since the club only possessed one player with major league experience in Jack Leary. Altoona was also perceived to be a Podunk town in the middle of nowhere by the majority of observers. How could the Union Association be legitimate if they had to host a team in tiny Altoona?

The National Association had faced this same issue years ago. The top clubs were located in large markets and boasted high salaried players but were forced to do battle with ramshackle entrants from such obscure locales as Keokuk, Iowa, Middletown, Connecticut, and Fort Wayne, Indiana. The dichotomy of these provincial squads facing off against the juggernauts from large markets had been one of the death knells for the NA. It was common for the smaller clubs to drop out early in the year, and if they did survive, they were so woefully overmatched that they stood little chance of winning more than a handful of games. Altoona's debut performance and perceived smallness harkened back to those dark days and was one of the potential threats to the viability of the new circuit.

Opening day wasn't entirely a wash, as Baltimore drew an excellent crowd and played a strong game that gave the locals a reason to get excited about the coming season. Their park at Belair Lot had also earned much praise. Another highlight was the performance of the Boston Unions, who showed themselves to be a surprisingly talented team with their dominant win over the Keystones. If Bond and Brown could hold up, there was no limit to how successful they could be. After this uneven opening day, the attention of baseball fans would now turn to the Lucas Grounds for the much-anticipated debut of the St. Louis Unions. President Lucas had adroitly scheduled his team's opening contest for Saturday, April 19, in hopes of drawing a large weekend crowd while also garnering the undivided attention of the baseball world.

6

✧✧✧✧✧✧✧✧✧✧✧✧✧✧

"The Finest!
The Nearest!
The Prettiest!"

"While there has been nothing particularly brilliant or noteworthy in
the opening games of the new Union Association, it has made a very
plucky and praiseworthy start, and it has got considerably beyond
the point certain wiseacres predicted it would not reach. The Nationals of Washington, the Boston Unions, the Keystones of Philadelphia
and the St. Louis and Chicago Unions are all playing very tolerable
ball, and although it is not up to the highest professional standard, it
promises better things, and that is doing very well for a young association."—*St. Louis Post-Dispatch*, April 26, 1884

Henry Lucas returned home from Cincinnati on the evening of April 18 to over-
see the final preparations of the Union Base Ball Park to ensure it was ready for
the debut of his prized nine the following day. The park was his contribution to the
advancement of architecture in the baseball world. The ambitious mogul of the St.
Louis Unions had invested some $15,000 in the grounds, hoping it would be the mar-
vel of Mound City and outdo the city's other baseball haven, Chris von der Ahe's
Sportsman's Park.[1] The grounds on which Sportsman's Park laid had been used to
play baseball as early as 1867. That year, August Solari had acquired the tract of land
at the northwest corner of Grand Boulevard and Dodier Street. Initially, the area
was home to Grand Avenue Ball Grounds, which fell into disarray after the collapse
of professional baseball in the city in the late 1870s.[2] Sportsman's Park was built by
von der Ahe in 1881 on the same tract of land and became the home for his St. Louis
Brown Stockings. The grounds would remain in near continuous use until 1966,
with several versions of the park being constructed on the grounds. From 1953 to
1966, the park was known as Busch Stadium, named for August Anheuser "Gussie"
Busch, Jr., head of Anheuser-Busch Companies, which had grown to be the largest
brewery in the world by 1957. Busch had purchased the St. Louis Cardinals in 1953
after their owner Fred Saigh was convicted of tax evasion and forced to sell the club
rather than face banishment from baseball.[3] Ironically, this was not the Busch family's first foray into the world of baseball. In the weeks leading up to the opening day
of the Union Association, Gussie Busch's grandfather Adolphus Busch, president of
the Anheuser-Busch company, had purchased a considerable amount of stock in the

St. Louis Unions and Union Base Ball Park. Busch purchased all the interests held by Henry Lucas's original partner, Ellis Wainwright, who opted out of his investment, perhaps sensing that Lucas's ambition was clouding his financial judgment.[4] The connection between the Busch family and major league baseball was first forged in the Union Association.

Lucas's investment had resulted in an impressive site. Capable of seating up to 10,000 fans, the park was touted as one of the largest in the country. Blue grass and clover were planted in the outfield, which was encircled by a cinder track for sprint and cycling races, which would give the park utility when baseball was not being played.[5] Multipurpose grounds were becoming the in thing for ballpark construction during the period. The trend started with von der Ahe's ambitious redesign of Sportsman's Park as a multifaceted entertainment complex rather than just a ball field. The ballpark also featured a large scoreboard at the southeast corner of the grounds that would post the score of the game and updates on other Union Association games transmitted via telegraph.[6] The grounds were also outfitted with a wooden grandstand, painted white, that stood at the northwest corner of the lot behind home plate.[7] The park was also home to a carriage yard that could fit 100 vehicles.[8] Lucas also took extra steps when it came to his players' comfort, as he also provided two billiard tables in the reception room of the clubhouse and shower rooms.[9] The clubhouse was staffed by a French cook enlisted to prepare meals for the players at "all hours of the day free of charge."[10]

Day two of Union Association play had provided Lucas with a reason for optimism, as the home debut of the Washington Nationals had drawn an excellent crowd of over 2,000 fans to a still-unfinished Capitol Park to witness their return match with Baltimore. A large number of youths witnessed the game from outside the park, climbing atop "the roofs of adjacent houses, tree-tops, fences and even telegraph pole cross-arms."[11] After his decisive defeat on opening day, Milo Lockwood was called on to pitch for the second consecutive start. Baltimore countered with Edgar Alexander Smith, an anonymously named pitcher, not to be confused with contemporary pitcher Edgar E. Smith, or Albert Edward Smith, a Yale alumnus, who played for the 1883 Boston Red Stockings and is confusingly listed as Edgar Smith in the record books. Smith hailed from St. Thomas, Ontario, which would become mildly famous the following year as the place where the famed Jumbo the Elephant was killed after getting hit by a locomotive.[12] Smith was likely recommended by a fellow denizen of St. Thomas, pitcher Bob Emslie, who would win 32 games that summer for the Orioles. Smith's tenure with the Unions would not be as fruitful as his fellow Canadian, and he earned his release in May. Smith was the first of 13 different men who would try and fail to take on the role of secondary pitcher to ace Bill Sweeney. Smith was unimpressive to begin his debut, allowing three runs through three innings before his teammates bailed him out in the bottom of the third. The visitors from Baltimore batted Lockwood all over the field for eight hits and eight runs in the inning, giving their rookie pitcher a five-run lead to start the fourth inning. Lockwood was replaced by Bill Wise, who kept the home club in the contest while they rallied to score four runs and bring the game to within one. In the late innings, Wise faltered and allowed single runs in the bottom of the seventh and the eighth. Down 10-7, the

Nationals scored one more run off Smith in the top of the ninth but could not complete the comeback.

The day's other contests saw rematches between Altoona at Cincinnati and Boston at Philadelphia. Altoona was once again outclassed, and attendance in the Queen City was dreadful. Some 400 odd fans witnessed the 9–2 thrashing of the "Famous Altoonas."[13] There was no salvaging the reputation of the visitors, at least amongst the eyes of those in Cincinnati, and the April 19 contest drew a paltry 250 fans.[14] In Philadelphia, the Keystones improved upon their dreadful opening day performance with a 7–6 victory over the visitors from Beantown. On the downside, the game drew another modest crowd of 500 fans.[15] Making his debut for the Keystones was Jersey Bakley, a talented local semi-pro pitcher. He had debuted as a 19-year-old with the Athletics in 1883, compiling a 5–3 record and 3.23 ERA in eight starts, but failed to earn a regular spot with the eventual pennant winners. Bakley was a potential boon for the Keystones since he was a talented young pitcher with some major league success. There was just one problem; in April, Bakley had signed a contract with the Littlestown, Pennsylvania, club of the Keystone Association. After signing with Littlestown, he received several other offers from pro clubs. Since the pitcher had accepted advance money from Littlestown, he was beholden to stay with that club or risk a blacklist. The naïve youngster had failed to report to Littlestown, claiming illness, eventually joining the Philadelphia Reserves, the Philadelphia League club's reserve nine, before officially signing with the Keystones.[16] Bakley's signing was an unwitting violation of the Union Association's pledge to "under no circumstances … sign a player who was under obligation to any other club, no matter of what organization."[17] Tom Pratt, the well-liked and congenial owner of the Keystones, had even issued a circular prior to the season outlining the core values of the organization, including respecting contracts:

The Keystone Club enunciates its principles in this, its initial season, by declaring that:

    I. Believing it has the right to exist it has come to stay.

   II. It recognizes the inviolability of contracts and would refuse the services of the finest player if under agreement with the smallest amateur club in the country.

  III. The reserve rule is not part of a player's contract, but is a mere club regulation without the former's consent, to take effect after the termination of such contract.

  IV. Its enforcement is exacted by the law of might, not right, and should be resisted by every manly player worthy the privileges of a freeman.[18]

It seems likely that Pratt and Keystones exhibited no malice towards Littlestown, and the contract confusion by Bakley was the result of youthful negligence by the young hurler.

The much-anticipated debut of the St. Louis Unions slated for the afternoon of April 19 was postponed thanks to a steady rainfall that began shortly after the visiting Chicago Unions arrived at the park. With no game to cover or box score to publish, the decidedly pro–Union newspaper, the *St. Louis Republican,* instead published a profile of Henry Lucas. The piece admirably described Henry Lucas's baseball credentials and managerial experience:

> Mr. Henry V. Lucas of the St. Louis Union club is a great lover of the national game and is probably the only base ball president in the country who ever plays himself. All last season he kept up a club, known as the Lucas amateurs, at his own expense and played third base on the nine himself, and played it well, too. At his beautiful suburban home in Normandy he had a fine ball ground laid out on his estate and had comfortable seats erected for the accommodation of a couple of thousand of people. On days when games were played he invited out a number of friends from the city and at the conclusion of the game they were treated to an elegant spread prepared under the supervision of his charming wife.[19]

The glowing account of Lucas was a common occurrence in the St. Louis papers. For all his hubris in taking on the baseball establishment, he was still a member of one of the city's most well-to-do families. His business pursuits were treated with the utmost respect, and he was considered an important figure in the city. The activities of him and his wife were regularly reported in the society pages of the local periodicals. He was perceived as having great credibility. His venture with the Union Association was not presented as a wild-eyed and impulsive gamble. Rather, Lucas's organization was reported on with great anticipation and fanfare. From day one, his fledgling club was given equal coverage with the established St. Louis Brown Stockings.

The postponed opener was rescheduled for the following day, Sunday, April 20. Lucas had placed an advertisement in the *St. Louis Republican* with a bold header declaring the club's grounds: "The Finest! The Nearest! The Prettiest!" and noted that attendees would receive one of ten thousand official Union Association guides published by Wright & Ditson.[20] Each guide included the league's official rules,

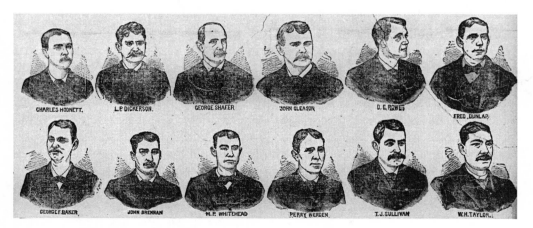

Woodcut illustrations of the St. Louis Unions, as they appeared on the eve of their Sunday, April 20, home opener. Top row, from left: Charles Hodnett, pitcher; Lewis "Buttercup" Dickerson, left fielder; George "Orator" Shafer, right fielder; Jack Gleason, third baseman; Dave Rowe, center fielder; and Fred "Sure Shot" Dunlap, second baseman. Bottom row, from left: George Baker, catcher; Jack Brennan, catcher; Milt Whitehead, shortstop; Perry Werden, pitcher; Ted Sullivan, manager; and "Bollicky" Billy Taylor, pitcher (*St. Louis Post-Dispatch*, April 19, 1884).

complete scheduling information for each major league, and a list of rosters for the UA's clubs. The guides are one of the few pieces of memorabilia still extant from the long-defunct organization. Despite temperatures near freezing, and a slow drizzling rain that lasted all afternoon, a reported crowd of around 10,000 fans made their way to the Union grounds to witness the contest.[21] Debates about the crowd size would ensue in the local papers for the days after, with the more critical lens of the *St. Louis Post-Dispatch*, alleging the attendance was actually around 5,000 while other estimates neared 12,000.[22] Perhaps the most accurate indicator of attendance was the notable success of that day's giveaway, as nearly all of the UA guides ended up in the hands of baseball enthusiasts, placing the attendance near the 10,000 mark. *The Republican* noted that the poor weather prevented what would "have been the largest gathering ever seen in a ball park in St. Louis."[23]

Facing off against the aging wonder, Chicago's Hugh "One Arm" Daily, his old Cleveland teammate, St. Louis's prize acquisition, second baseman Fred Dunlap led off the first game in franchise history for St. Louis. The patient second sacker drew a base on balls, which as per the Union Association's rulebook, took seven balls to earn a free pass. Orator Shafer followed with a ground ball that Chicago failed to turn into a double play, allowing Dunlap to reach second. Dunlap stole third base and scored on a passed ball by catcher Bill Krieg. Daily escaped the inning by striking out Buttercup Dickerson and getting Jack Gleason to ground out. Charlie Hodnett was in the box for St. Louis and retired Joe Ellick on a ground ball to second before allowing a hit to Krieg. Second baseman Moxie Hengel went out on a foul fly to Shafer. Hodnett threw a wild pitch allowing Krieg to go to second, but the catcher was thrown out at third after trying to steal on the next pitch. The following three innings were scoreless. St. Louis scored two runs in the top of the fourth off Daily, on a single by Gleason, and an error by Daily who dropped the ball on a Dave Rowe ground ball to first. Rowe stole second, and with runners on second and third, Billy Taylor drove both men in with a single. Chicago responded with a run in the bottom of the fourth, and St. Louis retaliated with two more runs in each of the fifth and the sixth while Chicago tallied just one more run, and the score stood 7–2 at the end of six innings. The continued rainfall, combined with freezing temperatures, darkness ensuing, and the now seemingly decisive lead, umpire Mike Hooper, an old veteran of Baltimore in the National Association, called the contest.[24] St. Louis outfielder Buttercup Dickerson recalled growing up in Baltimore and watching the former catcher: "I used to look through the cracks in the fence, and see old Hoop, catching [Bobby] Matthews. He was a dandy catcher too."[25] The final result was a 7–2 victory for the home club. The game was relatively well played considering the conditions, with the clubs combining for ten errors, a modest total by 1884 standards, in the days before fielders wore gloves. The hard-throwing Daily struck out nine batters to Hodnett's one. In spite of the loss, the visitors were praised for their immense size and strong play despite having never appeared together before.[26] The large Sunday crowd that turned out despite the poor conditions must have thrilled Lucas and provided proof of the validity of his idea.

The cold and wet spring weather continued for the coming days and resulted in more postponements. The Chicago Unions had expected to play four games in

St. Louis but could only complete one before venturing east to Cincinnati. The rain finally stopped as the visitors boarded their train at Union depot on April 23, with their superstitious manager Ed Hengel reportedly eying up members of his nine in search of a "Jonah," a bit of 1880s slang frequently used to describe a jinxed or unlucky ballplayer.[27] The rainouts were interpreted to be to the advantage of both clubs, as more lucrative Sunday games could be rescheduled later in the season. Lucas and the St. Louis Unions would next face off against the Altoona Unions in a four-game set that would close out the month of April. The Pennsylvania nine had arrived from Cincinnati on April 22, still licking their wounds after a resounding three-game sweep by the Queen City aggregate. Perhaps still naive about his club's talent level and prospects for success, Manager Ed Curtis was interviewed by the *St. Louis Republican*. On the subject of what he expected of his club going forward, he noted, "I won't say that we will win the pennant, for we have not as high priced a nine as some of the others, and therefore should not look too high. But we have a stalwart lot of young men, all steady and reliable, and all willing and earnest players. Therefore we expect to render a good account of ourselves."[28] He also elaborated on the financial standing of his club, noting that the club had a "staunch friend in the Pennsylvania Railroad company, who had furnished it with grounds without charge and presented it with lumber to build a grand stand and open seats."[29] Curtis spoke with great anticipation about the club's home debut which would come against the visiting St. Louis nine on May 2. Curtis noted, "when we play your team at home next week, if the weather is fair, there will be five or six thousand people out, for although our town is not as large as yours, we have the whole people with us and they intend doing all they can to make our season a successful one."[30]

Curtis's measured optimism was quickly dashed in their series with St. Louis. Three thousand fans turned out to the St. Louis grounds to witness the opening contest on April 24. The *Republican*'s game account described the affair: "the game while abounding in errors and very one-sided, was, nevertheless, very interesting and at times was enlivened by some very pretty plays."[31] St. Louis displayed their dominance putting 11 runs on the board before Altoona scored two runs late in the contest. Perry Werden, who was listed 6 foot 2 and weighed 220 pounds and would later earn the well-deserved nickname "Moose," was pitching for St. Louis. Werden would later reinvent himself as a mammoth power hitter in the minors, hitting an astonishing 45 home runs with a .428 average for Minneapolis in 1895. In 1884, Werden was still a 22-year-old pitcher making his professional debut. The young hurler was effective but not dominant, allowing nine Altoona hits and walking two batters. He allowed only one earned run in the contest, a late home run off the bat of Altoona pitcher Jim Brown. The visitors showed surprising hitting prowess, but the strong defense of the home club ensured that Altoona was unable to sustain a rally. The Altoona defense, in contrast, was porous and demonstrated the difference between the haves and the have-nots of the UA. The best clubs provided consistent defensive support to their pitchers virtually every game, while the worst clubs would often waste strong pitching efforts with error-filled sequences. This disparity was to be expected in an era when fielders still did not wear gloves, unearned runs were accrued in staggering amounts, and the ability to field a hard-hit ball cleanly was at a premium. The disparity in fielding quality was arguably the single determining factor in team quality and league quality in this era. Of the 33 clubs that appeared in the three major leagues in 1884, Altoona had the fifth-worst fielding percentage with .861 and posted the third-worst defensive efficiency rating at .562. For comparison, the average of these numbers across all leagues was .891 and .624. The St. Louis Unions, undisputedly the strongest club in the Union Association, would post figures of .888 and .642.

The remaining three contests of the series offered little hope of Altoona's ability to compete, as they lost by scores of 9–3, 7–1, and 8–1. The only noteworthy aspect of the series was the well-attended Sunday contest on April 27, which drew another massive crowd of 10,000 fans.[32] After seven games, Altoona was winless and had been outscored 60–17. The Lucas nine had demonstrated impressive dominance, winning their first five games, and would now travel to Altoona for the Pennsylvanians' home debut on April 30. The hot-hitting of Fred Dunlap, Buttercup Dickerson, and George "Orator" Shafer, all talented batsmen, with previous stretches of dominance in the National League, carried the way for the Unions. With a major league career dating back to 1874, Shafer had the most games played of any of the Union Association's acquisitions, with 573. He also had a reputation as perhaps baseball's most eccentric figure. Shafer earned his ubiquitous nickname due to his tendency to speak loudly to himself in the outfield, commenting on his own abilities with a befuddling mixture of scorn and praise. On one occasion, after making two errors in right field, he was heard muttering to himself:

> Old Shaf, you're gettin' no good. You're very, very bum, and if you don't look out I'll fine you fifty. Oh, what a puddin' you had on that ball, and you let her go flip-flap through your claws. If you do it again I'll kick your head off. Hello, there she is again! Now, Shaf, show 'em what you're made of. Zeet, that's the way to take her in. Good boy, Shaf. You're gettin' her all back. Keep her up. Don't get discouraged. You're old, but you're a little bit good.[33]

When he wasn't busy orating, he was busy mashing. He was a key cog in the powerful Unions' lineup, demonstrating the same skill at age 32 that he had in 1878 when he had hit .338 and paced the National League with a 184 OPS+.

While St. Louis was off to a roaring

George "Orator" Shafer was one of the quirkiest characters in baseball during his long career. He earned his nickname due to his tendency to engage in prolonged self-talk while patrolling the outfield. He was also one of the Union Association's top hitters, batting .360/.398/.501 and leading the league in doubles with 40 (courtesy Southern Illinois University Press).

start, the dreadful performance of Altoona signaled that the overall disparity in team quality was cause for concern. Other clubs were struggling, as the Nationals' record stood at just 2–7, and the club had been outscored 87–50. In Philadelphia, the Keystones' record was 2–5, and they had been outscored 54–41. On a positive note, Baltimore and Cincinnati, expected to be pennant contenders, were each off to hot starts. Chicago held a 2–3 record, including a 2–2 split of their series in Cincinnati, which pointed to their potential. Perhaps the league's greatest surprise was the outstanding play of the league's Boston franchise. The club from the Hub had gotten off to a stellar 5–2 start, exceeding preseason expectations that the hastily formed club would have trouble competing. The biggest surprise was the stellar pitching of Tommy Bond, who had won his first five starts and earned rave reviews, suggesting he looked like the man who had dominated the National League at the end of the previous decade. Bond's success on the mound was aided by several years of rest and a willingness to push the boundaries of the rulebook by releasing his pitches above the shoulder.[34]

The early season attendance returns were as uneven as the league's on-field play. Cincinnati had drawn poorly, averaging under 500 fans per contest, though their Sunday contest on April 27, a 4–3 extra-innings loss to Chicago, drew a solid crowd of roughly 2,000.[35] Philadelphians were similarly nonplussed by the exploits of their local Keystones, as they had also averaged under 500 fans over their first seven home games and were now engaged in a lengthy road trip that would keep them away until June 9. Conversely, Baltimore and Washington had each drawn very well and earned the support of the local fans and media. Each club had drawn over 1,000 fans per game, including multiple contests drawing over 2,000 fans. The response in St. Louis was exceedingly positive, with their two Sunday contests drawing 20,000 fans combined while their other contests ranged from 1,000 to 3,000. Chicago, Boston, and Altoona still had yet to play home games. It remained to be seen how the local fans in those cities would receive the clubs.

The critical response to the league ranged from unabashed praise in the Union organs like the *St. Louis Republican* and the *Cincinnati Enquirer* to the perpetually negative *Cincinnati Commercial*. O.P. Caylor's paper remained incredibly hostile towards the new league, whom they dubbed "the wreckers," while editorializing on the league's quality of baseball and working in stinging jabs about any and every aspect of the circuit on a near-daily basis. The *Commercial* also critiqued papers such as the *Cincinnati Enquirer* for embellishing the quality of play in the new organization:

> All manner of deception is resorted to by them in their foolish attempt to deceive the public … in a word, the Union clubs could not get players, had no opportunities, and with a few exceptions did not get them. The St. Louis club has two or three good reliable players. The Cincinnati Unions have Bradley, Hawes and Powell. The Washington Nationals have Baker. If there are any more even fair second-class players in their ranks we want to hear of them. There is no use trying to deceive a base ball public. They know ball players every time.[36]

For Henry Lucas, Justus Thorner, and Albert H. Henderson, the league's trio of power brokers, the early results of their risky venture illustrated opportunities for growth and causes for concern. Attendance was uneven, with several markets showing keen interest and drawing well while others seemed utterly disinterested, unmoved by novelty or curiosity in the new league. The league's directors had to hope that as the weather warmed and the baseball season got into full swing, fans in Cincinnati and Philadelphia would also warm up. The directors were optimistic that the home debuts in Altoona, Boston, and Chicago would draw more substantial crowds. The outmatched Nationals and Altoonas had demonstrated that their initial configurations were wholly outclassed.

In Washington, the resourceful Mike Scanlon had cast off the dead weight on his roster. He sought cheap and potentially viable new recruits, signing several amateurs from Maryland and Connecticut. One of his opening day outfielders was a man named Carroll, who had reportedly asked team captain Phil Baker "Where is left field, Mr. Baker?" prior to taking the field for the team's debut exhibition contest against Georgetown University in early April. Carroll evidently learned where left field was, but not how to play it, as he made four errors on eight chances across his four big-league appearances before being cast into oblivion. His first name remains undiscovered, though the most likely candidate is Thomas P. Carroll, an outfielder from Johnstown, who perished in the Johnstown Flood in 1889. Scanlon's frugality caused issues in terms of his team's competitiveness but also ensured that his club's costs were kept to a minimum.

Ed Curtis in Altoona was also searching for alternatives for his over-matched club, aided in part by a benevolent Henry Lucas. Curtis was offered several players from Lucas's reserve club, the Lucas Amateurs. Lucas was astute enough to recognize that his organization was only as strong as its weakest club. Throughout the season, Lucas, Thorner, and Henderson would regularly intervene in the affairs and finances of the league's remaining clubs.

7

One Month
in Altoona, Pennsylvania

"An eastern exchange says a naturalist has discovered that monkeys can be trained to play base ball. If this be true, the Union Association still have a fighting chance left."—Cincinnati Commercial, May 21, 1884

"The 'Famous' Altoona Club has announced that it will not play any more games on Sunday. The next announcement they make will be that they will not play any more games on week days."—Cincinnati Commercial, May 14, 1884

The winless Altoona Unions and the undefeated Lucas nine boarded the train at Union Depot in St. Louis on the evening of April 28 to make the journey north to Pennsylvania. The clubs were scheduled to play the first major league ball game in Altoona history on April 30. The first two weeks of the Union Association season had demonstrated the considerable disparity between the talent level of the Altoonas and that of Henry Lucas's star-studded nine. The teams had just completed a brutal four-game set in the Mound City that served as an object lesson in abject humiliation. The weak squad from the Mountain City had been thoroughly dominated, losing all four games by a combined score of 35–7. Add in the three-game sweep at the hands of Cincinnati that opened the year, and Altoona was the very definition of bush league. The winless squad had been hammered, allowing more than three times as many runs (60) as they had scored (17). If there was any respite for the club, it was that they would finally get to play at home, in front of an enthusiastic and supportive crowd.

Henry Lucas, who must have recognized the deficiencies of his most unworthy opponent, sought ways to help the nine. He recommended that Altoona's manager Ed Curtis sign second baseman Charlie Berry, one of the top players for the Lucas Amateurs, the St. Louis Unions' reserve squad. Berry, a 23-year-old from Elizabeth, New Jersey, with no minor league experience, didn't exactly move the needle, but he was a capable fielder and hitter. His son, Charlie Berry, would enjoy a lengthy career as a major league catcher, with a career that remarkably saw him debut 41 years after his father in 1925.

Despite Altoona's deficiencies, the club had a few bright spots. The club's

67

shortstop George "Germany" Smith, at age 25, now in his third consecutive season in Altoona, had performed exquisitely in the field and at bat, reaching base safely in the club's first eight contests. The *St. Louis Republican* described him as a "bonanza."[1] The club's hurlers, Jim Brown and John Murphy, had both performed somewhat admirably, particularly considering the absence of the club's regular catcher, Charlie Manlove. The young backstop had injured his hand while warming up on opening day and had yet to appear for the club.[2] Jerry Moore, the club's replacement behind the mask, was an excellent hitter but had proven to be a sieve behind the plate. He had shown little aptitude in handling the swift deliveries of Brown and Murphy. George Noftsker, a semi-pro from Shippensburg, Pennsylvania, had also demonstrated minimal defensive aptitude in spelling Moore. He was equally deficient as a hitter, having notched only one hit in 23 at-bats to start the season. Perhaps most disappointingly, Jack Leary, the team's sole player with prior major-league experience, had provided absolutely zero value to the club. Leary, who just two years before with Pittsburgh, had hit .286/.300/.349 for a 118 OPS+ while playing five positions, was struggling in a similar role with Altoona. As the club's leadoff hitter, he had only three hits thus far. He had also made two pitching starts, proving ineffective in both games.

Anticipation was high at Fourth Avenue Grounds on the afternoon of April 30, where over 2,000 fans gathered to witness the return of their hometown heroes.[3] The arrival of the now famous and still undefeated St. Louis Unions had "attracted hundreds from adjoining towns."[4] The local baseball enthusiasts were mystified at how badly their club had been manhandled thus far in the season. Indeed, it was an aberration. After all, Altoona was the class of the Western Interstate League in 1883. Just last July, with much the same roster, they had even beaten the Pittsburgh Alleghenys and their star hurler, Billy Taylor.[5] The demoralizing sweep in St. Louis was just bad luck, that's all. Now that they were home, their true colors could shine through.

Any and all hope for the home club was thoroughly extinguished in the top of the first inning. After receiving a warm welcome from the hometown crowd, Lucas's powerhouse got down to business. They quickly tallied four runs off Altoona's John Murphy in the top of the first inning. Two more St. Louis runs in the top of the second put their lead to 6–0. Altoona responded with one run off pitcher Charlie Hodnett in the bottom of the inning to make the score 6–1. Before the day was over, St. Louis had tallied nine more runs and the game concluded with a final score of 15–2. It was the worst loss yet for Altoona, and despite knocking 12 hits off Hodnett, could not muster a substantial rally. The only bright spot for the club was the stellar debut of Berry, who had two hits in four at-bats and played errorless ball at second base. For the Altoona faithful, St. Louis appeared to be the greatest team in the world. The superb play of the visitors was "relished by the audience, as the St. Louis club treated them to such batting as never before seen in Altoona, besides playing a great game in the field, having but one error charged to them."[6]

Two days later, the clubs met again in front of 600 fans. The pitching matchup would feature two former teammates and drinking buddies from the Alleghenys, Billy Taylor for St. Louis and Jack Leary for Altoona. Taylor had been in the pitcher's box last July 22 when Altoona defeated his Alleghenys by a score of 3–1. Leary, expected to contribute as a utility man and change pitcher, had thus far been a disappointment. Since his professional career began in 1877 with Erie of the League Alliance, Leary had appeared for six different major league clubs. He had appeared for at least eight more minor-league outfits. Despite his poor personal habits, he kept getting chance after chance thanks to his tremendous promise and versatility. In 1878, Leary was expelled by the Manchester, New Hampshire, club "for violation of his contract and drunkenness on the ball field."[7] In 1879, he was back with Manchester, earning a reputation as one of the finest pitchers in the country while being recruited by Cincinnati of the National League. Hall of Fame catcher Mike "King" Kelly would later recall that his major league career was saved by Leary's failure to appear in Boston for a game on June 21, 1879. Kelly later wondered, "What might have been the result if Jack Leary appeared on the ground in Boston? I would have been laid off and returned to Paterson [New Jersey] in disgrace."[8] Knowing his career was in peril, Kelly went four for five that day, and a star was born. In this case, Leary's absence had to do with an uproar in Manchester over his pending departure, which caused him to stay with the club. The love affair would not last long, as Leary again earned expulsion in July due to repeated drunkenness and often showing up unfit to play.[9] He joined the Rochester Hop Bitters and played without incident, eventually traveling west in the fall. In January 1880, he was living in California alongside fellow eastern-born carousers/ballplayers, "Hartford" Jack Farrell and Fred Lewis. The good times did not last long, and he was suspended by the California League due to drunkenness just a few months later.[10]

After his ban, he traveled back east, playing briefly in Topeka, Kansas, before being given a brief trial by Boston of the National League in August, pitching poorly in his only appearance. In 1881, he signed with the New York Metropolitans of the Eastern Championship Association and pitched well enough to be recruited by Detroit of the National League. Leary jumped his New York contract and made three appearances for Detroit, again earning his release after failing in his "promise to abstain from liquor."[11] The Metropolitans sought an injunction against Leary, and the case went all the way to the New York Supreme Court. In 1882, he joined Taylor and another future St. Louis Union/drinking man, Lewis "Buttercup" Dickerson, on the inaugural edition of the Pittsburgh Alleghenys. The club, which was replete with elbow-benders of the highest quality, was given the well-earned moniker "the Brewery Nine." It was here that Leary had shown his capabilities, playing five positions and hitting .286. His tenure was not without incident, as he earned a suspension in May for a drunken incident in which he cursed his manager Al Pratt with foul language.[12] In September, he was released and joined Baltimore, pitching effectively in three starts, going 2–1, with a 1.04 ERA. His low ERA is deceptive, as he did allow 22 runs in 26 innings, but a porous defense meant that only three of them were earned. Baltimore reorganized their club entirely for 1883, which meant that Leary was out of work. He signed with Louisville for 1883 and reprised his role as a utility man but proved much less effective than his time in Pittsburgh, earning his release in July after hitting just .188. In a veiled reference to his drinking, *Sporting Life* noted that his fondness for "in-shoots" caused his dismissal.[13] Despite this, he was given another trial by Baltimore but made just three appearances. A similarly uninspired tenure with Harrisburg of the Interstate Association was short-lived. He closed the season pitching in tiny Carlisle, Pennsylvania, where he showed little of his previous ability: "Leary, the once-noted pitcher, now with the Carlisle, Pa., Club, has been batted out, even by the amateur and semi-professional clubs he pitches against."[14] For those keeping score, he had earned expulsion or release due to his drinking in every season dating back to 1878. Despite his underwhelming play in 1883 and his well-known reputation for imbibing, he was signed up by Altoona in the off-season, when the club was still slated to play in the Interstate Association.

Now with Altoona standing winless at 0–8, the underperforming Leary had to have sensed he was running out of chances to prove his mettle. Perhaps motivated by his precarious situation and the opportunity to face off against his brewery buddy and pitching pal, Leary stepped into the pitcher's box in the top of first and did the unthinkable: he pitched a scoreless first. The Altoonas responded in kind, getting shut down by Taylor. Any aspirations of redemptive heroics quickly dissipated, however, as St. Louis tallied three runs in the top of the second. The onslaught was just beginning, and by the end of the afternoon, St. Louis had scored 16 runs, despite the absence of their star second baseman Fred Dunlap, who had gone to Philadelphia on personal business. Leary allowed 19 St. Louis hits in the 16–3 defeat, with every batter in the Mound City lineup hitting successfully off the beleaguered pitcher.

For Altoona manager Ed Curtis, the blowout and the dreadful performance by Leary and his cohorts was the last straw. Five players were released by the club the following day, including Leary, catcher George Noftsker, first baseman John Grady, third baseman Frank Shaffer, and utility man Harry Koons.[15] Grady and Koons would each resign with the club shortly after, likely due to the sheer lack of players available and willingness to sign with the hapless club. Leary's time in Altoona came to a rough end, as he was "assaulted by a number of toughs who handled him in a rough manner" before he left town.[16] Beaten on the ball field and beaten off of it. Leary quickly got another chance and signed with Terre Haute of the Northwestern League. Within days, he was already in hot water with his new club for his personal habits, with one observer noting, "Whisky and insubordination are what down Jack."[17] After another release, he was recruited by the Chicago Unions in mid–June, who were desperate for both middle infield help and another pitcher to support Hugh "One Arm" Daily. After a week sober, it was mockingly reported that Leary "has commenced vacillating again … he revolts at the idea of the violation of his temperance principles, and will not have them tampered with at any cost."[18] Leary underwhelmed the Windy City and quickly returned to drinking. He was released in early July alongside the similarly talented but equally inebriated shortstop Frank McLaughlin, who was making his own brewery tour of the Union Association, with stops in Cincinnati, Chicago, and Kansas City each truncated despite the evident promise that had seen him appear previously in both the NL and the AA.

Leary would head south to Augusta, Georgia, in 1885, where he was suspended for the season after going on a "protracted drunk."[19] 1886 saw more of the same, with Leary earning a June suspension from the Bridgeport, Connecticut, club for the balance of the season.[20] Leary's final pro season came the following year, when he spent part of the season pitching for his native New Haven club, joined by his old pal, Billy Taylor, once again earning his release in July, after going on a bender. His hometown paper summed up his career succinctly: "Liquor has been Leary's worst enemy."[21] In every season dating back to 1878, Leary was either suspended or released for his drinking. Leary's story is worth recounting because it is emblematic of the temptations that could befall a promising ballplayer in that era or any era for that matter. It also demonstrates the complete lack of support networks available to men like Leary. There was no addiction counseling in 1885 and no sense of alcoholism as anything other than a moral and personal failing. The only solution was to punish the alcoholic with a fine or threaten him with release and hope he got the message. The ballplayer was simply a commodity to be used and cast aside when he could not perform. Drink was the ruin of many a promising player, but as long as a man still had some ability, he would get chance after chance. Once he did not, there was little else for a man to do, with many of these once-great players living in abject poverty and addiction after their careers. In Leary's case, he found work as an oysterman in New Haven, where he passed away at age 48 in 1905, though it is not clear if he ever overcame his struggles. Lee Allen, the famed historian of the Baseball Hall of Fame and an intrepid researcher, discovered Leary's final resting place. In his writings, he offered a poetic epitaph of Leary's life: "When he was a young pitcher with Boston in 1880 the world was his oyster, and I think it probable that the oyster was his world later [in life]."[22]

In place of the released Leary, Joe Connors, a Paterson, New Jersey, native, who the Cincinnati Unions had recently released, was signed and made his debut on May 3. The results were much the same, with St. Louis taking a convincing 14–5 victory in front of a large Saturday crowd of over 2,000 fans.[23] After an off day, the teams met again for the final game. The result was another St. Louis shellacking by the score of 12–2 in front of 1,000 fans.

While attendance so far was relatively strong, there was a faction of the locals who remained perturbed by the club's participation in a Sunday game on April 27 while in St. Louis. Before the season, the club had acquiesced to not playing home games on Sunday. The conservative contingent amongst the locals had objected to the team's participation in the April 27 road contest and pressured management not to play any more Sunday road games.

Sunday baseball in 1884 was still the subject of much hand wringing and legal controversy. Many cities prohibited Sunday baseball and made it a criminal offense. For working-class patrons, Sundays were commonly the only day off during the week. While the off day provided opportunities for leisure, there was great importance placed on observing the Sabbath. In many parts of the United States, there were so-called "blue laws," which prohibited certain events from taking place on the Sabbath. In many cases, sporting events such as baseball games were not permitted. These laws were rigorously upheld in many Northeastern cities that were home to professional clubs, while the more western locales were typically more lenient.

As a result of blue laws, it was common even into the 20th century to find ballplayers and teams arrested for playing Sunday contests. Incredibly, in Philadelphia, the right to play Sunday baseball was not won until 1933.[24] During the 1884 season, no National League clubs played Sunday contests as it was against league rules. In the American Association, St. Louis, Cincinnati, Indianapolis, Columbus, and Louisville hosted Sunday contests. Three inaugural UA clubs, Chicago, St. Louis, and Cincinnati, also played Sunday home games. Kansas City and Milwaukee, who would join the Union later in the season, also hosted Sunday games. The incentive to play on the Sabbath was financially motivated. Workers on their off days would be free to attend a ball game, which typically meant large attendance. If Sunday games could be hosted legally and without significant backlash from the local religious community, they were incredible sources of revenue. Conversely, in the cities where blue laws were strictly adhered to, playing Sunday contests was more trouble than it was worth, as legal intervention, arrests, and the souring of the public were often the result. This was the case in Altoona. They had made the mistake of playing in a road contest on the Sabbath. In doing so, they alienated a contingent of their already dwindling fanbase.

After the debacle of the St. Louis home and home series, there was still reason for optimism. The club had yet to play at full strength. Notably, two of their projected starters, catcher Charlie Manlove and first baseman John Grady, had yet to appear. Manlove broke his hand warming up before opening, and first baseman John Grady hurt his knee in the pre-season. Pitcher Jim Brown had struggled with illness and had yet to regain his full strength. He was also struggling in the absence of his Manlove, his longtime battery mate. The club also had a few days off and would finally have time to rest before starting a two-game series on May 10 against Boston. The club from the Hub was playing very well to start the season, holding a 9–2 record on the strength of their rejuvenated Tommy Bond, who was pitching like he had nearly a decade before. Despite the quick start, most experts had pegged them to be significantly worse than either Cincinnati or St. Louis. The upcoming series offered the chance to play against one of the league's lesser clubs. *Sporting Life* summarized the situation: "it is, however, gratifying to know that an easier time is fast approaching—a time when the home team will get its percentage of games, barring further accidents

Irish-born Tommy Bond as a member of the Boston Red Stockings, circa 1879. Bond won 221 games and pitched over 3300 innings by the age of 24. After several years of ineffectiveness, he was recruited by old teammate Tim Murnane to be the ace of the Boston Unions. The hurler started off strong winning nine of his first 11 decisions before fading badly by mid-season (courtesy New York Public Library).

and mishaps, and a long time before snow blows again for the Altoona Unions to retrieve its losses and place itself in an enviable position."[25]

A large Saturday crowd of nearly 3,000 was at Fourth Avenue Grounds on May 10.[26] The pitching matchup was Jim Brown for the home team and Tommy Bond for the visitors. Bond entered the contest with a perfect 7–0 record, enabled by several years of sporadic pitching that allowed his arm to recover from the staggering number of innings he threw in the 1870s. The game seemed a mismatch on paper, but motivated by the large and enthusiastic crowd, and coming off four days or rest, the Altoona squad played their finest game of the season. In the fourth inning, the home team jumped out to a 6–1 lead and forced Bond out of the pitcher's box. Aside from a brutal display of defense by Altoona's third baseman Clarence "Cleary" Cross, another acquisition from the Lucas Amateurs, who made five errors, the game was "very spirited and was marked by sharp and brilliant plays."[27] Altoona held on to win their first-ever Union Association contest by a score of 9–4. The club's strong play continued through the first two innings of their next game on a beautiful Monday in front of a strong weekday crowd of 1,200.[28] The home team thrilled the crowd by scoring two early runs off Bond. Boston responded with a run in the third inning to make the score 2–1, but the wheels fell off for Altoona in the fourth. Boston scored seven runs off John Murphy, thanks to a combination of heavy-hitting by the visitors and sloppy fielding by the home team. With an 8–2 lead, Bond and the Bostons put the game on cruise control and won 10–3.

Boston headed out of town, and the Philadelphia Keystones arrived. The Keystones carried a record of 3–12, and much like Altoona had undergone significant roster changes. Multiple members of their opening day roster were cast away in an attempt to change the club's fortunes. The promise of a matchup against one of the Union Association's other also-rans did little to excite the imagination of the locals. Four hundred fans turned out for each of the first three games of the series, with Philadelphia taking two of the three contests. The series finale was scheduled for Saturday, May 17, and a large crowd was anticipated, but the club's increasingly hapless performance was affecting attendance. Altoona's first two Saturday contests each drew over 2,000, but the May 17 contest, which resulted in a 9–8 loss, drew an attendance that was described as "light."[29] For the Altoona faithful, the lure of Saturday baseball was outweighed by the stench of watching two awful ball clubs go tête à tête. If Altoona couldn't beat the Keystones, then who could they beat?

Amid the club's struggles, several changes occurred off the field. Hoping to make fan access to the ballpark easier, the Altoona street railway was extended to reach the park entrance.[30] Meanwhile, W.W. Ritz, the club's president and primary financial backer, resigned from his position.[31] The resignation of Ritz spelled trouble for the club, as he was concerned about its long-term economic prospects. He was no doubt disappointed by the performance of the club on the field as well. Ed Curtis, who was acting as the club's field manager, was also becoming dismayed. Curtis was not a baseball man, and hiring a dedicated and experienced ballplayer to manage on-field strategies might make a difference. Former National Association star, Ned Cuthbert, was offered the role of field manager in place of Curtis.[32] The 39-year-old turned down the opportunity and instead signed a $250 a month contract to play center field and serve as field captain with the Baltimore Unions.[33] When he turned down the role, pitcher John Murphy was given the role of field captain and handed complete control of the men on the ball field.[34]

The club's next series was scheduled against another UA bottom feeder, the Nationals of Washington. The Nationals arrived for a four-game series to commence May 21. The opening game took place in front of a small crowd and saw another blowout loss for Altoona by the score of 13–3. An off day allowed the team to regroup, and, remarkably, the 2–16 Altoonas would win their next three games against the Nationals. Murphy, invigorated by his newfound responsibility, won games on consecutive days, including an exciting 3–2 victory on the club's inaugural ladies' day game on May 24.[35] The club's 6–3 win to close the series on May 26 even brought the club out of last place for the first time in their five-week history. The Altoonas were on fire as they welcomed Baltimore to town for another four-game set. The clubs met in a well-played contest on May 27. Altoona won their fourth straight game, a thrilling 3–2 victory in 13 innings, described as "the finest game ever played [in Altoona]."[36] The club's solid play during their win streak suggested a club finally playing to its potential, but the challenge that the weaker clubs in the league continually faced was the herculean effort it took to win games. If Altoona got an excellent pitching performance, great defense, and timely hitting, they could squeak out a win against a good club. If any of those factors were missing, they were nearly guaranteed to get blown out, as demonstrated in the next game against Baltimore on May 29. The result was a 13–0 dismantling, with a motivated Bill Sweeney redeeming his loss the previous game and allowing just four hits. Somewhat curiously, President Lucas had traveled from St. Louis to witness the contest. The *Altoona Times* noted, "If he had opinions about the playing he kept them to himself like the polite gentleman he is."[37]

Lucas had spent the last few weeks fighting in court to prevent Tony Mullane from pitching for Toledo in the American Association. Mullane had appeared in two of Toledo's first three games in the opening series in Louisville. Lucas and his attorney Newton Crane filed a series of injunctions against Mullane to prevent him from appearing in any additional Toledo contests. Lucas and Crane cited Mullane for breach of the contract that the pitcher had signed with the St. Louis Unions in November 1883. Lucas first filed an injunction to prevent Mullane from appearing in St. Louis on May 5, 1884.[38] He then filed a further case to prevent the pitcher from appearing in the state of Ohio. On May 10, the case was heard in Cincinnati, where Judge William H. Horner ruled in favor of Lucas and the Union Association, filing an injunction prohibiting Mullane from appearing in any games in the state.

The injunction proved short-lived. On May 13, the case was brought before the United States Circuit Court in Cincinnati on a motion by Mullane's lawyers to overturn the decision. Judge John Baxter quickly overturned the ruling describing the case as a "controversy between a base ball club and a base ball player growing out of an alleged contract of employment, to enjoin the player from making his living by his rather polite occupation. It is not a case that commends itself to a court of equity."[39] Essentially Judge Baxter dismissed the case as too trivial to be given time in court since baseball was not a business but a sport.[40] Lucas was unhappy with the decision and quickly filed an appeal to the circuit court. Judge Baxter oversaw the appeal and again decided against Lucas and the St. Louis Athletic Association. The decision in the case would apply to Ohio, Indiana, and Kentucky, the states represented in the circuit, and would be "used as a precedent in other courts."[41] This ruling essentially put an end to the Mullane storyline for the season since he would now be permitted to pitch for Toledo without issue. The injunction in Missouri remained on the books until prior to the 1887 season and prevented the pitcher from appearing in St. Louis.[42] The Mullane case signaled that the members of the National Agreement did not view the Union Association as a legitimate organization. As a result, Union contracts would not be respected. It also demonstrated the hypocrisy of the baseball establishment, who were willing to conspire and induce Union Association players to break their contracts while crying foul when their rivals did the same.

With the Mullane business now behind him, President Lucas could now focus on the future of the league. The locals in Altoona had wondered why he would travel to Altoona to witness an ordinary contest, suspecting he might have other reasons to be in town. The question would be answered in the coming days. For now, the Altoonas were preparing for their upcoming contests. May 30 was significant on the baseball calendar since it marked Decoration Day, one of just two national holidays that took place during the season. This meant that a large crowd was all but guaranteed to come out to the ballpark, which meant a large gate for the home club. Under the Union Association's rules that required a 50–50 split between home and visitor clubs for holiday games, it also meant lucrative payday for the visitors.[43] Decoration Day, which eventually morphed into Memorial Day, began as a means of remembering the lives of soldiers killed in the Civil War. Surviving soldiers would pay tribute to their fallen comrades and decorate their graves with flowers, flags, and wreaths.[44]

The Union Association scheduled five games on Decoration Day 1884. Boston was in Chicago for a doubleheader while Philadelphia visited St. Louis, Washington, traveled to Cincinnati, and Baltimore was in Altoona. Boston split their contests in Chicago. The doubleheader drew a paltry 200 fans for game one and only 1,500 for game two.[45] The poor attendance was caused in part by the rival White Stockings doubleheader that drew a combined 6,000.[46] Cincinnati also drew a disappointing crowd of only 1,000, despite running unopposed.[47] The Queen City cranks had little interest in watching the only team worse than Altoona. Another relatively modest crowd of 2,000 was present in St. Louis for the home club's 17–1 destruction of the Keystones.[48] In Altoona, a capacity crowd of 3,000 filed into the Fourth Avenue Grounds to witness their contest with Baltimore. The strong crowd was composed of local workers and an onslaught of fans who traveled from Hollidaysburg, Tyrone, and other nearby towns.[49] The home club showed nerves in front of such a large crowd and quickly gave the game away with a series of poor errors, and the score was 6–0 after four innings. Altoona would allow five more runs, and Baltimore won the contest, 9–0. In the aftermath, it became clear Lucas's presence in Altoona was not coincidental. Rumors swirled that he intended to move the Altoonas to Kansas City, one of the largest markets in the country without a major league ball club.[50]

Baltimore and Altoona faced off the following day for another Saturday contest. The citizens of Altoona treated the day as an extension of the previous days' holiday, with virtually every shop in the city closed.[51] The enthusiasm carried over to the ball-park, where a good crowd of 1,000 turned up despite the combined 22–0 shellacking their heroes had received in the previous two games. Before the contest, a trio of disgruntled Altoona players, catcher Jerry Moore, utility man Taylor Shafer, and second baseman Charlie Berry, informed the club's management that they would not play in the contest until they were paid what was owed them.[52] Despite the promise that they would get paid their salaries that evening, the trio "remained obdurate, and an outsider had to be taken in to complete the nine."[53] Charlie Manlove, who had finally recovered from his broken hand, was slated to catch the game in place of Moore. George Daisy, a local player who had been an outfielder for Altoona the previous year, was enlisted to replace Shafer in left field. Altoona, now strengthened by the reunification of the Brown-Manlove battery, put forth one of their most exemplary efforts. Baltimore jumped to an early three-run lead, but Altoona clawed back to tie the score 3–3 in the sixth inning. The score held until the eighth inning when the newcomer Daisy, making his first and only major league appearance, dropped an easy fly in left field. The error kept the Baltimore inning alive, and Baltimore scored two runs on an extra-base hit. The final score ended up 5–3. *Sporting Life* summed up the contest: "the Altoona club outplayed their opponents, but luck was against them."[54] Luck was against Altoona the whole season, it seemed.

It was announced after the May 31 contest that the club had disbanded, thus ending the Altoona experiment in the Union Association.[55] Henry Lucas had arranged for Kansas City to take Altoona's place and complete their remaining schedule. The club's final record stood at 6 and 19, which upon their demise was good for sixth place, with both the Nationals and the Keystones sporting worse records at the close of May. The Altoonas had been outscored 216–90, with their eight losses to St. Louis by a combined score of 92–19, creating a large chunk of the outsized run differential. In reality, they were a run-of-the-mill lousy team in the Union Association capable of putting a fight against the middle and lower-tier clubs in the circuit. The club possessed a decent amount of talent, some of whom went on to play in the National League and American Association. George "Germany" Smith became a legitimate major league star and ranks as the greatest defensive shortstop of the 19th century. He signed with Cleveland the following month. Jerry Moore, the disgruntled catcher, briefly joined Terre Haute and eventually rejoined Smith in Cleveland. The battery of Charlie Manlove and Jim Brown was also much sought after. The pair somewhat naively signed contracts with both Indianapolis of the American Association and New York of the National League. After some controversy over their rights, the battery appeared briefly for New York later in June.

What, then, caused the demise of the Altoonas? The issue wasn't strictly attendance as the club drew well for their Saturday contests, though weekday games tended to draw poorly. Their Decoration Day contest was the highest drawing of any Union Association contest that day, with 3,000 fans in attendance. The market was small, but there was interest in baseball in the area. Lew Simmons, the manager of the Philadelphia Athletics, had boasted that the club's exhibition game in Altoona in 1883 had resulted in the second-largest gate receipts they had received that year.[56] It was a baseball town, and due to its locale as a gateway between the eastern and western railway systems, it was a frequent stopover for professional clubs. This factor proved critical in explaining the Altoona Unions' demise. In 1883, the club played numerous exhibition contests on their home grounds against clubs in both major leagues and various minor league contests. These contests were lucrative for Altoona as they were well attended and provided a steady source of income throughout the season. By joining the Union Association, Altoona ostensibly forfeited this income. The AA, NL, Northwestern League, and the Eastern League strictly adhered to the National Agreement's prohibition against playing contests with Union Association teams. The result was that a crucial source of revenue was now unavailable to the Altoona directors.

Another critical factor was the indignance of the local fans after Altoona played the Sunday contest in St. Louis back in April. *Sporting Life* posited that the aftermath of the game "knocked the bottom out of the financial success at home" as offended fans refused to support a team that they believed had chosen money over keeping the Sabbath.[57] The puritanism of the local fan base may have had an influence on their decline in attendance after a promising start, though it would seem that the club's on-field performance had as much to do with the decline in interest as anything. Opening the season with 11 straight losses was bad enough, but it was the eight consecutive blowouts at the hands of Lucas's acolytes that did the most significant harm. The contests harmed the public perception of the Altoonas and embarrassed the local fans. This humiliation led to a drop in attendance as crowd support was not nearly as strong after their opening series. Injuries to important players hampered the club, but it was clear that they were a third-rate club compared to St. Louis and Cincinnati.

The most crucial factor in the demise of Altoona was Henry Lucas. President Lucas had grown impatient with Altoona's poor play and the perception that it was not a big enough market. Towards the end of May actively sought out a new market to replace them. The Altoona directors, for their part, believed that Lucas and the Union directors had failed to live up to their promises to provide financial support as needed, which combined with the loss of revenue from playing exhibition games resulted in something of a mutual agreement. Lucas wanted to replace Altoona, and Altoona had lost their desire to stay in the Association.

8

$\diamond\diamond\diamond\diamond\diamond\diamond\diamond\diamond\diamond\diamond\diamond\diamond$

Going to Kansas City

"Kansas City has 100,000 population and no base ball club. The reason for this omission is said by a local paper to be because the grown people of that metropolis are too busy to sit in the sun and listen to eighteen men quarrelling with an umpire."—*Sporting Life*, May 28, 1884

The Altoona experiment was a dismal failure on virtually every level. The tiny market of some 19,000 people proved too small, the club's backers proved too impoverished, and the nine proved too over-matched to compete. For Henry Lucas, the failure was something of a relief. The league's weakest link was now broken, and the deadweight cast away. The search for a replacement had begun during the final week of May. Altoona manager Ed Curtis had written a letter to Lucas, informing him that the club was in a "bad way financially, and that if Mr. Lucas and Mr. Thorner … did not come to the club's aid it would not attempt to complete the season."[1] This description was a far cry from the picture of wealth painted by Curtis and W.W. Ritz at the March meeting in Cincinnati. Washington manager Mike Scanlon had boasted that Altoona's backers were willing to take losses up to $20,000 to complete the season.[2] Noting this discrepancy, Lucas investigated the Altoona franchise's financial status. After examining their books, he discovered that the "club's capital was but $1,500 and that it was in arrears to its players and to the Union Association for monthly dues."[3] A disgusted Lucas told the club's directors that neither he nor Thorner would put any money towards the club. He also threatened that unless Altoona's outstanding dues of $150 were paid, the club's membership in the league would be canceled. When the club did not pay their debt, they were removed from the league.

While Lucas was sorting out Altoona's affairs, he sent out feelers to interested parties who might want to enter a club in the Union. An application from Americus V. McKim, a Kansas City grain dealer and brewer with ties to the local Democratic Party, was quickly accepted and approved by the directors of the Union. A party from Kansas City, likely helmed by McKim, had applied for membership back at the March meeting. This application was rejected to make space for the Boston franchise so that the league would have an even east-west balance.[4] Had Lucas accepted Kansas City and booted Altoona prior to the season, he could have saved himself a lot of trouble. Kansas City was a logical market for the Union Association. As *Sporting Life* noted: "Kansas City has 100,000 population and no base ball club."[5] McKim had organized a local baseball league in February 1884. The fledgling amateur association was able to garner the support of 200 backers and raised $7,000, suggesting there was interest from the locals in the national game.[6] The city was a virgin, however, when it came to professional baseball. McKim and Lucas surely hoped that the city's large population flush with cattle money could support the venture. The city was also home to a 2,000 seat ball ground called the Athletic Park, which hosted contests in McKim's local league.[7]

The new market also enabled the Union Association to maintain an even balance of eastern and western clubs, as Kansas City was replacing the league's fourth western club. Another advantage was their willingness to play Sunday contests, which had proved such a sticking point for the departed Altoonas. The primary knock against Kansas City as a major league city was that it was 12.5 hours by train from St. Louis, the next furthest west club in the league. However, given Lucas and the Union directors' urgency to find a replacement for Altoona and the paucity of viable markets without baseball teams, Kansas City was as good a market as could be hoped for in June 1884.

On May 31, the evening of Altoona's disbandment, Lucas confirmed the acceptance of Kansas City into the circuit as their replacement. The initial plan was for the players on Altoona to be transferred to Kansas City to form the nucleus of the league's newest club.[8] Understandably, a number of players on the Altoona roster balked at the prospect of making the long and arduous venture to western Missouri to continue their baseball lives. Seventeen-year-old outfielder Taylor Shafer and second baseman Charlie Berry were the only Altoona alumni to make the voyage.[9] The duo's Missouri connections likely motivated their willingness to move. Shafer's older brother, the famed Orator Shafer, was starring for Lucas out west while Berry had played for the Lucas Amateurs earlier in the year and had ties in St. Louis. The remaining Altoona players reconstituted as an independent club, planning to recoup their costs by taking on all comers from teams under the National Agreement.[10] The prohibition against playing top clubs in the AA and the NL had prevented the club from picking up extra revenue. The effort proved short-lived as the club folded after just a couple of weeks in mid–June.[11] With the disbandment, the club's top players quickly found work with Germany Smith, Jerry Moore, Charlie Manlove, and John Brown, each signed by major league clubs. Pitcher John Murphy signed with Wilmington of the Eastern League.

Kansas City would begin play on June 7 at their home grounds against the visiting Chicago Unions. In the span of a week, McKim had to fill out a roster, get the grounds ready, and hopefully create a presentable product for the curious cowboys and cattlemen that made up the prospective fan base. With the help of Lucas, this mission was remarkably accomplished. McKim and Lucas met at Laclede Hotel in St. Louis on June 4 to formalize the organization and build a roster.[12] Harry Wheeler, an experienced outfielder who the St. Louis Brown Stockings had recently released, was signed to be the Kansas City captain.[13] Charlie Fisher and Jim Chatterton, two players from the Lynn of the Massachusetts State Association, were the next players signed.[14] Ernie Hickman, a live-armed pitcher and center fielder for the St. Louis Reserves, was recruited as the club's change pitcher. Two former Altoona players released in May, shortstop Cleary Cross and pitcher Joe Connors, were also signed. Cross had returned home to St. Louis and resumed his spot on the Lucas Amateurs while Connors had gone to the Cincinnati Union reserve club.[15] Catcher William "Nin" Alexander was signed from a club in Pana, Illinois.[16] Charlie Berry and Taylor Shafer, the Altoona transfers, completed the nine.

Just three days later, the nine took the field for the first professional baseball game in the history of Kansas City, Missouri. As game time approached at 3 p.m. on Saturday, June 7, a steady stream of curious Midwesterners sidled into Athletic Park to witness the debut of their new ball club. McKim and his directors, which included his secretary and later UA umpire Alex S. Crawford, had overseen a hasty expansion of the ball grounds at Athletic Park. The site could now hold up to 4,000 fans, doubling the original capacity.[17] The banner affair was graced with the presence of Henry Lucas, who had traveled from St. Louis alongside a group of Kansas City's new players.[18] Despite the opportunity to witness history, a somewhat lackluster crowd of 1,500 fans was in attendance.[19] This figure was disappointing since the amateur contests at the grounds in May had drawn a similar attendance. Nonetheless, the "goodly number of the sporting fraternity" was treated to a thrilling battle.[20]

Ernie Hickman debuted in the box for Kansas City, facing off against Chicago's change pitcher, Patrick Horan. The home club lost the coin toss and batted first. Left fielder Harry Wheeler stepped into the batter's box as the first batter in franchise history. He hit a fly ball that third baseman Charlie Householder muffed so badly that Wheeler reached second base on the play. He went to third on a passed ball and then scored on third baseman Cleary Cross's single, the franchise's first hit and first run occurring on the same play. Cross was thrown out trying to steal second, and Horan struck out Hickman and Berry to end the inning.

In the bottom of the first, Chicago retaliated with two runs on a sac fly off the bat of second baseman Frank McLaughlin and two passed balls made by Kansas City catcher Alexander. With a 2–1 lead after one, Horan bore down and held Kansas City scoreless through the next five innings while Chicago added two more runs to make the score 4–1 heading into the top of the seventh. Cross led off the inning with a base hit to center field and then stole second. He reached third on a passed ball by Chicago catcher Emil Gross. Cross scored when Berry hit a two-bagger to left field. Taylor Shafer followed up with a triple that scored Berry. He then scored on a long sac fly to center by Alexander that tied the score at four. Horan got out of the inning without any more damage. Chicago and Kansas City failed to score during the remainder of regulation, and after nine innings, the score remained tied. In the top of the tenth inning, Jim Chatterton hit a one-out single, stole second and third base, and then came home on a wild throw by right fielder Joe Ellick. With a one-run lead, Hickman returned to the box in the bottom of the tenth but could not hang on and secure the victory. Hickman got Gross to fly out to left field to open the inning. McLaughlin followed with a triple to left field and then scored on a double by shortstop Steve Matthias to tie the game. The eleventh inning was scoreless, and Horan shut down Kansas City in the top of the twelfth. Hickman's control wavered, and he opened the inning by walking Louis "Jumbo" Schoeneck. Gross followed with a hit to Cross at third base. Cross fielded the ball cleanly but threw so wildly to first that "Jumbo," the lumbering first baseman, who at 6-foot-2 and 223 pounds earned every ounce of his nickname, scored the game's winning run all the way from first. The final score stood 6–5 after 12 innings. The contest was played briskly and took just two hours and 15 minutes. Hickman had pitched very well in his debut, allowing just five hits in the extra-inning affair, though his defense was appalling behind him. Cross made five errors at third base, including the one that cost his club the game. The *Kansas City Daily Times* was charitable in noting the club was at a distinct disadvantage because of their hasty formation: "quite a number of the players had never seen each other, and several positions assigned were entirely new to them."[21] It was also noted promisingly, "yesterday's audience will convince the most skeptical that Kansas City can and will support a good base ball club."[22] The inaugural contest showed both the promise of their new club and the distinct limitations that arose from having to create a club out of thin air in one week.

The two clubs were slated to meet again on June 8. A crowd of 2,500 fans was sent home when a torrent of rain opened up after all of two pitches had been thrown, causing the game to be postponed.[23] Two thousand fans showed up the following day to see the home team face off against the remarkable "One Arm" Daily, but the game was a debacle from the start.[24] Joe Connors was handed the pitching duties for the game and allowed seven runs to cross the plate before the first inning mercifully concluded. Daily coasted to an easy 12–3 victory while also getting three hits in five at-bats. His brilliance caused one spectator to speculate: "wonder what he would do if he had both arms."[25] The sole highlight of the game for Kansas City was a home run by second baseman Charlie Berry, the first in team history. The uninspired performance by the home team would be the first of many for the new kids on the UA block.

Sensing that his nine could use some improvement, McKim and the club's field manager, Matthew S. Porter, enlisted some local recruits from the Kansas City Red Stockings, Willis Wyman and Bill Hutchison. Wyman was a utility man and pitcher who, until recently, had been mistakenly listed as Frank Wyman, an outfielder from Lynn, Massachusetts, in the record books. Hutchison was already well known in baseball circles as the famed shortstop and pitcher from Yale University. He captained that club in 1880 and led them to the American College Association Championship.[26] A native of New Haven, Connecticut, Hutchison moved to Kansas City after graduating from Yale. He was working in the railroad business and began his professional baseball career with a brief stint for Springfield of the Northwestern League in 1883.[27] The hurler started the 1884 season with the local Red Stockings before signing with Kansas City. He made his inauspicious major league debut against Chicago on June 10. The young pitcher was shaky and received poor support from his catcher Nin Alexander, who allowed four passed balls. Hutchison was not blameless as he allowed 11 hits and ten runs while his own club scored just three. The 24-year-old pitcher was not ready for primetime and returned to pitching for local clubs. He would make just one more appearance for Kansas City, starting the final game of the season on October 19. The unremarkable debut did little to hint at his future success. He reemerged as a top-flight pitcher in the Western League with Des Moines in 1887 and 1888 and graduated to the Chicago White Stockings of the

National League in 1889. Hutchison made a reputation as one of the hardest throwing pitchers in baseball. From 1890 to 1892, he led the National League in victories with staggering totals of 41, 44, 36, all while averaging nearly 600 innings a year. Thanks to this herculean workload and the rule change that extended the pitching distance to 60 feet 6 inches in 1893, he saw his ERA jump by more than two runs from 1892 to 1893. He was essentially done as an effective pitcher and, after a dismal stint with the lowly St. Louis Brown Stockings in 1897, his impressive career concluded. He returned to his adopted home of Kansas City, spending the rest of his life in the same place his major league career had started so inauspiciously on June 10, 1884.

Local enthusiasm was undiminished by three straight losses, and an impressive 3,000 fans attended the closing game of the series to witness a faceoff between Hickman and Daily.[28] The game was another close contest that mirrored the team's debut, with the two teams trading runs. Kansas City showed remarkable resilience in coming back from an early 5–2 deficit. The home team tied up the contest in the top of the ninth, making the score 6–6, but Chicago responded with the game-winning tally in the bottom of the ninth. The four-game series demonstrated that Kansas City had some flashes of potential but still had a long way to go towards being competitive on a game-to-game basis. The club had some decent talent, and Hickman looked like an up-and-comer, but the team defense had proven dreadful. The attendance for the series was solid, with nearly 8,000 fans attending the four contests. While Lucas likely lamented that Kansas City's on-field performance appeared to be no better than the lowly Altoonas, he must have been ecstatic with the strong attendance. The Kansas City nine were now scheduled to go on the road for more than six weeks, which was the inherent downside of playing in such a far-flung locale. It remained to be seen how the team would perform in the coming weeks and whether the goodwill of the local public would dissipate in light of the club's prolonged absence.

While Kansas City went on the road, dissension was bubbling over in St. Louis. The team's manager, Ted Sullivan, had a tremendous capacity to create conflict amid seemingly perfect situations. Lucas had recruited him to helm his fledgling club, and thanks in part to his guidance, the St. Louis Unions had cruised to an astonishing 28–3 record. In a situation that mirrored his resignation from the St. Louis Brown Stockings the previous year, Sullivan huffily resigned his post at the helm of a first-place club. The disgruntled leader cited the following reason for his departure: "Three of the leading spirits tried to run the club and opposed all others in it. I would not tolerate this, and as I was not backed up in my action by President Lucas, I tendered my resignation. The three I mean are [Fred] Dunlap, [Dave] Rowe, and [Orator] Shafer. They formed a faction, and the others could not agree with them, and as a result, there was nothing left for me to do but resign."[29] Not coincidentally, Dunlap, Rowe, and Shafer were the club's most experienced and highest-paid players, as well as its top performers. Each man undoubtedly recognized their influence and standing in the eyes of their benefactor, Henry Lucas. Sullivan was now free to find his next club. Dunlap was given the reins of the first-place club, which already held a virtually insurmountable lead in the inaugural Union Association pennant race.

The pennant race, or lack thereof, was possibly the biggest failing of the season thus far. St. Louis had raced out to a 20–0 record before losing their first contest on May 24 to the Boston Unions. Five thousand fans attended the game at Lucas's grounds and watched in amazement as the Boston batters battered St. Louis pitcher Charlie Hodnett for eight runs on 22 hits. His counterpart Tommy Bond struck out nine St. Louis hitters and worked his way out of jams all day, putting an end to the historic streak. The record of 20 consecutive wins to start a season would remain the all-time major league sports record for 131 years. On December 5, 2015, the National Basketball Association's Golden State Warriors won their 21st consecutive game to open the 2015–16 season.[30] It was a strange reversal of fortune for Bond and the Boston Unions, as just weeks earlier, they had given the Altoona Unions their first-ever victory. From the lowest of lows to the highest of highs.

By the end of June, St. Louis's record was a remarkable 38–4 while Baltimore was in second place, 11 games behind them with a 27–15–1 record. Cincinnati was in third with a 24–16 record, Boston fourth at 22–17–2, and Chicago fifth at 21–21–1. The lowly Nationals stood 12–19 while the Keystones held the league's worst record at 10–34. Kansas City was 3–8 after 11 games, while Altoona's final record stood at 6–19. While there was a four-team race for second place, the race for first was decided from almost the moment Henry Lucas's nine set foot on the field. There was growing concern about the massive disparity in performance between the league's top five clubs and the bottom three. Union critic O.P. Caylor described the circuit's lesser lights: "about the two bummest nines in the country are the Keystones and Nationals of Washington. [Umpire] John Kelly says the latter play like a lot of countrymen. Even the Altoonas have had a picnic with the Keystones."[31] This disparity in quality remained the default critique of the league throughout the season. The Altoonas, Keystones, and Nationals had developed a well-earned reputation for futility, which served to discredit the accomplishments of Lucas's dominant nine.

This futility translated into troubling attendance figures, particularly for the Keystones. An observer in the city wrote about the club's first home series in June against the Nationals:

> The Keystones … opened here last week to ninety-three paying people. Their second game attracted one hundred and ten people, and their third ten. This latter game was postponed on the plea of weather, although both the Athletics and Philadelphias played on that day. The Keystones are on their last legs, and will never go West again. Its burst up may be expected any day. The Unions, as far as this city is concerned is dead.[32]

With Altoona having gone under, it now looked like the Keystones might be soon to follow. It was hoped that the upcoming Independence Day contests and warm July weather would bring about better crowds and improve the financial fortunes of the lesser clubs.

9

◇◇◇◇◇◇◇◇◇◇◇◇◇◇◇

Independence Day
in Washington

"In every respect our recent meeting was a most satisfactory one, and the croakers will be sadly disappointed in their auguries of evil for the Union Association of base-ball players."—Warren White, July 2, 1884, after the Union Association meeting in Baltimore

"I have come to the conclusion that everything is fair in base ball as in war and I want my share of the fun while it is going."[1]—Henry Lucas

The month of July opened with a meeting of the Union Association brass in Baltimore on July 1. The primary order of business at the conference was assessing the financial situation of each club in the league. Secretary Warren White presented a report describing the financial condition of each club and their prospects for the rest of the season:

St. Louis—Large surplus in treasury, and prospects favorable for heavy excess of receipts over expenditures, as the games are well patronized.

Cincinnati—A trifle behind, but with games yet to be played confident of coming out on the right side of the ledger.

Chicago—Expenditures a trifle in excess of receipts, but confidence expressed of a successful season.

Baltimore—Crowds attending all games, and the clubs daily growing in popular estimation. July 1st the receipts and expenditures just balanced.

The National Club, of Washington, which has been classed by several papers as weekly on the point of disbanding. All obligations paid in full to July 1st, and a handsome surplus in the treasury, the club being almost level from St. Louis from a financial standpoint.

Keystone, of Philadelphia—Greatly encouraged by the prospect ahead, having twenty-four games to play, and a growing increase in popular favor manifested toward the new organization.

Boston had not made any money thus far, but the indications showed that there was no lack of interest in the club, and its patronage was steadily improving.

Kansas City was ahead financially, and assured of popular support at home.[2]

White's summation of the league's prospects was optimistic: "there could be no question that although some of the clubs might not make money this season, still they could be depended upon to stick to their colors to the last, and there would be no struggling permitted with the games yet to play by the various clubs."[3]

As the halfway point in the season approached, the Union Association was entering the most crucial stretch of its existence. A growth in attendance could stabilize the league's shakier franchises and ensure a successful close to the season while increasing the odds of the league surviving into 1885. The month of July 1884 would serve as a bellwether for the future of the Union Association. The July 1 meeting in Baltimore was something of a call to arms for the clubs in the league. Five of the league's eight clubs were determined to be in solid to excellent financial shape. The three remaining clubs were in varying degrees of financial peril. Boston was considered a good market, but despite the strong play of the underdog club, the club had failed to garner a significant following. The rival National League club was filled with stars and was battling for the pennant, so they garnered the lion's share of attention from the Boston public. Attendance had tailed off for the Unions after drawing 3,000 fans for their home opener on April 30. Their weekday contests were drawing 500 people at most, while the Saturday contests topped out at 1,000. Like many of the more puritanical eastern markets, the club also eschewed lucrative Sunday baseball. The club's directors petitioned the UA's directors at the Baltimore meeting for help to cover their costs and complete the season, claiming to be $4,500 behind on the season to date.[4] Recognizing the value of having a competitive club in a league that was short on them, the triumvirate of Lucas, Thorner, and Henderson agreed to cover the costs for the club and allow them to complete their schedule.[5]

Chicago was expected to be a great market, and A.H. Henderson was stable financially. Despite a fine ballpark, Sunday games, and the elite hurling of Hugh Daily, the club was losing money and mired in the second division. Early season reports that the club had failed to draw $200 in revenue per home game were cause for concern.[6] The club's attendance was miserable for their weekday contests, often under 300, while the Saturday contests had averaged just 500 fans. Only the Sunday contests had drawn well, with attendance ranging from 1,500 to a season-high 4,100 on June 1, a 5–4 victory over St. Louis. The Sunday interest failed to translate to the rest of the week. Their excellent Sabbath attendance can be attributed to the fact that the rival White Stockings were prohibited from playing Sunday contests. Henderson faced additional strain as the moneyman for two franchises. The Chicago club was draining him of his resources, even as the Baltimore franchise was covering costs.

Philadelphia was the weak link of the UA's current configuration. Despite a sizeable baseball-hungry population, the locals had zero interest in watching an inferior brand of ball. The Athletics were the defending champions and still in the thick of the AA pennant race, while the Philadelphia League club was much improved under the management of Harry Wright. The Keystones club had drawn crowds under 100 on several occasions, though their most recent series against the visiting St. Louis Unions averaged over 1,000 fans per contest. Nevertheless, the situation was bleak. The best that poor Tom Pratt could say about the poorly performing franchise was that he had a bunch of home games left on the schedule, and a strong showing could help recoup some of his costs.

The UA meeting also addressed the issue of player contracts. The decision was made to blacklist seven players and threaten three more with punishment unless they returned their advance money. John Hillery, Thomas Gunning, Billy Colgan, Fleury Sullivan, Frank Meinke, and Steve Behel were banned for jumping their Chicago Union contracts. Gus Alberts was banned for breaking his pact with the Washington Nationals. Trick McSorley, Ed Kent, and George Pinkney were given until July 10 to pay back the combined $750 in advance money they had received for signing with Henderson.[7]

Since the season had started, two more players had jumped their Union contracts. Will Foley, the veteran third baseman for Chicago, jumped to St. Paul in late May. The aforementioned Alberts, a promising young infielder, had jumped the Nationals after just four games to go to the Reading, Pennsylvania, club of the Eastern League in early June. There had also been widespread rumors that clubs were trying to induce Union players. Hugh Daily had recently claimed that he was offered $1,000 to break his contract.[8] Amid these defections and rumors, Henry Lucas put forth a resolution at the July 1 meeting that would alter the course of the 1884 season. The motion read,

> As the older base ball associations had seen fit not to respect the contracts of the Union Association and were continually tempting their players to break their contracts, the Union Association retaliate in like manner and hereafter secure such players as they may desire regardless of contracts already made with any club outside the pale of the Union Association.[9]

Lucas was still stinging from his loss in the Tony Mullane case and had thrown down the gauntlet against the National Agreement. The vengeful Lucas promised: "I'll not only go into the business of breaking contracts, but I'll break up the League and the American Association, too, if I am pushed to do my utmost. I have come to the conclusion that everything is fair in base ball as in war and I want my share of the fun while it is going."[10] Lucas also offered a sinister premonition of what was to come in the month of July: "Wait for a few days and you'll hear a howl all through base balldom that will make your hair stand on end."[11]

Lucas's promise proved to come true in the ensuing weeks. A number of high-profile defectors jumped to the rebel league from the National League and American Association. Additionally, the weakened financial situation of the Northwestern League and the Eastern League caused an influx of players from those leagues. Dozens of solid players joined the circuit throughout the summer months, resulting in a significant improvement in the quality of play in the league.

With the future hanging in the balance, the directors of the Union Association must have been thrilled on the evening of July 4, 1884. It is not an understatement to say that July 4, 1884, was without a doubt the greatest day in the history of the Union Association. The significance of Independence Day for a ball club was immense. July 4 was just one of two National holidays that occurred during the baseball season in 1884. Along with Decoration Day on May 30, these two days were frequently the most well-attended games of the year. In an era where the working class worked six days a week, these two holidays also offered a brief respite from the grind of life in the city. What better way to celebrate the birth of America than by attending a display of the National Pastime? For the clubs of the Union Association, Independence

Day would be a showcase of the best the league had to offer, and it was a near certainty that a good crowd would take in the festivities. To take advantage of this, four doubleheaders were scheduled that would see all eight clubs play two games each, one in the morning and one in the afternoon. Boston would host Kansas City, and Philadelphia would host Chicago. In a very unusual doubleheader, Washington would host St. Louis in the morning and then Cincinnati in the afternoon. St. Louis would then travel to nearby Baltimore for an afternoon game, while Cincinnati would travel to Washington.

In the nation's capital, the Nationals had earned a robust following amongst the city's baseball aficionados. Despite a 12–31 record, the club was winning the war for fans against the city's hastily formed AA franchise. The American Association had granted entry to a Washington club in December 1883. It was anticipated that the new club would provide some competition for the Nationals and weaken another Union Association market. The AA club was bankrolled by Lloyd Moxley, a theatre proprietor and the owner of the Athletic Park at 9th Street and T. Street N.W., which would be the home of the new nine. Day-to-day management of the club fell to the beloved John Hollingshead. "Holly," as he was universally known, was a long-time favorite in D.C. He had starred for the Nationals in the National Association and various other permutations of the club throughout the late 1870s. Moxley and Holly, tasked with building a club from scratch over the winter, were forced to pay out high salaries to inexperienced, unknown, or marginal players. The competition of the Union Association, the expansion of the American Association and Northwestern League, the proliferation of reserve clubs, and the formation of the Eastern League had made it a seller's market for players. There simply weren't enough good players to go around, and men like Holly were forced to overpay. As an example of the bind that Holly was in, he signed Thorndike "Thorny" Hawkes for the sum of $1,300. Hawkes was a 32-year-old semi-pro from Danvers, Massachusetts. He had last played professionally in 1879 when he hit .208 for the Troy National League club. Yet even he could command a salary of over $200 a month.

The battle for Washington fans saw the early advantage go to the Nationals. Since the Union Association started their season a full two weeks before the American Association, that meant the locals would get their first taste of professional baseball that year from the Nationals. Scanlon's club had an inherent advantage in terms of branding, as the Nationals name was well established, dating back to its inception in 1859. The 1867 version of the club was headed by baseball's first superstar and now the owner of the Boston Unions, George Wright. That club had completed a successful ten-game western tour through Columbus, Cincinnati, Louisville, Indianapolis, St. Louis, and Chicago.[12] This tour was a direct inspiration for the famed 1869 tour of the Cincinnati Red Stockings. The Nationals also appeared in the National Association in 1872 and 1873. The 1880 iteration of the club was beloved in the city when it was likely the best team in baseball outside the National League. A semi-professional iteration of the club had taken the field in 1883 under the leadership of Warren White and drew from a selection of the city's best local players.

Scanlon's club had the advantage of playing at the centrally located Capitol Grounds. The grounds were situated in a desirable location nearby the Capitol building and provided easy access to Washington fans in the city's core. Perhaps the most significant advantage the Nationals had was Mike Scanlon's notorious frugality. Scanlon's original salary list had totaled around $14,000, but a series of releases had cut his salary list in half. By mid-season, Scanlon's 11-man roster came for the bargain-basement price of $7,000.[13] That total would have put his club's average salary at $600–$700 per man and almost certainly made the club the lowest paid team in the major leagues.

April attendance for the Nationals was strong, with up to 4,000 fans attending the club's home debut on April 18. The rest of their games that month drew between 1,000 and 2,500 fans. Their American Association rivals, known most commonly as the Washingtons, opened the season at the Athletic Park on May 1, unopposed by the Nationals. They drew over 2,000 fans for the opening day contest against Brooklyn, which saw the home club cruise to a 12–0 victory. The club drew another 2,500 fans on May 2. On May 3, the AA club and Nationals went head to head at home for the fan's attention. The Nationals drew 1,000 fans for their game against Baltimore, while the Washingtons drew a superior crowd of 2,500 fans. This result was heartening for Moxley, who had gone to great lengths to battle the Nationals. He was in control of the local billboards and had purposely shut out Scanlon's club from promoting their games.[14] The Washingtons then traveled out of town while the Nationals drew 2,000 fans to their May 5 contest before going on a long road trip that would go into June.

On May 9, the AA club returned home to a modest crowd of 1,000 fans for their 7–2 loss against New York. On May 10, the two clubs met in a dreadful contest that ended up in the record books. Washington debuted a new battery from Massachusetts: Ed Trumbull, a hard-throwing hurler from Chicopee, and Alex Gardner, a catcher from Danvers. Gardner was likely recommended for a trial by the club's second baseman, fellow Danvers native Thorny Hawkes. Trumbull's wild and swift delivery proved impossible to handle for the nervous backstop. Gardner allowed a major league record 12 passed balls, and the result was a disastrous 11–3 loss that was truncated after seven innings. Gardner's futility and the generally poor performance of the home club caused such disgust from the local fans that a reported 1,000 fans left the park after the fifth inning.[15] Despite this protest, the club still drew decent crowds through the rest of the month in the Nationals' absence, including a combined 5,000 fans at the Decoration Day doubleheader on May 30.

Moxley's club had drawn well but had performed miserably. Their record stood at 4–17 at the end of May, and this left an opening for Scanlon's club to win over the crowds. The Nationals returned home for a four-game set with the Keystones from June 2 to June 7 that saw the club earn a rare series sweep, bringing their record to 9–22. The series averaged a modest 1,000 fans per game but gained the confidence of the locals. When they went on the road again for the next two weeks, they took the hearts of the D.C. faithful with them. From June 2 to June 19, the Washingtons played 11 home games, nine of them unopposed by the Nationals. Attendance records are only available for the June 16 game, when they drew 600 fans for a rare 1–0 victory against the AA's other dismal newcomer from Indianapolis.[16] The absence of attendance figures in a game account in 1884 typically meant that the crowd was small.

Given that the June 16 game only drew 600 fans while earlier unopposed games drew 1,000 or more, it seems like the locals had tuned out the fledgling Washingtons and cast their lot with the familiar Nationals. This stretch of June home games was crucial because it was the last time the Washingtons would appear at home until July 21. Significant revenue from homestands was needed to cover costs on long road trips. For Moxley and Holly, the poorly attended homestand would have put undue financial pressure on the club as they headed on the road for over a month.

While Moxley's nine left the capital, the Nationals returned home to begin a series against Kansas City on June 24. As the weather warmed up and faced with only one choice, the locals flocked to the Capitol Grounds. The club's return was met by what the *Cincinnati Enquirer* determined was the largest crowd of the season (no figure provided), who turned out to watch their heroes fall 2–1 to Kansas City.[17] The club drew 1,500 fans on June 27, then 1,000 fans on June 28. July 1 would see the powerful Henry Lucas's club make their first visit to Washington. A steady rainfall during the game's first half kept the attendance to a modest 800 fans, with St. Louis taking the contest by the score of 6–3. A larger audience of 1,500 fans came out on July 3 to see the home team fall again by a score of 12–7.

On the eve of the Nationals' Independence Day game, the club possessed a miserable 13–31 record. The mark put them ahead of only the Philadelphia Keystones among teams that had played a full schedule. The club combined weak hitting, sloppy defense, and poor pitching. Milo Lockwood, enlisted to be the club's ace and opening day starter, was supposed to be a hard-throwing strikeout artist. He had starred for Johnstown in 1883 but had been battered so far in 1884. In 11 appearances with the Nationals, the rookie had posted an ERA of 7.32 and won just one of ten starts. He earned his release in late May. Mark Creegan, the club's opening day catcher, was also released that month. The much-ballyhooed 19-year-old from California was only used behind the plate in three games and hit just .152/.176/.152 in nine appearances. It is always a bad sign for a ball club when the opening day battery is turfed within six weeks. Scanlon was utterly unafraid to make roster moves to improve his club and save money. The Nationals would end up using a staggering 51 players during the season, including 17 who would make just one appearance with the club.

Despite the roster churn, the club had some bright spots. Henry Moore, another California export, was a sad-eyed outfielder who proved to be one of the best hitters in the circuit. The 22-year-old Moore would end up hitting .336/.363/.414 for an OPS+ of 163 in his sole major league season. He is one of only three players in baseball history to hit .300 in their only major league season alongside minor league stalwarts Buzz Arlett and Irv Waldron. The explanation for his abbreviated career undoubtedly comes from his propensity for erratic and downright disruptive actions. Years later, his old teammate Bill Wise recounted an incident in Boston during which Moore performed "the queerest and meanest thing ever done on a ball field."[18] Denied a ten-dollar advance by Mike Scanlon prior to the game, Moore came to the plate with two out in the bottom of the ninth, with Phil Baker on first and Bill Wise on third. The Nationals were down 3–2. Wise explained what happened next:

He walked up to the plate, smacked the first ball pitched into the far corner of the lot, good for twice four bases, threw his hat on the ground and deliberately walked to the players' bench and sat down. Baker and I both raced to the plate but the Boston fielder finally overtook the ball and fielded it to first base, and the umpire declared Moore out, neither run counting under the rule, Boston winning the game 3 to 2....

Tim Murnane, who was present, said it was the most measly trick he ever saw perpetrated.... [Back in Washington] I was commissioned to interview the culprit and offer to remit the fine and suspension if he would agree to play his best for the remainder of the season, for we really needed his services. He seemed sorry for what he had done, and gave his promise, which he kept, playing gilt-edge ball for another month.[19]

The downright sociopathic action, while possibly apocryphal, demonstrates the kinds of actions Moore was known to take. It showed both his talent on the field and his ability to charm his way back into the good graces of his beleaguered teammates and managers. Historian John Thorn noted that this "pattern of insubordination, petulance, apology, expulsion, reinstatement, and renewed expulsion came to mark Moore's career."[20] Moore's later career had him venture back to his native California, where his standout play was regularly interrupted by deliberate attempts to upset the applecart, reportedly dropping fly balls intentionally or getting in fights with teammates. His post-baseball life became one of baseball's greatest mysteries, and until 2015, his final whereabouts were unknown. Thanks to the steadfast research of John Thorn, Peter Morris, Richard Malatzky, and Bruce Allardice, it was revealed that Moore passed away in San Francisco on June 3, 1902, at the age of 40.[21]

Moore's strong play gave the club some much-needed stability in the outfield. Captain Phil Baker, who had spent the 1883 season with the independent Nationals and Baltimore of the American Association, split time at catcher and first base and hit very well. He posted a batting .288/.309/.356 and a 125 OPS+ on the season. Baker threw with his left hand and ranks tenth all-time in games played by a left-handed catcher with 50. Bill Wise had also pitched for the Nationals in 1883 and the AA's Alleghenys. He was the other bright spot for the club, giving the club a credible pitcher, eventually winning 23 games against 18 losses, with a steady 3.04 ERA and a 99 ERA+. When he was not in the pitcher's box, he also played all three outfield positions, third base, and first base. Despite these three quality players, the club was still not expected to be a match for the St. Louis Unions on Independence Day, 1884.

Alex Voss, a tall pitcher and utility man from Georgia, who early in the season had been compared unrealistically to Buffalo star Dan Brouthers, was given the start in front of the excited crowd of 5,000 strong at the Capitol Grounds. Voss had recently buried a horseshoe underneath home plate, hoping to bring his team good luck.[22] He would face off against the Unions' change pitcher, Charlie Hodnett, a Mound City product, who had pitched effectively so far on the season. Perhaps motivated by the excitable crowd, the Nationals played their best game of the season. Voss allowed just five hits while his defense played a rare errorless game behind him. A Nationals' crank was heard to exclaim: "Voss has his toe weights on to-day," evidently 1880s slang for "he is pitching a great game."[23] The pitcher was ably supported by teammates, who jumped out to a 2–0 lead in the top of the first. St. Louis scored one run in response in the bottom of the first. The Nationals then scored ten unanswered runs, and the final score was 12–1 in favor of the home team. It was a remarkable result that delighted the hometown crowd. Baker and weak-hitting shortstop John Deasley each notched four hits on the day. Deasley was the younger brother of the well-known St. Louis Brown Stockings catcher, Pat Deasley. Wise in right field had three hits. Left-handed second baseman Tom Evers (whose nephew Johnny would later star for the Chicago Cubs), the mercurial Moore, Voss, and catcher Joe Gunson also had two hits each. Only third baseman Patrick Larkins and first baseman Aloysius C. "Pop" Joy failed to get a hit for the Nationals.

The club celebrated their victory and prepared for the afternoon game to begin at 4 p.m. against Cincinnati. The Queen City club was currently involved in a fierce battle for second place in the standings with Boston and Baltimore and was riding the momentum of their 9–2 dismantling of Baltimore that morning. The club made the short hour-long journey to D.C. for the afternoon contest. Bill Wise, the Nationals' finest pitcher, noted to be "feeling pretty well himself" for the matchup would face off against the diminutive Dick Burns, a talented 5-foot-7, 140-pound lefthander.[24] Burns had struggled as a 19-year-old rookie with Detroit in the National League in 1883, going just 2–12, but had proved to be a valuable addition for Cincinnati. Burns offered a nice bit of relief to the aged right arm of the club's high-priced ace, George "Grin" Bradley, who would umpire that afternoon's contest after the scheduled arbiter failed to appear.

Five thousand fans were in attendance for the afternoon game to witness another display of hot hitting by the Nationals. The club got started early with a four-run outburst in the top of the second, helped by sloppy Cincinnati defense that resulted in all four runs being unearned. The Nationals gave all four runs back in the bottom of the second. The Nationals' tiny catcher, Ed McKenna, struggled to handle the swift delivery of Wise. In the top of the third, McKenna was summoned to right field by captain Baker, who took over behind the plate. This move changed the tide of the game, as Wise and the Nationals defense stabilized. The gutsy Joe Gunson made three tremendous catches in the outfield after being "knocked insensible by a swift wild-pitched ball in the fourth inning."[25] The next three innings were scoreless, with the two teams tied 4–4. In the top of the seventh, the Nationals strung together a rally with safe hits by Moore, McKenna, Voss, and Wise. By the time the inning ended, the Nationals had scored three runs. They would add one more in the top of the ninth and hold on for an 8–4 victory. The woeful Nationals had beaten the two best teams in the Union Association, much to the delight of the thousands of fans who attended the festivities.

The outstanding success of the Independence Day doubleheader was a turning point in the war between John Hollingshead's Washingtons and Mike Scanlon's Nationals. The Washingtons were engaged in a lengthy western road trip, getting their brains beat in by the rest of the American Association. The trip was an unmitigated disaster on the field, with the denizens of the nation's capital winning just two of 22 contests. While the Washingtons were away, the fans flocked to Capitol Park to see the Nationals play. Over the next two weeks, from July 5 to July 19, the club played nine home games. Attendance records exist for eight of the nine contests showing that the club averaged 2,225 fans per game. This figure was more than double their average attendance from earlier in the season. *Sporting Life* noted,

"Washingtonians have not been slow to show their appreciation of the good work done by the boys, for they have turned out in goodly numbers to see the games."[26] For the club's July 14 game, a 4–2 victory over Chicago, no attendance number was published, but one account mentioned that every seat on the grounds was full.[27] The Nationals rewarded their fans by going 6–3 during this stretch. On July 21, the Washingtons returned to Athletic Park for their first home game in over a month. The game was played head to head against the Nationals' contest with Boston. The attendance for the two games revealed the standing of the two clubs in the hearts of the locals. The AA nine drew just 200 fans to watch them play the lowly Alleghenys from Pittsburgh. Conversely, the improving Nationals drew 2,500 fans to their contest. It was clear that the Nationals were winning the war.

At the end of July, the final stake was driven in the hearts of Lloyd Moxley's club. The Washington owner came down with an illness late in the month and resigned active management of the club to Harry Ford.[28] His players were also grumbling about the late payment of the salaries.[29] Losing Moxley was demoralizing, and the sharks of the baseball world began to circle. The Washingtons, despite their terrible record, were not entirely bereft of talent. Rookie shortstop Frank Fennelly had burst onto the scene as one of the top hitters in the American Association with a .292/.343/.436 with a 165 OPS+ while also playing excellent defense. At just 24 years old, he was highly coveted. Another rookie, outfielder Frank Olin, had gotten off to a blazing start, hitting .386 in 21 games after debuting on July 4. Pitcher Bob Barr had also performed decently, with a 3.45 ERA and an 87 ERA+ in 281.1 innings.

The club was reportedly in the hole for $2,000, with $1,500 of that being outstanding player salaries.[30] With little hope of recouping these losses or presenting a competitive club the rest of the season, the club's backers called it quits. On August 2, after a 6–5 defeat to New York, the club officially disbanded. Fennelly was sold to the Cincinnati Red Stockings for a reported $1,000.[31] Pitcher Bob Barr had received offers in the range of $350 a month from Baltimore and St. Louis.[32] He would eventually join lowly Indianapolis for an undisclosed sum. Frank Olin and catcher John Humphries visited Mike Scanlon's headquarters to discuss possibly joining the Nationals.[33] In recognition of the hardship facing the now unemployed members of the Washingtons, the benevolent Scanlon arranged for a benefit game featuring members of the Nationals and the disbanded Washingtons. The players were divided into squads made up of Washington locals and players from abroad. The contest between the Home Boys and the Visitors was a close one, with a fair audience witnessing the out-of-towners take a 3–2 contest. The game was a modest success, and Scanlon was able to distribute $35 to $40 to each departing player.[34]

The swift demise of Moxley's club was a victory for the Union Association in D.C. Scanlon's crew had won out thanks to three main factors. First, the Nationals' name had credibility among the city's baseball fans, and the club had improved significantly throughout the summer. Second, the central location of the ball grounds meant that fans in the city's downtown core had easy access to the grounds. Third and most importantly, Scanlon kept his costs exceptionally low. A club that drew 2,000 fans a game and paid out some of the lowest salaries in baseball was bound to be a success. The Nationals had vanquished their American Association foe.

10

◇◇◇◇◇◇◇◇◇◇◇◇◇◇◇◇

Baltimore's Battle

"The Fourth was a great day at Union Park ... by actual count there were over ten thousand people at the park during the day, nearly three thousand seeing the morning game and over seven thousand being present in the afternoon. The Union management deserves this large patronage, for it has not only secured for Baltimore a fine team, but has in many other ways done all in its power to elevate the game. Now that people have gotten into the habit of going to Union park, there is no reason why the crowds to witness future games should not be large."—*Baltimore American*, July 5, 1884

While the Washington Nationals were waging a successful war against the American Association, their neighbors in Baltimore were engaged in a similar fight for the attention of local baseball fans. Baltimore was an inaugural member of the American Association in 1882, under the management of Henry Myers and C.C. Waite. The fledgling club was bereft of talent and finished in last place with a 19–54 record. The club drew a reported 36,000 fans across 34 home games.[1] Major concerns arose about both the club's finances and the quality of the organization. As a result, the club was asked to withdraw from the league following the season.

In 1883, a former National Association player named Billy Barnie and a new set of Baltimore-based backers successfully applied to join the American Association for the coming season. The new organization was an entirely new entity, undergoing a complete overhaul of the roster. Only two players from the 1882 roster, Jack Leary and the immortal Nick Scharf, would make appearances for the 1883 Orioles. The end result was an equally dreadful 28–68 record and another last-place finish. More positively, attendance more than doubled, increasing to 110,000 over 49 home games.[2]

Heading into 1884, Baltimore's baseball fans had experienced two dismal seasons in the American Association and a complete change in ownership. Despite an uptick in attendance, there were still doubts about the quality of the club. The Baltimore Union directors, A.H. Henderson and his brother William C., had reason to believe that these pliable fans could be turned into Union loyalists. This outcome would be especially possible if the Orioles got off to a slow start and the new Union club played well out of the gate.

It is important to realize that the American Association of 1884 was not some monolithic entity that could not be toppled. They were a two-year-old upstart with several fragile organizations, including Baltimore, Pittsburgh, and Columbus. They had also added four brand new clubs. Much like the Union Association, there was a significant disparity in talent between the top of the heap and the cellar dwellers. Their main strategic advantage over the Union Association was a two-year head start and getting first dibs on several markets. The circuit also featured clubs in the two largest cities in the country, New York and Philadelphia. They also had a formal but fragile relationship with the National League, having signed the National Agreement prior to the 1883 season. The advantages conferred by a two-year head start and the protections given by the National Agreement were significant but not insurmountable.

The Union Association directors had targeted players on AA and NL teams who were experiencing dissension and disarray. Though Cleveland in the NL and Pittsburgh in the AA had both been frequent targets of UA raids, Baltimore ended up ceding the most players to the new circuit. Three of Baltimore's reserved players, shortstop Lou Say, John "Rooney" Sweeney, and Jerry McCormick, were scooped up by Union clubs, though each had been taken off the reserve list before signing. Outfielder Dave Rowe, who had hit .313 in 59 games with Baltimore in 1883, was one of the first signees by Henry Lucas. UA clubs picked up five other players who had seen time with the Orioles. This included three catchers, John Kelly with Cincinnati, Phil Baker with the Nationals, George Baker (no relation) with St. Louis. Baltimore pitcher/infielder Jack Leary was the sole player with major league experience on the Altoona opening day roster, while Boston signed Tom O'Brien to play second base. Two more members of the Orioles, Frank "Gid" Gardner and Cal Broughton, would also make appearances in the Union Association in 1884. In total, 11 different members of the 1883 Orioles appeared in the UA in 1884.

After losing four regulars (Say, Rowe, Sweeney, and McCormick) from the 1883 club, little was expected of the Orioles in the coming season. Yet Billy Barnie's nine turned out to be one of the great surprises of the American Association in 1884. The primary source of their improvement was the ascendence of their young starting pitchers, 21-year-old Hardie Henderson and 25-year-old Bob Emslie. In 1883, Henderson was 10–32, with a 4.02 ERA and 85 ERA+, while Emslie was 9–13 with a 3.17 ERA and 108 ERA+. In 1884, Henderson went 27–23, with a 2.62 ERA and 131 ERA+ while striking out 346 men in 439.1 innings. Emslie was equally impressive and went 32–17, with a 2.75 ERA and 125 ERA+ in 455.1 innings. The club also benefited from the strong play of Joe Sommer, Jimmy Macullar, and Tom York, who proved to be capable replacements for the departed Say, Rowe, and McCormick.

The drastic improvement of the Oriole's pitching staff meant they were no longer a sad-sack nine. Henderson's Unions now faced stiff competition from their AA rivals. The clubs were closely matched as July started. On July 4, the Unions were 28–16–1, good for the second-best record in the Union Association, though they were already a distant 12 games behind Lucas's superlative club in St. Louis. The Orioles entered play that day with a 26–15–2 record, good for sixth place in the American Association. Despite being in sixth place, they were just two games out of first place. Both Baltimore nines were among the strongest clubs in their respective leagues. However, while the Union Association race was all but over, the Orioles were embroiled in a seven-team race for first. The baseball-loving denizens of the Monumental City had flocked to see the Orioles. Through 25 home games, the club had drawn over 100,000 fans, good for an average of over 4,000 per game. The club had left town on June 18 and embarked on a month-long road trip. Conveniently, the Unions were set to arrive home to begin a month-long homestand in Baltimore that would see the club play 19 consecutive games at their home grounds at Belair Lot. This homestand would be a crucial stretch and go a long way towards determining the club's financial viability going forward.

The Unions had drawn well in 16 home games heading into July, averaging close to 2,000 fans per game, including a season-high of 5,000 for opening day. While their overall attendance was less than half that of the Orioles, they were drawing better than most Union clubs. Only the Nationals, St. Louis, and the recently added Kansas City club could claim better attendance. Baltimore was proving to be a baseball town, and there was room for the Union nine within it. On the field, the club was led by the brilliance of Bill Sweeney. The 26-year-old pitcher had been hurling for various clubs across the country dating back to 1878. He had ventured to California in 1879 and developed his pitching skills in relative obscurity. He had shown enough promise to earn a spot with the Philadelphia Athletics in 1882, eventually going 9–10, with a 101 ERA+ as a change pitcher and spare outfielder. He paired up with catcher Ed Fusselback in 1883 for Peoria in the Northwestern League. The duo was amongst the cadre of Peoria's reserved players signed by the Henderson syndicate in the fall of 1883. Sweeney had proven to be one of the great finds of the season, and the Unions were content riding his right arm as far as it would take them. The club's failure to find a reliable second starter would be their Achilles' heel and undoubtedly brought a premature end to Sweeney's career. The reliable righty paced the UA in wins (40), games pitched (62), games started (60), complete games (58), innings pitched (538.0), hits (522), home runs allowed (13), and batters faced (2270). He also struck out 374 batters alongside his stellar 2.59 ERA and 128 ERA+. He also never pitched in the major leagues again.

He joined Cleveland of the Western League in 1885 after being removed from the blacklist he had been on since he jumped from Peoria to Baltimore in 1883. He compiled a 2–5 record in limited time before the league folded in mid–June. Sweeney rejoined Fusselback on the Oswego club in upstate New York and then shut himself down in September, hoping to rejuvenate his arm with extended rest.[3] He showed little of his old form in 1886 and was let go by Oswego in July, thus ending his formal professional career. A *Sporting Life* editorial in summer 1886 lamented his lack of speed while pitching for a semipro team in Little Falls, New York, claiming it was keeping him from "the top rungs of the profession."[4] Such was the life for many a talented pitcher in the 1880s: meteoric success, debilitating arm troubles, and condemnation to obscurity in the baseball hinterlands.

The Unions' lineup also featured two future stars making their major league debuts. Emmett Seery was a 23-year-old left fielder who had spent part of 1883 with Henderson's independent Chicago Union club. He was Baltimore's top hitter, whose best qualities were his speed and plate discipline, both of which enabled him to star for Indianapolis later in the decade. Yank Robinson was another excellent find for Baltimore. He had been snagged from East Saginaw of the North-western League in fall 1883, after a failed stint with Detroit in 1882. Robinson was a diminutive spark plug who could play three infield positions with exceptional range. He could even fill in at pitcher and catcher. Robinson was another speedster with excellent plate discipline. He later became a key cog for the St. Louis Brown Stockings dynasty, winning four straight pennants from 1885 to 1888. Robinson paced the Union Association in walks with 37 at a time when it took seven balls to get to first base.

With these three cogs, the club was among the strongest in the circuit. Thanks to Henderson's approach of signing Northwestern Leaguers, the team was built in a much more cost-effective way than the approach of Henry Lucas. This combination of modestly paid but talented youngsters and solid attendance meant Henderson's club was in solid financial shape. The July 1 meeting had revealed the club was at least breaking even or even slightly profitable.

Like Washington, Baltimore was also slated to play a July 4 doubleheader that promised to be lucrative. Two to three thousand fans turned out to Union Park for the morning contest between the Unions and rival Cincinnati. The versatile Robinson was in the pitcher's box for Baltimore to give the tired Sweeney a break. Cincinnati countered with their ace, George Bradley. Baltimore opened up with a run in the top of the first, but Robinson quickly relinquished the lead. He allowed one run in the first, one in the second, and two in the third. After a scoreless fourth, Robinson allowed three more runs. The problem plaguing the youngster was the wildness of his "cannon ball delivery."[5] He threw three wild pitches, though he struck out nine Cincinnati hitters. The result was a disappointing 9–2 defeat halted after eight innings, so Cincinnati could make their hasty departure and arrive in good time for their afternoon game in Washington.

The Unions had to regroup for the afternoon and await the arrival of the St. Louis nine to Union Park for the afternoon game. Having been stunned by a blowout loss to the Nationals that morning, the Lucas congregation was undoubtedly motivated for the afternoon contest. A weary Bill Sweeney took the reins for Baltimore, having started 28 of his club's first 43 games, including one stretch from May 14 to June 9, when he started 14 of 17 games. Sweeney had pitched exceptionally against the rest of the league, but he had fared poorly against St. Louis, losing all four contests in their first series in May. This included blowout losses by scores of 20–6 and 16–8.

St. Louis arrived only a few minutes before the game for their first appearance in Baltimore. Eight thousand fans had filled "every niche and corner" of Union Park in eager anticipation of the much-ballyhooed front-runners.[6] The St. Louis club arrived on the field "in their white suits, with maroon stockings and caps [looking] like old gladiators."[7] The immense and anxious crowd gave them a warm reception but burned with an intense desire that their hometown heroes would rise to the occasion and defeat the Roman Empire. Another 1,000 fans witnessed the game from surrounding "house-tops, telegraph poles, the steeple of No. 6 engine house, fences and other points of vantage overlooking Union Park."[8] Truly, the city was baseball mad on Independence Day 1884.

St. Louis enlisted their ace "Bollicky" Billy Taylor, an outstanding hurler and equally skilled hitter. Taylor's tendency to inebriate kept him from establishing himself as a star in the majors. Taylor had gotten his start in baseball with the Ted Sullivan's fabled Dubuque club in 1879. This was the same club that had given the legendary Charlie Comiskey and Old Hoss Radbourn, their starts in baseball. That

Ted Sullivan managed the 1879 Dubuque Red Stockings, one of the finest clubs in the nation. The Iowa nine featured a lineup of future major league stars, including Hall of Famers Charles "Old Hoss" Radbourn and Charles Comiskey as well as future Union Association stars Jack Gleason and Billy Taylor. Top row, from left: Tom Loftus, second baseman; Charles "Old Hoss" Radbourn, pitcher; Charles Comiskey, first baseman; and Bill Lapham, first baseman. Middle row, from left: Tom "Sleeper" Sullivan, catcher, and Laurie Reis, pitcher. Bottom row, from left: Harry Alveretta, center fielder; Bill Gleason, short stop; Jack Gleason, third baseman; and Billy Taylor, left fielder (Library of John T. Pregler, Dubuque).

outstanding club also boasted Tom Loftus, now a player-manager for Milwaukee of the Northwestern League. Loftus was a baseball lifer, later managing five major league clubs. The redoubtable Gleason brothers, Jack and Bill, were also on that squad. Jack was now plying his trade at third base Lucas while his brother Bill was starring at shortstop for Chris von der Ahe's Brown Stockings.

After Dubuque, Taylor ventured further west like his mound counterpart Bill Sweeney and pitched in California in 1880. He joined the inaugural version of the New York Metropolitans in the Eastern Championship Association in 1881, alongside future stars like Hugh "One Arm" Daily, Denny Driscoll, Thomas "Dude" Esterbrook, and Tom Mansell. Taylor also appeared for three National League clubs in 1881, struggling in brief stints with Worcester, Detroit, and Cleveland. He jumped to the American Association in 1882, where he enjoyed a strong season as a utility man, splitting time in the outfield, infield, and at catcher. Taylor hit .278/.297/.447, good for an OPS+ of 148 in 71 games for Pittsburgh. The Alleghenys retained his services in 1883, and he was slightly less effective, appearing in 83 games with a .260/.278/.350 batting line for an OPS+ of 107. He also saw his first substantial mound duties in the majors, compiling a 4–7 record and a dismal 5.39 ERA for a dreadful Alleghenys squad that finished in last place. Taylor and teammate Buttercup Dickerson were among the first players signed by Lucas. The duo had been derisively labeled as "tanks" by the *National Police Gazette* for their propensity to load up on alcohol.[9] So far in 1884, Taylor and Dickerson had been on their best behavior and were expected to be key contributors in St. Louis's July 4 matchup against Baltimore.

The game opened with a scoreless first inning. St. Louis opened the scoring with a run in the top of the second. Baltimore responded with a run in the bottom of the inning off Taylor. Baltimore scored two in the bottom of the third, and St. Louis tied up the game in the top of the fourth off a home run from Taylor. He was a skilled hitter and hit .366/.389/.548 for St. Louis on the season. Baltimore responded with three runs in the bottom of the fifth to make the score 6–3 and then added another run off Taylor in the sixth to make the score 7–3 for the home team. The visitors retaliated with four runs off a tired Sweeney in the top of the sixth to tie and then took a one-run lead in the seventh. While Taylor had not pitched well, he was now gifted a lead, and it was expected that he would close out the game. Faced with a deficit, Baltimore was energized by the exuberant hometown crowd. The weak-hitting 39-year-old Ned Cuthbert, who had strangely taken on center field duties despite his advanced age, led off with a surprising single. Henry Oberbeck flew out to Dave Rowe in center field, at which point the game took a turn. As the *Baltimore American* put it:

> Then the show began. Seery came to the bat and was loudly cheered, as Baltimore's chances of victory largely depended on what he and Fusselback would do. He sent the St. Louis fielders hunting leather on a two-base hit, and Fusselback followed with another two-bagger, bringing Cuthbert and Seery home. Robinson got his base on called balls, and a long single hit by J. Sweeney allowed Fusselback to score. A base hit by Phelan brought Robinson home, and Phelan scored on a safe hit by Levis, who was left on second.[10]

Buoyed with a four-run lead going into the top of the ninth, a gassed Sweeney was entrusted to pitch the ninth and go for the complete-game victory. The four-run lead soon turned to two on consecutive hits by Gleason, the anemic hitting catcher George Baker, and equally inept hitting shortstop Milt Whitehead. Sweeney summoned every last bit of strength and regrouped enough to survive the inning, sending the 8,000 strong into ecstasy with a surprising 12–10 victory. The thrilling spectacle nearly had a tragic bent. A shed behind the left-field fence, on which 100 fans were perched to watch the contest, had cracked. The panicked crowd leaped from the shed and onto the Union Park grounds. The *Baltimore Sun* noted that "one little fellow [was] caught on the fly by Dickerson, the St. Louis left fielder."[11] Thankfully, there appear to have been no injuries.

The success of the Baltimore Unions' doubleheader at the gate was hoped to boost interest in the nine for the rest of the season. Initial returns were positive, as 3,000 fans witnessed the hometown club batter a returning Cincinnati club on July 5, with a box score that read 13–5. The scheduled umpire, David F. Sullivan, only appeared on the grounds with the home team up 2–0 in the second inning. Because of his late arrival and the deficit faced by the visitors, Sullivan's request to treat the ongoing contest as official was rejected by Cincinnati.[12] Sullivan instead awarded the game to Baltimore via forfeit.

Another 2,000 fans turned out on July 7 to see the club fall 5–1 in a rematch of July 4 between Sweeney and Taylor. Attendance dipped to 1,000 for their July 9 loss to St. Louis, and 2,000 fans attended the closing game of the St. Louis series on July 12, a 4–0 loss for the home club. Perhaps nonplussed by their three straight losses to the superior St. Louis squad, the Baltimore cranks did not turn out in great numbers to see the first appearance of another Missouri squad at Belair Lot. The lowly Kansas City Unions entered play on July 14, with a dreadful 3–16 record. A decent crowd of 1,500 curious onlookers witnessed their expected defeat by a blowout score of 15–2. Kansas City's pitcher was Dick Blaisdell, a much-hyped prospect, who had jumped to the Unions from the Lynn club of the Massachusetts State Association, garnering a blacklist.[13] The victory marked the beginning of a 16-game winning streak for Baltimore that would run from July 14 to August 8 and see the club take a 10-game lead over Boston and Cincinnati in the battle for second place.

On July 16, Kansas City fell 17–5 in front of 1,300 fans. The game marked the beginning of one of the strangest careers in baseball history. A mystery man only known as Scott made his debut as Baltimore's new right fielder. The mysterious Scott was recruited to replace the disappointing Henry Oberbeck, who had parlayed a high-profile lawsuit against Chris von der Ahe in the offseason into a role with Baltimore. Oberbeck was quietly let go after the July 14 game and was picked up by the needy Kansas City nine, who were hungry for anyone with a pulse who claimed to play baseball. The mysterious Scott marked his debut with two hits in five at-bats while batting ninth and playing errorless ball. Scott's name would appear in the lineup for 12 more games, all of them Baltimore victories, including a thrilling 13–12 win on July 19 that saw Scott hit a home run. After getting two hits and scoring two runs in four at-bats in the club's 8–3 victory over the Nationals on August 5, Scott disappeared without a trace, his place being taken by Bernie Graham. Strangely, Scott's presence in the lineup was never marked by any mention of where he came from, and his departure received no mention. The mystery man appeared in 13 games, had 55 at-bats with a solid for 1884 batting line of .226/.255/.340 and 90 OPS+, including a double, a triple, and a home run. He made only one error in 13 games in right field, good for a fielding percentage of .909, against a league average of .816 for the position. Most importantly, the club had won all 13 games with him in the lineup. Scott's disappearance from the lineup without a mention, his common last name, and the complete lack of any biographical details or clues have ensured that his eternal anonymity is all but certain.

Baltimore drew reasonably well for the remaining home games in July, ranging from 1,000 to 2,000 fans per contest. Their success was overshadowed by the returning Orioles, who drew 4,000 fans for their first home game in over a month on July 17. On July 18, the club drew 5,000 more running directly opposite the Kansas City-Baltimore Union Association contest, whose attendance figures went unreported. Despite the stellar play of the Unions and the considerable success of Independence Day, it was still clear that the Orioles were the number one draw in Baltimore going into the home stretch of the baseball season. It can be reasonably assumed that the tight AA pennant race and higher quality of baseball in that circuit had given the incumbents the edge.

11

◇◇◇◇◇◇◇◇◇◇◇◇◇◇

"Bollicky" Billy
and the "Wizard"

"I have come to the conclusion that everything is fair in base ball as in war and I want my share of the fun while it is going."[1]—Henry Lucas, as quoted in *Sporting Life*, July 9, 1884

President Henry Lucas's decree that his circuit would now go into the business of breaking contracts at the July 1 meeting sent a ripple throughout the Union. Each club in the circuit was now given another means to acquire players. There was now a chance for players to be freed from an unhappy situation or escape a club on the verge of collapse. While Lucas's promise of vengeance against the establishment signaled significant changes on the horizon, the first player to jump was a pitcher from Lynn of the Massachusetts State Association. Dick Blaisdell was recruited from Lynn in early July, along with his catcher, Henry Oxley.[2] The pair signed with Kansas City, though Oxley quickly reneged on his deal. It seems likely that the battery was recommended by either Jim Chatterton or Charlie Fisher, two former Lynn players who appeared for Kansas City that season. The scoop was hardly a difference-maker, as Blaisdell only lasted four games with the club, though he would act as an eastern talent scout later in the month to earn his keep.

Henry Boyle was the next to jump, signing with St. Louis on July 7. Henry Lucas signed the promising Boyle for $200 a month from the Reading, Pennsylvania, team. The Eastern League club was on the brink of collapse and had urged Boyle to find a better situation.[3] Boyle, a young and hard-hitting first baseman, had never pitched regularly, having made only one appearance in the box in 1883 with Reading. Upon joining St. Louis, Fred Dunlap was impressed by the young player's strong arm and excellent control. He took a chance and put Boyle in as the starting pitcher in his very first appearance with the club. Dunlap and Lucas were getting desperate for pitching after all.

In the past ten days, the St. Louis Unions had lost both of their starting pitchers. Young Charlie Hodnett, a Mound City amateur, had pitched wonderfully in four games for the St. Louis Brown Stockings in 1883. He had failed to earn a regular role on the club, which boasted two top starters in Tony Mullane and George "Jumbo" McGinnis. Hodnett was given a chance by Lucas in 1884 and was outstanding. He compiled a 12–2 record with a 2.01 ERA and a 151 ERA+ for the Unions. However, the burgeoning star's durability proved to be his downfall, as he missed significant time in June. After getting thrashed 12–1 by Washington on July 4, he was sent home with an ailing foot. He never played professional baseball again. He found work as a printer for his father's newspaper, the *St. Louis Times*, before passing away in poverty at the young age of 30 in 1890.[4]

Hodnett's loss was a significant blow to St. Louis, but it was the sudden departure of the club's top starting pitcher, Billy Taylor, that had put the club in a massive bind. Taylor had proven unexpectedly dominant in the pitchers' box for St. Louis. He had replaced the production of expected ace Tony Mullane and was a critical reason that Lucas's nine was at the top of the standings. Taylor had long been a problem child, but he was playing to his full potential for the first time in several years. "Bollicky" Billy had done it all for Lucas, equally adept as a pitcher and a hitter. As the club's top hurler, he went 25–4 in 29 starts with a 1.68 ERA and a 180 ERA+. He also acted as a proto-relief ace and paced the UA in saves with four. When he wasn't pitching, he played first base and was one of the top hitters in the league. He put up a stunning slash line of .366/.389/.548 and a 212 OPS+ in 43 games.

His departure from the Unions was a byproduct of the same motion that Lucas had put forth not to respect contracts. With this now a codified policy of the Union Association, the clubs in the National Agreement ramped up their recruitment efforts, aggressively trying to induce Union players to break their bonds. Taylor was the first star to take the bait. "Bollicky" Billy had already developed a well-earned reputation as a stereotypical ballplayer: uncouth, impulsive, carefree, and frequently intoxicated. He now added disloyal to this list of suitable adjectives. It was first reported that Athletics manager Lew Simmons had induced Taylor to jump to his club on July 2. The manager had also tried to lure Taylor's battery mate George Baker as part of the coup but was rebuffed. The pitching hungry Athletics had offered Taylor a reported $300 advance with a promise of $700 more if he broke his contract and $2,000 in total to complete the rest of the season in the City of Brotherly Love.[5]

Taylor was an impulsive character, prone to fast living and hasty decisions. Taylor's off-season in 1883 tells you all you need to know about the type of person he was. On October 17 of that year, he was arrested after a dispute with a Pittsburgh jeweler over a $750 diamond pin. Taylor claimed to have been gifted the pin, while jeweler Charles Brown claimed to have loaned it to Taylor on the promise of future payment. Upon getting bailed out of jail by Pittsburgh owner H.D. McKnight for $1,500, Taylor refused to return the pin to the jeweler, claiming to have been "subjected to contumely and disgrace."[6] Just over a week later, on October 26, Taylor was the umpire in an eventful ballgame in Pittsburgh between two touring teams from Philadelphia, entirely made up of members of the female persuasion. The matchup between the Brunettes and the Blondes ended up with the Blondes on top by a score of 23–5. The following day, Taylor and some of his teammates played in a game against the female squad, with Taylor only throwing left-handed and batting with one hand on the bat. The managers of the female ball club were arrested for putting on an immoral exhibition in this battle of the sexes. Taylor became enamored with a member of the blonde team, a 16-year-old named Rosa Garrity of Lancaster, Pennsylvania. Three days later, on October 30, the two were married. As the story went:

He was smitten with one of the female nine, a petite blonde named Rosa Garrity, and very pretty. She accepted his invitation to a buggy ride and once on the road Rosa poured into Willie's ears the simple story of her life. She was scarcely sixteen years of age, and being fond of romp had run off from home at Lancaster, Pennsylvania, and joined the ball club. During the ride, it transpired that the mother of Taylor and the father of Rosa had come over in the same ship from the old country many years ago. Taylor suggested she leave the ball club. This she at first refused to do, but when Taylor accompanied the request with an offer of marriage on the following night, she relented. The ball club left the city without her, and on Tuesday last, just three days after their first meeting, Willie and Rosa were made man and wife. The fact has just leaked out and while Rosa has gone to her parents to acquaint them of the change in life, the new husband is awaiting her return to his bosom.[7]

Two days after getting married, Taylor was given his release from the Alleghenys, his recent arrest no doubt playing a role. Taylor was joined on the unemployment line by two other teammates, Buttercup Dickerson and Denny Driscoll. McKnight released the trio despite their evident abilities. *Sporting Life* described the reason for their dismissal: "the three men ... have been guilty of the most outrageous breaches of discipline, and who did more to demoralize the club than all else put together, have been released, to the relief of the rest of the nine, a number of whom openly avowed their intention of refusing to play next season if these men were retained."[8] A week later, on November 8, Taylor signed with Lucas and the rebel Unions for $2,000 for the 1884 season. Within the span of three weeks, Taylor had been arrested, met his future wife, gotten married, been released, and then risked banishment by signing a $2,000 contract with the upstart league. Such was life in Billy Taylor's world.

Now playing the best ball of his career and starring for the world-beating St. Louis Unions, the restless Taylor was on the verge of jumping ship. Taylor had taken the $300 advance from manager Lew Simmons on July 2 and disappeared while St. Louis was on their eastern road trip shortly before their Independence Day doubleheader. Henry Lucas recounted what happened next with Taylor:

Well I tell you how it was. When I was in Baltimore [for the July 1 Union Association meeting] I heard Taylor had left the club.... I soon received a telegram from Taylor stating he was in Washington and ready to pitch the game there. I did reply to it, and when I reached the hotel in Baltimore about noon of the Fourth [of July] I found Taylor there. He shook hands with me and said he was feeling very bad, as he had just been to New York where he had found his wife leading a life of shame. He told me he had received an offer from Simmons of the Athletics and had taken $500 advance money, but had spent it all. He would still continue to play with the club, but wanted me to return Simmons the money advanced him and I could keep it out of his [Taylor's] salary.... Now I have since learned that Simmons only advanced Taylor $300, and I don't intend to return it. Taylor is $375 in debt to me and I see no reason why he should be so anxious to pay Simmons and take his time about paying me. If Simmons will pay me the amount Taylor had drawn ahead, he can have him. I have got more work out of Taylor, I believe, than any other man ever has, and more than Simmons is likely to get out of him.[9]

Taylor returned to Lucas's club, perhaps hoping that the owner would change his mind and cover the debt to Simmons. He made around for a couple more appearances for Lucas, including one final appearance on July 7. Taylor pitched a stellar four-hit 5–1 victory over Washington. Taylor then fled the club for good and joined the Athletics. He made his debut in Toledo on July 11, with a fine 5–2 victory.

The Athletics' signing of Taylor was motivated by their lack of pitching depth. In June, their promising young pitcher, Al Atkinson, had left the club to recuperate from a mysterious ailment. Atkinson traveled to his native Illinois to rest. It was there that he was recruited by the Chicago Unions and signed in mid–July. His was another defection in a month full of them, with players jumping to and from the Union Association. Taylor's tenure with Philadelphia proved quite fruitful, even if the defending champion Athletics failed to keep pace in the pennant race. Taylor pitched 260 innings for Philadelphia while completing all 30 of his starts. He put up an excellent 2.53 ERA and 134 ERA+. His .252/.272/.342 batting line paled in comparison to his UA batting line, though his 93 OPS+ in the AA was still very good for a pitcher. Taylor's historic and unique 1884 season saw him finish in the top ten in WAR in the AA with 5.4 and the UA with 6.1.

Continuing the trend of contract jumping was Taylor's buddy Lewis Buttercup Dickerson. Buttercup was an excellent hitter when sober and had hit exceptionally in the Union Association. In 46 games, he had hit .365/.388/.445 for an OPS+ of 180, but the threat of lushing and unreliability was always there. The Baltimore native had been banned from the National League because of his addiction in 1881.[10] He demonstrated his recklessness when he abandoned Lucas after the club's 4–0 victory in his hometown of Baltimore on July 12. Rumors had him going on a prolonged bender while visiting old friends before succumbing to his greatest friend, whisky.[11] While back home, he also broke his UA contract and signed with Billy Barnie and the Baltimore Orioles in the AA. Barnie stated that he signed Dickerson as retaliation for the recent defection of his own alcohol-infused infielder, Frank "Gid" Gardner.[12] The infielder had jumped to the Chicago Unions after being suspended indefinitely by Barnie. Lucas responded to the loss of Dickerson with an attitude of good riddance. Lucas's organ, the *St. Louis Republican*, noted that the Union was dumping all its lushers into the "American Association vat."[13]

With Taylor gone, Lucas scrambled for his replacement. In the short term, the inexperienced Henry Boyle showed some promise. The young addition won a decisive 8–2 victory against Baltimore on July 9 in his first appearance for the club. The recently departed Charlie Hodnett boasted both of Boyle's pitching ability and his appearance, noting he "is the best looking man on the team, and that while he is of rather slim build and stands six feet high, he weighs no less than 174 pounds."[14] Boyle soon earned the nickname "Handsome Henry," a sobriquet that would last the remainder of his career. He won his second start on July 12, an impressive 4–0, one-hit shutout on July 12, once again defeating Baltimore. For a new pitcher with nearly zero pitching experience, the rookie was off to an exceptional start. He made his third consecutive start on July 14. The result was a sloppy 12–10 loss to Boston, suggesting that perhaps Boyle still had something to learn.

Henry Lucas still needed a second pitcher to stabilize his threadbare pitching staff, which now consisted of just Henry Boyle, who had all of four professional starts to his name. His first recruit was John Cattanach, a 21-year-old from Providence. The youngster had made one disastrous start for Providence on June 5, allowing seven

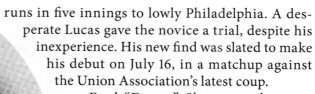

runs in five innings to lowly Philadelphia. A desperate Lucas gave the novice a trial, despite his inexperience. His new find was slated to make his debut on July 16, in a matchup against the Union Association's latest coup.

Fred "Dupee" Shaw was the newest member of the Boston Unions as he strode into the pitcher's box at Boston Athletic Grounds. The left-handed marvel from nearby Charlestown, Massachusetts, was making his Union debut, just a few days removed from jumping the lowly Detroits of the National League. If you listened to the Detroit papers, Shaw was a spoiled malcontent, refusing to take the pitcher's box and help his team. Shaw felt he was being overworked by being asked to take the pitcher's box every second day. Things came to a head during a controversial contest against Philadelphia on July 8.

Shaw's performance that day was poor. He reportedly tossed the ball lazily to the Philadelphia batters and laughed as his deliveries were pounded all over the field.[15] In the second inning, manager Jack Chapman sent his catcher Charlie Bennett out to talk with Shaw. After a brief conference, Shaw indicated he wanted to stay

"Handsome" Henry Boyle was thrust into pitching duties in July 1884 with St. Louis after the defection of ace Billy Taylor. The talented Boyle had never pitched regularly in professional baseball, but he enjoyed a strong rookie season going 15–3, with a 1.74 ERA for the pennant winners (courtesy Southern Illinois University Press).

in the box. Gifted with a rare three-run lead by his light-hitting lineup, he promptly gave up four runs in the third inning in a manner that raised the suspicions of his manager:

> In that inning, he fumbled an easy grounder and allowed a batter to reach first. He tossed the ball up to the batters and grinned when they hit it. After two runs had been scored and two men were on bases, he threw the ball high over [Milt] Scott's head and to the bank seats, both men scoring on the error. In the last two or three innings, after the game was irrevocably lost, he commenced pitching with his usual speed and effectiveness. This made it very palpable that he had been making no effort to win the game.[16]

Chapman fined him $30 for his poor play and for disobeying team rules.[17]

An incredulous Shaw bought a train ticket and traveled to his native Boston on July 9, fed up with Chapman and unwilling to pay the fine. Chapman thought he was tanking on purpose, but it is very plausible that Shaw was simply exhausted. The pitcher faced a daunting workload that was exacerbated by a dreadful defense. Detroit was the worst fielding club in the NL, with a fielding percentage of .886 and a defensive efficiency rating of .611. The porous defense turned outs into baserun-ners with regularity, and Shaw was forced to pitch out of jams and put more strain on his arm. At 5-foot-8 and 165 pounds, the slightly built Shaw was among the hard-est throwing pitchers in baseball. Thanks to the National League's rule change, his delivery was made even faster by the freedom to pitch overhand for the first time that year. He had started 28 of 53 Detroit games, completed 25 of them, and pitched 227.2 innings, and the season was not even half done. He was both tired physically and tired of getting his brains beat in game after game. The $30 fine was simply the last straw, and with the rebellious Union Association now an option, he was con-sidering a change of scenery. Shaw made one last-ditch effort to make amends with Chapman, requesting a $300 advance and rescindment of the fine.[18] His demands were quickly rejected, and the Boston Unions came calling. They offered Shaw the chance to pitch in his hometown with a pay raise to boot. His decision to leave Chap-man and Detroit was an easy one.

For Tim Murnane, Shaw's disgruntled Detroit departure could not have come at a better time. He was dealing with his own disgruntled and exhausted pitcher. The once outstanding Tommy Bond had enjoyed something of a renaissance in the early months of the season. Bond had been effectively out of baseball for the better part of four years, having last pitched regularly in the majors in 1880. His once-promising career, which included three straight forty-win seasons and back-to-back pennants in 1877 and 1878, had come to a crashing halt. His demise resulted from the arm troubles that came from throwing 3300 innings by the time he was 24 years old. Returning from his extended hiatus, he was pitching like a new man. He had racked up a stellar 10–2 record in his first 12 starts, including the remarkable 8–1 victory on May 24 that snapped St. Louis's win streak at 20 games to start the season. His per-formance deteriorated from that point. He had won just three more games while los-ing seven, which brought his record to a more modest 13–9 through the end of June.

On July 1, Bond and his battery mate and old friend, Lew Brown, announced to club management that they would not continue playing until their past due sal-ary was paid. Boston owed Bond $208 in back salary and Brown $180.[19] When man-agement refused to make the payment, Bond and Brown quit the club. The club directors formally released the duo, claiming, "That their tendency to be disturb-ing elements in the team more than balanced their good work."[20] Not coinciden-tally, Bond's release came at a time when his performance had waned, and the club's financial state was in question. Bond was the club's highest-paid player and also a noted malcontent, often calling attention to "trivial issues."[21] After his release, the pitcher signed with Indianapolis of the American Association but had nothing left in his right arm. He went 0–5 in five starts with a 5.65 ERA before he was released, never appearing in the majors again. He compiled an impressive 234–163 record and a 2.14 ERA in 3628.2 innings for his career. Almost all of his success came by the age of 24.

Bond's departure left Boston with James Burke as their only capable starter. In May, the club had picked up Burke after their presumed change pitcher, Char-lie Daniels failed to live up to the task. Brown University alumnus Fred Tenney was signed to replace Bond, and the collegian put forth a strong effort, winning three of his four starts. Despite Tenney's promise, Boston manager Tim Murnane knew he needed a workhorse to replace Bond and Shaw was just the man he was looking for.

Shaw reportedly signed with Boston on July 12. For Murnane and the Boston directors, the signing was a life preserver both on the field and off. The Unions were struggling at the gate. At the July 1 meeting in Baltimore, Boston president Frank E. Winslow had announced that "his club would have to cut short its career on account of a lack of funds to pay salaries and general expenses."[22] Only the intervention of Henry Lucas, Justus Thorner, and Albert Henderson saved the club. The three men each agreed to cover a quarter of the club's losses for the balance of the season. Boston was drawing poorly and failed to capture the imagination of the city's baseball cranks. Bostonians were far more enthralled with the pennant race brewing in the National League between the home club and nearby Providence. The club's July 4 doubleheader against Kansas City, which was unopposed by their more famous rival, only drew a combined 2,500 fans. Even the terrible Keystones in Philadelphia had attracted a great crowd of 8,000 total fans for their Independence Day contests. Boston's attendance typically averaged around 500 per game. Their pitiful attendance occurred despite their solid performance, an abundance of promising young local talent, positive coverage in the local media, and 25-cent tickets.

The signing of Shaw would solidify Boston's pitching staff for the rest of the year while also generating buzz in the Hub. Murnane and company surely hoped fans would turn out in droves to watch Shaw. He was the controversial hometown hero whose dazzling delivery had earned him the sobriquet "the Wizard." When Shaw strode onto the field to face the league-leading St. Louis nine on July 16, the Boston directors must have felt pangs of disappointment in seeing that only 1,500 fans had shown up to the game. That was the same attendance as the opening game of the series just two days before, on July 14. Shaw's ballyhooed arrival had done nothing to boost attendance, and if anything could be credited with the turnout, it was the St. Unions, the league's best drawing card.

Shaw would face a significant challenge in the St. Louis nine, easily the league's best-hitting lineup. To coincide with Shaw's signing, the Unions also reinstated Lew Brown to serve as his catcher. Brown was anxious to rejoin the club, and despite his poor off-field habits, he was still an excellent receiver and one of the few people qualified to handle Shaw's difficult deliveries. The reinstatement was a wise choice by Murnane and paid immediate benefits in Shaw's debut. Shaw was warmly applauded by the 1,500 fans in attendance when he took to the pitcher's box in the top of the first. The Wizard dazzled both the crowd and the powerful St. Louis lineup with an array of left-handed curves. Shaw's curves were as confounding as his famed wind-up, which he later claimed to be the first pitcher to incorporate into his delivery. One observer noted, "Shaw's preliminary motions are enough to give a timid batsman the delirium tremens."[23] Shaw's pre-pitch actions were described as follows by Al Spink, founder of *The Sporting News*:

> After considerable swinging and scratching around with his feet, during which he would deliver a lengthy speech to the batter, to the effect that he was the best pitcher on earth and the batter a dub, he would stretch both arms at full length over his head. Then after gazing fixedly at the first baseman for a moment, he would wheel half around and both arms would

fly apart like magic… [H]e would wind his left arm around again and let the ball fly, running at the same time all the way from the box to the home plate.[24]

Catcher Brown was making his first appearance in several weeks and was rusty early on. He struggled a bit with Shaw's delivery in the first inning, allowing a runner to reach first when he missed a third strike, but after that, he caught on quickly. Shaw's teammates gave him an early lead scoring four runs off of John Cattanach, the jittery rookie from Providence. Young Cattanach settled down and would allow just one more run the rest of the way. However, the debuting Shaw was nearly unhittable, allowing just three St. Louis hits and striking out 14 batters while allowing one unearned run. The conclusion was a 5–1 victory for Boston. The short-handed St. Louis nine put Cattanach back in the box the following day on July 17. St. Louis battered pitcher James Burke and took home a sloppy 8–5 win in front of just 200 fans. The game was overshadowed by the Boston and Providence game taking place that afternoon, which drew 3,722 fans.[25]

In his second start with Boston two days later, on July 19, Dupee Shaw put forth one of the most remarkable pitching performances in baseball history. The contest between Boston and St. Louis would go down as the finest game in the brief history of the Union Association. Shaw was facing off against Henry Boyle, who was responsible for anchoring the pitching staff of the best team in the league just ten days into his pitching career. On this day, he proved up to the task. Shaw and Boyle traded goose eggs through six innings, with Shaw's deceptive deliveries proving even harder to hit than in his debut. Shaw's hurling sent the St. Louis batters into fits, particularly the excitable Orator Shafer, St. Louis eccentric star, who

Lefthander Frank "Dupee" Shaw was the famed inventor of the pitching wind-up and was known during his prime as "The Wizard" for his dazzling array of curves. Shaw jumped to the Boston Unions after a falling out with Detroit manager Jack Chapman. Shaw is pictured unusually throwing right-handed. The photograph was taken while he was on the downswing of his career during a minor league stint in Newark in 1889 (Library of Congress).

"cut up some wonderful antics in his frantic efforts to hit the ball."[26] St. Louis short-stop Milt Whitehead and right fielder Jack Brennan each struck out three times. When the game concluded, Shaw had struck out an astonishing 18 hitters. This figure remained the single-game record for a left-handed pitcher until September 15, 1969, when Steve Carlton struck out 19 New York Mets. Shaw's performance was undermined by the sloppy defensive support his teammates gave him in the field. On three separate occasions, St. Louis got runners to third base because of sloppy defense, and on each occasion, Shaw ended the threat with a strikeout. In the top of the seventh inning, Shaw struck out Jack Gleason, but the ordinarily reliable Lew Brown dropped the third strike. The heady Gleason got all the way to second base. Dave Rowe advanced Gleason to third on a sacrifice hit. The upside of Shaw's superb pitching was that he was nearly unhittable at his best, but the downside was that it could make his catcher's job a nightmare. With Gleason on third, Shaw uncorked a wild delivery allowing the baserunner to score and put his club down 1–0. That run would end up being the game's lone tally and marred a truly historic performance by Shaw. The game concluded with a final score of 1–0. Shaw had struck out 18 hitters and allowed just one hit, a single off the bat of light hitting Joe Quinn. The rookie first baseman was making a solid impression for St. Louis, honing a reputation as a bright and steady player in the mold of his mentor Charles Comiskey.

Henry Lucas was awed by Shaw's otherworldly performance and was determined to get an ace of his own to replace the departed Billy Taylor. It seems very probable that Lucas was the source for a brief article that appeared in the *Boston Herald* on July 20, 1884, just a few columns over from the box score that documented Shaw's historic performance the day before. The title of the report read: "Is Radbourne Going to St. Louis?"

12

◇◇◇◇◇◇◇◇◇◇◇◇◇

The Hoss and the Playboy

The brilliance of Dupee Shaw's first two appearances against St. Louis had given Henry Lucas a sense of urgency to find an ace pitcher of his own. Lucas turned to Rhode Island for his answer. Providence was embroiled in a heated pennant race with their most hated rival in nearby Boston. Managed by the steady and resourceful Frank Bancroft, the club's record stood at 43–18–1 on July 19, just 1.5 games behind first-place Boston. Despite their strong play, there was trouble brewing for the club behind the scenes. The club's financial situation was a significant concern. The city was the smallest market in the National League, with an 1880 population of 104,857. The club had been among the finest teams in the National League since its inception in 1878. They won the pennant in 1879 and had never finished below third place in the standings. The Providence club drew relatively well, finishing as high as second in attendance in both 1879 and 1880. In 1883, the club's attendance of 61,314 was good for just sixth in the eight-team league. Their modest attendance figures were acceptable when the NL had multiple clubs in smaller cities, but the league's composition had changed drastically in recent years. Facing pressure from the American Association, the NL jettisoned the Troy and Worcester clubs after the 1882 season and replaced them with teams in New York and Philadelphia. Baseball's arrival as a big business was putting smaller clubs like Providence into an untenable situation. With the larger market NL teams drawing well over 100,000 fans, small market clubs like Providence were facing the squeeze.

On the field, the club's success was driven by the fantastic work of their two star pitchers, the gruff and experienced Charles "Old Hoss" Radbourn, and the impulsive and outlandish youngster, Charlie Sweeney. The two men achieved their brilliance in disparate ways. Radbourn relied on guile, wisdom, and sheer determination to get National League hitters out. Young Sweeney used incredible speed to blow away his competition. Both men were in the midst of remarkable seasons, but the friction between the two stars was starting to boil over. The trouble had been brewing since spring training when it was reported that the duo had "become jealous of each other."[1]

The pair's relationship remained icy through the first month of the season, with each man determined to outdo the exploits of the other game by game. On June 6, Radbourn took to the box in a match against defending champion Boston and put forth one of the all-time great performances in a 16-inning 1–1 tie game against his rival "Grasshopper" Jim Whitney. The *Providence Journal* proclaimed the contest to be a "phenomenal game, the like of which will probably never be seen again."[2] On June 7, in front of a crowd of 7,387 at the South End Grounds, Sweeney took the box for Providence. Determined to make the world forget Radbourn's performance the previous day, Sweeney pitched a masterful game. The hurler struck out a record 19 Boston hitters, with a devastating array of "outs and ins, drops and rises … some of the most deceptive curves imaginable."[3] Sweeney was hailed as a hero. When the nine returned home that evening, horse-drawn carriages and Herrick's Providence Brigade Band were waiting. Sweeney was carried on the shoulders of the excited crowd while the band played "Hail to the Chief," and the excited cranks of Providence lit up a battalion of lighted flares. *Sporting Life* reported on the chaotic scene: "[the] streets were one vast blaze of red fire and the crowd packed the sidewalks thicker than sardines."[4]

Radbourn, for one, was deeply annoyed at the attention given to Sweeney. The taciturn star had labored brilliantly in his first three seasons with Providence. He wasn't about to let some arrogant young kid steal his thunder. Radbourn brooded for the next six weeks while the local fans taunted him with pleas to break Sweeney's strikeout record.[5] Sweeney's meteoric rise and public adoration had alienated Radbourn, who felt the accolades should be his. He was also unhappy about his salary. In October 1882, he had signed a contract with the St. Louis Brown Stockings of the American Association. After he was threatened with a blacklist, he reneged on his agreement and returned to Providence.[6] His 1883 season had been his best season thus far. The indefatigable hurler had pitched remarkably, leading the majors with 48 wins and 76 appearances. He also finished second in innings with 632.1 and in ERA at 2.05. For his efforts, he had asked for $4,000 in the off-season. This figure was a large sum for the time, but he was certainly deserving, given his stature and ability.[7] Providence turned down his request, and he ended up signing for $2,000 in November.[8] Radbourn entered the season unhappy with his pay, and now he was unhappy with Sweeney, who had stolen his rightful laurels. His discontentment grew even further when Sweeney missed time with a sore arm, forcing Radbourn to pick up the slack. With Sweeney injured, Radbourn made 10 of 12 starts from June 28 to July 14 while relieving the ailing Sweeney in the club's July 8 game. During this stretch, Radbourn compiled a modest 6–4 record, impressive given the circumstances but disappointing for a club in the thick of a pennant race.

Bancroft tried to rub salve on the situation by poaching the promising youngster Joseph "Cyclone" Miller from the Chicago Unions. Miller had debuted for Chicago on July 11 with an impressive complete-game victory that saw him strike out 13 batters while allowing just four hits and two runs to the Boston Unions. In another Lucas-inspired raid, A.H. Henderson had enticed Miller, along with first baseman Bernie Graham and second baseman James "Chippy" McGarr, to jump their contracts with the Worcester club of the Massachusetts State Association. Manager Bancroft snagged Miller immediately after his impressive Union debut and slotted him in as the club's alternate hurler. Miller debuted on July 15 with a 4–3 loss at Boston. On July 16, while Dupee Shaw was debuting in nearby Boston, Radbourn faced off against Boston at home. The admittedly biased *Boston Daily Globe* noted, "Radbourn was in no condition, physically or mentally, to pitch."[9] He lost a 5–2 decision to Boston's ace Charlie Buffinton, marred by a disastrous eighth inning that saw him argue with the umpire and his catcher Barney Gilligan. Radbourn had allowed a walk and then became increasingly flustered after Gilligan made an error. After a fumble by his third baseman Jerry Denny, he became upset. He then was called for a balk on an apparent third strike and took his ire out on the umpire. The *Boston Daily Globe* described the scene: "This seemed to break up Rad, and then he pitched the ball so wild that no man could hold it, and two men came home."[10] He was immediately suspended after the game by Bancroft and accused of poor play. He was summoned before the team's directors and asked to give account for his disappointing play in recent weeks. The *Fall River (Massachusetts) Daily Evening News*, which often leveled snarky criticism towards the Providence club, empathized with Radbourn, editorializing:

> The strongest opponents that the Providences have to contend against are the base ball scribes, the patrons and directors. The former abuse them or sicken them with adulation; the patrons sink in their boots and stay at home after they lose a game while the directors kill their "refractory" players by fining them, or disciplining them unreasonably. They killed [former pitcher John] Ward and have broken Radbourne's spirit. It is a hard city to play in.[11]

Cyclone Miller made two consecutive starts in place of the now-suspended Radbourn on July 17 and July 18, winning both. Another youngster, Ed Conley, won a 6–1 decision over the lowly Philadelphia Phillies on July 19. Sweeney re-emerged, making two relief appearances during this stretch, but was perturbed at having to make any emergency appearances. In the days after Radbourn was suspended, Henry Lucas, who was in Boston with his club, offered him a $5,000 contract to pitch the remainder of 1884 and the entire 1885 season for the St. Louis Unions.[12] With a suspended Radbourn mulling over the offer, Sweeney was called upon to resume his role as ace and keep Providence in the pennant race. Despite the turmoil behind the scenes, they remained just 1.5 games behind Boston. The situation took a turn for the worse on July 21, when Providence played an exhibition game in Woonsocket, Rhode Island. Sweeney arrived at the contest in the presence of a woman, purportedly of ill repute. He refused to pitch in the contest, appearing instead in center field.[13] The pitching starved club used three pitchers, including Miller, Paul Radford, and backup catcher Sandy Nava, to grind out a sloppy 11–2 victory over the semi-pro O.S.R.C. club. After the contest, Sweeney refused to travel back to Providence with the club. He stayed behind to consort and carouse with the residents of Woonsocket before returning home on the late train.[14]

The following day, Sweeney agreed to pitch against Philadelphia. The plan was that Cyclone Miller would be called upon to relieve him if necessary. The resulting contest at the Messer Street Grounds would be the source of controversy for decades to come. Sweeney's actions on that Tuesday afternoon would come to define his career and reputation for the remainder of his life. The *Providence Morning Star* opened their game account evocatively: "The 450 people who went out to the Messer street grounds Tuesday afternoon to witness a good ball game, came away deeply disgusted with the perfidy and treachery of Sweeney, who with malicious deliberation placed the home club in such a dilemma that they were forced to drop the game."[15] Sweeney pitched effectively through seven innings and was ably supported by his teammates, holding down a 6–2 lead while allowing just five hits against the seventh-place Phillies. Bancroft played it safe with the four-run lead and called upon Miller to relieve the starter while Sweeney would finish the contest in right field. The temperamental hurler refused the assignment and berated manager Bancroft with a tirade of "vile and insulting language."[16] In an act of petulant defiance, Sweeney discarded his uniform and called Bancroft a "son of a ------."[17] The club's business manager, J. Edward "Ned" Allen, was enlisted to induce Sweeney to get back into uniform, threatening to lay the pitcher off without pay. The arrogant Sweeney laughed at the threat and claimed he could make more money by not playing for Providence. Sweeney's refusal to play meant Providence had to finish the game with just two men in the outfield. Gifted this unusual opportunity, Philadelphia hitters took full advantage and scored eight unearned runs in the ninth inning off a shell-shocked Miller and the demoralized Providence squad. All the while, the borderline sociopathic Sweeney watched the game from the crowd, laughing at the misfortunes of his club while their lead was squandered.[18] Despite the hisses and derision of the crowd, Sweeney remained unfazed, eventually sauntering off after the game in the company of two women, likely prostitutes, utterly unconcerned with his future, his reputation, or the fate of his team.

The club suspended Sweeney immediately after the debacle. The Providence directors were comfortably ahead financially on the season and contemplated disbandment. With a $17,000 surplus in the treasury, and their two star hurlers under suspension, it seemed foolish to continue. The *Providence Morning Star* lamented: "the pennant is no doubt out of the reach of Providence this year."[19] In a last-ditch effort to save the season and keep their pennant hopes alive, the club directors reached out to Radbourn. The grumpy hurler had fended off the advances of Lucas in the ensuing days. Despite his displeasure with his salary, he was a man of his word. He agreed to meet with the directors about a possible return. The savvy Hoss, recognizing the power of his leverage, put forth a series of demands in exchange for his return to the club. First, he asked for the reserve rule to be stricken from his contract, enabling him to become a free agent after the season and finally get paid what he was worth on the open market. Second, he asked for Sweeney's expulsion from the club. Third, Radbourn would be paid a salary equivalent to two pitchers since he would now be called on to pick up the slack of pitching almost every day down the stretch. The agreement ostensibly took his salary from $2,000 to $4,000 on the year. As an additional concession, Providence agreed to pay him another $1,000 on the year, bringing his 1884 salary to $5,000, seemingly out of fear that he was on the verge of jumping over to the Union Association. In return for their investment, Providence would get a newly reinvigorated and determined Radbourn. The pitcher made a bold promise, "I'll pitch every day and win the pennant for Providence, even if it costs me my right arm."[20]

Radbourn was back in the pitcher's box on July 23, pacing his club to an 11–5 victory over third-place New York. Radbourn's dominant stretch of pitching over the season's remaining 51 games from July 23 to October 15 has become the stuff of legend. The unstoppable Hoss started 41 games and compiled a 35–4–1 record, including 18 straight victories from August 7 to September 6. Providence regained first place on August 7 and held on the rest of the way, eventually taking the flag by 10.5 games over Boston. He was a man of his word. Radbourn's record in 1884 was truly astonishing, 59 wins, 12 losses, 73 complete games, 678⅔ innings, 441 strike-outs, 11 shutouts, and a 1.38 ERA, good for a league-leading 205 ERA+. It was the most remarkable pitching season in history.

His petulant rival, Charlie Sweeney, was now persona non grata in Providence. Still in town a day after the incident against Philadelphia, he was chastised by the *Providence Evening Press* for his hubris and lack of morals: "Sweeney is still about town, and wherever he goes the women whom he escorted to the ball game on Tues-day are seen with him. The conduct of this fellow is shameful, and he will regret it when he fully wakes up to its enormity."[21] In any other season, he would have had to come groveling back to Bancroft and his teammates, begging their forgiveness in hopes of pitching again. However, this was 1884, and the Union Association and Henry Lucas were waiting with arms open. Lucas didn't care about a player's past indiscretions; he simply cared about what a man could do on the field. The magnate had salvaged Billy Taylor and Buttercup Dickerson and could do the same with Sweeney. Lucas had been pursuing Radbourn for weeks, and now, with Hoss off the table, he turned his attention toward recruit-ing Sweeney. On July 24, Sweeney officially signed with St. Louis for a $2,000 salary to complete the 1884 season, then $3,000 for 1885 and $3,000 for 1886.[22]

The newest member of the St. Louis Unions promptly left Providence and traveled to Kansas City to meet up with this new club. Arriving in time for the club's July 28 game, Sweeney was placed in left field and showed his hitting prowess with two hits in the club's easy 8–2 thrashing of their dis-mal cross-state rivals. On July 29, Swee-ney made his first appearance in front of 1,000 Kansas City fans. He did not disap-point, taking the contest by a score of 9–1. Sweeney struck out four while allowing just four hits. He also knocked out three hits in five at-bats, showing off his considerable hitting ability. Not only was he starring on the mound, but he was also replac-ing the offense of the departed pitcher/everyman, Billy Taylor.

The club returned to St. Louis, and after sitting out the July 31, 20–1 thrash-ing of Kansas City, Sweeney made his

The controversial Charlie Sweeney was Henry Lucas's big acquisition in summer 1884. The talented and temperamental Sweeney had bristled at sharing pitching duties with Old Hoss Radbourn in Providence and jumped to the Union Association after he was suspended due to insubordination (courtesy Southern Illinois University Press).

home debut on August 1 against the same club. About 2,000 fans came out to the Lucas grounds to witness the debut of the brooding new acquisition. A motivated Sweeney was a dominant Sweeney, and he demonstrated the unlimited potential of his thunderous right arm by holding Kansas City hitless through five innings. Provided with an early three-run lead, he eased up a bit later in the game, eventually allowing a hit in the sixth to break up the no-hitter. Only an eighth-inning run broke up his shutout and the game's final score was 4–1. Sweeney struck out ten on the day, including striking out the side on two separate occasions. He allowed just five hits while getting two hits of his own. The *St. Louis Globe-Democrat* boasted that between Sweeney and catcher George Baker, "the Unions now have a battery equal to any in the country."[23] In the short term, Lucas's gambit had paid off; Sweeney was motivated, happy, and looking for vindication. In addition, since he had barely pitched in July, his weakened right arm had been given time to rest. His old manager Frank Bancroft remained skeptical and warned that Sweeney was damaged goods: "Lucas has secured a poor bargain in Sweeney, his arm has given out and he can only throw underhand."[24]

As a tumultuous July concluded for the Henry Lucas and the Union Association, there remained two and a half months of baseball left. While the pennant race was all but over, there was still a great deal of uncertainty about what the circuit would look like come October. While St. Louis, Washington, and Kansas City had proven financial successes, it remained to be seen whether the likes of Philadelphia, Boston, and Chicago would continue to fight the uphill battle towards profitability. The month of August would be another crucial period towards determining the future of the league.

13

The Bell Tolls
for the Keystones

"The Keystones were to the Union association like a rotten twig to a sound tree. Their cutting off therefore instilled new life into the association."—*St. Louis Republican*, August 9, 1884

When Tom Pratt arrived at Keystone Park at the corner of Broad and Moore on August 7, he knew that the Union Association dream was over. The likable Pratt must surely have regretted his decision to dump his stock in Philadelphia's National League club in order to start up the Keystones last fall. After all, the venture was running thousands of dollars in the red, and the season still had two months left to go. His friends had warned him against getting involved with Henderson and Lucas and the Union scheme, and it turns out they were right.

Pratt's Keystones were a failure on every level. On the field, the club was a disaster. The decision to stock their roster with long-dormant veterans, whose names were once sacred to Philadelphians, had proven to be a bad one. The irascible Fergy Malone, the club's opening day catcher, whose last big-league experience came in 1876, lasted just one day behind the plate. Five passed balls and a bruised ego later, the 39-year-old transitioned to a role as the club's manager. Thirty-four-year-old Levi Meyerle, baseball's first-ever batting champion, seven years removed from his last major league contest, was the club's opening day first baseman. He lasted just three games. Evidently, seven years of rust could not be shaken off. Henry Luff, a talented but well-traveled 31-year-old veteran of four major league clubs, was signed on as an outfielder. He had been banned from the American Association in 1883 after a drunken arrest in July.[1] Luff lasted only 20 games with the Keystones, his tenure ending shortly after his arrest in Cincinnati during a drunken night on the town, which saw him pull a knife on a carriage driver.[2] Billy Geer, another temperamental and unsavory character, lasted nine games before jumping the club to join the Brooklyn club in the American Association.

Geer's story is worthy of its own book. His penchant for theft and forgery derailed a promising career. Geer and Luff had been teammates in 1875 with New Haven of the National Association when Geer's criminal tendencies first appeared. The duo was arrested for stealing some women's dress coats and a police officer's revolver, earning a lifetime ban from the National Association for their troubles.[3]

116

Geer played professionally until 1887, despite frequent interruptions, suspensions, and arrests. After his career was over, he spent the next 35 years as the leading check forger in the United States. Geer was in and out of prison and used upwards of 20 aliases or more while traveling from state to state and even to Europe and Argentina, scamming local businesses everywhere he went.[4] The ex-ballplayer was a well-bred graduate of Manhattan College. His background helps explain the ease with which he could convince strangers of his trustworthiness. It also makes his choice to become a con artist all the more mysterious. Until recently, his final resting place was also a mystery, thanks to his frequent use of fake names and extended stints in jail. Thanks to the diligence of Bill Carle, Peter Morris, and the SABR Biographical Research Committee, Geer was finally tracked down, having died in Chicago on September 30, 1928, under the alias of Bruce Barrington.[5] Nineteenth-century baseball was filled with all sorts of strange birds.

The quick departure of five members of their opening day lineup was made even worse by the performance of expected ace, Sam "Buck" Weaver. The right-hander was the club's marquee signing. He was never an elite pitcher, but he had won 26 games in 1882 and 24 games for the Louisville Eclipse in 1883. His signing was Pratt's response to the lavish spending of Lucas, but he failed to replicate his success with the Keystones and was the club's biggest bust. Weaver's woes were tied to his dead arm, no doubt thanks to the previous year's 400.2 innings of work. He won just five games for the Keystones, posting a dreadful 5.76 ERA, 50 ERA+ while allowing 13.6 hits per nine innings. He also gave up an astounding 146 runs in just 136 innings of work. His failure to be even remotely effective against the diminished competition of his new league was disastrous for the competitive hopes of Pratt's nine. His final appearance came on July 16, when he was pounded for 20 hits and 19 runs at home against the Cincinnati Unions.

These failures in selecting veterans aside, the Keystones' management demonstrated a knack for plucking young talent from Philadelphia's vibrant semi-pro and amateur baseball circuits. Much like Boston, the Keystones had given opportunities to local players and bore the fruit. Baby-faced outfielder William "Buster" Hoover tortured the twirlers of the Union Association. He batted a scalding hot .364 in just his second season of professional baseball. The mark was good for second place in the league, behind only the league's premier player, Fred Dunlap. Burly Jack Clements, who was listed as 5–8, but carried 204 pounds on his stocky frame, had proven equally promising as the club's backstop. The curmudgeonly left-handed catcher debuted at the tender age of 19, plucked from the amateur Continentals club, quickly making a name for himself for his unusual usage of a sheepskin chest protector.[6] In 1884, this was still a cause for concern amongst sportswriters and fans, who were set on upholding a demanding standard of physical toughness for the gladiators of professional baseball. Clements made his mark as a steady catcher and skilled batter, putting up an excellent .282/.317/.429 batting line and a 158 OPS+ as a teenager. He would later star for the Phillies, and in 1895, he hit a sizzling .394, setting a record that still stands as the highest single-season batting average by a catcher. Clements would also set the unbreakable record of most games caught by a left-handed catcher with 1,076.

In the absence of Weaver, the hard-throwing but inconsistent 20-year-old Jersey Bakley had emerged as the club's rubber-armed number one pitcher. Bakley had thrown over 300 innings and struck out 204 batters but also paced the league in walks, earned runs, and wild pitches. Twenty-four-year-old Bill Kienzle had emerged as a strong outfielder for the Keystones, while 22-year-old Jerry McCormick, a defector from the American Association, hit .285 and played relatively well at third base. This quintuplet of Philadelphians made up a solid young core. Two local 18-year-olds, Tom Daly and Al Maul, each received trials with the Keystones in June, and although they were quickly released, the pair would enjoy long major league careers that lasted into the 20th century. Daly's 80 appearances for the 1903 Cincinnati Reds made him the last active Union Association player. Maul's career ended with a three-game stint on the 1901 New York Giants, and when he passed away on May 3, 1958, at 92, he was the oldest Union alumnus.

As bad as the club was on the field, the results were even worse at the box office. The club had drawn poorly from the start. The home opener against Boston drew between 400 and 500 fans. To put it in context, at 25 cents per ticket, the club needed to draw 300 fans just to cover the $75 guarantee to the road team. That did not account for the cost of salaries, equipment, travel, or any other expenses. Before the season, the *Philadelphia Record* published a breakdown of what the Keystones would need to make per game to cover their anticipated expenses:

> The outside games are played under a small guarantee, which barely covers traveling expenses, so that the games on which each club must rely for support are the fifty-six home games. The season is seven months—that's an average of eight games per month. I suppose the salary list of the Keystone club is from $1,400 to $1,600 a month, and other expenses will run the cost of the venture close up to $2,000 a month. The guarantee to visiting clubs, $75, has got to be paid besides. So you see the games of the Keystone club here in Philadelphia must average receipts of $325 per game to bring the club out even at the end of the season, without a dollar of profit. That is, there must be an average attendance of over 1,000 for each game. On some few days, like the Fourth of July, there will be large crowds, but I don't see how they are going to keep the average up to such a high figure.[7]

An examination of available attendance records shows that the club topped 1,000 fans at only eight home games all season. Only the July 4 doubleheader victory over Chicago had drawn anything resembling a large crowd. Those contests drew 4,000 fans each because neither of the rival Philadelphia clubs was in town that day. The club drew fewer than 100 fans on at least one occasion, with 93 attending the June 9 contest against Washington.

The club's poor performance at the box office was undoubtedly affected by the city's two other major league clubs. In 1884, Philadelphia was the second-most populous city in the nation, but it could not possibly support three major league clubs. The fate of Tom Pratt's nine was sealed almost from the start, made worse by the club's glaring ineptitude. To put it bluntly, Philadelphians did not want to watch a third-rate club, no matter how many local players and aged heroes were on the field.

The disappointment of the Keystones season came to a head with one final game at Keystone Park on August 7. The clumsy Keystones took the field against the Boston Unions, much as they had on opening day when the visitors demolished them by a score of 14–2. The home team demonstrated considerably more spirit in this final game. They clawed back from a 6–1 deficit to get within one run in the eighth inning before two more Boston runs in the ninth put the game away. The 8–5 loss brought the lowly Keystones record to 21–46, good for seventh place in the league, ahead of only the disbanded Altoonas and the Kansas City club that had replaced them.

As the game ended and the 200 odd fans in attendance made their way home from Keystone Park, Pratt finalized his decision to disband the club. Buster Hoover and Bill Kienzle refused to play again for the club unless their salaries were promptly played. The Keystone club owed their players approximately two weeks' worth of pay, about $700.[8] Pratt's venture had put him in the hole for $10,000 to $12,000. He had spent $5,000 to build Keystone Park. With his losses mounting and no hope of recouping his investment, Pratt pulled the plug on the season. In an August 13, 1884, editorial in *Sporting Life*, Pratt offered the following summation of his reasons for folding the Keystones:

> The action taken by the Union Association at its Baltimore meeting hurt my club. I have been going down into my pocket to keep the club alive and would be willing to continue if I could see anything gained in the end. But now that it is to be an open fight for players, the biggest pocketbook getting the best, there is little chance for me, as I can't afford to pay $5,000 salaries down my way. The club was not making money now, and with the present state of affairs never would. Why, if I was to develop a first-class player one of the other associations would come and steal him.[9]

Pratt's contention that it was President Lucas's decision to induce players to break their contracts that had led to the club's demise is interesting. On the surface, the Keystones did not lose any players to raiding clubs and had no one jump their contract from the club aside from Billy Geer. However, there may be something to Pratt's belief as NL and AA clubs had been approaching Union players for months now. It was only a matter of time before some of his players jumped, especially since he was having trouble paying their salaries on time.

The Keystones disbanded on the evening of August 7, and the dispersal of players began almost immediately. Hoover and Clements were quickly snatched up by Harry Wright and joined Philadelphia's rapidly improving NL nine. Clements's contract was transferred in return for covering a $500 debt owed by the Keystones for the lumber used to construct Keystone Park. Bakley was rumored to join Providence to spell Old Hoss Radbourn, but he could not sign owing to his blacklist for jumping his contract with the Littlestown, Pennsylvania, club. Kienzle ended up with Trenton of the Eastern League. Pratt ensured that despite his losses, he would pay the players in full: "I felt very sorry for the boys, for we were in arrears in salaries. Every player shall be paid in full however, as I have made arrangements to that effect."[10] In a last-ditch effort to salvage the baseball season, he made a hasty application to have the Keystones join the Eastern League but was promptly denied. The well-liked Pratt had "the sympathies of everyone in his misfortune. If he had followed the advice of his best friends he never would have had anything to do with the Unions."[11]

For the league's opponents, this was one step closer to the collapse of the wreckers, as the *Philadelphia City Item* put it: "to use Brother Caylor's language, 'the bell is ringing for the Union,' and other clubs will soon follow the Keystone."[12] For Henry

Lucas, the Keystones collapse presented both a crisis and an opportunity. Finding a club willing to take over Philadelphia's schedule for the rest of the season would be a challenge. However, with the Northwestern League and Eastern League both facing financial difficulties, there was now a chance to poach a team wholesale and have them replace the Keystones. He quickly reached out to John T. West the owner of the Wilmington, Delaware, club. Wilmington was dominating the Eastern League, but tepid fan support had resulted in losses of nearly $3,000 on the season so far.[13] Lucas and Union secretary Warren White sent numerous telegrams to West and the club directors trying to curry their favor and hasten an agreement which would see the Eastern League leaders replace the Keystones.

Why were Lucas and White so fixated on Wilmington, a city of just over 40,000 people that had proven to be lukewarm about professional baseball? The primary reason appears to be location. Wilmington was just 30 miles from Philadelphia. It would require minimal re-jiggering of the schedule since any Keystone home games could easily be played in Wilmington without disrupting travel plans for visiting clubs. Additionally, Wilmington's stellar record in the Eastern League suggested they might be a stronger club than the departed Keystones.

The next few days saw Wilmington management hem and haw at the prospect of joining the Union Association. Jumping ship from the Eastern League would mean missing potentially lucrative exhibition games against AA and NL clubs since the UA was not part of the National Agreement. They might also risk losing some of their top players since joining a new league would result in the voiding of their Eastern League contracts and render their roster veritable free agents. The Eastern League was a signatory of the protective National Agreement.[14] On the positive side, perhaps joining the UA would boost fan interest in the short term, since it would create a sense of novelty. It might also be worth embarking on a new challenge. Wilmington was running away with the pennant, winning 50 games against just 12 losses. The Eastern League was also incredibly unstable. The circuit had started with eight teams but had already seen Baltimore, Harrisburg, and Reading disband while Richmond jumped to the American Association to replace the departed club from Washington. A club in Brooklyn lasted just two games and was expelled. There was no guarantee that the EL would finish the season, so the UA presented a fresh start and one last chance to salvage their investment for West and company.

While Wilmington debated the merits of joining the Unions, Lucas was also considering another entrant to replace the Keystones. The Quincy club of the Northwestern League was one of the strongest in the circuit with a 45–23 record. Despite their quality, the club was behind almost $4,500 on August 2, when the league shuttered due to the disbandment of Muskegon and league-leading Grand Rapids.[15] League organizers quickly tried to reconstitute the league with remaining clubs required to pay a $500 bond to ensure the completion of the season.[16] Quincy manager George W. Brackett had little interest in participating in what was bound to be a financial disaster. His club could not recoup its costs because of the extensive interstate travel needed to complete the season schedule. Brackett telegraphed the club's resignation from the Northwestern League on August 10. The following day, Quincy applied to replace the Keystones in the UA. Brackett and team management had also decided to disband the club if they failed to gain entry to the Union Association.[17]

What ensued in the following days was a unique and possibly unprecedented event in the history of baseball. The aggregate from Quincy traveled to St. Louis, where they would face the league-leading Lucas nine in what was ostensibly a play-in game. If Quincy could prove their mettle on the field, they were in line to earn a spot in the Union Association. If they failed to earn the favor of Lucas and gain entry into the league, the club would be disbanded forever.

Quincy, Illinois, boasted a population of 27,268 in 1880, a small market for a professional club, but it had several things going for it as a potential replacement for the Keystones. First, the Northwestern League was the strongest minor league in the country in 1884, and Quincy was one of its best teams. There was ample reason to believe that Quincy's roster could certainly compete in the UA, or at least fair no worse than their predecessors. Second, Quincy was in close proximity to two of the UA's western markets, located just 130 odd miles from St. Louis and approximately 275 miles from Kansas City. This must have been enticing to Lucas since making sure road trips were less time-consuming and cost-intensive was a top priority.

On Thursday, August 14, the Quincys showed up at Union Park in St. Louis to face off against Lucas's titans in this one-of-a-kind battle. Nearly 1,000 fans showed up with great curiosity to see what the Quincy men had to offer. St. Louis would not make this easy, as they ran out their regular lineup to face the proud upstarts. This lineup included the league's greatest star, Fred Dunlap, and the tempestuous, tumultuous, and talented twirler, Charlie Sweeney. In the weeks since his jump from Providence, Sweeney had pitched well, compiling a 6–1 record in seven starts and doing his part to ensure St. Louis remained at the top of the standings.

Quincy countered with Bob Black, their promising 21-year-old right-hander, who had pitched quite well in 1884. Black's greatest weapon was a deceptive curveball that kept Northwestern League hitters guessing.[18] His record stood at 12–11 with an ERA of 1.49 on the season. He was supported at catcher by Lawrence "Law" Daniels, another 21-year-old with a reputation for defensive brilliance that would eventually culminate in a two-year major league career later in the decade. The battery got off to a rocky start thanks to some poor defense by Quincy shortstop Frank Spill. The aptly named Spill scooped up a hot grounder by Dunlap to open the game but threw wildly to first baseman Jerry Sweeney, allowing Dunlap to reach second. Dunlap advanced to third on a passed ball and then scored on a hit to right by center-fielder Dave Rowe. Black snuffed out the opening inning rally and escaped with just one run on the board. Sweeney mowed down the light-hitting Quincy lineup, allowing only a base hit to Conny Lynch in the second inning. Black matched Sweeney's excellence and held the hard-hitting Unions from scoring again until the top of the fifth. The incomparable Dunlap opened the inning with a hit and then advanced to third on another passed ball. He scored on Orator Shafer's out to first base. Third baseman Jack Gleason made another hit and advanced to third on a wild pitch. With the game about to be blown open, Black got Rowe and left fielder Henry Boyle out to end the inning.

Quincy finally got a rally going in the bottom of the fifth. Lynch hit a double to left field and then advanced to third on Black's sacrifice fly. St. Louis catcher Jack Brennan failed to hold one of Sweeney's deliveries, and Lynch came scampering home to open the scoring for Quincy. Sweeney buckled down and retired the next two Quincy batters to end the inning. Black got into a bases-loaded jam with one out in the seventh inning but worked his way out of it. In the end, the Unions proved too much to handle and finally broke through for three runs in the final two innings. Down to their last three outs, Sweeney showed how good he was and retired the gritty Quincys one, two, three to close out the contest.

The final result was 5–1, but a close look at the box score reveals an impressive performance by Quincy. In an era when errors were commonplace, the Quincy defense made just one error to St. Louis's two. The *St. Louis Republican* offered high praise for the Quincys: "the visitors played as pretty a game as the most critical could desire. Black and Daniels, the Quincy battery, is as good as any that has visited the grounds this season, the former striking out no less than seven of the strong hitters of the home club, and Daniels was frequently applauded for his brilliant work."[19] Would their effort be enough to gain Quincy a spot in the Union circuit? The *St. Louis Post-Dispatch* offered their support for the Quincy bid: "Based upon their exhibition of yesterday the Quincy's appeal is well founded, and there should be [no] argument regarding their admission to the Unions. The nine is proficient and their city is a convenient and central point on the Union circuit."[20]

Lucas promised to contact Quincy management by 6 p.m. on August 15 and inform them of the status of their application. As Manager Brackett waited eagerly for a telegraph from St. Louis, the minutes turned to hours, and by noon on August 16, still no word had been received.[21] In modern parlance, Lucas had ghosted Brackett and his Quincy club. With no response, the difficult decision was made by Brackett to disband the club after an offer from the city of Winona, Minnesota, to transfer the club fell through because of the proposed cost of $1,400 a month required to field a squad of ten players.[22] Despite the sad news of the club's disbanding, multiple players on the squad had major league offers. After the Quincy–St. Louis game, pitcher Black signed with the Kansas City Unions.[23] He would soon be joined by first baseman Jerry Sweeney, utility man Pat Sullivan, and outfielder "Stooping" Jack Gorman. Outfielder Conny Doyle turned down an offer from Kansas City and signed with Pittsburgh of the American Association.

Lucas's decision to reject the Quincy bid was likely for two reasons. First, the failure of the Keystones necessitated the need for another eastern club to maintain the balance of four eastern and four western clubs. Second, the Quincy market was prohibitively small, and one would hope that Lucas had learned something from the Altoona debacle. Another factor was that Wilmington management finally capitulated to the barrage of requests to join the Union. On August 14, Wilmington's owner, John T. West, met with UA secretary Warren White to discuss the offer.[24] The carrot that enticed West was a promise to cover the club's travel expenses on its western road trip, including board bills, train fare, and salaries.[25] West wanted a guarantee that the Wilmington club would be profitable should they enter the Union Association, and White's proposal seemed to fit that bill.

A team meeting was held on August 15, with the directors explaining the plan and getting a near-universal consensus from the players about the proposed plan to join the league. The only holdout was their egocentric pitcher Ed "The Only" Nolan, who asked for time to consider his options. On Sunday, the club officially disbanded, and every player on the roster save for Nolan and infielder Andy Cusick signed Union Association contracts. With pen to paper, on August 18, it became official, Wilmington was in the Union Association, and Delaware would have a major league team.[26]

14

◇◇◇◇◇◇◇◇◇◇◇◇◇◇

A Matter of Dollars and Cents

"I presume we will be blacklisted, but we have been playing ball for glory long enough; it is now a matter of dollars and cents."—Charles Briody, Cincinnati Unions catcher

On August 8, the same day that news broke about the implosion of the Philadelphia Keystones, another struggling club was reaching its nadir. The struggling Cleveland National League nine arrived in Grand Rapids, Michigan, for an exhibition game with the local club of the Northwestern League. Cleveland manager Charlie Hackett knew the writing was on the wall for his club. Attendance at home was poor, salaries were high, and the debts were getting larger by the day. There was a great deal of uncertainty about whether Cleveland could finish out the season. Even though some 1,200 paid fans were in attendance at Grand Rapids Base Ball Park for the game, the revenue from the exhibition would do little to change the club's financial fortunes. A worrying report had appeared in that day's *Louisville Courier-Journal*:

> There are now strong surface indications that the Cleveland League team will disband in a short time, owing to its poor showing in the race, and the lack of patronage in consequence. The team has been at Chicago all this week, and all kinds of rumors have been afloat regarding its future movements. Enough is known to warrant the statement that in all probability the windy city will be the last place the team will play as a Cleveland organization.[1]

The sharks could smell the blood in the water. Rumor had it that H.D. "Denny" McKnight, president of the American Association and its Pittsburgh franchise, had gone to Chicago to sign the Cleveland roster to exorbitant contracts.[2] It was believed that McKnight had focused his efforts on signing a trio of Clevelanders: star shortstop "Pebbly" Jack Glasscock, workhorse pitcher Jim McCormick, and the club's rotund backup catcher Charles "Fatty" Briody. The trio respectfully declined the offer, and manager Hackett breathed a sigh of relief as the team departed for Grand Rapids. Little did he know that Grand Rapids would be Cleveland's Waterloo.

It was about an hour before game time in Grand Rapids when the unthinkable happened. Jack Glasscock, Jim McCormick, and Charles Briody had put their pens to paper and signed a contract in the presence of Justus Thorner, president of the Cincinnati Unions. Thorner had been planning the coup for weeks after a failed offer to purchase the trio's release from Cleveland.[3] In late July, he had sent sportswriter and club secretary Frank Wright to Buffalo to negotiate with the trio while

Cleveland was in town for a series with the home club. Wright continued to negotiate with the players in Chicago. On Thursday, August 7, Thorner and the Cincinnati Union Base Ball Club made a truly enticing offer. Each of the three players would receive $1,000 upfront to defect from the National League to the Union Association.[4]

Hackett and the players on the Cleveland team caught wind of the situation when the three defectors refused to board the team carriage that would bring the team to the Grand Rapids ballpark. When the trio arrived at the park 30 minutes before game time, they refused to appear on the field. They had now signed with Thorner. The trio's now-former manager was enraged at the betrayal but determined to get the men on the field. Otherwise, his club would have to forfeit, and they wouldn't get their much-needed share of the gate. Hackett negotiated with Thorner and three men, who initially held out for $25 each to appear but eventually were convinced to play that day for the princely sum of $10 a man.[5]

The defectors appeared on the field for the exhibition game, which resulted in a sloppy 7–5 victory for Cleveland. The contest also marked the final game for the first-place Grand Rapids club. The club disbanded immediately following the game, having lost $2,500 on the year despite their 48–15 record.[6] Five Grand Rapids players immediately joined Detroit, including future 30-game winner Charles "Pretzels" Getzien. The news of the Cleveland defections reached the wire that evening, with the *Cleveland Plain Dealer* being the first to report on the players' departure and the advance of $3,000 given to the men as an inducement to jump ship.[7] Further details surfaced the following day, on August 9. The *Cleveland Leader* noted that "Thorner has advanced considerable money to the three men as an inducement to jump the League, and has guaranteed them a liberal salary for two years."[8] Catcher Charles Briody provided his reasoning for jumping: "I presume we will be blacklisted, but we have been playing ball for glory long enough; it is now a matter of dollars and cents."[9] Thorner boasted about his move and promised a revolution was coming to the baseball world: "Next year … the leagues will be making terms with us. From the beginning we took a bold stand and intend to keep it up."[10] Thorner had made his big move, one that strengthened his club while striking a near-fatal blow to his cross-state rival from the National League.

After the defection, disparaging rumors were floated that Glasscock had been drinking as of late, which had influenced his jump. This gossip was quickly refuted by his brother-in-law, William Welfeld, in an article in Jack's hometown paper, the *Wheeling Register*: "The charge that Glasscock had been drinking is a gross slander, and Glasscock's conduct has been in every way honorable and straightforward."[11] Welfeld also outlined a proposed plan by the Cleveland directors to have the players run the club as a cooperative, as well as their willingness to sell Glasscock to another team:

> While the club was in Cleveland, Glasscock was sent for by one of the directors, and asked to talk to the boys about taking the club on their own hands and running it. Glasscock promptly answered that he did not believe the boys would consent to it, and said he would be glad of his release. "On no," was the reply, "we can get a thousand dollars for your release." That set Glass to thinking. He came to us and asked what he should do saying he objected to being sold like an animal…. Glasscock could not help arriving at the conclusion that he

would be sold like a slave if he did not leave…. He believed the club might disband after the players in it had been sold to the highest bidder. Then he resolved to leave the team to derive what profit was to be made out of the change for himself.[12]

Pitcher Jim McCormick was reported to have asked for his release in July, evidently dissatisfied with his recent performance.[13] Reports in late July had surfaced that Cleveland management had put out feelers to other clubs about buying the release of some of their players. The pair of Glasscock and McCormick were relatively well paid by Cleveland, with Glasscock's salary listed at $1,800 and McCormick's at $2,500. Briody was believed to be making $1,400 for the year.[14] The three men do not appear to have been irked by their salaries, but rather by the failing circumstances of the Cleveland club. There was a significant chance that the club was going to disband. Glasscock believed that the club's top players would simply be sold off to the highest bidder. Because of the uncertainty, the trio took matters into their own hands and jumped ship rather than be sold like chattel. Thorner recognized their unhappiness and offered sufficient reason to defect. Apart from the $3,000 paid up front, Thorner also signed the men to pro-rated contracts that were significantly higher than they were currently being paid. McCormick would be paid $2,500 for the remaining two months of the season to shore up Cincinnati's pitching. Glasscock would get $1,500 to play shortstop, while catcher Briody would get $500.[15]

Justus Thorner's reasoning for acquiring the trio was built around his desire to field an elite nine for the 1885 season. Thorner and President Lucas were compatriots committed to bettering the Union Association and improving their respective situations. From Thorner's perspective, the defectors would help his team in the short term and hopefully boost attendance. Since Lucas's club had all but wrapped up the pennant race, Thorner had already set his sights on 1885. He had boasted to Lucas about his plans for the coming season: "next spring…. I will have the best nine in the country, as well as the best grounds."[16] His plan was remarkably similar to Lucas's pre-season tactics. President Lucas was over the moon for his friend in the Queen City:

> I have nothing to say, except that I feel better over [Thorner's] success in getting McCormick, Glasscock and Briody than if some one had given me $10,000…I don't take any pride in contract-breaking as a regular business, but it is a good thing to succeed when self-preservation forces you to engage in it. There is also great pleasure in going into the enemy's camp, capturing their guns and using them on your own side.[17]

Lucas's joyous response to his friend Thorner's coup was influenced by the fact that the defections significantly weakened an already unstable Cleveland club. Lucas knew the situation well; after all, it was his theft of their star second baseman Fred Dunlap in November 1883 that had set the course for the tumultuous season currently being endured in Cleveland.

While both Lucas and Thorner wanted to build up their own league, there was another side benefit of the assault on Cleveland. If the Cleveland franchise were weakened enough, it increased the chances of the club being dropped entirely. If they were dropped, it would create a much-coveted opening in the National League, which a club from the Union Association might fill. *Sporting Life* published an accusatory editorial from pages of the *Cleveland Herald* that spelled out Lucas and Thorner's intentions to enter the National League at the expense of Cleveland and the other Union Association clubs:

> It is the opinion of those who watch the schemes of the Union wreckers and figure on them, that the leaders among that choice assortment of base ball clubs are building for the future. All the life there is in the Association is confined to St. Louis and Cincinnati ... the two evidently worked together for some purpose and the purpose is no less a one than admission to the National League. They work on the idea that strong clubs in such strong cities as Cincinnati and St. Louis will be eagerly accepted in place of Detroit, Buffalo or Cleveland, and seek to fortify themselves so as to go to the National League fall meeting in such shape that there will be little chance of the offer being rejected. Admittance to the League would gratify Lucas's ambition and give Thorner, of Cincinnati, a chance to "get even" for the slight, real or imaginary, given him by the Cincinnati American Association Club. Of course, the minor clubs of the Union Association would be duped if such a deal was made, but it is evident that Lucas and Thorner would willingly wreck their present partners in wrecking for the sake of their pet scheme.[18]

In light of the Keystone club's collapse and mounting expenses for the league, both Lucas and Thorner appeared to be looking beyond the Union Association for 1885.

The trio of Cleveland newcomers would make their Union Association debut on Sunday, August 10, in Cincinnati against Lucas's St. Louis Unions. What better way to see what the new additions were made of than to face off against the very best the league had to offer. McCormick and Briody would form the battery for Cincinnati, going up against the battery of St. Louis ace Charlie Sweeney and catcher George Baker. St. Louis led off the game, and McCormick pitched a scoreless first. Sweeney was up to the task and copied his fellow defector by retiring the side. Jack Gleason led off the top of the second with a double and then advanced to third on a sacrifice fly by the hard-hitting Sweeney. Gleason then scored on a wild pitch, giving the visitors a 1–0 lead heading into the bottom of the second. The home team, evidently inspired by their new recruits and a large and supportive hometown crowd, erupted in the second inning totaling eight hits and six runs off the usually unhittable Sweeney. The 6–1 deficit was too much for St. Louis to overcome, and McCormick held on to take the contest by a final score of 7–4. Glasscock was undoubtedly the star of the show, getting two hits in three at-bats, drawing a walk while scoring one run, and playing errorless ball at short. McCormick was shaky in the high-profile matchup, allowing ten St. Louis hits and four runs, though just one of those was earned. He avoided any big innings and helped his own cause at the plate, getting two hits, including a triple. The light-hitting Briody, who had batted just .169 in 42 games for Cleveland, was held hitless but made eight putouts and had two assists while making just one error. The *Cincinnati Enquirer* presented the occasion as a banner day for the franchise:

> McCormick, Briody and Glasscock made their initial appearances, and that the Cincinnati Union team, as presented yesterday, made a more than favorable impression with the 4,105 spectators is not half telling the story. The plaudits that followed the many good plays made, and the enthusiasm manifested on all sides, sum up the success of yesterday better than it can be made clear by newspaper talk. The representative club here of the new base-ball association, as it now stands, is second to none in the country.[19]

The reported attendance of 4,105 was a drastic increase over the club's previous home game on July 25, which had drawn a paltry crowd of 200 fans. The impressive turnout for the trio's debut was aided by the fact that it was also a Sunday contest. The win also moved the club into a tie for third place with Boston, with a 35–29 record. They were still 21.5 games behind the league-leading St. Louis Unions and ten games behind Baltimore for second place. While a pennant was out of the question for Thorner, the defection drastically improved his club for 1884 and the years to come.

The *New York Clipper* tried to paint the defection of Glasscock, McCormick, and Briody as addition by subtraction for Cleveland, singling out McCormick's negative influence:

> What was thought to be the Cleveland Club's severe loss in the secession of their strong "battery" is evidently turning out to be a gain to the club, for not only is the team playing better ball than before, but, besides, a degree of sympathy for the club has been elicited which bids fair, in increased patronage, to more than compensate for the loss of the three seceding players. One cause for the improved play is the absence of the clique-ism which had previously marred the success of the team. McCormick virtually ruled the team.[20]

For a moment, this seemed to ring true. The club responded to the departure by winning three of four games against lowly Detroit, but such improvement was short-lived. The club won just two of their next 21 games, which included a 12 game losing streak. Improved team chemistry could only do so much to negate the loss of two Hall of Fame–caliber players in their primes.

The debut of the big three also marked the final appearance of another National League defector on the Cincinnati roster. The enigmatic first baseman Martin Powell had been reserved by Detroit for the 1884 season but failed to sign a contract. In January 1884, after being recruited by Frank Wright, the same man who had wooed the

"Pebbly" Jack Glasscock made headlines in August 1884 when he defected from Cleveland to join Justus Thorner's Cincinnati Unions, along with Jim McCormick and Charles Briody. In 38 games with Cincinnati, the shortstop hit a scorching .419 and played his customary excellent defense (Library of Congress).

Clevelanders, Powell joined Thorner's club for $2,500. Powell had hit .338/.380/.429 with a 150 OPS+ as a 25-year-old rookie in 1881. He had failed to reproduce those results at the bat in 1882, hitting just .240/.280/.278 for an 80 OPS+. In 1883, he rebounded somewhat with a steady batting line of .273/.318/.344 for an OPS+ of 104. The first sacker led the NL in games played with 101 and also led the league's first basemen in errors and double plays. He wasn't a star player, but he was a player with potential and good personal habits. He had hit exceptionally well in Cincinnati, batting .319/.364/.378 in 43 games, good for a 138 OPS+. Powell's durability, which had proven

impressive in 1883, was lacking in 1884. He had missed 31 games with a variety of ailments and, at one point, was said to have malaria.[21] The era's sportswriters used malaria as a catchall term to describe ailments such as cold and flu, but it could also be used as a subtle reference to a player having caught a venereal disease.[22] The straight-laced Powell, described in the early season as "very quiet and unobtrusive," was most likely suffering from a bad cold rather than a social disease.[23] He may have also been suffering from the early stages of the tuberculosis that would take his life less than four years later at the age of 32. Whatever Powell's illness, it sapped his strength. After going 3 for 5 with three runs in Cincinnati's 12–10 win in Washington on July 12, he did not appear again for the club until the big three's debut on August 10. Powell went one for four with a run and played errorless ball in the contest. After the game, it was announced that he would not be traveling with the club when they caught their 6 a.m. train to Kansas City the following morning.[24] Powell was released by the club shortly after. Thorner and manager Sam Crane likely dumped his contract to cut costs considering the club's recent expenditures. Powell sued the club on August 25 for $1,000, claiming that was the amount owed him for the rest of the season, though it is unclear if this suit was ever resolved.[25]

Big Jim McCormick was one of the great workhorses of the 19th century. The hurler compiled a 265–214 record in 4,275.2 innings with a sterling 2.43 ERA. After jumping to the Union Association, he paced the circuit in ERA (1.54), shutouts (7), ERA+ (213), and WHIP (0.786) (Library of Congress).

The reinvigorated Cincinnati Unions caught the early train to Kansas City to make the nearly 600-mile journey. Cincinnati made its debut in Kansas City on August 13, in front of a strong crowd of 1,800 curiosity seekers. The locals put up a strong fight but fell by a score of 6–4 as McCormick pitched another steady effort while Glasscock played like a superstar. He went four for five out of the leadoff spot while making just one error at shortstop. Cincinnati followed up with a 5–1 win, with Dick Burns on the mound while McCormick appeared in center field. Cincinnati followed up with a loss in an exhibition game to Kansas City by a score of 10–5 on August 15. The unusual decision to play an exhibition game mid-series was likely an attempt to squeeze in an extra game and some additional revenue for both clubs, especially considering that the home club was drawing very well. The two teams closed out the series in front of an enormous Sunday crown of 8,000 fans, with McCormick pitching his very best game yet. He shut out the light-hitting Kansas City nine on just four hits while striking out nine. Cincinnati supported their star twirler with a consistent attack that saw the club score seven runs. The win brought Cincinnati's record to 38–29. Though they remained

Charles "Fatty" Briody was a capable defensive catcher with Cleveland who joined Glasscock and McCormick in their jump to the Union Association. The portly backstop hit .337 in 22 games in the UA, a vast improvement over the .169 batting average he posted for Cleveland. Briody's success at bat points to the weaker pitching he faced in the UA. He is pictured with the 1887 World Series champion Detroit Wolverines, one of the greatest clubs of the 19th century (courtesy Detroit Public Library).

in a dead heat with Boston, the club's five-game win streak had allowed the club to gain 2.5 games on Baltimore in the race for second place. The club then traveled home to welcome the struggling Chicago Unions for their next set to begin on August 19.

15

The Windy City Blows Out of Town

In just one week, the Union Association had undergone significant changes. The Keystones had folded; the Wilmingtons had agreed to join in their stead, and Justus Thorner had staged his great coup and was the talk of the baseball world. Meanwhile, the circuit's Chicago franchise was in a state of disarray. Chicago Union owner Albert H. Henderson had miscalculated the desire of the Chicago fans to patronize a club other than their beloved Chicago White Stockings. The club drew well for their seven Sunday games, averaging over 2,500 fans for those contests. However, the club's home attendance for non–Sunday games was frequently in the 200–300 range. Their contest on July 29 against Cincinnati drew just 100 fans. The great disparity in attendance between Sunday and non–Sunday contests revealed two things. First, Chicago was hungry for Sunday baseball. Whatever moral stance the National League was taking by not allowing Sunday games, it cost them money. Second, despite the desire of Chicago fans to watch the Unions on Sunday, they had very little interest in buying tickets to their games the rest of the week. Another issue may have been the location of the Union ballpark, located at 39th Street and South Wabash. One observer commented the park was "five miles from the city," which accounted for attendance figures that ranged from 100 to 140 for the weekday games.[1] The distant location hindered the efforts of the Unions to gain a foothold in Chicago, and the result was dismal attendance. The poor attendance proved catastrophic to Henderson's business plan.

On August 13, it was reported that Henderson had lost $12,000 so far this season. However, these losses likely included costs associated with his dual ownership of the Baltimore and Chicago franchises.[2] Footing the bill for two clubs was proving to be too much. Chicago's underwhelming performance on the field matched their failure at the box office. The local newspapers were so indifferent that they frequently did not print full box scores while the *Chicago Daily Inter Ocean* took to including their coverage in a section titled "Minor Games."[3] Despite the marvelous performance of ace Hugh "One Arm" Daily and the acquisition of the promising right-hander Al Atkinson, who had defected from the Philadelphia Athletics, the club had failed to play winning baseball. Chicago's lineup included a never-ending parade of middle infielders, with 14 different men appearing at the second sack, including two appearances by Daily, who only had one hand. Ten different players made appearances at shortstop, including Daily, who was also enlisted to play short-stop for one game. Two obscure additions highlight the club's futility in search of middle infield help. Dan Cronin, a veteran infielder from Boston with minor league experience, was signed up by the club during their visit to Beantown in July. Cronin appeared in one contest on July 9, getting one hit in four at-bats, but showed up to the game without cleats and attempted to play without spikes in his shoes.[4] The result was four errors in five chances, including a wild throw caused by him slipping while trying to release the ball. He was let go after the contest. He was replaced at second base by a mystery man known only as Richardson for their July 10 contest. Richardson fared no better, striking out four times in four at-bats, though he at least only made one error on three chances. Cronin would make one more appearance for the St. Louis Unions on July 14, making two errors in his only two chances in left field. His career fielding percentage was .143.

It was only the presence of Hugh Daily that kept the Unions from being cast among the league's weakest clubs. Daily was in the midst of an astonishing campaign that would see him strike out 483 batters and was highlighted by a series of remarkable performances. On May 14 and May 18, he became the first pitcher in major league history to throw consecutive one-hitters, beating the Washington Nationals in both contests.[5] During one stretch, he completed 33 consecutive starts. On July 7, less than a month after Charlie Sweeney had set the single-game strikeout record, Daily took the mound in Boston against the Unions. He matched and nearly bested Sweeney's feat by striking out 19 Boston hitters, walking zero while allowing just one hit, his third one-hitter of the season.[6] Daily actually struck out 20 Boston batters that day, but his catcher Bill Krieg dropped a third strike with two outs in the fifth inning and threw wildly to first, allowing Pat Scanlon to reach base on an error. The rules at the time signified that a dropped third strike counted as a strikeout, but since there was also an error on Krieg's throw, the strikeout was not credited in the record book. Daily followed up his remarkable performance with another one-hitter three days later, giving him back-to-back one-hitters twice in the same season.[7] For all of Daily's brilliance, his team just wasn't capable of supporting him. In July, Daily posted a 5–5 record, despite a 1.04 ERA. He also had 108 strikeouts while allowing just 50 hits and seven walks in 94 innings.[8]

Aside from Daily, the Unions did feature several quality players. Louis "Jumbo" Schoeneck was a huge man by the standards of the time, at listed dimensions of 6'2" and 223 pounds. The 22-year-old was one of the league's top hitters, putting up a .317/.332/.404 line good for a 146 OPS+. Emil Gross, an excellent hitting catcher, had been blacklisted by the National League due to a contract dispute with Philadelphia. In June, he finally joined Chicago after lengthy negotiations and hit a scorching .358 in 23 games before leaving the club in July for unknown reasons. Gross had a strange career and a reputation as a lusher but also came from a wealthy family and was heir to a rumored $50,000 worth of Chicago real estate.[9] It seems likely that his wealth made him especially difficult in contract negotiations. After leaving Chicago, he played in the low-level minors to close out the season, never returning to professional baseball. Despite his ample resources, he was reportedly too stubborn to pay the $500 fine that would earn his reinstatement to the National League.[10] His career was over at 26, with an outstanding .295/.329/.427 batting line and 146 OPS+ as a catcher.

Another noteworthy member of the club was Frank "Gid" Gardner, a troubled carouser whose talent tantalized teams again and again. The *National Police Gazette* described him in 1888: "Gid Gardner is a good ball player, but he is also a good drinker, and between the two, he manages to pull through the season after a fashion. Although nearly every club he has played with has had to suspend him for drunkenness, he has always caught on to another job as soon as he is set adrift."[11] The circumstances that brought Gardner to the Unions were befitting of his reputation. Gardner began the year with the Baltimore Orioles, appearing in 41 games for the club. In June, he was arrested and put in jail for assaulting a woman, which earned him a suspension by the manager Billy Barnie.[12] Gardner was released on bail and returned to the club, but he got in more trouble on the club's road trip just a week later. He was arrested and jailed in St. Louis when he and two teammates "found themselves pretty badly loaded [with alcohol] in a disreputable house" and got involved in a melee among the prostitutes and the other johns.[13] The *Baltimore Sun's* account of the incident gave the specifics: "Gardner accompanied Madame Abbey to the Four Courts and tried to appease her wrath and smooth the matter over, whereupon she struck him a hard blow to the face."[14] For Barnie, this was a final straw, and he stated that "Gardner has been a disturbing element in his nine and only his fine ball playing has kept him in the ranks."[15] Gardner's unseemly behavior was not enough to keep him out of work for long. The Unions recruited him, and he debuted for the club on July 16. He hit decently for Chicago, putting up a line of .255/.302/.349 and an OPS+ of 118. He also avoided further trouble while with the club, despite the temptations present in a city like Chicago.

The club's failure to draw put the team in a dire financial situation. The club was reportedly evicted from their ballpark at the 39th Street Ground on August 1, being three months in arrears on rent.[16] There was little hope of recouping losses on the season and little hope that the situation would improve. Henderson's drastic losses necessitated a drastic solution. On August 13, while his club was on an eastern road trip, he traveled to Pittsburgh with league secretary Warren White to negotiate a lease with the group of directors that controlled the Exposition Grounds ballpark. The plan was to move the Chicago franchise to Pennsylvania to complete the season. The *Cincinnati Enquirer* reported, "Matters have progressed so far that a proposition made by them [White and Henderson] will be before the directors of the association controlling the grounds at their next meeting. Lovers of the game [in Pittsburgh] say they are willing to contribute money to the support of a first-class club, and that they are tired of the American Association management and its practices."[17]

Al Pratt, the man involved with the initial attempts to put a Pittsburgh franchise in the Union Association back in September 1883, had nothing to do with this new scheme. Instead, Harry O. Price, a 43-year-old sporting man, took the reins. Price was fresh off signing a five-year lease on the Exposition Grounds and had first been rumored to be angling for a Union Association franchise in January 1884 after Pratt's withdrawal.[18] That plan did not come to fruition. In mid–July 1884, Price explained his plan to manage a "first class" club at his Exposition Grounds during the coming 1885 season.[19] Price's motivations for getting involved in baseball appear to have been as a means to generate revenue for his Exposition Grounds. Price was a hustler, regularly booking races, circuses, and other events on the grounds, hoping to recoup the $50,000 he had spent in developing the grounds.[20] Price seemed to hunger for attention and was often spouting fanciful stories about his future plans. On August 9, the *Pittsburgh Press* reported Price was building a baseball park on his grounds and that "in all probability the Providence League team will be transferred to this city."[21] No doubt, Price was the source of that report. Just two days later, the *Pittsburgh Post* reported that the Cleveland league club might be on its way to Pittsburgh. Price's fingerprints were all over this report as well:

> The truth of the matter is that Messrs. H.O. Price & Co. some time since concluded they would make an effort to give Pittsburgh a good team. It was their intention to enter the new Union association irrespective of any other club, league or association. Matters had proceeded so far that Messrs. McCormick, [Briody] and Glasscock had pledged Mr. Harry Price not once, but several times, that in case they departed from the Cleveland club they would enter a club he might organize. With these three players for a nucleus, it was the intention to gather such a base ball organization as any city might rejoice in, and therefore it was with no little chagrin and disappointment Mr. Price heard Saturday that these men had gone to Cincinnati.[22]

The veracity of Price's account must certainly be called into question. Why would the trio of coveted players risk their baseball futures on a baseball team that didn't even exist? Whatever Price lacked in honesty, he made up for with relentless optimism. He predicted that the defection of the trio would enable more players to jump and increase his chances of forming a strong nine in the Smoky City:

> Pittsburgh people want the best, and it is our intention to make up a strong nine. It is just possible that the break this trio has just made will enable us to secure good players with more ease. You see the way one sheep jumps the whole flock goes, and it may be that now the ball has commenced to roll, and other league players might follow. It's too early to talk about places, but it is not improbable there will be another team here next season, and it is more than probable if there is another it will belong to the Union Association.[23]

Albert H. Henderson and Warren White came to Pittsburgh to meet with prospective owners about a club transfer. Price, whose name was all over the newspapers, was the man they sought out. Price's enthusiasm, boundless optimism, and desire to field a team made him the perfect candidate to foist the struggling Chicago Unions upon. Pittsburgh itself was a promising baseball market in 1884. The city was the twelfth largest in the country in 1880, with a population of 156,389. When combined with the 78,862 people just across the river in Allegheny, the market now included nearly 250,000 people, putting it just behind Cincinnati for the eighth-largest metropolitan area in the country. From the Union Association's perspective, it could fill the void left by Altoona's departure as a viable stop for clubs traveling to and from the eastern seaboard. It would also eliminate the extra travel time needed to visit Chicago, located far north of the circuit's western clubs in Cincinnati, St. Louis, and Kansas City. The train travel from Pittsburgh west to Kansas City was much simpler to organize.

Pittsburgh was also home to an American Association franchise, the

Alleghenys, that had failed to impress patrons since their formation under the guidance of Al Pratt in 1882. The club peaked with a 39–39 record in their inaugural season drawing 42,000 fans in 35 home games while finishing in fourth place. In 1883, the club fell to seventh, with a 31–67 record, though attendance increased, with the club drawing 85,000 fans in 49 home games. The 1884 squad was even worse, going just 30–78 while attendance fell to 60,000 for 56 home games. The club had earned a reputation as a rowdy and erratic bunch, and aside from the hard-hitting and hard-drinking Ed Swartwood, offered little in star power. The 1884 club employed five different managers and fielded 34 different players during the season. From the Union's perspective, the AA franchise was in disarray, and a strong Pittsburgh club in the UA could supplant the Alleghenys as the premier baseball team in the city.

The meeting with Price went well, as Henderson and Price agreed to an arrangement just a few days later that would have the Chicago Unions transferred to Pittsburgh to complete the remaining Union Association schedule. On August 19, it was announced that the newly christened Pittsburgh Unions would be under the direction of Price and the Exposition Park Association. Henderson would remain club president while splitting profits and retaining equal partnership.[24] Henderson would still be involved in the management of the club, and it was reported that he would relocate his headquarters from Chicago to Pittsburgh.[25] The club would play their first game in Pittsburgh against the St. Louis Unions on August 25. Price promised a first-class experience for fans: "Mr. Price says he will make his park a base ball resort in every respect. The ladies will have neat dressing rooms in charge of colored attendants, and the people who pay only twenty five cents to get in will get on the grand stand and have a chair to sit on."[26]

The newly appointed Alleghenys manager, "Hustling" Horace Phillips, warned his new challenger that he would not go down without a fight. He claimed to have the backing of the American Association and vowed that the new league would "transfer players at any time to defeat the ends of the Union."[27] Given that the president of the American Association, Denny McKnight, was also the primary stockholder of the Pittsburgh club, it seemed plausible that the AA would furnish support for the local club. Price seemed aloof to these threats and sped forward in his plans to put the finishing touches on the ballpark at the Exposition Grounds, which would play host to its first UA game in less than a week.

Henderson's finalization of the transfer of the club to Pittsburgh and partnership with Price coincided with an announcement about the Union Association's plan for 1885. A report out of St. Louis noted that President Henry Lucas and Cincinnati president Justus Thorner had arranged for a complete reorganization of the Union Association for next season. The circuit would feature eight clubs while also forming an alliance of eastern and western leagues, similar to that negotiated in the National Agreement, which had aligned the AA, NL, and both the Northwestern and Eastern leagues. Thorner and Lucas would also form a large guarantee fund to assist any clubs in need. The fund would also go towards player acquisitions that would strengthen the league as a whole. The current $75 guarantee would give way to the road team receiving 30 percent of the gross gate receipts. It was also noted that the new configuration would only feature teams in larger markets, with three teams of over 100,000 each, two teams of 200,000 each, and the remaining three at 300,000 each.[28]

The plan put forth by Lucas and Thorner demonstrated the duo had learned from some of the challenges the league had undergone thus far. Notably, strengthening weaker clubs and ensuring they could complete the season was essential to building stability and credibility. With Altoona and Philadelphia disbanded and the Chicago relocation, the league was perceived as teetering on the brink of oblivion. The formation of some sort of alliance similar to the National Agreement was also a solid idea. It could protect clubs from raids and create a pool of players to draw from since the teams in the proposed alliance could buy and sell players from each other. Since the Union Association was pro–Sunday ball, moving to a 30 percent guarantee might help visiting clubs reap the benefits from the well-attended contests. Conversely, visiting clubs also stood to lose out on poorly attended contests. For example, under the proposed scheme, if a game drew a crowd of 100 paying fans at 25 cents, it would yield $25 in gross gate receipts. It would provide the visitors with just $7.50, a pitiful sum and only 10 percent of what they were due to receive under the current $75 guarantee structure. Virtually all the financial risk would be borne out by visiting clubs under the new plan.

The reorganization plan also seemed to demonstrate the increased influence that Justus Thorner had gained in the circuit. Thorner was now Lucas's right-hand man, while Albert H. Henderson's role in the league had diminished considerably as the season progressed. Thorner's relentless enthusiasm for the venture supplanted Henderson's more steady approach and more closely mirrored the personality of Henry Lucas. Henderson had sunk $12,000 into the venture with little hope of recouping his losses. He was looking for a way out, hence the alliance with Harry Price in Pittsburgh.

Since the club was already on the road, the players on the Chicago roster willingly traveled to Pittsburgh to continue their baseball season. Manager Ed Hengel left the team, however, and became an umpire for the circuit. Hengel had guided the Unions to a disappointing 34–39 record. In his stead, Price and Henderson enlisted Joe Battin, the recently fired Allegheny player-manager, to take the club's reins. Battin was one of baseball's best-known players with a well-traveled career that dated back to 1871 when he debuted as a 17-year-old for Cleveland of the National Association. Battin had been at the center of the game-fixing scandal that had spelled the end of the old NL version of the St. Louis Brown Stockings in 1877. This scandal created a vacuum for professional baseball in St. Louis that had indirectly led to the rise of Chris von der Ahe and the American Association and the insurgent Union Association under the guidance of Henry Lucas.

The National League did not formally ban Battin for his role in the scandal, but he never played in the league again. Battin spent the next few seasons in the minors before returning to the major leagues in 1882 with Pittsburgh of the American Association. The fledgling league had provided homes to many players who had been blacklisted formally and informally by the NL. Battin resumed his major league career as a light-hitting and exquisite fielding infielder from 1882 to 1884. He also served as the club's interim manager for parts of the 1883 and 1884 seasons.

Battin was the club's player-manager from July to August 1884 after Bob Ferguson was fired. He put up a respectable 6–7 record as manager but was let go on August 6, 1884.[29] Battin was reported to have signed with Detroit of the National League but did not appear for the club.[30]

Battin's signing was officially announced on August 23, two days before the Pittsburgh Unions' home debut. He would take on the role of field manager and starting third baseman. Despite the turmoil of their impending relocation, Chicago's final series against Cincinnati saw them play well, taking two of three games. This recent success offered Pittsburgh fans some hope that the club would be competitive. Over 3,000 fans showed up on August 25 at the Exposition Grounds to watch the new home nine face off against Lucas's club. The attendance was excellent for a Tuesday game, though a pre-game rainstorm reportedly kept some fans away.[31] Hugh "One Arm" Daily was in the box for Pittsburgh. With Chicago, he had put up a season for the ages. The hard-throwing right-hander with a devastating curveball had pitched exquisitely as one of the club's few bright spots. He alone had kept the team competitive despite the many holes in their lineup. The aged wonder, 36 on opening day, had shown surprising durability and ended up pitching over 500 innings in 1884. This feat was especially remarkable considering his 1882 and 1883 seasons had each been interrupted by complaints of a sore arm.

With Daily on the mound and UA luminaries Henry Lucas and Justus Thorner in attendance, the Pittsburgh crowd witnessed one of the finest games of the season. The reputed "best team in the world," the St. Louis Unions did battle with Daily and his nine in a hotly contested matchup. It was a banner day for Price and his venture:

> No club ever before was accorded such a flattering reception in this city ... long before the band reached the ground to give its little concert the crowd began to gather. A half hour before the game was called there were 2,500 people in the grand stand. The grounds were marvelously fine and everyone was surprised at the transformation.[32]

The local fans were immediately enraptured by their new idols: "the home club appeared ... clad in bright, new suits of white flannel with the title 'Pittsburgh Unions' in crimson on their breasts. The thousands present leaped to their feet and cheered as the new team crossed the lawn."[33] Battin, for his part, received a hero's welcome, making his first appearance since his release by the Alleghenys: "Battin was the last to appear and the applause was renewed. Every time he touched the ball, which was quite often, his popularity was attested."[34]

The game itself was a tense affair. For five innings, Daily and his rival Perry Werden pitched scoreless ball. Werden was a talented young pitcher from St. Louis who would later become a power-hitting first baseman and the greatest minor leaguer of the 19th century. Werden's eventual claim was rivaled only by the current Pittsburgh Union catcher, Bill Krieg. The catcher was a Notre Dame alumnus who would later win three batting titles in the minor leagues, including an 1895 season when he hit .452 for Rockford. No less an authority than Bill James thought Krieg to be the best minor leaguer of the 1880s.[35]

In the bottom of the sixth inning, Jack Gleason got a base hit and reached second on an error by second baseman Charlie Berry. He then scored on a long hit by Handsome Henry Boyle, giving St. Louis a one-run lead. Werden held this lead until the top of the eighth inning. Joe Ellick hit a triple and then scored on a single by Harry Wheeler, a much-traveled outfielder, best known for his key contributions for the pennant-winning 1882 Cincinnati Red Stockings. Wheeler was now playing for his third different team and fourth different home city in 1884. Werden and Daily maintained the tie through the ninth and then the tenth innings. In the eleventh, Wheeler drew a rare walk on seven balls, stole second, and then scored on a long single by Gid Gardner. The run put the home club up 2–1. Big Jumbo Schoeneck, the club's top hitter, came to bat with Gardner now on second, having taken the base on St. Louis's attempt to throw out Wheeler at the plate. Schoeneck hit a single, and Gardner scored on another bad throw by St. Louis. The 3–1 lead caused the crow to erupt with a noise that "would have done credit to a national convention."[36] St. Louis responded with a run in their half of the eleventh, but Daily held on to the one-run lead and gave Pittsburgh the victory in fine fashion. Daily had struck out just three batters but only allowed seven hits to his high-scoring rivals and was supported behind the plate by the able Krieg.

The debut was a huge success by anyone's standards. The large and enthusiastic crowd was treated to a close, extremely tense contest, with the cherry on top being a victory for the home club over the best team in the league. Little did Harry Price, or any of the 3,000 fans in attendance, realize that this would be the high point in the brief history of the Pittsburgh Unions. Less than a month later, they would be dead.

16

◇◇◇◇◇◇◇◇◇◇◇◇◇

A Curse Falls
Upon Delaware

It all started so promisingly. The Wilmingtons had dominated the Eastern League, and Henry Lucas and the Wilmington locals were confident that the club would be a drastic improvement over the Philadelphia Keystones, the club they were replacing. In the days leading up to Wilmington's Union Association debut, the *Wilmington Morning News* had boasted optimistically, "the Wilmington club ... is a formidable member of the Union Association."[1] Many words could describe Wilmington's tenure in the Union Association, but formidable would not be one of them. Delaware's brief foray into major league baseball was marked by a series of bizarre, unfortunate, and increasingly outlandish events that would make even the most hardened skeptic believe in curses.

The club made its Union debut in Washington, facing the lowly Nationals on August 18. The Nats record stood at 24–46 on game day, good for sixth place in the UA. The Eastern League champion Wilmingtons were weakened by the absence of two of their starters, their ace Ed "The Only" Nolan and infielder Andy Cusick, who remained unsigned after the team switched leagues. Twenty-one-year-old Dan Casey was in the pitcher's box for Wilmington, facing off against Washington's recently acquired ace, the hard-throwing Californian, Charlie Geggus. Casey and his older brother Dennis had come to Wilmington from Binghamton, New York. The brothers quickly became two of the key cogs in the Wilmington lineup that had paced the Eastern League. Elder Dennis hit .370 in 57 games in the EL, while Dan, in his first year in professional baseball, had gone 10–2 in 13 starts with a sterling 1.91 ERA. The club also boasted the mercurial Thomas Burns, who later garnered the unique nickname "Oyster." The 19-year-old wunderkind hit an EL leading 11 home runs, batted .337, and played great defense at shortstop. Burns also took the mound as the club's change pitcher and was equally impressive, winning seven of his nine starts with a minuscule ERA of 1.47. Burns earned a reputation as a firebrand due to frequent confrontations with teammates and umpires, but he was a tremendous young prospect.

The Wilmingtons showed up at their very best for their debut, but so did the Nationals. Geggus had finally given the club a starting pitcher who could keep them in each game. What ensued was a hard-fought back-and-forth contest. The Nationals opened the scoring in the first inning, netting one run. Wilmington tied the score

139

in the bottom half of the inning. Casey and Geggus matched each other with scoreless innings until the bottom of the fourth when Wilmington scored another run on a passed ball. The Nationals pulled ahead in the sixth inning on hits by first baseman Phil Baker, center fielder Abner Powell, and former Keystone shortstop Jerry McCormick, who the club had acquired after Philadelphia's implosion earlier in the month. An error by Wilmington catcher Bill McCloskey caused the go-ahead run to score.

The Nationals lead held until the bottom of the eighth, when Wilmington rallied to score two runs and take a 4–3 lead on hits by Dan Casey, left fielder Tom Lynch, and a passed ball by Nationals' catcher Joe Gunson. Dan Casey held off the Nationals in the top of the ninth for the win. Wilmington was victorious in their first-ever game in the Union Association. The *Washington National Republican* offered high praise for the newcomers: "The Wilmingtons are a fine set of ball players, and gave a beautiful display of fielding, and won favor by the quiet, gentlemanly deportment."[2] This thrilling victory one-run victory over one of the league's worst teams would prove to be the high point of Wilmington's tenure in the UA. Things were about to go downhill and fast.

Reports appeared after the game that the unsigned Nolan and Cusick had jumped ship to Philadelphia of the National League.[3] In light of the rumors, Wilmington faced off against Washington again on August 19 in what *Sporting Life* described as "a hot contest."[4] One thousand one hundred fans were in attendance to witness the contest at Washington's Capitol Park. The game was a close one. John Murphy, who pitched effectively for the Altoonas before they disbanded, took the box for Wilmington. Abner Powell was in the box for Washington. Powell had recently joined the Nationals from Peoria of the Northwestern League alongside his battery mate Chris Fulmer. Wilmington opened the scoring in the bottom of the second. In the bottom of the third, they loaded the bases with nobody out but failed to score. This failure proved crucial, as the Nationals pulled ahead with two runs in the top of the sixth. Wilmington tied the game 2–2 in the bottom of the seventh, but the Nationals responded with two runs in the top of the eighth. The result was a 4–2 loss. Even in defeat, the tight contest demonstrated the solid teamwork and strong defense that were hallmarks of the Wilmingtons during their Eastern League dominance.

That evening, the Wilmingtons got some good news when it was reported that holdout Andy Cusick had decided to rejoin the club at a salary of $150 a month rather than join Philadelphia. Nolan remained unsigned while he pondered the Philadelphia offer.[5] The good news was coupled with some bad news. Baltimore of the American Association had reached out to Oyster Burns and Dennis Casey, the club's two strongest hitters, with enticing offers to leave Wilmington for Monument City.[6] It was first reported that the duo had rejected the offer, but an August 21 report had Baltimore manager Billy Barnie confirming he had signed the pair of promising youngsters. Burns signed for $700 to play out the remaining two months of the season, while Casey signed for $600.[7] While the Wilmingtons cried foul, as far as Baltimore was concerned, Casey and Burns were fair game. When Wilmington opted out of the Eastern League, they had opted out of the protection of the

National Agreement. Opting out meant that their players could jump to NL and AA clubs without risk of reprisal, despite having signed new contracts to appear in the Union Association. Wilmington was left with no recourse. The defection proved to be disastrous to the morale of the league's newest addition.

Burns and Casey were two of the club's best players, and both would enjoy major league success. Burns would go on to stardom as a hard-hitting outfielder for Baltimore and Brooklyn during the next decade. Big Dennis Casey proved to be a solid hitter in two seasons with Baltimore, posting a 129 OPS+ before his major league career was derailed due to his poor base running and free-swinging ways, which drew the ire of Baltimore management.[8] The departure of the two men and the continued absence of The Only Nolan left the club shorthanded for game three of the Washington series on August 21.

The club hastily recruited Jim McElroy, an erratic and lightning-armed Californian, who had joined the Philadelphia League nine earlier in the season to much hype. He had proven not ready for fast company, as he went 1–12 in 13 starts while walking more men than he struck out and uncorking 46 wild pitches in just 111 innings. McElroy was in the box for Wilmington and proved just as ineffective in the Union Association as he had in the National League. He was scheduled to face off against Charlie Geggus. Both McElroy and Geggus were alumni of the baseball program at Saint Mary's College in Moraga, California. Saint Mary's College first fielded a baseball team in 1872 and, in the years since, developed a reputation as a baseball factory. To date, the college has produced 63 major-league players, most notably Hall of Famers Harry Hooper and Hank O'Day. In 1884, six St. Mary's alums, including McElroy and Geggus, pitcher Ed Morris, catcher Fred Carroll, pitcher O'Day, and outfielder Jim Fogarty, debuted in the major leagues.

Despite facing a familiar rival in Geggus, McElroy failed to show the potential that brought the wayward pitcher eastward just a few months before. While he did not walk a single hitter nor throw a wild pitch on the day, he allowed six earned runs and ten hits in five innings. He was replaced by John Murphy, who allowed six unearned runs in the remaining four innings. The demoralized Wilmingtons, who had fought valiantly in the first two games, completely fell apart. Despite the return of the slick-fielding Andy Cusick, the club was no match for Geggus. Perhaps inspired to prove his superiority over his fellow Californian, Geggus struck out 13 batters and pitched a no-hitter to the delight of the 1,800 fans in attendance. In the bottom of the seventh inning, Wilmington's Tom Lynch hit a ground ball to second baseman Tom Evers. The left-handed Evers threw wildly to first base. The ball became stuck under some seats, enabling Lynch to round the bases and score. The little league home run broke up Geggus' shut-out bid. The game was called on a mercy rule after eight innings, with the score 12–1 for the Nationals. Since the contest only lasted eight innings, Geggus' no-hitter does not appear in the current record book.

Wilmington's pitiful play continued on August 22, when Dan Casey, who had pitched so well in their Union debut just days before, was battered for 14 runs on 14 hits. The Wilmington bats continued their slumber, as Abner Powell allowed just four hits and zero runs in the 14–0 victory. Casey's poor performance must have come as a surprise to the Wilmingtons. In another devastating blow, the pitcher's dismal start would mark his final appearance with the club. Casey was suffering from an undisclosed illness and was sent home to his native Binghamton, where he could recover.[9] Casey eventually blossomed into a star pitcher in the ensuing years for the Phillies, winning a career-high 28 games in 1887. After four games, the Wilmingtons were 1–3 and had lost the three most talented members of the starting lineup. However, there was help on the way, and it went by the name of The Only Nolan.

Edward Sylvester "The Only" Nolan was born in Canada in 1855 but was raised in Paterson, New Jersey. The husky pitcher earned his unique moniker in 1877 while pitching for Indianapolis of the League Alliance. During that one magical sea-

son, the 22-year-old Nolan pitched an astonishing 76 complete games, winning 64 of them, including 30 by shutout. One of those 30 shutouts was a no-hitter against the same Columbus, Ohio, club he had starred for in 1876. Nolan's final record was 64–4, with eight ties and an ERA of 0.50. The young phenom was so successful that year that he came to be referred to as The Only Nolan. The nickname likely came from the theatrical world, where entertainers were often billed as "The One, the Only." For that one extraordinary season, Nolan was an entertainer of the highest magnitude.[10]

That year would prove to be the peak of Nolan's career, but the nickname stuck with him the rest of his life, even as he failed again and again to replicate the same ability to dazzle fans or get hitters out. When Indianapolis joined the National League in 1878, Nolan endured a tumultuous season, winning just 13 of his 38 starts while leading the league in walks allowed. The most notable events of his rookie season were the two suspensions he received. One was for a charge of game-fixing, for which he was acquitted, and another for consorting with a prostitute after lying about visiting a sick brother.[11] Nolan went to California to spend the next two seasons and then was lured back to the National League

Pitcher Dan Casey was one of the few bright spots for Wilmington during their time in the Union Association. His stint in the UA was cut short due to illness, but he emerged as a star hurler in the National League later in the decade, winning 28 games in 1887, while leading the league in ERA with a 2.86 mark (Library of Congress).

for 1881, signing with Cleveland. After going 8–14 on the year, he was suspended by the National League for "confirmed dissipation and general insubordination," which caused him to miss the 1882 season.[12] He joined Pittsburgh of the American Association in 1883 but lost all seven of his decisions.

The combination of ineffectiveness, alcoholism, and gambling should have spelled the end of his career, but The Only Nolan had an incredible knack for convincing others of his abilities. This skill brought him to Wilmington for the 1884 Eastern League season. Owing to weaker competition and a rejuvenated right arm, he went 19–5, with a 1.42 ERA and 150 strikeouts in 203 innings. With the Jim McElroy experience proving a disaster and the departure of the ailing Dan Casey, the Wilmingtons desperately needed a competent arm if they were going to endure the season. Nolan was the club's only option, and he knew it. While he might have felt sympathy for his struggling teammates, Nolan was first and foremost a mercenary, skilled in the art of the hold-up. Club owner John T. West convinced Nolan to rejoin the club for a significant raise from $125 per month to $325 a month for the rest of the season.[13]

It was under these circumstances that Nolan traveled to Washington and emerged from his weeklong absence. He made his first Union appearance in centerfield for the final game of the Wilmington-Nationals series on August 23. The result was another disappointing one for Wilmington. John Murphy took the box for Wilmington and staked the Nationals to an early 5–0 lead. Washington added five more runs in the later innings. Once again, Wilmington could muster little offense against the dominant pitching of Geggus. Only a late four-run rally in the bottom of the ninth broke up the shutout. The final score was 10–4.

Wilmington was slated to travel to Boston for an afternoon game on August 25. The club stayed too long in New York City during their travels. As a result, the club failed to arrive in time for the contest at the Boston Union grounds. The game was forfeited to Boston. The club finally arrived at the grounds around 4 p.m., where the two clubs decided to play another contest in lieu of the earlier forfeit.[14] Nolan made his Union pitching debut and pitched reasonably well, allowing just two earned runs and six hits, but sloppy play by Wilmington in the field resulted in four unearned runs for Boston. At bat, the Wilmington hitters were completely dominated by Dupee Shaw. Boston's mystifying left-hander allowed four scattered hits in a six-inning 6–0 shutout, which was called because of darkness. After an off day, the clubs met again on August 27, with Shaw and Nolan facing off again in a rematch. The final score was 7–1 for Boston, though it belied Nolan's impressive yet erratic performance. The deceptive deliveries of Nolan kept Boston hitters guessing, but unfortunately, he also kept his own catchers guessing. Nolan struck out 13 men and allowed just six hits but also threw four wild pitches while his catchers Andy Cusick and Bill McCloskey combined for seven passed balls.

The clubs met again the following day, with Fred Tenney, a Brown University alumnus, in the box for Wilmington. Tenney had pitched one game for the Nationals in June under the alias of "Art Thompson" before a brief stint with the Boston Unions in July. The college boy was effective, allowing just six hits and striking out nine of his former teammates. The Wilmington batters finally offered a little support, spelling the newcomer to a 4–0 lead in the bottom of the second. Boston chipped away at the deficit, aided by the sloppy catching of Tom Lynch, who made several errors and allowed multiple passed balls on Tenney's delivery. Boston scored two runs in the top of the third and then two more in the sixth. In the seventh, Boston catcher Lew Brown hit a double off Tenney. Ed "Cannonball" Crane, the burly right fielder for Boston, hit a single which advanced Brown to third. Lynch gave up another passed ball, which allowed the winning run to score in the painful 5–4 loss. The defeat dropped Wilmington's record to 1–8. Strangely, despite Tenney's credible performance, he was not picked up by Wilmington. The college hurler managed the unique feat of appearing for three different Union Association teams, Washington, Boston, and Wilmington, without ever leaving his native Boston. Tenney appears to have been content to stay at home. He wound up leaving baseball behind entirely for a career in education, culminating in a role as the Superintendent of Schools in Fall River, Massachusetts.[15]

Shaw closed out the series on August 30, striking out nine men in a two-hit shutout. Wilmington ably supported John Murphy with solid defense, as they allowed only three runs. If you were a club mired in as deep a rut as the Wilmingtons were in August 1884, a 3–0 loss was a moral victory. The 1–9 Wilmingtons had endured the defection of their two best players in Oyster Burns and Dennis Casey, lost Dan Casey to illness, and forfeited a contest. The Eastern League champions had become the laughingstock of the Union Association, and they had yet to play a home game. In a situation that mirrored the brief tenure of the Altoonas earlier in the year, the battered, bumbling, and beleaguered Wilmingtons suffered through a brutal road trip to start their existence before finally arriving at home, with the optimism of the hometown fans thoroughly extinguished.

As the club returned home for the commencement of their series against the red-hot Cincinnati Unions on September 2, expectations could not be lower. The Unions were already a strong club and had been bolstered by the big three from Cleveland, shortstop Jack Glasscock, pitcher Jim McCormick, and catcher Charles "Fatty" Briody. Since the trio debuted on August 10, the club had gone 11–3 and won their last six games. For the series' opening contest, Jim McCormick would face off against the pathetic Wilmingtons. Six hundred loyal and masochistic fans congregated at Wilmington's Union Street Park. The Only Nolan was entrusted to silence the Cincinnati hitters. On this fateful day, the first major league home game ever played in the state of Delaware, Nolan and the Wilmington lineup were up for the task.

Nolan's pitching was spectacular, as he struck out 13 hitters. Second baseman Charlie Bastian, usually a weak hitter, was the star of the Wilmington offense, getting three hits in three at-bats off McCormick, falling a single short of the cycle. Bastian also scored three runs and played errorless ball at second base. His home run over the right-field fence in the seventh inning proved the deciding run, as Nolan and the defense held the powerful Queen City lineup to just two runs. The final score of 3–2 for the home club was a remarkable upset. Wilmington's performance on the day showed a glimmer of the ability that had helped the club dominate the Eastern League. At their best, the club combined solid pitching and excellent defense while adding in some timely hitting. Unfortunately, the early departure of Oyster Burns and the Casey brothers, three credible future major league stars, had prevented the club from demonstrating its full potential.

September 3 saw some 800 fans show up for the matchup between Cincinnati's change pitcher Dick Burns and John Murphy. Buoyed by their strong play in the series opener, Wilmington got off to a fast start, erasing an early Cincinnati lead with two runs in the bottom of the second. Wilmington advanced their lead to 3–1 in the bottom of the fifth while Murphy held the Cincinnati lineup in check. Cincinnati clawed back two runs in the top of the seventh to tie the score, but Murphy escaped the inning, still pitching well. The tables turned in the bottom of the seventh when Murphy was hit by a pitch. Burns' delivery had struck Murphy's lower back and caused him to writhe in agony on the ground. Since this was 1884, players seldom came out of the game unless they were fully incapacitated. Murphy remained in the contest, but the beaning proved to be costly. He was walloped in the final two innings, which allowed Cincinnati to score four late runs and take a 7–3 decision.

That evening, tragedy nearly befell Wilmington outfielder John J. "Rusty" Cullen, a veteran ballplayer from California. The incident occurred at the Clayton House, where the Wilmington players were boarded. At around 11:30 p.m., Cullen and third baseman Jimmy Say were heading down a darkened hallway toward the elevator as they made their way to their rooms to retire for the night. Cullen found the elevator door was open, to his surprise. Believing the elevator was still functioning, he stepped into the darkened elevator. Much to his dismay, the elevator car had gone up, and Cullen fell nearly 20 feet down the shaft and landed in a pile of filth.[16] A local physician, Dr. Carrow, was summoned to examine Cullen and found that remarkably, he had suffered no broken bones, though he had injured his back and was badly bruised and cut all over his body.[17] The veteran was lucky to be alive, though the injury was severe enough that he did not play again that year. Cullen recovered from his injuries and was well enough to join "Bollicky" Billy Taylor's barnstorming team on a trip to Cuba that winter before spending several more years in the minor leagues. Cullen's fall can be seen as a metaphor for the Wilmington franchise. The club took a stab in the dark by joining the Union Association but had seen their fate come crashing down, and they had ended up in a pile of filth.

The injury to Murphy on the hit by pitch and the near-death of Cullen foreshadowed another traumatic occurrence in the following day's game. With Cincinnati up 5–3 in the fourth inning, shortstop Jack Glasscock came to bat to face The Only Nolan with a runner on third and one out. After taking the first pitch, the star shortstop took a big cut at the second pitch, making glancing contact off Nolan's hard delivery. The ball ricocheted off Glasscock's bat and flew backward with tremendous force, striking umpire Patrick J. Dutton in the mouth. This was the days before umpires used facemasks, and so the 26-year-old umpire's face was completely exposed to the foul tip. The *Wilmington Morning News* described the blow:

> [Dutton] stood still one moment and then fell backward like a log. The spectators thought that the man was killed and everybody became greatly excited. Players ran for ice water and called for a physician. Dr. A.E. Frantz was fortunately present and immediately ran to the prostrate man's assistance. He found that Dutton had received a compound dislocation of the

lower jaw, which had pressed together the windpipe, and the man was rapidly suffocating. His eyes and tongue were already protruding. The physician after repeated efforts reduced the dislocation, but during the operation, the injured man was seized with two nervous spasms, during which he writhed in great agony. Plenty of cold water was applied to revive him, but for a while without effect. He was then removed to the shade of the left field fence, where a few draughts of liquor finally brought him back to consciousness after a half hour's work.[18]

Dutton was taken to convalesce at the nearby Clayton House. The game was nearly resumed with Wash Williams, a journeyman ballplayer in town looking for a job after his release by the Richmond, Virginia, club, replacing Dutton as the umpire. However, it was quickly decided that it would be inappropriate to restart the game with a man's life in the balance, and the game was officially declared a draw. Owing to the quick intervention of Dr. Frantz, Dutton made a speedy recovery and was well enough to go for a walk that night. He was found to have a cut on his severely swollen upper lip and several loosened teeth but otherwise was none the worse for wear.[19] Amazingly, Dutton would be back behind the plate just six days later, serving as the umpire for the September 9 game between Kansas City and Boston. Tragically, Dutton passed away from unknown causes five years later, at just 31 years old, in his native Hartford, Connecticut.

The near-death of Dutton might have scared off the Wilmington fans for the team's next game on September 5. Umpire George Seward was called upon to replace Dutton as the official for the day's game. Seward was a former major league catcher who had umpired in the NL and the AA before joining the UA. A repeat of the near-tragedy that befell Dutton occurred in the third inning when Seward was struck in the back of the head by a foul tip off the bat of Cincinnati second baseman and manager Sam Crane.[20] The blow knocked Seward to the ground, but despite being stunned for several minutes, the determined umpire and former catcher quickly recovered, and the game was resumed. The talented but erratic former Keystone, Jersey Bakley, was recruited to pitch for Wilmington and made his first appearance. Bakley pitched decently and was given solid defensive support, including three double plays. He still gave up six runs while the Wilmingtons only scored one. John Munce, a Philadelphia minor leaguer, who also made his living as a song and dance man, was in the lineup replacing Cullen in the outfield. The final 6–1 score brought the club's record to just 2–11, with the world-beating St. Louis Unions coming to town.

The two teams met on September 8 for the series-opening contest. St. Louis had typically drawn excellent attendance everywhere they went, but in Delaware, the bloom was off the rose, and any excitement about professional baseball had all but dissipated. As a result, only 800 fans appeared on the grounds to satiate their curiosity about the strength of Henry Lucas's club. The dismal attendance figure was the club's season-high during their time in the Union Association. Thanks to a solid effort by John Murphy, the contest was unexpectedly competitive. Murphy allowed only four runs but was out-dueled by Charlie Sweeney, who struck out 11 batters and paced his club to a 4–2 victory. Thankfully, for the first time in several days, there were no near-death experiences involving persons related to the Wilmington ball club.

The remaining three games in the series were each blowout losses, with Wilmington losing by scores of 9–3, 11–3, and 7–1. The series finale drew only 200 fans. The citizens of Wilmington did not want to watch their poor, cursed squad get manhandled by the rest of the Union Association. Owing to the poor attendance and performance of the Delaware club, Henry Lucas had realized that the Wilmington experiment was a bust. Lucas's promise to cover Wilmington's salary, road guarantees, and travel expenses on their upcoming western road trip would cost him $6,000 with little return on investment.[21] The Eastern League champions were the worst club in the Union Association. They had lost their best players to defection, illness, and accident. To top it all off, no one in the city of Wilmington seemed to care. The Wilmingtons were on life support.

On September 12, Wilmington traveled to Maryland to play the Baltimore Unions. Away from home, the Wilmingtons played a strong game against the talented club from Monument City. The visitors fell 4–3 in 10 innings after an errant throw to second by catcher Andy Cusick allowed Baltimore's Emmett Seery to score the winning run. Bill Sweeney's 16-strikeout performance was the undoubted highlight of the game and dropped Wilmington's record to 2 wins and 16 losses. The club then traveled to Chester, Pennsylvania, to play the Chester club, a solid semi-pro club, for an exhibition game on September 13. The Delaware nine took the game by a final score of 7–3. If you want to examine the hierarchy of baseball in terms of quality of play in 1884, Wilmington's track record can be instructive. They were the very best team in the Eastern League by a long shot, but they were also the very worst team in the Union Association by a long shot. On the verge of disbanding and missing four of their best players, they easily defeated a top semi-pro club. The Chester club had actually defeated the Philadelphia Keystones in June by a score of 7–1. What does that say about the Keystones?

The Wilmingtons were slated for a four-game set back at home against the lowly Kansas City Unions to begin September 15. *Sporting Life* intimated that Wilmington had been formally asked to withdraw from the UA. Secretary Warren White was tasked with ensuring that the club was replaced before they made their western road trip later in the month.[22] Milwaukee of the Northwestern League was the rumored replacement. The city boasted a strong club in a good market and had been left in precarious circumstances by the collapse of the Northwestern League.

Any chance of survival for Wilmington was extinguished at 4 p.m. on September 15. When the Kansas City and Wilmington clubs arrived at the grounds around 3:30 p.m., there were but a handful of people in attendance. Manager Joe Simmons of the Wilmingtons was dismayed by the smattering of fans and saw that he could not pay the $75 guarantee to the road club. Simmons called his club off the field and told them they were disbanding.[23] The club's directors were not interested in digging deeper into their pockets to pay for a losing venture.

Wilmington's secretary James M. Bryan paid out all outstanding salaries owed to the players. Only Andy Cusick and catcher Emanuel "Redleg" Snyder agreed to the proposed 20 percent reduction in salary.[24] A proposed Union Association meeting, initially slated for early September, during which Wilmington was to receive financial aid, had been postponed several times.[25] Wilmington had lost $3,000 during their time in the Eastern League. The club directors had paid out another $1,500 during their month in the UA and were unwilling to wait any longer for Lucas to fulfill his promise.[26] From the perspective of the Wilmington directors, the postponement of the league meeting was a cynical ploy by Lucas. He wanted to force Wilmington out by reneging on his promise to foot the bill for the club's western road trip.

Thus ended the strange, winding, and cursed story of the 1884 Wilmington baseball club. They went from dominance to futility and suffered their best players' defection while losing others to illness and near-death experiences. They experienced the hope of a fresh new start in the Union Association. They had also been subjected to the betrayal of Henry Lucas. He had promised to be a savior of baseball in Wilmington but ultimately proved to be its destroyer.

A representative of President Lucas sought to refute the charges laid against him.[27] He claimed somewhat incredulously that Lucas had no contact with the Wilmington directors during their time in the league and had made no promises to cover expenses. In fact, Lucas and most of the Union Association clubs had voted against allowing Wilmington to enter the league. It was Secretary Warren White, who had admitted Wilmington at his own behest, much to Lucas's surprise. An investigation into Wilmington's acceptance was to be undertaken at the league's upcoming meeting, but since Wilmington disbanded, there was no need to look further into the matter. In Lucas's version of events, Wilmington was admitted into his league without his approval, even though virtually every decision made by the Union had occurred with his decided influence. The definitive truth of the situation is lost to history, though one must undoubtedly take Lucas's perspective with a huge grain of salt.

The legacy of Wilmington's tumult-filled time in the Union Association was unexpectedly rich. The club gave birth to a surprising number of substantial major league talents. Thomas "Oyster" Burns and Dan Casey went on to baseball stardom later in the decade. Big Dennis Casey was a hard hitter whose abbreviated major league career was followed by a lengthy minor-league odyssey that lasted into the 1890s. The Casey brothers' greatest legacy may be as the purported inspirations behind the famed poem "Casey at the Bat," though that has never been definitively proven. Jersey Bakley, Charlie Bastian, and Jimmy Say were all picked up by the Kansas City Unions after the club folded. Bakley would achieve modest success pitching for Cleveland franchises in the AA, the NL, and the Players' League. Bastian later played several seasons for the Philadelphia Phillies, earning a reputation as a good field-no hit infielder. During his time with the Phillies, Bastian would be joined by fellow Wilmington alumni, Dan Casey, Tom Lynch, Andy Cusick, and the one and "The Only" Nolan. Nine players on the Wilmington roster would play again in the majors after the club folded. The figure would be ten if you included Dan Sheahan, a Washington, D.C., outfielder who made a token and currently undocumented appearance as an injury replacement for the Baltimore Unions on August 27, 1884.

The demise of the Wilmington franchise left a hole in the UA, and that would soon grow even bigger, as it was reported that the Pittsburgh franchise was also on the verge of disbanding. The loss of these clubs put Lucas and the directors in the unenviable position of having to find two clubs willing to join the flailing Union Association. This was no easy task given the double-cross instituted by Lucas against the Wilmington directors. Milwaukee had already expressed interest in joining the Union, but who would the second team be?

17

◇◇◇◇◇◇◇◇◇◇◇◇◇◇

The Union
Goes North ... Western

After the Pittsburgh Unions made their stellar home debut on August 25, Harry O. Price must have felt very confident about the prospects for his venture into the baseball world. The club had drawn a big crowd of 3,000 fans for a weekday game and had responded with an impressive victory over St. Louis, the best team in the league. The two clubs met again on August 26 for a rematch. Lucas's pet, Charlie Sweeney, took the mound against the enigmatic and electric young hurler Al Atkinson. Twenty-three-year-old Atkinson had made his major league debut on May 1, 1884, for the Philadelphia Athletics. Less than a month later, on May 24, he pitched a masterful 10–1 no-hitter against the lowly Alleghenys that saw him hit the leadoff hitter Ed Swartwood with a pitch and then retire the next 27 batters in a row. Swartwood had scored on a passed ball after stealing second and getting to third on a put-out. The no-hitter was a testament to Atkinson's potential, though he still had some work to go in becoming an ace. Atkinson was modestly effective for the Athletics going 11–11 with a 4.20 ERA and 81 ERA+. His performance may have been hindered because of homesickness or illness. He was a native Illinoisan and had left the club in July with a purported illness. He traveled west to his home state, first joining the Chicago White Stockings' reserve club and then defecting to the Chicago Unions.[1] He pitched well for Chicago as a change pitcher for Hugh Daily and gave the club another strong arm. He was expected to do the same in Pittsburgh.

Atkinson's club got out to a fast start in front of the 3,000 fans in attendance, scoring three runs in the top of the first inning thanks to two St. Louis errors and a couple of extra-base hits. St. Louis clawed back for three runs in the bottom of the fourth. They added two more in the bottom of the fifth to take a 5–3 lead that held until the top of the ninth. Pittsburgh scored one more run on a Jumbo Schoeneck double, but Sweeney scuttled the rally and held on to secure a 5–4 victory. Perry Werden and Hugh Daily met for a rematch on August 27, just two days after their exciting duel in the series' first contest. What happened this afternoon was the polar opposite of that dramatic affair. The game was a dreadful contest that saw Daily hit very hard, allowing 15 hits and 11 runs. The 2,000 fans witnessed a nearly remarkable comeback by the home squad, as they scored six runs in the bottom of the eighth to erase a 9–3 St. Louis lead and tie the game. Daily allowed two runs in the top of the ninth. Pittsburgh came to bat down by two runs in the bottom of the ninth. Werden,

150

who had struggled all day, got one out. Field manager and second baseman Fred Dunlap was unsatisfied and sent Werden to right field, taking to the pitcher's box himself. He was jeered by the home fans for his perceived arrogance. Dunlap had never pitched in a major league game before, but in 1884, he was seemingly capable of anything. Dunlap's hunch proved right as he was effective enough to get the final two outs, allowing only one run and saving the game. Dunlap's one save on the season would be good enough for second place in the Union Association, behind his old teammate Billy Taylor, who finished with four. It was the rare category that "Dunnie" failed to lead the league in that season.

The club's August 28 game was rained out, but the day was still eventful for Pittsburgh. Gid Gardner, who had avoided trouble in Chicago, could not handle the temptations that the Smoky City offered. He was fined $100 and released by the club after going on a drunken bender.[2] George Strief, an experienced second baseman, who had split the season between the St. Louis Brown Stockings and the Kansas City Unions, was signed to take his place on the roster. The August 29 contest was attended by 1,500 fans who witnessed a lopsided 7–2 loss by the home club. The matchup was highlighted by Sweeney's ten strikeouts and his defense's errorless play. The recently released Gardner was back in the Pittsburgh lineup, appearing in right field and getting two base hits off Sweeney. Gardner's ability to get into trouble was matched only by his ability to talk his way back into the good graces of those he offended.

After four well-attended games, Pittsburgh closed out their series with St. Louis in front of 1,000 fans on August 30. The club fell 4–3 in another tight extra-inning contest, with Henry Boyle taking the victory over Hugh Daily. After five home games at the Exposition Grounds, the Pittsburgh Unions had earned the favor of the locals. Attendance was very strong, with over 10,000 fans attending the five-game set. When the club was in Chicago, they had not drawn 1,000 fans to a game save for their Sunday contests and the second game of the Decoration Day doubleheader on May 30. Yet Pittsburgh had topped that mark in each of their first five home games. Price's gamble seemed to have paid off as the club embarked on a lengthy road trip that would span nearly four weeks.

The club traveled to Boston, where they continued their competitive play, taking three games of four from the strong Boston club to begin the month of September. The final game of the series was played on September 4. The club should have had ample time to travel to Washington to begin their next series on September 8. For reasons unknown, the club failed to arrive in Washington in time, and the opening contest of the series was awarded by forfeit to the Nationals. The Unions struggled in the Nation's capital, losing three, including the forfeited contest. They managed one tie, a six-inning 3–3 contest that was shortened by darkness after a lengthy delay was caused in the second inning by the maiming of Pittsburgh catcher Bill Krieg by a pitched ball.[3]

As the club headed to Baltimore for another series to commence on September 13, trouble was brewing back home in Pittsburgh. The *Pittsburgh Press* detailed the precarious financial situation Price was in thanks to his investment in the Exposition Grounds, quoting an unnamed sporting man with knowledge of the situation:

[Price]'s in a very big hole and wants to get out the best way he can. He expended $50,000 in fixing up the park, and yet has never had a profitable day since he opened it. He dropped big money on his running meeting and lost heavily by the fire-works experiment. He has worked hard to make the place a success, but somehow or other the people don't attend, no matter how great the attraction.[4]

Price's investment in the park was a money loser. Despite solid attendance during the Unions' homestand, there were not enough events scheduled at the park to generate revenue to offset his costs. Albert H. Henderson was still club president and entitled to half of any revenues that Pittsburgh generated. While the club was on the road, Price was not making any money, as the club was just collecting their $75 visitors' guarantee for each away game.

The lengthy road trips necessitated by the circuit's geographic composition and the limitations of train travel put many teams in difficult financial situations. The $75 guarantee rule was a blessing and a curse for visiting squads. Pittsburgh would be compensated equally, no matter the attendance during their road contests. The team's series in Boston was almost certainly not well attended, making such a guarantee a sufficient reward for coming to town. Conversely, the Washington series was very well attended, including a season-high 4,000 fans on September 9. Yet, Pittsburgh received the same guarantee as they had in the Boston series. The league's guarantee rule impacted every club in the Union Association. Teams bore significant expenditures during the month-long road trips while their sole source of road income was the $75 guarantee for each contest. Well-attended contests offered no additional benefit, and poorly attended games might result in the guarantee not even being paid, as had been the case in Wilmington.

Rumors circulated that the Pittsburgh Unions were on the verge of disbanding. Price was quick to refute these reports: "There is nothing in it and the first I heard of it was through the paper in question. Why, Mr. Thorner…[was here on] Saturday arranging for two games with our club at the Exposition grounds on the 25th and 26th of this month. After that date I expect the club to remain here and play all the Eastern Union Association clubs."[5] Publicly Price spoke of wanting to finish the season in Pittsburgh, though another report in *Sporting Life* stated that Price would move the club to Cleveland for the 1885 season and drive out the National League club by charging just 25 cents a game.[6]

Any intrigue surrounding Price's machinations would soon be put to rest. The Union Association held an emergency meeting on September 19, 1884, in Washington, D.C., to deal with the departure of Wilmington and the admission of the Milwaukee club from the Northwestern League to replace them. The independent Omaha Union Pacifics were reportedly seeking entry to the league.[7] With two clubs seeking to join and only one spot in the league, Albert H. Henderson decided to disband the Pittsburgh franchise and create room for another western club.

The timing of Henderson's decision was aided by the fact that Pittsburgh was still in Baltimore completing their series. Henderson made the announcement that evening at the Howard House, the boarding house where his Pittsburgh club was staying. Henderson stated that the "disbandment was not caused by any financial trouble."[8] It was noted that he had lost money on the Chicago venture, but the club's transfer to Pittsburgh was financially successful. Henderson clarified that "the Pittsburg and Baltimore Unions were under the same management, and the former club was disbanded in order to strengthen the latter. Furthermore, the Milwaukee and Omaha Clubs were seeking admission into the Union Association, and the removal of one Pittsburgh Club would make the necessary room, as the Wilmington club already disbanded."[9] No record exists of Price's thoughts on Henderson's decision to disband before returning home, though his confidence remained unaffected by the debacle. By the end of the month, he was reported to be in pursuit of a National League nine.[10]

A handful of players were transferred from Pittsburgh to Baltimore. Catcher Tony Suck, pitcher Al Atkinson, third baseman Joe Battin, shortstop Joe Ellick, outfielder Harry Wheeler and first baseman Jumbo Schoeneck. George Strief and Bill Krieg were also reported to have been transferred, but they seem to have refused the offer.[11] The temperamental Hugh Daily also did not join the club, despite the chance to pitch for his hometown team in Baltimore. While the Baltimore club was being reconstituted, the matter of the admission of Milwaukee and Omaha to the Union Association was being ironed out. Milwaukee was a strong club in a good market, left out in the cold by the collapse of the Northwestern League earlier in the month. For the club's directors, led by team president John C. Iverson, the offer to join the Union Association was a way to make a bit of extra money to close out the season with little risk. Their proposed Union schedule included 16 home contests and zero road games.

The application of the Omaha Union Pacifics to join the Union Association remains enigmatic over 135 years later. The "UPs," as they were commonly referred to, were arguably the strongest independent club in the country in 1884. The club had defeated the St. Louis Brown Stockings by a score of 7–0 on July 18. The club had also tamed the powerful St. Louis Unions, taking a 3–2 victory in St. Louis on August 18. The club featured a mixture of Union Pacific Railroad employees and players for hire, often given clerical positions with the railroad. They played their home games at St. Mary's avenue park, where they frequently drew upwards of 1,000 fans a game. The UPs had also done battle with Henderson's Chicago Unions semi-pro club the previous summer. In their current iteration, the club was in the middle of a seven-game series against St. Paul of the Northwestern League. The UPs took the series four games to three, led by a lineup that contained future and former major leaguers, including Russ McKelvy, John Sneed, and Joe Visner. On September 15, 1884, the *Omaha Daily Bee* first reported on the likely possibility of Omaha joining the Union Association: "Acting Manager [T.K.] Sudborough has entertained overtures for the past few days whereby the Union Pacifics play the circuit of the Union league, beginning September 20th."[12] It was expected that the club would readily accept the terms, which included completing a road trip through the western markets of the UA, with no guarantee of any home games.[13] The timing of the UA directors reaching out to Sudborough lines up with Pittsburgh's arrival in Baltimore, when rumors of the club's disbandment first appeared. On September 17, it was confirmed that the club would enter the Union Association on September 20, with the UP's traveling to Milwaukee, St. Louis, Cincinnati, Kansas City, and then back to Milwaukee to complete the season.[14]

Omaha and Milwaukee both made formal applications to join the league at the September 19 meeting. On September 23, Lucas optimistically noted that Milwaukee had formally been added to the UA roster to replace Pittsburgh: "Yes, the Milwaukees are with us, and will remain with us, I think, for many a year to come. Their association is on a good financial basis."[15] All along, the plan had been for Omaha to replace the Pittsburgh franchise and complete their schedule, but it was now being reported that Milwaukee would take over for that franchise. Meanwhile, Wilmington's spot remained vacant. In his pronouncements about Milwaukee, Lucas failed to mention Omaha, which just a few days before was a lock to join. Had Omaha's application been rejected? Or had they not been able to come to terms with Lucas and Secretary White's demands that the club complete an extensive western road trip without the benefit of any home games? The answer, unfortunately, is lost to time. When Lucas went silent about Omaha's application, so did the local Omaha media. After mentioning the club's certain admission on September 17, the *Omaha Daily Bee* made no further mention of the club or their application for the next few days. Aside from a no-show against a local club on September 21, the UP's would not be heard from again until mid–October when they played an exhibition series against a club from Evansville, Indiana.

So if the Omaha Union Pacifics were not joining the UA to replace Wilmington, then who would? The answer came on September 25, when St. Paul was enlisted to replace Wilmington and complete their delayed western road trip.[16] St. Paul was one of the two still extant members of the Northwestern League, alongside Milwaukee. While Milwaukee had been one of the defunct circuit's stronger teams, finishing with a 42 and 30 record, St. Paul was decidedly not. The woeful club compiled just a 24 and 48 record and was outscored by 173 runs. Omaha was undoubtedly the stronger club, having defeated St. Paul in the close seven-game series and holding victories over the two Mound City major league clubs.[17] St. Paul's willingness to complete Wilmington's still pending western road trip may have given them the edge over Omaha. St. Paul's Union stint would see them visit Cincinnati, St. Louis, Kansas City, and then close out the year in Milwaukee.

Financially, the club was stable, having broken even on the year as of August 2.[18] St. Paul had joined the Northwestern League as part of the six-team expansion prior to the 1884 season. On September 18, it was reported that the club was on the verge of disbanding if they could not find any new opponents. They had just completed a tour of Midwestern cities that included a series in Milwaukee and the previously discussed seven-game set in Omaha.[19] Henry Lucas and the UA directorship offered no inducements to the St. Paul's management to join. The club simply agreed to make the trip for the promise of the UA's guarantee of $75 per road game. Despite this minimal provision, team management felt that "no losses will be incurred, the guarantees being sufficient, it is said, to cover ordinary expenses."[20] The club would bring along just 11 men and manager Andrew M. Thompson. In essence, this would be a barnstorming tour for an adventurous group of ballplayers eager to keep their season alive.

18

Cream City Chronicles

As Mike Scanlon and his once-moribund squad from the nation's capital rode the train from Washington to Milwaukee on the evening of September 26, 1884, they had to have been ecstatic. The club had concluded the final home game of the season the day before with a dominant 10–2 victory over the strong Boston Unions. The large crowd of 3,000 fans at the Capitol Grounds was out in full force, including a large cadre of ladies who had become devoted fans as the season had progressed. The home club had gone out in "a blaze of glory" in their home finale, aided by the recent addition of the Hugh Daily, who allowed just one earned run and struck out seven in the victory.[1]

Daily had come to Washington from Pittsburgh after the Henderson-owned clubs merged the week before. It can be inferred that Henderson was looking to cut costs and granted the high salaried hurler his release, choosing to cast his lot with Pittsburgh's other hurler, the younger and cheaper Al Atkinson. It is also possible that Daily, whose 36-year-old right arm had logged 484.2 innings so far that year, wanted a break to assess his options. Regardless of the reasons, Daily was a free agent, and his services were sought by the American Association's Pittsburgh nine. The Alleghenys sought to sign him and his battery mate Bill Krieg, pending reinstatement by the National Agreement's Arbitration Committee.[2] Pittsburgh's pursuit was a longshot as the animus of the established leagues towards blacklisted contract jumpers like Daily had not subsided. It would remain a contentious issue in the offseason. The one-handed wonder telegraphed Scanlon on September 21 following an exhibition game between the Nationals and the disbanded Pittsburgh Union nine that drew 3500 fans.[3] Daily let Scanlon know he would be available to pitch for the club the following day against Cincinnati. His arrival had come at a time when the Nationals were playing their best baseball of the season.

The club had endured a disastrous start, but had improved steadily as the season progressed. April and May had seen the club go 6 and 21 with a -95 run differential before stabilizing somewhat in June, posting a 6–8 record with a +2 run differential. In July, the club went 10–9 with a +11 run differential, aided by a long homestand, the improved pitching of Bill Wise, and the hard-hitting of outfielder Henry Moore. In August, the savvy Scanlon, who was equally relentless and frugal in churning through his roster looking for ways to improve, finally found some pitching depth. He acquired two talented hurlers, Abner Powell and Charlie Geggus. Powell had joined the Nationals alongside his catcher, Chris Fulmer, after jumping

Peoria of the Northwestern League. Peoria had fined the duo and blacklisted them when they refused to pay up. The 24-year-old Powell was a solid addition for Washington. He had spent the prior season with the independent Chicago Unions after being released from a trial by Providence. Powell's major league career was relatively brief, concluding with several appearances for Baltimore and Cincinnati in 1886. He would go on to a lengthy and memorable minor league career that lasted until 1899, eventually finding a permanent home in New Orleans, where he earned the nickname "the Father of New Orleans Baseball."[4]

Powell was an imaginative thinker and was responsible for several innovations, including the implementation of a regular Ladies' Day, the detachable rain check ticket stub, and the use of a tarpaulin to cover the field during rainy weather.[5] He was also a key figure in the success of the Southern Association, thanks to his early investment in multiple clubs in the league. Much as Henry Lucas, Justus Thorner, and Albert Henderson had subsidized the lesser the lights of the Union, Powell did the same for the Southern Association. Powell had convinced young sportswriter Grantland Rice to leave Nashville and work at the *Atlanta Journal*, a move that launched the nationwide fame later attained by Rice.[6] Powell eventually left the world of baseball in 1905, ending a 22-year odyssey that had seen him succeed as a player, manager, and owner.[7] He lived until the age of 92, giving frequent interviews and serving as an ambassador of the early days of baseball. His influence was so significant that in 1950 on the occasion of Powell's 90th birthday, no less an authority than Connie Mack wrote to his old friend, "You, Abner, have contributed more to the game than any other man alive today."[8]

Powell ended up a solid contributor to the Nationals, posting a 6–12 record with a 3.43 ERA and 88 ERA+ while also playing center field, right field, second base, shortstop, and third base. Across 48 games, he put up a strong batting line of .283/.294/.387 and a 129 OPS+. Scanlon's other pitching find was Charlie Geggus. He had been signed from the recently disbanded Reading club of the Eastern League and was a veteran of the vibrant California baseball circuit. Geggus had undoubtedly been recommended to the Nationals by Henry Moore, who had teamed with the hurler on the San Francisco Mystics several years before. The 22-year-old made his pitching debut on August 11 in Boston. After falling behind 3–0 in the first thanks to his early wildness, Geggus pitched scoreless ball the rest of the way, striking out 14 bewildered Boston batters, allowing just five hits on the day. Geggus had already appeared in several games at shortstop for the Nationals, so his astonishing pitching debut found no place in the record books, as it was not his first major league game. Nearly 126 years later, another Nationals pitcher, Stephen Strasburg, would replicate his strikeout total in his major league debut. For context, Karl Spooner and J.R. Richard are co-holders of the record for most strikeouts in a major league debut with 15. Geggus' dominance continued in the following weeks culminating in a 12–1, 13 strikeout, eight-inning no-hitter over Wilmington on August 21. Buoyed by the elite pitching and frequent double-digit strikeout performances of their newfound star, the Nationals went on a 13 game undefeated streak from August 19 to September 12, with 11 wins and two ties. The rookie would finish third in the circuit with 7.9 strikeouts per nine innings, behind only Dupee Shaw and Hugh Daily. Despite his impressive performance that year, he would never play another major league contest. He appeared in the Eastern League in 1885 before returning to California. One commentator noted Geggus had a significant weakness in that he would "fret and become excited when he [did not] strike out ten or fifteen men in a game."[9] Perhaps this lack of composure prematurely shortened his pro career.

The Nationals' strong play had also built the club a strong following at home, where the club was regularly drawing over 2,000 fans per game. At the conclusion of their final homestand, the Nationals record stood at 43–53–2, a significant improvement from their early-season woes. Since June 1, they had even outscored their opponents 386–352. They certainly were not a great team, but with a pitcher like Geggus, they could compete against anyone. They had reason for optimism heading into Milwaukee for the debut of the league's newest club.

Milwaukee had performed inconsistently during the Northwestern League season. The Wisconsin nine had suffered under the erratic management of James McKee, struggling to an 18–23 record until McKee was fired in late June.[10] McKee had briefly managed the 1883 Chicago Unions before he was replaced by Ed Hengel. McKee was replaced in Milwaukee by Tom Loftus, a 28-year-old outfielder from St. Louis, who had made brief appearances in the National League and American Association. Loftus would eventually go on to a long career as a manager in the American Association, National League, and the American League before passing away at 53 years old in 1910. Loftus took over the day-to-day management of the club, and the club's performance improved dramatically, allowing the club to claw above .500 and to the periphery of the league's pennant race. When the Northwestern League disbanded on August 7, the club's record stood at 30–26.[11] Milwaukee had been one of the few teams in the league that drew well enough to pay out the league's $75 guarantee to visiting clubs, drawing as many as 3,000 fans on several occasions.[12] A proposed scheme was put forth by the directors of the Northwestern League to reconstitute as a four-team league and complete a second season. Milwaukee's directors agreed to the plan on the condition that Sunday games were permitted. With their conditions met, Milwaukee commenced this second season with just three other participants: Minneapolis, Winona, and St. Paul. The season was to comprise 24 games, with each club playing eight games against the other three clubs. Milwaukee was the class of this newly configured organization and posted an 11–4 record before the league died a second time when Minneapolis folded on September 2.[13] With virtually every other minor league club in the country disbanded, the Wisconsinites were arguably the strongest independent club in the country, rivaled only by the Omaha Union Pacifics and the nine in St. Paul.

The strength of Loftus's club was in its pitching staff. His team boasted a three-headed monster composed of two lefthanders, Ed Cushman and Charles "Lady" Baldwin, and one righty in Henry Porter. Cushman was a 32-year-old veteran from Ohio who was among the highest-paid players in the league, making $2,100 on the season.[14] He had been worth every penny, posting an unbelievable 22–1 record with a 0.61 ERA while striking out nearly one batter per inning. Baldwin was a 25-year-old who grew up in western Michigan. His unusual nickname "Lady" was derived from his quiet demeanor and pristine personal habits that included his refusal to swear or come in contact with either tobacco or liquor.[15] Baldwin compiled a 1.17 ERA for Milwaukee but received poor support from his teammates and finished with a 9–10 record, with 78 of the 100 runs he allowed being unearned. Henry Porter was a 26-year-old pitcher from Vermont, who had starred for the Bay City, Michigan, club earlier in the season, posting a 19–10 record and 0.75 ERA, before the club disbanded on July 22 despite a 39–16 record. Porter was snapped up by Loftus and continued to pitch wonderfully, compiling a 10–2 record with a 0.86 ERA in Milwaukee.

Loftus's trio of pitchers had dominated the Northwestern League. Since pitching was perhaps the single most crucial factor in the success of a club, it stood to reason that the nine would be competitive in their new league. The Northwestern League was a pitching factory in 1884, as it spawned future major league stars John Clarkson, Pretzels Getzien, Dave Foutz, and Bob Caruthers, along with Milwaukee's trio. Cushman, Baldwin, and Porter were supported by three excellent defensive catchers in Cal Broughton, George Bignell, and Anton Falch. Broughton and Falch were both Wisconsinites. Falch later became a Milwaukee police officer and was credited with saving many lives by preventing a catastrophic accident when he "grappled with a runaway team hauling a heavy truck wagon with one wheel off, barely missing a lot of people and grazing a streetcar."[16] Bignell had teamed with Porter as his personal catcher on the Bay City club and enjoyed the same role on his new club.

The club's left fielder, Steve Arnold Douglas Behel, often listed in contemporary papers as S.A.D. Behel had signed with the Chicago Unions in the offseason. He had been one of the handful of signees to jump Henderson's club before the season and was blacklisted by the Union Association at the July 1 meeting. In the late season turmoil of the UA, Behel's blacklist was forgotten about or conveniently ignored. Second baseman Al "Cod" Myers was signed by Milwaukee on the eve of their first Union Association game for a salary of $150 per month, having been wooed by Loftus ever since the disbandment of Myers's Muskegon club on August 7.[17] He immediately became the club's best position player. At just 20 years old, he was in his first season in professional baseball and would later star in the National League.

The opening contest of Milwaukee's Union Association tenure took place on September 27. Charlie Geggus faced off against Henry Porter in front of 1,800 fans who gathered at the Wright Street Grounds. The crowd was strong even though the contest was played in direct opposition to a well-attended horse race.[18] The Nationals had traveled west shorthanded, as their recent acquisition, Hugh Daily, chose to sit out the rest of the season. The workhorse had his eyes fixed on resting up, hoping to be 100 percent for the 1885 season. Captain and catcher Phil Baker and pitcher Bill Wise were also absent from the club because of illness, though both men planned to re-join the club for the Cincinnati series in October.[19] Despite the absence of three of their top players, the Nationals remained confident as they expected to manhandle the UA's newcomers, with Manager Scanlon expecting a series sweep.

The opening contest was a beautiful pitching duel as Porter and Geggus traded zeroes until the top of the seventh. Milwaukee's third baseman Tom Morrissey hit a one-out double to start the rally. Morrissey was from Janesville, Wisconsin, an early baseball hotbed in the Midwest. Morrissey's older brother John had starred for the town's 1877 League Alliance club that featured seven players who would go onto major league careers. Among them were Baseball Hall of Famer John Ward, Canadian Baseball Hall of Famer Bill Phillips, the greatest dentist in baseball history in A.J. "Doc" Bushong, a great defensive catcher who ran a dentistry practice in the offseason. The elder John Morrissey had passed away just a few months prior on April 29, 1884, due to that most common of 1880s afflictions, consumption. Centerfielder Cal Broughton followed up with a double to drive Morrissey home and open the scoring. Broughton went to third on a wild throw and scored on a sacrifice hit by Porter. Catcher George Bignell drew a rare base on balls, stole second, and then scored on a hit by shortstop Tom Sexton, bringing the score to 3–0. This lead was enough for Porter, who was virtually unhittable in his major league debut, allowing just one hit off the bat of his pitching counterpart while striking out 13 batters. Geggus allowed just seven hits on the day, though he only struck out two Milwaukee batters, undoubtedly causing him to pout and lose focus. Porter dominated the shorthanded Nationals, who constructed a somewhat makeshift lineup with a mysterious player known only as Franklin appearing in centerfield for the club. Porter was also provided outstanding defensive support, with only two errors made by his fielders.

Lefthander Ed Cushman got the nod against Abner Powell for the Sunday contest the following day. Rain fell until game time at 3 p.m., and despite the poor weather, "over 2,000 lovers of ball, with umbrellas and rubber coats, went over two miles to see the game."[20] The fans in attendance were rewarded with a historic performance by Cushman in his UA debut. The overpowering Cushman struck out 12 Nationals hitters while allowing zero hits. Powell allowed just five hits, though a sloppy defensive effort by his defense spoiled his strong performance. After six scoreless innings, the Nationals defense allowed five runs in the top of the seventh, resulting in a 5–0 final score. Cushman's no-hitter was not his major league debut, as he had started seven games for Buffalo of the National League the previous year. His shutout was the third no-hitter of the Union Association season. Geggus had pitched the circuit's first no-hitter, his eight-inning gem, against Wilmington on August 21. Five days later, Cincinnati's Dick Burns pitched the league's second no-hitter on August 26 in Kansas City.

Henry Porter was given the ball for the third contest of the series on September 29. He pitched another good game, striking out 11 more Nationals hitters and squelching a late rally by the visitors to complete a 7–5 victory and send the 1,800 Milwaukee fans home happy. Milwaukee had demonstrated that their pitching staff was elite in their first three outings. Another victory was expected by the 1,800 fans who attended the final matchup of the series on September 30. Lady Baldwin pitched a solid game but was undermined by the astonishing 14 errors made by his defense, and the contest was taken by the Nationals 5–3. Second baseman Al Myers led the way with four errors while shortstop Tom Sexton and first baseman Thomas Griffin contributed three errors each. Charlie Geggus pitched a good game for the visitors, striking out eight batters while allowing just six hits and one earned run. The local fans blamed the loss on the umpiring of former Chicago White Stockings and Baltimore Unions' pitcher Tom Lee. The pitcher was a Milwaukee native who had returned home following his release after the Baltimore-Pittsburgh merger.[21] Regardless of the reason for the loss, the Milwaukees had established that they were a strong club and could hold their own in the new league. Their next opponents, the visiting Boston Unions, were expected to pose a tougher battle than the departed Nationals had.

Two thousand fans turned out on October 3 to witness another historic performance by Henry Porter in the opening contest. Facing off against Dupee Shaw, Porter showed up the wizard and struck out an impressive 18 batters, matching Shaw's 18-strikeout performance from earlier in the season. Porter's catcher, George Bignell, set a major league record that still stands by handling 23 chances on the day.[22] Despite the efforts of the battery, the visiting Boston Unions rescued a victory from the jaws of defeat with a three-run rally in the bottom of the ninth to win the contest 5–4. Cushman responded the following day with a nearly unmatched performance, striking out 16 hitters and taking a no-hitter into the ninth inning, when Ed Callahan, the Boston right fielder, broke it up with a bloop single over first base to lead off the inning.[23] Cushman had come achingly close to pitching consecutive no-hitters, beginning his UA career with 17 consecutive no-hit innings. Johnny Vander Meer would eventually accomplish the feat of consecutive no-hitters for Cincinnati in 1938. Cushman's effort resulted in a 2–0 victory as he out-dueled Tommy McCarthy, the Boston outfielder and change pitcher, who put forth his finest effort of the season. The man who broke up the no-hitter was Ed Callahan, a Boston semi-pro, who had made an emergency appearance for the St. Louis Unions back on July 19 in Boston. From there, he was picked up by Kansas City and taken west. Callahan made three appearances hitting .364, then umpired a contest between Boston and Kansas City on September 28. He then joined Boston as they continued their western road trip, where he closed out the season by hitting .385 in four more contests. Callahan's whirlwind season ended with his return home to Boston. He never pursued professional baseball again, despite his apparent hitting abilities. Callahan's big league career comprised three months, three teams, eight games, a .333 batting average, and an umpiring gig. It was the type of career that could only happen in the Union Association.

Milwaukee played their second Sunday contest on October 5, drawing a crowd of 2,500 to 3,000 fans. The game would see a marquee rematch between pitchers Shaw and Porter. The game was controversial and saw the breakup of the inseparable battery of Porter and Bignell. An indignant Bignell grew frustrated with the wild hurling of his partner and removed himself from the contest in the second inning after having his fingernail torn off by a fast delivery from Porter.[24] Porter's wildness cost the club two runs in the inning. Cal Broughton was moved from center field to behind the plate to complete the contest and supported Porter ably. He allowed zero passed balls despite his lack of familiarity with the wild hurler. Porter struck out another ten Boston hitters but was outmatched by his rival Shaw, who struck out 11 Milwaukee batters and won the contest 3–1. Outfielder Steve Behel was felled by an injury late in the contest, wrenching the tendons in his left leg while sliding into third base during Milwaukee's failed ninth-inning rally. Behel missed the next few games while the club released the disgruntled Bignell. Cushman and McCarthy faced off again to close the series, and the home team took the contest by a score of 6–2, with a modest crowd of around 800 fans witnessing another strong but not history-making performance by Cushman. He struck out eight Boston batters and allowed just four hits. After eight contests, Milwaukee's record stood at 5–3. With a couple of breaks, they could easily have gone undefeated.

The ailing Baltimore Unions arrived in town for Milwaukee's next series starting on October 9. The men from Monument City had been in something of a freefall since their thirteen-game winning streak had ended on August 16. Since that date, the club had gone just 11–21, including an 11 game losing streak from August 27 to September 11. Their merger with the Pittsburgh Unions was expected to rejuvenate the club and help them secure second place in the UA. The influx of the best players from Pittsburgh was supposed to have strengthened their weak spots. In particular, ailing workhorse Bill Sweeney would finally have another quality pitcher to spell him in Al Atkinson. Since the so-called "New Baltimores" took the field for the first time on September 20, the club had posted a mediocre 6–5 record in 11 games. Alarmingly, all six of those wins had come against lowly Kansas City, and they had been thoroughly outclassed in a three-game sweep in St. Louis at the end of September. The Lucas squad was the bane of Sweeney's existence in 1884. He went just 1–10 against St. Louis while posting a 29–11 record against the rest of the league.

On the eve of their series in Milwaukee, Baltimore's record stood at 57–42–1, 28.5 games behind the league-leading St. Louis Unions, who held an 88–16–1 record. They were a full seven games behind the streaking Cincinnati nine, who seemed to have second place locked up with a 64–35 record. The Baltimore nine was now in a close fight for third place with the Boston nine, who were only two games behind in the win column with a 55–46–2 record. Milwaukee technically held down third place by winning percentage with their 5–3 record and .625 winning percentage topping the .576 mark held by Baltimore. The Baltimore-Milwaukee series would go a long way in determining Baltimore's place in the final league standings and give the Milwaukee nine more evidence to determine where they stood in the UA hierarchy.

Henry Porter faced off against Bill Sweeney in another solid pitching matchup to open the series. Despite the promise of a pitcher's duel, only 800 fans turned out to witness the contest. Milwaukee entered the eighth inning, hanging on to a slim 4–3 lead. Sweeney, the Baltimore ace, had pitched steadily, but the staggering number of innings he threw all year had taken their toll. Sweeney was well north of 500 innings on the season and had struggled down the stretch. The home team broke open a 4–4 tie with three runs in the bottom of the eighth and won the contest 7–4. Porter's strikeout ways continued as he added 14 more punch-outs to his portfolio. Through five starts, Porter had struck out an astonishing 66 batters through 44 innings, for a staggering ratio of 13.5 K/9 that would be just as impressive in today's game.

The clubs met again on October 10, with Lady Baldwin matching up against Al Atkinson in front of 1,500 fans. Baldwin earned his first major league victory with a four-hitter as Milwaukee cruised to a 5–1 win. Baldwin also totaled 13 strikeouts in an effort that hinted at his future stardom for Detroit in the National League later in the decade. Baldwin debuted with Detroit in 1885, finishing the season with an

11–9 record with a 1.86 ERA. He also posted a league-leading 0.920 WHIP and 6.8 K/9. In 1886, Baldwin was the best pitcher in baseball, winning 42 games against 13 losses for second place Detroit while leading the league with 323 strikeouts. Arm injuries curtailed his promising career, as he won just 13 games in 1887 for Detroit, who finally took home the National League pennant. His career ended prematurely in 1890, another victim of overwork.

The evening of Baldwin's first big league win, Milwaukee's directors telegraphed St. Paul manager Andrew Thompson in Kansas City. They informed the manager of the Minnesota nine that the upcoming series in Milwaukee had been canceled owing to expected cold weather. The four games would have closed out the Union Association season for both clubs. The cancellation brought another premature end to the season for the last members standing of the Northwestern League. It seems plausible that the cancelations were also motivated by the fear of poor attendance in Milwaukee, since the visitors from St. Paul had already appeared in the Cream City many times that year.

On October 11, Porter faced off against Sweeney again and carried a three-run lead into the seventh inning. The home nine and their fans argued that the game should be called since it was too dark to continue. The visitors, hoping for a comeback, successfully pressured the umpire, B.F. Adler, to continue the game. The Baltimoreans rallied for five runs to take the contest by a score of 8–5. Porter only managed five strikeouts in the contest, a far cry from his established rate. Like Baldwin, Porter's brilliance in the UA was a precursor to future stardom. The right-hander was much sought after in the offseason and eventually signed with Brooklyn of the American Association. The hurler won 33 games in 1885 and followed it up with 27 more in 1886. His career quickly went downhill in the ensuing years. He went 15–24 in 1887 and then lost 37 games in 1888 for Kansas City. He closed out his major league career in 1889 with a 0–3 record for the lowly Missouri nine, another overworked hurler cast to the scrap heap.

Cushman and Atkinson, both of whom had thrown no-hitters earlier in the season, would be the matchup in the final game of the series, a Sunday contest in front of 4,000 fans on October 12. Cushman was his usual dominant self, allowing just four hits and two runs while striking out seven. The home club took the contest 5–2, thanks to four hits and three runs during a seventh-inning rally that erased a 2–1 Baltimore lead. Cushman would join Baldwin and Porter in the major leagues as arguably the most talented of the three hurlers. Despite his evident ability, he would enjoy only modest success over the course of his career and failed to establish himself as an elite pitcher. His finest season saw him post a mediocre 17–21 record and 3.12 ERA in 1886 for the New York Metropolitans. His career concluded at age 38 with another 17–21 season for Toledo of the American Association in 1890.

After 12 contests, Milwaukee boasted an impressive 8–4 record. On the field, the club owed much of its success to the abilities of its pitching staff. The club was not an offensive dynamo, though both Al Myers and Cal Broughton hit over .300. It was the club's run prevention abilities that truly stood out. They had allowed a microscopic 2.8 runs per game in a league where teams averaged 5.8 runs a game. The club's talent level was near to Cincinnati and St. Louis at the close of the season. Few clubs in baseball could boast three pitchers as good as Cushman, Baldwin, and Porter. The team had drawn very well at the gate, with anywhere from 24,000 to 31,000 fans attending the 12 home games thus far. Milwaukee's roster was reportedly paid $3,000 a month, the second-highest salary in the league behind the Lucas nine.[25] Despite the high salary, the club had made $3,000 in profits over the 12 contests, demonstrating that the decision to enter the UA under such favorable circumstances was correct.[26] With the St. Paul series canceled, baseball season in Milwaukee was officially over. The season had proven that Cream City was a baseball town, and much was expected in 1885, particularly if the club remained in the Union Association. For the circuit's other Northwestern League emigre from Minnesota, the results were not nearly as fruitful.

19

◇◇◇◇◇◇◇◇◇◇◇◇◇◇◇◇◇

The Vagabonds
from Minnesota

While the Milwaukee experiment was an unqualified success for the Milwaukee directors and the heads of the Union Association, the St. Paul experience was a forgettable one for all parties. The fundamental difference in the tenures of both clubs was simply that Milwaukee's proposed schedule included 16 consecutive home games. In comparison, their former rival in the Northwestern League was asked to play 16 road games to complete the Union Association schedule. The difference in revenue was significant since the Milwaukee directors could reap the profits of the expected strong gates at their home grounds while not paying any travel expenses. Conversely, St. Paul would only receive the standard $75 guarantee for each of their road contests. Unlike the propositions that Lucas had offered Wilmington to cover salaries and road expenses, St. Paul received no such enticement.

Another critical difference between the two clubs had to do with their overall quality. Milwaukee was a solid competitor in the Northwestern League, finishing in fifth place in the first half of the season and finishing in first place in the second half. They possessed a superlative pitching trio of major league caliber. By the close of the league's second season, the club was playing their best baseball of the season. St. Paul's tenure in the circuit was less rosy. The club started the season under the management of 21-year-old pitcher Robert Lemuel Hunter, listed in the record books as Lem Hunter, who had pitched one game for Cleveland in September 1883. Hunter earned his release from Cleveland after a feisty brawl with Hugh "One Arm" Daily, with the rookie criticizing the veteran's pitching and drawing his ire.[1] Hunter's abrasive tendencies came to light once again in July 1884. Hunter had lost the room, and several players on the club had sought to have him replaced.[2] He responded by arranging for the release of team captain Will Foley, who had jumped his contract with the Chicago Unions to join St. Paul in May.[3] Hunter had perceived that Foley was the ringleader of the coup and hoped that his release would undermine the player's revolt. The result was the complete opposite, as every member of the club signed a petition to have Hunter fired and presented it to management. The petition resulted in Hunter being relieved of his duties, bringing the boy manager's tenure to an end while also ending his playing career at the age of 21. Hunter was from a wealthy family in Ohio and returned there. When he passed away at the age of 93 on November 9, 1956, he was the last surviving member of Cleveland's first National League franchise.

The friction on the club seemed to be resolved by the removal of Hunter. Andrew M. Thompson, one of the club's directors, was given the task of managing the club. Thompson had served in the Civil War as a drummer boy while still a teenager in Illinois.[4] The club had gone 24–48 in the first half but finished with a 7–7 record in the second half. Thompson organized a series of contests with the Omaha Union Pacifics in September, taking his team on the road in search of any stray contests. There were few midwestern clubs still in existence at that point in the season, as Thompson and the St. Pauls desperately tried to keep their season going.

When the club was granted entrance into the Union Association in late September, the roster was a lean one comprising just 11 men. Second baseman Moxie Hengel served as the field captain to compensate for Thompson's lack of baseball experience. Hengel was a scrappy and heady infielder who had spent the early part of the season with the Chicago Unions, under the management of his brother Ed Hengel. He evidently failed to impress his sibling and was released by the club in May, quickly joining St. Paul along with the contract jumping Will Foley. Hengel was a light hitter but highly regarded for his defense at the second sack. The club's best position player was likely infielder Billy O'Brien, who had hit .281 on the season and would play several seasons in the National League and American Association later in the decade. Catcher Charlie Ganzel ended up having the most significant impact on baseball history, later achieving fame with the legendary Boston Beaneaters dynasty, which fought tooth and nail with the rowdy Baltimore Orioles for baseball supremacy in the 1890s.

St. Paul's pitching staff comprised three men, though it had been seriously hindered by injuries and hasty departures. For much of the Northwestern League season, the club's ace was Elmer Foster, who compiled a 17–19 record. He also posted a microscopic 1.18 ERA, though his 5.71 runs allowed per nine innings suggests he was the victim of a porous defense. Foster's season was cut short by an arm injury that ended his pitching career and cost him the chance to appear in the Union Association. He later reemerged as a utility man for several seasons in the American Association, National League, and minor Western Association. Their other top pitcher was "Stooping" Jack Gorman, a talented and versatile player from St. Louis who had spent time with Quincy and Kansas City earlier in the year. Gorman joined St. Paul as a replacement for Foster. He earned his nickname from his strange pitching delivery: "when about to deliver the ball he gets down almost on his knees, then suddenly rises and sends the ball in with terrific force."[5] He had been the club's ace in their September series against the Omaha Union Pacifics, winning two of his three starts in their seven-game series. St. Paul blew a 3–0 series lead and lost the series 4–3. His performance drew the attention of the Allegheny club, who signed the pitcher for the rest of the season.[6]

After the Omaha series, the St. Paul club was in limbo. The club played what was expected to be their final contest on September 21 against a local club named the Red Caps. The following day, with St. Paul's season essentially over, the local paper published an epitaph to the Northwestern League that read:

Northwestern League
Born
In Chicago, October 27, 1882
Died
In St. Paul, September 21, 1884
This promising youth crossed the dark river by degrees, and among the ailments
were internal dissensions, self-conceit, public apathy, geographical extensiveness,
numerical ponderosity, extravagance and lonesomeness.
Requiescat in Pace.[7]

For players like Gorman faced with an end to their season and an unknown future ahead, there was no reason to turn down an offer from another club, even with the prospect of the St. Paul's admission to the Union Association on the horizon.

The departure of Gorman left the club with only one regular pitcher. Lou Galvin was a 21-year-old St. Paul native in his first season in pro-ball. Galvin split time between the outfield and the pitcher's box in the latter half of the Northwestern League and was one of the club's two primary pitchers in the Omaha series earlier in the month, winning one of three starts. Galvin compiled a 2–7 record in the Northwestern League, though his 2.03 ERA suggests he pitched better than his record. Billy O'Brien made rare mound appearances when not playing in the field. He showed some promise as he compiled a 2–0 record in Northwestern League play, allowing just 3 earned runs in 18 innings of work. Despite O'Brien's live arm, Manager Thompson preferred to use the hard-hitting O'Brien in the field. As the club prepared to head to Cincinnati to begin their Union experiment on September 27, they desperately needed another pitcher to carry the load.

The current record book lists former Altoona Union, Jim Brown, as the man who filled the void for St. Paul, but currently, no evidence is known to exist that proves it was him. Brown had joined New York in the National League briefly in June. After that stint, he appears to have gone back to Philadelphia and pitched semi-pro ball the rest of the season. It is more likely that Ed Brown, a Chicago native, filled the role of St. Paul's number one pitcher. The Chicago Brown had spent half of the season with Toledo of the American Association, appearing in 42 games while compiling a dismal .176/.187/.196 batting line. He also compiled a seemingly apocryphal pitching line in his one start of the year. On May 7, Brown faced off against the St. Louis Brown Stockings and was pounded for 19 hits while walking four men and hitting another. He was left in the contest to die and faced a staggering 53 batters before the game mercifully came to a close, with the final score being 16–0. Brown had fared better in his one pitching appearance in 1882 when he allowed one run on two hits in two innings of work for St. Louis. Ed Brown had joined St. Paul in July after his release from Toledo and stuck around for a couple of weeks as a third baseman and change pitcher.

The only biographical note that appears about the pitcher who would start five contests for the St. Paul Union club was a tidbit stating that he came from "the famous Franklin club of Chicago."[8] The Franklins were a semi-pro team made up of printers, who bore famed Benjamin Franklin's surname as the source of their nickname. Ed Brown had first started playing in the Chicago amateur and semi-pro ranks in 1874. During the latter half of the 1880s, Brown played for the Franklin club, and he also worked as a printer in the offseason.[9] These facts would seem to confirm that the St. Paul player was Ed Brown and not Jim Brown as currently listed. Such are the intrigues, ambiguities, and frustrations of researching 135-year-old team rosters.

The *Cincinnati Enquirer* tried to put its best spin on the quality of the St. Paul club. On the eve of their debut contest in the Queen City, the paper wrote: "The St. Paul club is said to be very strong and recently defeated the Union Pacifics, of Omaha, in three straight games. The Omaha club, in turn, had won balls from both the St. Louis Union and American clubs."[10] The paper neglected to mention that the club had then lost four straight contests to Omaha. It was also noted that the club had finished in second place in the Northwestern League, failing to indicate that the club held a modest 7–7 record at the time and giving no mention of their struggles in the league's first half.[11] Strengthened by the trio of Cleveland defectors, the home club had been on a remarkable tear since their debut on August 10. In 29 games, the club had compiled a 23–6 record, with one of those losses coming by forfeit. This stretch included consecutive four-game sweeps on the road of their rivals for second place in Baltimore and Boston. The club from Porkopolis was playing their best baseball of the season and had just returned home from a lengthy eastern road trip that had spanned the whole month of September. The debuting nine from St. Paul would have their hands full with what now stood as arguably the strongest nine in the Union Association.

Despite the dominant performance of Cincinnati in recent weeks, their absence did not make the heart grow fonder for the city's baseball enthusiasts. A small crowd estimated at just 300 fans attended the opening game of the series. It was a far cry from the hero's welcome bestowed upon the rival Lucas nine in St. Louis the following day when 8,000 fans showed up at the park to witness their beloved nine's triumphant return after a lengthy road trip.

The novelty of seeing the UA's newest entrant live in the flesh was diminished by the rainy weather. Heavy overnight rain and morning showers nearly postponed the contest and at least partially explained the poor crowd for the afternoon contest. By mid-afternoon, the weather had cleared up a bit, and the park was in good enough shape to play. Sawdust was added to give better traction around the bases and to the batters' and pitchers' boxes, respectively.[12] Brown and Ganzel were the battery for visitors, facing off against little Dick Burns and Joe Crotty for the home nine. Cincinnati's star shortstop, Jack Glasscock, was given the day off and was replaced by George Bradley. Cincinnati opened the scoring in the top of the second with two runs, one coming on a little league home run by Bill Harbridge, thanks to a throwing error on a routine grounder to second baseman Moxie Hengel. Cincinnati's second run came on another throwing error, this time by outfielder John "Scrappy" Carroll. St. Paul responded with a run on a sac fly in the bottom of the third. The game remained close for the next several innings, as St. Paul's hurler proved baffling to the home team. Brown allowed just seven hits on the day and struck out ten batters while also hitting two doubles. His defense played creditably after the disastrous second inning, but two more errors in the eighth led to three more Cincinnati runs and a final score of 6–1.

Rain fell over the next two days, postponing two contests between the clubs at Union Park, which the *Cincinnati Enquirer* now boasted was the prettiest park in the country and "the finest field in the world."[13] Six hundred fans witnessed Big Jim McCormick face off against Brown on September 30, and the result was another 6–1 victory for Cincinnati. McCormick allowed just three hits on the day and his defense made just one error. Brown was less effective than in his debut but pitched credibly and earned raves noting that he was "quite the pitcher, and in the two games he has pitched against the Cincinnati Unions he has kept the boys 'guessing' very hard to make safe hits."[14] The catching support of Charlie Ganzel was equally impressive. The young catcher was faced with the unenviable task of catching the deliveries of a live-armed hurler whom he had never caught before. It is not surprising that the mettle Ganzel had shown thus far would be one of the building blocks of his eventual stardom. He later made his name as the brainy backstop for two of the nineteenth-century's greatest teams, the 1887 National League champions from Detroit and the 1890s Boston Beaneaters.

The clubs met again on October 1 to close their series, with George Bradley facing off against Lou Galvin. Galvin was making his debut in the Union Association. A rumor was floated that he was the sibling of the famed hurler James "Pud" Galvin, perhaps designed to inflate his reputation and potential. However, Galvin was a St. Paul native and bore no relation to his hurling compatriot of the same surname. The 22-year-old was unprepared for the task and spotted the visitors a 4–0 lead after three innings. By the end of the fifth, the visitors were down 7–0, a score that turned out to be the final. Cincinnati's George Washington Bradley pitched like it was the centennial, returning to his 1876 form with a two-hit shutout while hitting a double of his own. Galvin's control proved to be his downfall, as he allowed four base on balls, a high total for the era when seven balls were required for a walk. The additional baserunners made the 11 hits he allowed even more costly.

For Cincinnati's Justus Thorner, the poorly attended contests must have caused some concern. Despite the increased strength of his club and the ongoing improvements to the ball grounds designed to enhance the fan experience, the club had failed to gain a substantial audience. Thorner's attempts to usurp local attention from his former pledges in the American Association were proving futile. The Union club's attendance had seen a slight bump after acquiring the big three from Cleveland, with the trio's home debut on August 10 representing the club's high water mark for attendance. Their debut contest drew a reported 4,105 fans to the much-hyped Sunday contest versus the St. Louis Unions. However, the existing attendance figures for the club's remaining August contests had the club averaging under 1,000 fans per contest. The club's August 31 contest against Kansas City drew a disappointing 1,100 fans for an unopposed Sunday contest. Although the club was given ample coverage and attention in the *Cincinnati Enquirer*, the team's attendance had failed to improve. Under the editorial guidance of team secretary Harry M. Weldon, the paper's sporting pages had taken to publishing woodcuts and biographies of the team's players to build interest. The paper also provided detailed and favorable coverage of the club's exploits, often giving them top billing over the rival Red Stockings. The *Cincinnati Commercial* was still skeptical of the Union Association and the Thorner nine but had softened their brutal diatribes against the wreckers. Their sports section now sprinkled in the occasional dig rather than launching long screeds. This change in approach was likely caused by the realization that the Union club was quite strong at this point in the season and posed little threat commercially to the established Red Stockings.

At this juncture in the season, there were even calls for the two nines to face off in a postseason series to determine which club would reign supreme. This melting of hostilities between the Union Association and the parties adhering to the National Agreement resulted in Thorner putting forth a challenge to any club in Ohio to play a best of three series after the season for a purse of $1,000 to $5,000 a side plus the gate receipts.[15] While Thorner waited for a response, he booked exhibition contests against the newly formed Nashville, Tennessee, club, the first professional team in the history of that city, for October 10 and 11.[16] He also scheduled two contests against the Louisville Colonels of the American Association that would take place on October 18 and October 19, after the close of the season for both leagues. These would mark the first contests that would take place between a Union club and an established club in either of the two major leagues. Louisville president James A. Hart had petitioned A.G. Mills, the chair of the arbitration committee that enforced the National Agreement, for the right to play against Union Association clubs. Hart claimed that since the Louisville players' contracts were up on October 15, they should be free to play teams outside of the National Agreement.[17] Mills delivered a measured response to Hart, stating:

> If your men play as the Louisville Club, of the American Association, games with Union club would fall within the prohibitions of the National Agreement, but clarified that the mere fact that a player is under reservation (and not under contract) to a National Agreement club, does not forbid him to participate in a game against a Union club, but such an act would be injurious to us and a direct benefit to the common enemy.[18]

Mills' statement seemed to leave an opening for Union clubs to play against teams featuring players from National Agreement clubs, though it would be frowned upon.

For Andrew Thompson, the manager of the St. Paul club, his team's debut series in the Union Association had not gone quite as well as he had hoped. After three contests, the hallmark of the St. Paul club was its anemic hitting. The St. Paul nine had totaled just 13 hits and two runs so far. The club was not a strong hitting club, even in the Northwestern League, but facing off against pitchers, the quality of Bradley, McCormick, and young Dick Burns had proven to be too much. On the bright side, the club's defense had performed commendably. Their two pitchers, Brown and Galvin, had shown the ability to get hitters out and prevent contests from turning into complete debacles. They had proven not to be an embarrassment thus far, though that might change as the Minnesotans traveled to St. Louis for their next slate of contests.

St. Paul's debut in St. Louis came about on October 3 in front of 1,500 fans. Brown faced off against Charlie Sweeney, and the result was a close battle between the seemingly disparate clubs. Brown struggled to get the heavy hitters in the St. Louis lineup out. Second baseman Fred Dunlap was in the final stretch of one of the more remarkable performances in baseball history to that point. The exceptional second sacker hit his league-leading twelfth home run over the left-field fence in the third inning. Dunlap had been the splashiest acquisition made by Lucas in the off-season. He was a 25-year-old burgeoning megastar, equally skilled as a hitter and in the field. He would soon be given the well-deserved title "the King of Second Basemen." As the driving force in the powerful Unions lineup, he completed the season with an unfathomable .412/.448/.621 line. His 256 OPS+ has only been bested by Barry Bonds, who accomplished the feat on three occasions in 2001, 2002, and 2004. Of course, it is absurd to compare Dunlap's 1884 season to Barry Bonds' finest work, but the record just demonstrates how superior he was to his peers in the league for this one season. Dunlap also

paced the circuit with 160 runs scored, 185 hits, 13 home runs, and 279 total bases. At second base, he was equally exquisite, leading all second basemen with 54 double plays, 341 putouts, and 300 assists. His .926 fielding percentage was nearly .50 points better than the league's runner up, Baltimore's Dick Phelan. Dunlap's range factor was 6.41, well ahead of Washington's Tom Evers at 5.71. Dunlap's offensive WAR of 6.7 was 2.7 better than his nearest competitor, teammate Orator Shafer. His 1.4 defensive WAR was the best by any non-catcher. His total of 7.8 WAR was the best mark by any non-pitcher in all of baseball that year. While his statistics for the year were obviously inflated by the demonstrably weak overall talent level of the UA, make no mistake, Dunlap was an elite player. His first four seasons in the National League from 1880 to 1883 saw him finish fourth, third, tenth, and sixth in WAR amongst position players. He also cemented his reputation as baseball's premier second baseman. Dunlap's remarkable 1884 performance at-bat, on the field, and as team manager after Ted Sullivan quit, had proven that Lucas's investment was indeed a wise one.

On the strength of Dunlap's home run and several extra-base hits by Dave

Fred Dunlap enjoyed one of the most dominant seasons in baseball history with the St. Louis Unions in 1884. He led the league in numerous hitting categories, while playing exceptional defense at second base for Henry Lucas's pennant-winning club. The King of Second Basemen was the highest paid player in baseball throughout the rest of the decade before injuries cut his career short. He is pictured while with the 1887 World Series champion Detroit Wolverines, one of the greatest clubs of the 19th century (courtesy Detroit Public Library).

Rowe, Brown was knocked out of the box in the fifth inning, down 6–0. Third base-man Billy O'Brien was brought in to replace Brown and tasked with keeping St. Paul in the contest. He did a fine job, holding St. Louis scoreless for two innings before allowing two runs in the top of the seventh. The score now stood 8–1, and with dark-ness encroaching, the St. Paul batters finally showed signs of life after nearly four whole games, erupting for four runs off Charlie Sweeney. The late rally brought the score to 8–5. At the close of the seventh, with the time now 5:30 p.m., the umpire called the game due to darkness at the behest of Dunlap. St. Paul's resilience was per-haps best personified by Ganzel, who continued to earn raves for his backstop play. He earned regular applause from the appreciative fans and showed suitable pluck while also getting two hits on the day.[19] Rain prevented the two clubs from playing on October 4, with the contest rescheduled for October 13. The clubs met on Sunday, October 5, in front of a strong crowd of 5,000. Sweeney faced off against Brown in what turned out to be a brisk and abbreviated affair. The pair of hurlers brought their A-game, with Sweeney striking out the first six batters he faced before trading places with left fielder Henry Boyle so that he could save his arm for the club's pending exhi-bition series against Cincinnati. Sweeney's willingness to think of the team's needs demonstrated a surprising amount of growth, considering his dubious response to a similar situation had caused his controversial departure from Providence in July. Boyle struck out another three St. Paul batters over the next three innings while allowing zero hits. St. Paul broke up the parade of zeroes with an unearned run on a sequence of St. Louis errors in the fourth. St. Paul's Brown was also effective, strik-ing out three, allowing only a base hit to Sweeney. After five innings, the score stood 1–0 for St. Paul when heavy rain came down over the field. Despite feverish attempts by the local grounds crew to make the field presentable, the game was called. St. Paul had won their first-ever Union contest against the league champions to boot, and they did it while being no-hit by the combined efforts of Sweeney and Boyle. St. Paul now departed for Kansas City while Cincinnati arrived in St. Louis to begin an exhi-bition series.

Lucas welcomed Thorner's nine to St. Louis for the first contest in the head-to-head series for Union Association supremacy on October 6. While the pen-nant race had long been decided in the Mound City's favor, the acquisition of the Cleveland trio by Thorner had rendered his Cincinnati club "almost invincible."[20] With no more contests on the Union schedule, Thorner and Lucas agreed to hold a two-game exhibition series in St. Louis. May the best man win. At this point in the season, there was little to choose between the two clubs. Cincinnati had the better pitching depth, with McCormick, Bradley, and Burns each winning 20 games on the season, while St. Louis had the more potent offense. Dunlap's superiority at the bat was now rivaled by his old double-play partner Jack Glasscock, who had shown a similar capability to dismantle UA pitching, hitting .419/.444/.564 across 38 UA contests. St. Louis was strengthened by the addition of two former St. Louis Brown Stockings, outfielder Fred Lewis and catcher Tom Dolan. Lewis was a well-known drinking man who had palled around the west coast earlier in the decade with our old friend, Jack Leary. Lewis had hit .323/.366/.418 in 73 games for the Brown Stock-ings, but a recent suspension after a drunken arrest had caused him to jump to the

Union Association.[21] His addition gave the already powerful Union lineup another weapon. Dolan was unhappy with losing his starting role on the Brown Stockings to Pat Deasley and bristled at the criticism of owner Chris von der Ahe. Lucas offered the disaffected backstop a salary of $400 a month for the rest of the season, and Dolan broke his AA contract of $1,400 to join the Unions.[22]

The contests between the circuit's top dogs were highly competitive affairs. McCormick and Sweeney faced off on October 6 in front of a crowd of 4,000. St. Louis scored a run in the top of the first to open the scoring off McCormick, thanks to a leadoff triple by Dunlap and a sac fly by Shafer. The score held until the bottom of the sixth when left fielder Bill Hawes scored for Cincinnati after an error by Dave Rowe on a long fly ball off the bat of Bill Harbridge. The game was marked by a series of exciting rallies, with each club threatening to blow the game open, only to be stifled by timely strikeouts and outstanding defensive plays. The score remained tied until the bottom of the ninth. Harbridge opened with a double to right field. With darkness looming, Fred Dunlap, sensing impending doom for his club, pleaded with the umpire to call the game. Unmoved by his petitions, umpire Harry McCaffery allowed the game to continue. Harbridge was advanced to third on a sacrifice by the next batter, the pitcher McCormick. Catcher Charles Briody hit a ground ball to shortstop Milt Whitehead, and Harbridge, running on contact, raced for home. Whitehead rushed a wild throw that catcher Jack Brennan could not handle and Harbridge scored the winning run, giving the visitors from the Queen City a hard-fought 2–1 victory. The contest was well played, with the circuit's two premier clubs combining for just six errors while McCormick held the vaunted Lucas club to just four hits. Sweeney was less dominant, though he struck out eight Cincinnati batters, including striking out the side in the seventh inning.

Another 4,000 fans showed up to witness the second contest on October 7. The game was similarly close, with Sweeney facing off against George Bradley. St. Louis opened the scoring with two runs in the bottom of the first, thanks to two costly Cincinnati errors. Sweeney was dominant, mowing down the visitors with regularity. He struck out nine on the day while allowing just three hits. Second baseman Sam Crane drove in a run on a single in the bottom of the sixth to cut the St. Louis lead in half, but that was the only blemish on Sweeney's record. The visitors fell by a final score of 2–1 in another hotly contested pitcher's duel. The crafty Bradley allowed just five hits despite striking out zero batters. The series to determine the best club in the circuit had ended in a draw. Cincinnati took game one while St. Louis took game two, each game resulting in a nail-biting 2–1 score.

While the clubs were equals on the field, the financial success of Lucas's club was diametrically opposed to the increasingly sunken costs falling upon Thorner's shoulders. Despite his best efforts to field a strong team, build a fine park, and promote the club in the press, fans had failed to flock to the Union Grounds and support his venture. While Thorner may have wanted to blame the rival AA nine for his club's poor attendance, the two clubs had only played home games in opposition to one another on five occasions. Thorner's nine had trouble grabbing attention from the hotly contested and congested AA pennant race that saw five teams, including Cincinnati, in the mix into October. As a result, Porkopolitans frequented the Red

Stockings' games and displayed apathy towards Thorner's nine. Conversely, in St. Louis, Lucas's club had captured the imagination of the local fans, who came to the park in droves despite the presence of the rival Brown Stockings. Thorner desperately wanted to achieve the success that Lucas was experiencing, but the citizens of Cincinnati did not seem to care about his desires.

The size of the respective markets may have played a role as well. Cincinnati was the eighth-largest city in the country in 1880 with 255,139 people, while St. Louis was the country's sixth-largest with 350,518. This difference of almost 100,000 citizens could very well have explained why the St. Louis market could draw 15,000 to 20,000 folks to the ballpark on a given day to witness the rival AA and UA games. Meanwhile, the very best-attended Red Stocking games were drawing 5,000 fans. The peak combined attendance in Cincinnati occurred on August 10, when the Red Stockings and Unions each played Sunday home games in direct opposition. The game marked the debut of the Cleveland defectors, and the matchup with St. Louis allowed Thorner a rare victory at the gate as 4,105 fans showed up to Union Park. The rival Red Stockings drew an estimated 2,000 fans to witness their 10–6 win over Toledo. On their very best drawing day, a Sunday no less, the two Cincinnati clubs drew just over 6,000 fans to witness the two contests. Despite the Queen City's pedigree as the birthplace of professional baseball, by the 1880s, St. Louis was the superior baseball town. There really was not enough interest to support two clubs in Cincinnati. The poor attendance did not deter Thorner, who continued to gamble that his investment in a first-class nine would pay off in 1885 when he promised to field the best club in the country.

20

◇◇◇◇◇◇◇◇◇◇◇◇◇

The Wild West
and the Race for Third Place

In the afterglow of their surprising victory at St. Louis, Andrew Thompson and his St. Paul nine made the 12-hour journey westward to Kansas City to enter the literal Wild West for a series with Ted Sullivan's ever-changing aggregate. The indefatigable Sullivan had churned through dozens of never-weres and never-will-bes in search of a roster that could at least finish a ball game without setting the ballpark on fire. The keen-eyed Sullivan had taken over the on-field management of the club from Matthew Porter in mid–July after he purchased a half interest in the club from director Americus V. McKim.[1] Sullivan was given complete control over roster moves. The impatient and astute manager set out to find winning ballplayers, who also happened to be unsigned, a Sisyphean task if there ever were one. Virtually every ballplayer who could draw a breath in the summer of 1884 was signed to some club at the major league, minor league, or semi-pro level.

If anyone could accomplish this feat, it was Sullivan. He had been one of baseball's pioneers on the western frontier and later wrote several books detailing his life in baseball. His books provide fascinating insights into the development of professional baseball in the west but are frequently marred by a disturbingly casual racism that is jarring to read. Sullivan knew the western baseball circuit like the back of his hand. His ability to identify diamonds in the rough in the hinterlands of the baseball world was his greatest asset. As skilled as he was at finding talent, his ability to play well with others was his greatest weakness. He had left the dominant St. Louis Unions in June after a dispute over leadership of the club, which was the only reason he was free to cast his lot in Kansas City.

Under Sullivan's guidance, the Kansas City club had not exactly experienced a renaissance. By the end of July, the team's record stood at just 4–28. Thanks to Sullivan's unrelenting scalpel, only one player, 17-year-old Taylor Shafer, remained on the team from the lineup that took the field for the franchise's first game just six weeks before on June 7. Shafer was the younger brother of St. Louis star Orator Shafer, one of the men Sullivan had feuded with in St. Louis. The younger Shafer would only last a couple of more weeks with the club as Sullivan drastically overhauled his lineup week to week. There were two primary reasons for Sullivan's aggressiveness. First, it was both cost-effective and low-risk to bring in players on trial and hope they might produce and cast off anyone who did not. Second, by July, many minor league clubs had started to go under, and many talented players were free to pursue new opportunities. One of the strongest clubs in the Northwestern League, Bay City, went bust on July 22, despite holding a 39–16 record and being in the thick of the pennant race. Their pending disbandment set off a feeding frenzy of sorts, and Sullivan was the prime beneficiary, signing up four men from the club, Jerry Turbidy, Jim Cudworth, Joe Strauss, and James "Jumbo" Davis.[2] Another Northwestern League recruit, 19-year-old catcher Clarence Baldwin, was signed by Sullivan for the seemingly exorbitant sum of $350 per month for the rest of the season.[3] The salary made the teenager the highest-paid player on the team. Baldwin's high salary resulted from his status as a much sought-after catching prospect. Demonstrating the naivete and recklessness that became the hallmarks of his career, Baldwin had signed with Henry Lucas prior to the season, receiving a $200 advance from the magnate.[4] Baldwin had spent 1883 with Quincy of the Northwestern League and had been reserved by that

Ted Sullivan had a well-earned reputation as one of the finest organizers and team builders of the era. From the 1870s to the 1910s, Sullivan organized leagues, managed teams, scouted players, and acted as a raconteur, writing several books documenting the development of baseball in the western United States (courtesy Southern Illinois University Press).

club. He re-signed with Quincy but also wrote a letter to Lucas claiming he had not signed. Baldwin chose to remain with Quincy rather than face banishment as part of the National Agreement. A seemingly remorseful Baldwin wrote another letter to Lucas offering to pay $200 debt once he started drawing a salary.[5] Baldwin remained with Quincy until August, earning a blacklist from the Northwestern League when he jumped to Sullivan's Kansas City nine. Reports surfaced that he still owed the outstanding debt to Lucas, who apparently forgave the youngster as a favor to his friend Sullivan. Shortly after signing with Kansas City, Baldwin was arrested one morning for outstanding debts in Quincy and then spent the afternoon at a house of ill repute.[6] Baldwin, known colloquially as "Kid," was summed up thusly by the Quincy newspapers: "The Kid is a bad egg."[7]

Baldwin provided much-needed stability to Kansas City's wonky pitching staff despite his unsavory off-field reputation. Sullivan had heretofore supplied the pitcher's box with a never-ending series of swift throwing amateurs that had caught his eye. The club's staff was aided significantly by the addition of Baldwin's Quincy battery mate, Bob Black, who joined the club in mid–August upon the disbandment of the Illinois nine. Black assumed the role of ace, posting a modest 4–9 record across 123 innings of work with a steady 3.22 ERA and 88 ERA+. While none of these marks were particularly impressive, Black boasted strikeout potential with decent control, as his 6.8 K/9 and 5.47 K/BB ratios attest. Black's four victories tied Ernie Hickman for the team lead, and though he would never play in the majors again, he enjoyed a lengthy minor league career that lasted until 1903.

Sullivan further raided the corpses of the decomposing Quincy roster, signing another battery in pitcher "Stooping" Jack Gorman and catcher Pat Sullivan. His greatest find was the battery of William Walter "Peek-A-Boo" Veach and catcher Harry Decker. The pair joined K.C. in late August after the disbandment of the Northwestern League's Evansville franchise, which had joined the circuit on July 30, won four of five games, and promptly disbanded on August 4. Veach was a talented young twirler from Indianapolis. He made 12 starts for K.C., posting a 3–9 record, with 2.42 ERA and a solid 117 ERA+ in 104 innings of work. Veach earned his unique moniker of "Peek-A-Boo" thanks to manager Sullivan, who had set up signals to designate pick-off plays for Veach when a runner was on base. The inexperienced Veach made such an obvious and detectable show of waiting for, observing, and implementing the signals, that opposition players took note of it and bestowed him with the nickname.[8]

Catcher Harry Decker could have an entire autobiography written about him thanks to his fascinating double life. Decker was a talented ballplayer from Lockport, Illinois, whose promising career was derailed by his penchant for bigamy, contract jumping, and forgery. His baseball career stalled out by the age of 26 in 1891, having appeared for six different major league teams. Decker also invented and patented a padded catcher's mitt in 1887, ostensibly the same technology used to this day. While the design should have made Decker wealthy, he was an impatient man and sold the rights to the patent for $50 to Al Spalding's sporting goods company.[9] Decker was also credited with inventing a new kind of turnstile, which became the standard for ballparks, fairgrounds, and racetracks. However, one report has him ripping off the design after stealing a turnstile from the Philadelphia Phillies' ballpark.[10] Decker's post-baseball career was filled with a litany of criminal activities, including theft and forgery. At the same time, he demonstrated the womanizing tendencies that had earned him the nickname the "Don Juan of the Diamond."[11] Decker served time in insane asylums and prisons, often using the alias Earle Henry Davenport. Decker often claimed to have gone insane either after a blow to the head during his time as a catcher or after he was kicked in the head by a horse.[12] One of his prison records even notes that he had first been institutionalized in 1883 when his baseball career had just started. His ability to charm others combined with an unrelenting hubris bordering on psychopathy was astonishing. The man could spin a sob story, win the heart of a wealthy dowager, and once even earned early release from prison by faking tuberculosis. After a stint in San Quentin, where he played for the prison baseball team, he was released in 1915. At this point, he vanished from history. Despite the persistent efforts of numerous talented researchers, including Peter Morris, the veritable expert on the subject of Decker, his whereabouts remain unknown. It was once said about him, "he changes his name each time he boards a train."[13]

Sullivan's team had shown a modicum of improvement with the additions of Decker, Baldwin, Black, and Veach. Sullivan made further changes to his squad in the aftermath of the Union Association's own dysfunction. He signed pitcher Jersey Bakley, shortstop Jimmy Say, and second baseman Charlie Bastian after Wilmington folded. The collapse of Pittsburgh and their merger with Baltimore made both Lou Say and Joe Ellick free agents, and they joined the K.C. squad. The additions had paid off with improved performance, and October would see the club actually post a positive run differential while compiling a 5–6–1 record in 12 fall contests. By the close of the season, Sullivan's squad had used an astonishing 51 players. Quite literally, the fans in Kansas City were rooting for laundry.

Despite K.C.'s generally poor on-field play and constant changeover of the roster, the club had won the affections of the locals. The club drew modest crowds of 500–1,000 for their weekday games but thrived on Sundays with attendances ranging from 5,000 to 8,000. Some reports even boasted of 10,000 fans in attendance at the Sabbath games. These raucous Sunday contests earned the local fan base a reputation for wildness, intensity, and exuberance that made opposing players uncomfortable. Boston Union manager-turned-sportswriter Tim Murnane later recounted an incident during one of these contests:

DECKER, C., Philadelphias

OLD JUDGE
CIGARETTE FACTORY.
GOODWIN & CO., New York.

The troubled Earle Harry Decker was a talented catcher whose promising career was derailed by his frequent run-ins with the law. He was a bigamist, a check forger, and a thief; his knack for getting into trouble was matched by his ability to talk his way out of it. He served time at San Quentin State Prison in California, where he starred for their baseball team. Upon his release in 1915, he disappeared and his final resting place remains undiscovered (Library of Congress).

I remember an occurrence in the fall of '84. The Boston Unions were playing a Sunday game in Kansas City. There was a tremendous crowd present and among the rest were several cowboys. A dispute delayed the game and the cowboys became a little anxious.

Bang! Bang! Went a revolver in one corner of the field–the cowboys' salute.

[Catcher Lew] Brown got nervous, turned pale, came to me and said:

"Say, for goodness' sake give them anything they want—Bang! Bang!—Or we will all be shot before we get through."[14]

Financially, the club was one of three that was clearing a profit alongside St. Louis and Washington. The contrasting approaches of Lucas and his high-budgeted dream team versus the frugal acquisition of ball-playing marginalia by Scanlon and Sullivan proved that there was more than one way to make money in this game.

Sullivan's club was playing its best baseball of the season as the series with St. Paul began. On October 8, just 300 fans in heavy overcoats showed up to the Athletic Park for the opening contest on a freezing cold afternoon. St. Paul won their second straight game with a 9–5 victory. The St. Paul lineup showed a rare display of hitting acumen, battering K.C. pitcher Jersey Bakley, making four runs in the second inning, and necessitating his replacement in the third by Barney McLaughlin. Bakley was released by Sullivan after the contest, bringing to an end a tumultuous season for the 20-year-old Bakley. He led the UA in losses, earned runs, wild pitches, and walks while seeing action for Philadelphia, Wilmington, and Kansas City. After several years in the minor leagues, Bakley re-emerged as the ace for Cleveland of the American Association in 1888, winning 25 games against 33 losses. Bakley stayed with the club after their move to the National League in 1889 and defected to the city's awful Players' League franchise in 1890. He is one of just 19 men to appear in four different major leagues. He also holds the unbreakable record of appearing in three different leagues in three consecutive seasons while representing the same city.

The clubs met the following day in front of another modest crowd of 500. This time the home club took the contest cruising to an easy 7–2 victory highlighted by Peek-A-Boo Veach's 11 strikeouts. The clubs met again on October 12 in front of a much larger Sunday crowd of 5,000. The series' final contest was a sloppy one, with the two clubs combining for 20 errors. Neither side was to capitalize on the other's defensive shortcomings. After St. Paul scored and tied the game 4–4 in the ninth inning, the contest was called due to darkness. With the cancellation of the St. Paul-Milwaukee series requested by the Milwaukee directors due to cold weather, the Minnesotans traveled back to St. Louis for one final contest to close the season.

On October 13, St. Paul arrived in St. Louis after a 12-hour journey from Kansas City. The exhausted nine was handily defeated by a score of 14–1 in seven innings by a motivated St. Louis nine. The home club was eager to atone for their 1–0 loss to the visitors the week prior. Their final game now completed, St. Paul's final record stood at 2–6–1. The club returned home to Minnesota minus Billy O'Brien, who had signed with Kansas City. It was reported that Andrew Thompson's crew had lost money on the year. However, the losses were primarily incurred during their time in the Northwestern League, where they had frequently played in tiny markets that could not pay out guarantees.[15] The premature close to the season ended the career of the most enigmatic franchise in major league history. They are the only major league club to play entirely on the road, and the state of Minnesota had to wait until April 21, 1961, to host their first major league home game.

While the UA's Northwestern League additions ended their seasons early, the remaining six clubs completed their schedules over the season's final week. The league's eastern nines each traveled westward to complete their schedules by October 19. First and second place were already decided, with St. Louis taking the crown and red-hot Cincinnati entrenched in second. However, by winning percentage, Milwaukee's 8–4 record gave them a slight edge at .667 to .647. Boston and Baltimore were embroiled in a close race to determine third place. Thanks to the scheduling turmoil caused by the disbandment of four different clubs, neither club ended up playing a full 112 game schedule on the season. Boston faced an uphill battle in their quest for third, as their remaining contests would come against Cincinnati and St. Louis. Baltimore was slated to appear in Cincinnati for a three-game set concluding on October 16.

Boston's series in Cincinnati had begun with a surprisingly high-scoring contest on October 9, with each team's respective ace, Jim McCormick and Dupee Shaw, unable to reign in the opposition. The result was a 10–6 victory for the home team. Baltimore lost their contest in Milwaukee the same day, and Boston remained three games back in the standings with a 55–47–2 record to Baltimore's 57–43–1 record. Baltimore lost their contest on October 10 by a score of 5–1, while Boston had an off-day allowing them to gain a half-game in the standings. Cincinnati had traveled to Nashville to play two contests against the newly formed pro club in that city, the Americans, on October 10 and 11, resulting in two victories for the Queen City nine. In a rare occurrence, Boston was credited with a forfeit victory as the road team on October 11 since the home club failed to appear for the scheduled home game. It is unclear why Cincinnati double-booked themselves to play in Nashville and Cincinnati on the same day. Still, the forfeit victory failed to gain Boston any ground in the standings, as Baltimore took an 8–5 decision over Milwaukee.

On Sunday, October 12, both Boston and Baltimore lost, by scores of 11–5 and 5–2, respectively. The Sunday contest in Cincinnati is most noteworthy for the brilliant feat accomplished by Boston's star rookie Ed "Cannonball" Crane. Prior to the game, it was announced that Crane would attempt to break the record for the longest throw, currently held by former Cincinnati Red Stocking outfielder John Hatfield, who had set the mark with a throw of 133 yards, 1 foot and 7¼ inches (400 feet, 7¼ inches) on October 15, 1872. Nearly 12 years to the day in the same city where Hatfield had first made his fame, Crane would attempt to break the record. Some claimed Crane was the longest thrower in the profession. His friends back in Boston had boasted that he could beat the record for the right amount of cash.[16] In the moments before the contest began in front of over 1,600 fans at the Union Grounds, Crane made his attempt. The *Cincinnati Enquirer* described the effort:

> The distance scored by Hatfield was first staked off from the home plate in a direct line to center field, and a stake driven in that ground. Crane took his position in deep center field and threw in toward the building. The ball was so much veered about by the wind, which in that position was against him a little, that it was impossible to judge the throw accurately. After making three attempts in this position, Crane changed his base to left field, and made three more throws, the last of which was the longest. As it was now time to call the game, stakes were driven in the ground at the point where he stood, and also where the ball landed on the fly.[17]

The distance was measured after the contest under the supervision of two city surveyors, who each confirmed that Crane's toss had bested the mark set by Hatfield.[18] Crane's throw was officially measured at 135 yards and seven inches (405 feet 7 inches). Crane had made the throw under the same conditions as Hatfield by throwing across the wind. The feat was declared as the new record in newspapers nationwide. Strangely, in the years following the throw, Hatfield's mark remained the official one, with Crane's listed as unofficial. Crane had used the Union Association Wright & Ditson baseball, which was lighter than that thrown by Hatfield. Some old-timers believed that since Crane used a lighter ball, his record was not legitimate.[19] Regardless of that fact, on October 12, 1884, Crane was the champion thrower in the world of baseball.

The performance of Crane in 1884 was nothing less than exceptional. The 22-year-old rookie had begun play on the Boston sandlots. He was easily the finest player on the Unions, providing tremendous offense and versatility. At this point in his career, Crane was an exceptional athlete. He played five positions for Boston that season: right field, left field, catcher, first base, and pitcher. If a Rookie of the Year award existed in the Union Association, Crane would have been a prime candidate. His primary rivals would have been the Keystones' baby-faced outfielder Buster Hoover, and Washington outfielder Henry Moore. The powerful Crane finished second in the league with 12 home runs and posted a .285/.308/.451 line, good for a team-high 152 OPS+. This mark was good for fifth place in the league. He also finished in the top ten in virtually every offensive category. Defensively, his powerful throwing arm enabled him to throw out 21 runners in just 57 games in the outfield. It wasn't all roses, as he was a significant liability behind the plate, pacing the league in errors with 64 and allowing 69 passed balls in just 42 games. Crane struggled for the next few seasons, failing to replicate his offensive prowess. He eventually transitioned to the pitcher's box and earned a certain level of stardom with the New York Giants later in the decade. His career soon unraveled due to a penchant for the high life. His skills eroded due to overeating and alcoholism, and he was out of the majors by 1893. Failing to resuscitate his career, he spiraled deeper into the bottle and was found dead in a Rochester hotel of a suspected drug overdose on September 20, 1896, at the age of 34.

In the afterglow of Crane's remarkable throwing feat, Boston and Cincinnati played one more contest to complete their series on October 13. The contest pitted George Bradley against Boston's Tommy McCarthy. The 20-year-old McCarthy was used as an outfielder primarily but saw time in the pitchers' box after the release of the club's number two pitcher James Burke in mid–September. Burke's departure had come as something of a shock. He had pitched over 300 innings for the club and won 19 games with a 2.85 ERA and 106 ERA+. Burke had something of a meltdown during a 13–4 loss to Cincinnati on September 15. The temperamental pitcher became upset when Crane, who was catching that day, failed to throw the ball back to him in the desired location. Rather than attempt to catch the ball, Burke stood in the pitcher's box sullenly, letting the ball go into the field. This all happened with runners on base, mind you, and it happened not once but twice. Two Cincinnati runs scored as a result. Manager Tim Murnane was appalled by Burke's actions and released him after the contest. In turn, Murnane leaned heavily on Shaw and tried to spell his star with McCarthy. The youngster was another of Murnane's local Boston finds, joining the club on July 10 after working as a piano mover in his hometown.

The diminutive McCarthy was in the early stages of what would eventually turn into an excellent major league career. To date, he is the only Union Association player to make the Baseball Hall of Fame. His induction is problematic for Cooperstown enthusiasts as McCarthy is almost universally regarded as the worst player to receive the honor. His career numbers pale in comparison to virtually every other player in the Hall. McCarthy is thought to have earned induction because of his role as one of "the Heavenly Twins" alongside Hugh Duffy on the famed 1890s Boston Beaneaters. The duo was elected together in 1946. McCarthy also had a reputation as an exceptional baseball mind, being credited by John Ward as the inventor of the hit-and-run play and the outfield trap while also being adept at sign stealing.[20]

CRANE, P., New Yorks
OLD JUDGE
CIGARETTE FACTORY.
GOODWIN & CO., New York.

Ed Crane was a great all-around athlete, whose tremendous throwing arm enabled him to set a world's record for the longest throw on October 12, 1884, before his Boston Unions faced off against Cincinnati. Crane enjoyed a wonderful rookie season in the UA, hitting 12 home runs and posting a 152 OPS+. He later made his mark as a star hurler for the New York Giants at the end of the decade (Library of Congress).

The great irony of McCarthy's induction is that he was arguably the worst regular player in the Union Association during his rookie year. McCarthy posted -1.0 offensive WAR thanks to his .215/.237/.244 batting line and 62 OPS+ in 53 games. In 48 appearances in the outfield, McCarthy posted another -0.3 defensive WAR, fielding .794 against a league average of .816. As a pitcher, McCarthy made seven appearances, losing all seven contests. He compiled a 4.82 ERA and 63 ERA+ and another -1.4 WAR on the mound. That gave McCarthy a combined WAR of -2.7 in just 53 games. Several UA pitchers would exceed this mark on the year, notably Jersey Bakley, who brought up the rear with a -5.3 WAR for his pitching efforts. Seventeen-year-old teammate Mike Slattery gave McCarthy a run for his money posting a -2.4

offensive WAR, though his total was achieved in 106 contests. Somewhat unexpectedly, Slattery too would emerge as starting outfielder on a pennant winner later in the decade with the 1888 New York Giants alongside his old teammate Ed Crane. The common denominator for both men was that they were exceptional athletes. Slattery stood an impressive 6'2" and 210 pounds while McCarthy would later lead the league in stolen bases. Murnane likely gave both youngsters ample playing time because their athleticism hinted at untapped ball-playing ability, not unlike the toolsy prospects of today, who get extra chances due to their raw athleticism.

For the October 13 contest, McCarthy displayed his customary futility, allowing 15 total runs on ten hits and nine errors by his defense while blowing an eight-run second inning lead. His pitching rival George Bradley also had a rough outing allowing 11 Boston runs on 17 hits and nine errors by his defense. The loss combined with an off day for Baltimore left the club three games behind their rival, as Baltimore headed to the Queen City for a three-game series while Boston traveled to St. Louis. On October 14, Baltimore was shutout 8–0 by Jim McCormick in Cincinnati. Boston called on Dupee Shaw to face off against his fellow defector Charlie Sweeney to open their final series in St. Louis. Shaw, who had dazzled hitters earlier in his tenure in Boston, would be called upon to start all four games in the St. Louis series. Neither McCarthy nor Crane had been able to spell "the Wizard." Ever since the surprising release of Burke on September 15, the Boston nine had entered a tailspin, and Shaw's performance had lagged accordingly. They had won just seven of 20 contests since Burke's dismissal, including the forfeited victory on October 11, taking the club from a record of 50–35 to 56–49. This stretch

Twenty-year-old Tommy McCarthy's inauspicious rookie season in the Union Association marked him as one of the worst players in the circuit. Despite the slow start to his career, he became one of baseball's biggest stars, first with the champion St. Louis Brown Stockings and later for the dominant Boston Beaneaters in the 1890s. McCarthy's role as one half of "the Heavenly Twins," alongside Hugh Duffy, was the main catalyst for his Hall of Fame induction in 1946. To date, he is the only UA player in the Hall of Fame and is considered one of its weakest inductees (Library of Congress).

had included being on the wrong end of a surprising four-game sweep in Kansas City at the end of September. A tired Shaw had started 12 of the last 19 games, with uneven results. On this day, Shaw struck out nine men and allowed just six hits, but thanks to sloppy defense by first baseman Tim Murnane and third baseman John Irwin, his effort was wasted. The pair combined for five costly errors while St. Louis scored seven runs, six of them unearned. Charlie Sweeney struck out 11 batters, as his defense accounted for nine errors, but Boston only tallied five runs, and the result was a 7–5 defeat for the visitors.

On October 15, Baltimore played Cincinnati in what turned out to be the final regular-season game for both clubs as the October 16 contest was called off due to weather. The home nine took a tightly contested 5–4 victory, with George Bradley hanging on for the one-run victory after Baltimore rallied from a five-run deficit to get within one. Cincinnati finished the season with a 69–36 record and a firm grip on second place. The cancellation of the October 16 game clinched a third-place finish for Baltimore, leaving Boston with little to play for but pride. Meanwhile, the Queen City nine would close out their season with a series of exhibition contests. Two would come against the American Association's Louisville Colonels on October 18 and 19. They would also play two more games on October 21 and 22 against St. Louis in a return matchup for their series in Mound City earlier in the month.

Baltimore's season had come to a close with a somewhat disappointing 58–47–1 record. The Marylanders had held second place for three straight months from June 8 to September 8. An 11 game losing streak from August 27 to September 11, which included a four-game sweep by the ascendant Cincinnati club, knocked them out of position and into the battle for third with Boston. The expected boost they were to have received from merging with the Chicago-Pittsburgh franchise failed to produce victories. Bill Sweeney's early-season dominance diminished due to overwork, while newcomer Al Atkinson was inconsistent. Baltimore was also thoroughly outplayed by the league's strongest clubs. Baltimore won just one of 15 contests against St. Louis and just four of 10 against Cincinnati.

In a somewhat ignominious end to the season, it was reported that the "Baltimore Union nine were cut adrift in this city without the payment of their last month's salary. Henderson owed the nine about $700. Several of the duped players borrowed money with which to get out of town."[21] This sudden disbandment brought Albert H. Henderson's baseball syndicate to a forgettable close, with both his clubs having gone kaput. He lost a reported $12,000 on the venture. O.P. Caylor offered his thoughts on Henderson, "We warned the public and base ball players early in the year against Henderson. It has always been his principle to claim more than he is able to accomplish."[22] Caylor's harsh words aside, Henderson was understandably disappointed with the outcome and left the world of baseball for good. He turned his ample creativity towards the world of invention. In 1885, he helped create the technology that allowed Baltimore's first electric streetcar line to function and later earned his medical license.[23]

Two games were scheduled for the season's final day on October 19. Boston would face off against St. Louis while Kansas City would host Washington. Eight thousand were in attendance in St. Louis for another Sunday affair at the Lucas grounds. Motivated by the large crowd, Boston's Dupee Shaw was at his best, summoning whatever strength remained in his barely mobile left arm. "The Wizard" dazzled one more time, allowing just four hits to the powerful Lucas club, while his two-run double in the fourth inning of Charlie Sweeney gave him some breathing room. Boston played one of their finest games of the season and won the day by a score of 5–0.

Another throwing contest was arranged to take place before the game. Ed Crane was called upon to see if he could top his throw of the previous week.[24] Lucas and Murnane had bet $50 that Crane could beat 135 yards on his toss.[25] Despite his best efforts, Crane fell short of his previous mark. His longest toss came in at 134 yards and five inches, and Lucas and Murnane were out $50.[26] The throw was still impressive, though, as he topped the Hatfield mark once again. After the game, Boston's record stood at 58–51–2, two games back of Baltimore, but now tied with their rivals in the win column. St. Louis finished the season with an astonishing 94–19–1 mark and a .832 winning percentage, still the highest mark of any pennant winner in baseball history. Twelve hours away in Kansas City, the home club laid the boots to a demoralized Washington Nationals in front of 5,000 raucous fans. Kansas City won 12–1 behind a superb pitching performance by future Chicago ace Bill Hutchison, who took home his first major league victory. The victory brought their record to 16–63–3, while the Washington loss put their final mark at 47–65–2. Little did anyone realize at the time, but the games on October 19 would be the final official contests in Union Association history.

21

◇◇◇◇◇◇◇◇◇◇◇◇◇

The Associations Face Off

Justus Thorner had the utmost faith in his ball club as the members of the Louisville club came to town for their exhibition series on October 18–19. Thorner's nine had outperformed every club in the Union Association down the stretch. They had traveled to St. Louis earlier in the month and split an incredibly close two-game series with the eventual pennant winners. The upcoming contests would be history-making as they marked the first contests between a Union Association club and an American Association club. Louisville agreed to play exhibition contests against three UA clubs, Cincinnati, Kansas City, and St. Louis, to close out their season and earn extra cash. The chairman of the National Agreement arbitration committee, A.G. Mills, expressed his disapproval of Louisville's plan to play Union clubs, but he could do little to stop it. The club's player contracts had ended on October 15. Even though their players were still reserved for 1885, they were no longer under contract and the authority of the National Agreement.

Under the guidance of Mike Walsh, Louisville had just completed a surprising season. The Kentuckians finished in third place with an excellent 68–40 record while remaining in the pennant hunt until late in the season. The club was led by their supremely versatile hurler, Guy Hecker. The native of Youngsville, Pennsylvania, completed an incredible season, leading the American Association in virtually every major pitching category. This included wins (52), ERA (1.80), appearances (75), games started (73), complete games (72), innings pitched (670.2), strikeouts (385), batters faced (2649), ERA+ (171) and WHIP (0.868). At the bat, he also excelled, posting a batting line of .297/.323/.430 for an OPS+ of 148. His combined WAR of 17.8 on the season is the fifth-best total of all time, while his 52 wins rank only behind Old Hoss Radbourn (59) and John Clarkson (53). Hecker would famously capture a batting title in 1886 with a .341 average becoming the first and only pitcher ever to accomplish such a feat. Louisville's other superstar was Pete Browning, a hard-hitting and poor fielding third baseman who would soon be moved permanently to the outfield, where his struggles in fighting fly balls earned him the nickname "Gladiator." Browning was one of baseball's greatest hitters and most enduring characters. His career .341 batting average is the highest of any eligible player not in the Baseball Hall of Fame. Famously particular about his bats, Browning sought a young cabinetmaker named John Andrew "Bud" Hillerich to craft his willows. The Louisville Slugger was born, named after the famed hitter.[1] At this point in his career, he was 23 years old and had won the first American Association batting title as a rookie in 1882. He was coming off another strong season with a batting line of .336/.347/.472 for an OPS+ of 173. The club's lineup possessed substantial depth, with both John "Monk" Cline and Jimmy "Chicken" Wolf, each posting an OPS+ over 130. The club's only weak link was first baseman George "Jumbo" Latham, who batted a paltry .169/.197/.198 in 77 games at first base. The team's offense produced a 107 OPS+, good for third in the league, but their greatest strengths were pitching and defense. The Colonels posted a 142 ERA+, the best of any staff, and paced the league in defensive efficiency (.670) and fielding percentage (.912). By comparison, the Cincinnati Unions had a 109 OPS+, good for second in the league amongst teams completing a full schedule. The Unions posted a 138 ERA+, also the league's second-best mark. Defensively, they were second in the UA in defensive efficiency (.632) and fielding percentage (.882). Louisville was likely the strongest club that Cincinnati had faced all season, only rivaled by Lucas's superb outfit.

Because of the prohibition that prevented clubs in the National Agreement from playing against Union Association nines, the Union clubs played precious few games against non–Union competitors. Before the season began, several clubs outside the National Agreement were threatened with punishment if they agreed to play games against Union clubs. Namely, they would be prevented from playing lucrative contests against clubs in the agreement. These threats led to the cancellation of several planned games between lower minor league and semi-pro clubs and Union entrants.[2] Thus, there is scant evidence of how the UA nines stacked up against clubs outside their jurisdiction.

Only a few semi-pro clubs took the chance of playing against UA clubs. In April, the Philadelphia Keystones played two contests against the local Foley amateur club, winning handily by scores of 12–4 and 21–6.[3] The Foleys featured second baseman Elias Peak, who later joined the Keystones and had a long minor league career. The Keystones split a two-game set against an independent club in Richmond, Virginia, on June 4–5, losing the first game 11–9 and winning the second 6–2.[4] The club also played a contest against the Chester, Pennsylvania, club on June 17. Chester had started the season in the Keystone Association before becoming an independent club. The team played a one-off contest in front of 100 fans in Chester against the Keystones and won 7–1.[5] The Chester club featured several Philadelphia semi-pros, including future Orioles outfielder William "Lefty" Johnson, and Joseph Wiley, who would each see brief Union Association action in the following weeks. That they could defeat the Keystones says a lot about the quality of the Keystones. Though in defense of Philadelphia, they used an unproven 18-year-old amateur from Philadelphia named Al Maul as their starter in that game. Maul was not ready for prime time or whatever a June 1884 exhibition game in Chester might be called. He would later enjoy a long major league career as a pitcher for numerous clubs. The Chester club also faced off against the Wilmingtons on September 13, losing the final game in Wilmington's history by a score of 7–3.[6]

The Portsmouth Athletic Association, a Virginia semi-professional club, regularly entertained visiting UA clubs throughout the season. The Portsmouth club played host to the Washington Nationals, the Kansas City Unions, the Baltimore Unions, the Chicago Unions, the Keystones, and the Cincinnati Unions.[7] The club featured no future major league players and compiled a 1–8 record against Union clubs while being outscored 92–29. Their only victory came against Baltimore on August 12. The game was a controversial affair that saw the local scorer miscount the number of Portsmouth runs. After the contest, the locals petitioned the scorer to change the tally, turning a Baltimore extra-inning win into a Portsmouth regulation victory.[8] A final exhibition contest took place between the Kansas City Unions and a top-flight St. Louis semi-pro club, the Prickly Ash Bitters, on October 26. The game was the final one played by a Union club in 1884 and ended in a 1–1 tie.[9] The Ash Bitters featured several players with major league experience, including Thomas Gorman, Harry Decker, and John Peters. The limited evidence suggests that the Union clubs (save for the Keystones) were generally a cut above the local semi-pro outfits, though a fine pitching performance by the home nine or a lackadaisical effort by the visitors could make things competitive. The Louisville contests would give a better indication of the actual quality of the Union Association.

Game one saw Guy Hecker pitted against Jim McCormick in what promised to be a close contest. Louisville opened the scoring in the bottom of the first. Pete Browning struck out to lead off the inning. Chicken Wolf hit a weak grounder to second baseman Sam Crane, which he fumbled, allowing Wolf to reach base. Hecker hit a double that was misplayed by Dick Burns in center field, allowing Wolf to score and Hecker to reach third. A passed ball by catcher Charles Briody scored Hecker to give the visitors a 2–0 lead. McCormick walked Joe Gerhardt, but Monk Cline hit a fielder's choice, and catcher Dan Sullivan struck out to close the inning. The lead remained 2–0 until the fourth when Dick Burns singled and reached second on a passed ball by catcher Sullivan. Lou Sylvester hit a hard single to right field that drove Burns home, making the score 2–1. Sylvester stole second but was caught in a rundown between second and third thanks to a nice pickoff throw by Hecker. Bill Harbridge walked, and McCormick singled to put runners on first and second. Briody's sacrifice hit put runners on second and third with two out. Hecker snuffed out the rally by striking out Elmer Cleveland. A series of Cincinnati errors in the fifth inning allowed Louisville to increase their lead. Browning hit a hard line drive for a one-out double. First baseman Mox McQuery made a terrible muff, dropping a throw from shortstop Jack Glasscock on a grounder by Wolf. Hecker hit a bloop single over second base that scored Browning. "Move Up" Joe Gerhardt lived up to his nickname and drove home Hecker with a single. Monk Cline drove in another run on a single to make the score 5–1. Hecker was not at his best, allowing ten hits on the day, but worked out of jams and snuffed out late rallies in the final two innings, holding on for a final score of 5–3. The *Cincinnati Enquirer* noted that the Union club looked nervous, and their defensive play cost them the game, with only League veteran Jack Glasscock displaying his usual poise.[10] On a positive note, Cincinnati showed a surprising ability to hit Hecker, and it was only their failure to get a timely hit with men on base that prevented them from completing their rally. One thousand six hundred fans attended the historic contest. It was written that the game was played honestly, with none of the players appearing to be hippodroming or giving a lesser effort.[11]

Game two took place on October 19, in front of over 2,500 fans, who flocked to the park to watch the fall Sunday matchup. The contest saw a rematch of the previous day's starting pitchers, with Hecker and McCormick in the box once again. Rooney Sweeney, the former catcher for the Baltimore Unions, was enlisted to catch Hecker in place of the regular catcher Dan Sullivan. Despite it being his first time catching Hecker, Sweeney demonstrated considerable skill in handling the pitcher's deliveries. The contest opened with Louisville at the bat. Browning hit a single to center to open the game. Browning tried to steal second, and Briody's throw beat the runner, but the ordinarily reliable Jack Glasscock dropped the throw. Chicken Wolf's sacrifice moved Browning over to third, and McCormick's wild pitch allowed the runner to score the contest's opening tally. Once again, the nerves of the Unions were getting them in trouble. The experienced McCormick bore down and escaped the inning. Cincinnati tied the game in the bottom of the third. Mox McQuery reached first on a wild throw by Phil Reccius, the Louisville third sacker. Sam Crane, Cincinnati's player-manager, hit a ground ball that led to a force out at second and a near double play, but first baseman Wally Andrews dropped the throw, allowing Crane to reach safely. Crane stole second and was driven home on a hard hit Jack Glasscock grounder that Joe Gerhardt could not handle.

The home club blew the game open in the fourth inning with "a great show of red-legged men skinning around the bags."[12] Bill Hawes opened the inning with a single. Bill Harbridge hit an easy ground ball to Gerhardt that took a funny bounce over the first baseman's head, putting runners on first and second. Jim McCormick helped his cause with a single driving in Hawes. Catcher Briody followed with another hit that drove home Harbridge. The score was now 3–1, and Hecker caught McCormick napping at second base, but his wild throw allowed his rival to advance to third. McCormick scored the fourth run on another wild throw by Hecker, who was fielding a bunt off the bat of Elmer Cleveland. McQuery hit a grounder to third, and Reccius threw home to catch the slow-footed Briody, but his toss was wild, and the score was now 5–1. McQuery reached third base on the play and scored on a sacrifice out. The score was now 6–1. Cincinnati scored another run in the inning, but the existing game account does not explain how. Thanks to timely hitting and a cavalcade of Louisville muffs, the home team now had a commanding 7–1 lead. Cincinnati added another run in the eighth inning, with McQuery scoring on a Sam Crane single. Louisville continually threatened to mount a comeback, thanks to several Cincinnati errors, but could not hit McCormick, who allowed just four hits on the day. The final score stood 8–1.

For Justus Thorner, the contest was sweet validation. His club of wreckers and outcasts had defeated one of the strongest clubs in the country. It had made a mockery of the deliveries of the top pitcher in the American Association. Guy Hecker, who was no doubt in a weakened state, having thrown nearly 700 innings on the season, proved eminently hittable, allowing 21 base hits across the two contests, including 11 in the day's loss. McCormick, by contrast, was only nearing 600 innings on the season. On this day, Big Jim demonstrated the skill that had made him one of the top pitchers in baseball. In his two-and-a-half months in Cincinnati, he was equally effective, pacing the Union circuit in ERA (1.54), ERA+ (213), WHIP (0.786), and hits allowed per nine innings (6.5). With McCormick in the box, the Cincinnati Unions were one of the best clubs in the country in October 1884. Even the *Cincinnati Commercial*, which had railed all season long against the usurpers, presented an utterly mundane account of the contest, failing to make anything even resembling a jab against the Union Association.[13] Silence was as good as praise in this case.

Thorner's club now prepared for a two-game exhibition return set against St. Louis in the Mound City. The contests were slated for October 21–22 and would close the Cincinnati season. In appreciation for the exemplary efforts by his nine over the season's final months, Thorner feted his team on October 20 with a carriage ride through the streets of Cincinnati, which included a stop to horse racing grounds at Chester Park and a visit to the city's workhouse.[14] The day was completed with an informal reception and dinner, all expenses paid by the grateful Thorner, who undoubtedly hoped the generosity would inspire his team to victory against his friend and rival Henry Lucas.[15]

The opening contest on October 21 saw Jim McCormick match wits with Charlie Sweeney. St. Louis went to bat in the top of the first, with "Sure Shot" Fred Dunlap leading off. Dunlap demonstrated his continued dominance, nailing a pitch off his former teammate into deep right-center field for an inside-the-park home run. Orator Shafer followed with a bloop single to left field. Dave Rowe tripled to left and scored Shafer. Rowe tried to score on a Fred Lewis sac fly to left field to Bill Hawes. The leftfielder fielded the ball cleanly and fired a strong throw home to catcher Briody, who tagged out Rowe and completed the double play. McCormick settled down and struck out Henry Boyle to end the inning. The two runs would be all that Sweeney needed as he pitched an exquisite game, allowing just five hits while striking out four hitters. McCormick managed to settle down and allowed only five more hits the rest of the way, but the damage was done in the top of the first. The victory gave St. Louis a two games to one edge in their exhibition series, as the clubs had split the two games in St. Louis earlier in the month. The contest also marked the first time Cincinnati had been shut out since the debut of the Cleveland trio on August 10. Since their debut, the two evenly matched rivals had split their four contests. Before their defection, Cincinnati had gone just 3–12 against Lucas's club, which points to how vastly improved the club was with Glasscock at shortstop, McCormick in the box, and Briody behind the plate. Not surprisingly, the addition of two Hall of Fame caliber players in their primes made their club much better. Briody had done well, too, hitting .337/.344/.404 for a 139 OPS+ while posting an astonishing 1.5 defensive WAR in just 22 games at catcher. It seems likely that the numbers might overstate his defensive contributions, but he had proven his worth to Cincinnati.

The two clubs were set to face off on October 22, but cold and rainy weather caused the game's cancellation and concluded the season for Thorner's nine. It was announced that Sam Crane, the club's player-manager, had signed a contract with the Indianapolis club of the American Association for the 1885 season. Crane had been a free agent when he signed with Cincinnati. Since the American Association had not blacklisted him, he was free to sign with another club once his Union contract had ended.

Crane had come to Cincinnati after suffering an injury with the New York Metropolitans in May. He was released by New York and signed with Cincinnati without penalty, soon emerging as a much-needed leader on the club, which had struggled under Dan O'Leary. The incumbent O'Leary was a talented raconteur and organizer but a questionable leader of men, as liable to get drunk with his men as discipline them. O'Leary had come to the club after a dispute with the directors of the Indianapolis club in the offseason. O'Leary had managed the team as an independent club in 1883, reputed to be the best-unaffiliated nine in the west.[16] After a pre-season blacklisting by Indianapolis, he was signed by Thorner to act as a player-manager. Under his guidance, the Unions had gone a disappointing 20–15. Amidst rumors of his drinking and gambling on games, he was let go.[17] It did not help that he missed time with a bout of malaria, likely code for a social disease since O'Leary was not one known for restraint.[18] One oft-told yarn about O'Leary's tenure with Cincinnati had him sending a small boy to fetch a pitcher of beer for him after a game. President Thorner soon arrived in the clubhouse to meet with his manager. When the boy returned, O'Leary poured the pitcher of beer over the boy and chastised him, saying, "The next time I send you for milk, get it."[19]

Under Crane's management, the club went 49–21, a vast improvement over the carefree O'Leary. The 30-year-old impressed everyone with his intelligence. Crane was never much of a hitter, but he was a well-respected player. His career was interrupted somewhat by a bizarre series of events in 1889 when he was arrested in Scranton on charges of adultery and larceny after allegedly stealing $1,500 from a fruit dealer.[20] He was acquitted later that year, but not before his name was besmirched in headlines across the country. He played one more major league season in 1890 before transitioning into the field of writing. Like fellow UA player-manager Tim Murnane, Crane became one of the nation's leading sportswriters. Crane's syndicated column appeared throughout the country, and he famously championed Cooperstown as a suitable place to memorialize baseball's history.[21]

While Cincinnati and St. Louis were facing off for baseball supremacy, Louisville traveled to Kansas City to continue their exhibition tour against the inferior Kansas City Unions. Thanks to an argument about the suitability of the weather, the matchups never came together. The Kentuckians then traveled to St. Louis for a much-anticipated three-game matchup against Henry Lucas and his nine scheduled for October 24–26. St. Louis had held down the first place spot virtually the entire season. From April 27 to October 19, St. Louis was the league's pre-eminent force, though they had posted a relatively pedestrian 11–8 record over the season's final month. This included a four-game losing streak, as well as losses to lowly St. Paul and Washington. They were still the finest team in the circuit on their best day, but they were a ragged bunch by this point. Charlie Sweeney was tired while the club's second pitcher, Henry Boyle, was still learning how to pitch. With nothing to play for, the club coasted through the final month, lacking their usual sharpness. It remained to be seen if they could match the efforts of their counterparts in Cincinnati during the Louisville exhibition contests.

Boyle was called upon to open the series in the pitcher's role against Phil Reccius, who was enlisted to give Guy Hecker a day off. Reccius had pitched effectively as the club's change pitcher and long reliever, pacing the AA in games finished while posting a solid 2.71 ERA and 114 ERA+ over 129.1 innings. But he was no Hecker.

Boyle had pitched very well for St. Louis in his rookie season, posting a 15–3 record, with a 1.74 ERA and 174 ERA+ while holding the fort down for several weeks in July after the unexpected departure of ace Billy Taylor and before the arrival of Charlie Sweeney. His record was inflated since he was primarily called upon to face the weaker clubs in the league. However, it was still a remarkable achievement considering he had never pitched regularly at any level until July. Boyle never became a workhorse in the mold of McCormick or Radbourn, but he achieved some level of success in his major league career, notably winning an ERA title while pacing the NL in ERA+ in 1886.

For such a big contest as this, Sweeney would typically have been called to pitch. However, Fred Dunlap was out of the lineup because of illness, so the versatile Sweeney was forced to play second. Without Dunlap's leadership, the St. Louis nine did not give their best effort in support of Boyle. The ordinarily hard-hitting lineup failed to capitalize on the deliveries of Reccius while making crucial errors behind Boyle. The final score stood at 7–2 for Louisville. The *St. Louis Republican* lamented the home club's listless play and failure to hit the visitors' secondary hurler: "It was not any very fine exhibition of pitching by Reccius, but their weakness at the bat, which prevented the Unions securing more hits. As a rule they batted as if they did not care whether they hit the ball or not."[22]

St. Louis's lackluster play was surprising given how well they showed up against Cincinnati. Dunlap returned to the lineup for the second contest in the series, hoping to avenge his club's loss. Hecker and Sweeney took the mound, and the home club responded with a dominant performance, evocative of their early-season exploits that had captivated the baseball world. Hecker was hit hard early and hit hard often. By the end of the third, the contest stood 8–1. The Louisville hitters, in comparison, "were all like a lot of school boys in the hands of Sweeney."[23] The moody hurler allowed just two hits on the day while striking out 13 hitters. The game was called after eight innings because of darkness, and the score stood 15–1 for the home nine. Every St. Louis batter got a hit off Hecker. Dunlap led the way, adding another excellent performance to his resume, getting four hits in six at-bats with two doubles and two runs scored off one of baseball's best hurlers. The decisive victory featured Lucas's nine at their best. They took full advantage of an exhausted Hecker, who had pitched well over 700 innings on the season and was not up to his usual standard. At the same time that the St. Louis Union batters were abusing Hecker, Providence ace Old Hoss Radbourn was busy dismantling the AA champion New York in game three of the first-ever World's Series. Radbourn led his nine to a 12–2 victory in six innings, completing a three-game sweep of New York. In the three contests, Radbourn allowed just three unearned runs in 22 innings and closed the season, having pitched 700.2 innings himself. Hecker was no Radbourn, but really, no one was.

The final contest of the series was to have taken place on October 26, and despite a promise from Henry Lucas that he would buy every member of his squad a new hat if they won, the game was canceled due to poor weather. This disappointing postponement brought an end to a remarkable season for St. Louis. Louisville's exhibition series in Cincinnati and St. Louis were the only contests between UA and major league clubs that year. Pennant-contending Louisville, led by one of the best pitchers in the country, posted a .500 record in the four exhibition contests. This suggests that Cincinnati and St. Louis would have been competitive against other major league clubs in their current iterations. Indeed, both nines possessed some elite talent in established major league stars like Dunlap, Glasscock, Shafer, McCormick, and Sweeney. In 1884, having an ace workhorse was the surest path to victory, and both clubs had that. McCormick was one of the great workhorses of the decade. He won 265 games over 4,275.2 innings for his career, with a 2.88 ERA and 118 ERA+. There is a solid case to be made that McCormick is the best nineteenth-century player not in the Baseball Hall of Fame. His counterpart, Sweeney, had pitched tremendously in both the NL and the UA, though his career was soon derailed by arm troubles, alcoholism, and attitude issues. However, in 1884, there was no question Sweeney was an elite pitcher.

The results of the exhibition contests should be taken with a grain of salt; however, as late-season games played in poor weather by exhausted ball clubs were not wholly indicative of a club's talent level or game in, game out consistency. It is also almost certain that the AA was a weaker circuit than the NL in 1884, at least partially evidenced by Providence's dismantling of New York in the World's Series and the AA's expansion with four new clubs joining the fold. Small sample size be damned. These four games, played in October 1884, and forgotten to history, are the only definitive evidence we have about how a Union Association club would fare against an NL or AA club. They tell us that, at the very least, the top two clubs in the UA could hold their own against one of the top teams in baseball in 1884.

22

◇◇◇◇◇◇◇◇◇◇◇◇◇

The Real Games Begin

The off-season of 1884 was pivotal for Henry Lucas, Justus Thorner, and the rest of the Union Association's leadership. The league had survived a tumultuous first season, filled with uncertainty. The league started with eight teams, and by the season's close, 12 teams in 13 different cities had been represented in the Union. It now remained to be seen what the configuration of the circuit would look like in 1885. Thorner and Lucas had announced plans for an eight-team circuit back in August, but that was before Pittsburgh and Wilmington bit the dust.

The league's directorship took a big hit to start the off-season. Albert H. Henderson, the owner of the Baltimore franchise, was out. Baltimore's disgraceful actions at the close of the season in Cincinnati, leaving their players stranded and owing back pay, had signaled a drastic change of heart for the disgusted mogul. Henderson had been a stalwart supporter of the league but had given up as the season closed. Henderson's conglomerate, which included the investment of his brother, William C. Henderson, had lost an estimated $12,000 combined on the Baltimore and Chicago franchises. Henderson had also invested in the Boston Unions and likely other clubs as well. Baltimore was believed to have nearly broken even on the season, while the Chicago-Pittsburgh experiment resulted in the bulk of his losses.

On a fundamental level, Henderson's approach to roster construction and financial management was at odds with the approaches taken by his fellow directors. Henderson had chosen a middle road between the lavish spending of Lucas and Thorner and the frugality of Mike Scanlon and Ted Sullivan. The result was disastrous financially, particularly considering his decision to sponsor two franchises rather than one. The Henderson brothers' prospects for the coming seasons were summed up in a letter dated December 2, 1884, from William C. Henderson to William "Yank" Robinson, the budding star of the Baltimore Unions:

> Robby there will not be any Union Club in Balto [Baltimore] at least as far as Willie [William C. Henderson] knows and he generally does. So you can bet there will not. Willie could not see enough money in it, so he has given up the idea and intends going into the Wholesale Hat Business with a good solid firm where he knows that at the end of the season there will be no owings.[1]

Baseball was a risky business, and that proved to be the theme of the offseason.

In late October, the American Association underwent a huge shake-up. On October 25, the Toledo club disbanded with reported losses of $10,000 on the season.

The Ohio nine, whose signing of Tony Mullane had proven to be a thorn in Henry Lucas's side, had struggled to a mediocre 46–58 record and an eighth-place finish in the American Association after taking home the 1883 Northwestern League pennant. Toledo's single-season of major league play is singularly noteworthy for the presence of the Walker brothers, Moses Fleetwood and Welday. The brothers officially broke baseball's color barrier by being the first openly black players to appear in the major leagues. William Edward White, a mixed-race Brown University alumnus, who often passed as white, was technically the first African American player to appear in the majors, thanks to his one game for Providence on June 21, 1879.[2] The departure of Toledo and the Walker brothers re-instituted the major league color barrier that would remain in place as a tremendous blight on the game of baseball until Jackie Robinson's debut in 1947.

The disbanding of the Toledo nine saw the sharks swirl, with Chris von der Ahe quickly signing up Tony Mullane, second baseman Sam Barkley, outfielders Curt Welch and Tom Poorman, and manager Charlie Morton. For the second straight off-season, Mullane double-crossed Herr von der Ahe, this time by also signing a contract with the Cincinnati Red Stockings. His standing for the coming season would be decided at the American Association meeting in December.

Just days after the disbanding of Toledo, the *Cincinnati Enquirer* published an article under the provocative title "Sold Out. Columbus Sells Its Players Like Slaves to Pittsburg."[3] The surprising Columbus nine had finished in second place in the circuit, after a dismal sixth-place performance in 1883. The club was profitable, and the team directors had over $7,000 in their treasury at season's close.[4] Pittsburgh, now under the management of "Hustling" Horace Phillips, who had managed the Columbus nine in 1883, offered his former club either $3,000 to secure the rights to their battery of Ed Morris and Fred Carroll or $6,000 to have his pick of the team.[5] Columbus president P.J. Sullivan jumped at the offer with the blessing of the club's stockholders, who saw the opportunity to make a quick 40 percent return on their investment.[6] The deal was closed on October 30 and brought an end to the Capital City's first major league franchise. Sullivan justified his decision, claiming that if he did not sell out now, he would be on the hook to pay out $2,500 in advance money to his roster come December. Sullivan also cited the rumored restructuring of the American Association as a reason for his decision. The proposal would likely leave Indianapolis, Richmond, and his own club out in the cold.[7] There were even allegations that the pennant-winning Metropolitans of New York might move to Brooklyn and replace the AA club there, creating another opening in the circuit.[8]

Despite the uncertain future, the franchises in Richmond and Indianapolis continued onwards, fully expecting to be members of the American Association in 1885. Richmond had signed manager Joe Simmons, formerly of the Wilmington nine, to take the reins of their club and hopefully provide a stronger outfit for the coming season. The Virginians had compiled a 12–30 record in 42 games in the American Association after replacing the Washington club in August. Indianapolis had disappointed in the Association after spending the 1883 season as arguably the strongest independent club in the country. The club went just 29–78 and changed managers late in the season. Bill Watkins had joined the club as a second baseman after the disbanding of the Bay City club, which he had also managed. He eventually took on the role of manager for Indianapolis late in the 1884 season and would helm the club in 1885. With an entire offseason to improve his club's fortune, the 26-year-old Canadian was exceedingly active in rebuilding the club in his image. He signed Sam Crane, the Cincinnati Unions' player-manager in October, to be his second baseman. Many other players were also in negotiations with Watkins. The uncertainty surrounding the makeup of the AA for the 1885 season would be an ongoing storyline in the coming weeks.

The National League had its own concerns, as its two weakest franchises in Detroit and Cleveland had significant red flags attached to them. Detroit had finished in last place with a 28–84 record, and as *Sporting Life* put it: "the outlook is not very bright for a strong team here next season. The present one has some very good players in it, but ... most of them are anxious to get away from here, and have been for some time."[9] The defection of Dupee Shaw in July after his dispute with manager Jack Chapman was emblematic of the toxic and losing culture that permeated the club. Despite Chapman's limitations in player relations, he was purportedly excellent at managing the team finances and kept the team in a stable financial position.[10] Their financial standing was impressive considering that Detroit was the worst drawing club in the league, with just 32,000 fans attending the club's 56 home games.[11] The team's president, William G. Thompson, was disgusted with his team's circumstances. He cited the disloyalty of players and their exorbitant salary demands as the reasons for his club's futility. In a scathing editorial, he described his players as "the most ungrateful set of men I have ever

CRANE, 2d B Washington

COPYRIGHTED BY GOODWIN & CO. 1887.

GOODWIN & CO. New York.

Sam Crane joined the Union Association after he was released by New York of the American Association. He signed with the Cincinnati Unions to play second base and soon took over for Dan O'Leary as the team's manager. He posted a 49–21 record and guided the club to a second place finish. After his career, he joined Tim Murnane as a former UA player-manager turned national sportswriter (Library of Congress).

met, and I am done with them ... they are paid from \$12 to \$25 each per game they play, and then they go and sell the games to the pool-box gamblers."[12]

Cleveland, meanwhile, had been the club most adversely affected by the Union Association. They had turned from a pennant contender in 1883 to a moribund organization on the verge of folding in 1884. The club had been weakened by the pre-season defection of Fred Dunlap and Hugh Daily but was absolutely decimated by the mid-season jump of Jack Glasscock, Jim McCormick, and Charles Briody. No major league club had lost so many top players to the rival league. As the off-season unfolded, it was revealed that the attack on Cleveland by Lucas and Thorner was not coincidental. Both Lucas and Thorner were deeply invested in their clubs' success. Perhaps even more so than that of the Union Association as a whole. For both men, any losses incurred in 1884 were meant to build a foundation for long-term success for their respective clubs, whether they remained in the Union Association or joined another league.

As early as October 1883, it had been reported that an anonymous bidder in St. Louis had attempted to buy the Cleveland franchise and move it to St. Louis. No doubt, this was Lucas, who soon latched onto the Union Association. Lucas would do whatever it took to overtake Chris von der Ahe's Brown Stockings. Thorner was motivated by his previous failures in the National League and the American Association. Putting the Cleveland nine out of business might create an opening in the National League. The spot could then be filled by St. Louis or Cincinnati. On a league level, the directorship of the National League was in the midst of a transition from the odd mixture of large markets and minuscule locales that had comprised the league early in the decade. The addition of New York and Philadelphia in 1883, resulting in the jettisoning of Worcester and Troy, symbolized this trend towards favoring larger markets. If this trend continued, it would seem that from the NL's perspective, Cincinnati and St. Louis would be more enticing locales than Detroit and Cleveland. If an opening presented itself, Thorner and Lucas were ready to capitalize.

It is tempting to cast Lucas and Thorner in a Machiavellian light based on their machinations. Lucas's attempt to purchase Cleveland in October 1883, his signing of Dunlap shortly thereafter, and Thorner's acquisition of the Glasscock, McCormick, and Briody in August 1884 all point to a concerted attack on the Ohio club. It is difficult to assert that Lucas and Thorner were actively conspiring to undermine the Union Association or leverage it to gain entry into the National League. The pair seem to have been pragmatic about their continued involvement with the UA. They both aimed to ensure their clubs would see play in 1885, no matter what the league. Their presence at the December 1884 meeting confirms they were trying to keep their options open for 1885. Rumors had started to appear in summer 1884 about their intentions to abandon the Union. Since their entry into the NL was entirely dependent upon forces outside their control, continuing to push for an 1885 Union season was a way to hedge their bets. However, if Detroit and Cleveland disbanded or were dropped by the NL, there was little doubt that the pair would pursue the opportunity to change leagues.

The Union Association directors watched the tumult with great fascination.

With Baltimore out of the running, the league now contained seven clubs. The season had finished with an uneven balance of three eastern teams (Washington, Boston, and Baltimore) against five western teams (St. Louis, Cincinnati, Kansas City, Milwaukee, and St. Paul). Given the complete dependence upon train travel, this unequal balance was untenable for scheduling purposes and gave credence to the notion of a proposed 1885 Union Association as an entirely western-based league.[13] Another critical factor was the uncertainty surrounding the remaining two eastern clubs in Boston and Washington. The Boston Unions had been a surprise success story, having earned universal acclaim for their on-field play and gentlemanly demeanor. Financially, however, the club had struggled. They relied on financial support from Lucas, Thorner, and Henderson to stay afloat early in the season. By the close of the campaign, the club had lost a reported $10,000 on the year.[14] One correspondent speculated that there would "be no Union nine in Boston in 1885. The managers of last season paid too dearly for their membership in the Union Association."[15] With little chance of usurping their National League rivals for the attention of Boston's faithful, there was not much appetite amongst the club's directors to invest any further funds in the venture.

In Washington, Mike Scanlon's venture had proven to be very profitable. The Nationals had been the second most profitable in the league behind Lucas's club, and the club had won the war against the American Association's venture in the nation's capital. Scanlon and the Nationals' directors appeared ambivalent about remaining in the Union Association, citing shabby treatment bestowed upon his club on their final western road trip while visiting Cincinnati and St. Louis. During the trip, the Nationals were treated poorly by the Union's top dogs. They also chafed at biased officiating that went against them. Scanlon also felt cheated out of gate receipts by Thorner and Lucas.[16] This brewing distrust was exacerbated by the proposed Union plan that would see visiting clubs paid out 30 percent of total gate receipts in 1885, which Scanlon virulently opposed.[17] Should the Nationals depart from the Union Association, they had two options for 1885. First, Scanlon had previously applied to join the American Association in fall 1883, when there was some doubt about the Union Association coming to fruition. It seemed very probable that he would make an application again, given his position of financial strength. Second, there was also serious discussion about the reformation of the Eastern League, which had gone bust shortly after Wilmington joined the Union Association.[18] Both the Nationals and the Boston Unions were rumored participants. The budget-conscious Scanlon undoubtedly savored the opportunity to play in an eastern-only circuit and save money on travel expenses.

With the uncertain futures of Boston and Washington, speculation was brewing that the league would abandon their eastern markets entirely and become a wholly western organization. Conflicting reports noted that there were plans to try again in Philadelphia and Pittsburgh, including one that claimed Henry Lucas would purchase the old Keystone grounds and place a club there.[19] A report out of St. Paul on October 21 indicated that the 1885 season would see Union teams in St. Louis, Cincinnati, Indianapolis, Milwaukee, St. Paul, Minneapolis, Omaha, and Kansas City.[20] The unexpected departure of Columbus gave birth to rumors that the

Unions would place a club in that city.[21] President Lucas continued to seek opportunities to improve his club, offering a three-year contract for $10,000 with a $1,000 advance to reigning home run king Ed Williamson of the Chicago White Stockings.[22] The slugger had hit a record 27 home runs on the season. His total was aided by the minuscule dimensions at the club's Lakefront Park (left field 186 feet, center fielder 300 feet, right field 190 feet) and a change in the park's ground rules that meant any ball hit over the fence would count as a home run.[23] The previous season, aided by the same dimensions, but under the ground rules that counted any ball hit over the fence as a double, Williamson had smashed the all-time doubles record with 49. The home run record was of dubious legitimacy but would hold until 1919, when Babe Ruth broke it with 29. Regardless of the record's validity, Williamson was a tremendous athlete and one of the finest all-around players in baseball, playing excellent defense at third base. White Stockings outfielder George Gore was also reported to have received an offer from a Union club.[24] Neither man ended up signing, but the fact the Union clubs were pursuing reserved players was a sign that they intended to continue their war for players.

In Kansas City, Ted Sullivan was very active in the player market, seeking to improve his team's competitiveness. With the Boston franchise in limbo, he signed their ace Dupee Shaw and second baseman Tom O'Brien. Shaw signed for a sum of $3,200 for the coming season, though perhaps to hedge his bets, he unsuccessfully applied for reinstatement to the National League.[25] William "Yank" Robinson was much sought after and also agreed to terms with Kansas City.[26] The club also outbid the Philadelphia National League club for the services of second baseman Charlie Bastian, who had finished the season on Sullivan's club after the disbanding of Wilmington. Sullivan won his rights for $2,000 and a $500 advance.[27] A key reason for Sullivan's lavish attempts to spend his way to success was the impressive financial success of the club's inaugural season. Buoyed by raucous Sunday crowds, excited to experience the novelty of professional baseball, Sullivan and co-owner A.V. McKim raked in the dough, turning a profit to the tune of $6,000.[28] The figure was remarkable since the club had formed in haste at the beginning of June and generally put forth an awful on-field product. Sullivan was a great baseball mind and also highly competitive. Now flush with cash, he saw the coming season as an opportunity to improve his club's fortunes. An improved club would hopefully maintain fan interest as well. There were also plans to move their park closer to downtown Kansas City and install a 5,000-seat grandstand.[29]

For all his efforts to build a winner in Cincinnati, Justus Thorner had lost $11,000 on the season.[30] By contrast, the rival Red Stockings turned a $9,000 profit.[31] Despite his losses, Thorner was optimistic about the club's prospects in 1885 and boasted of his plans to field the best club in baseball. To that effect, he re-signed his top players, including George Bradley, Bill Harbridge, Bill Hawes, and the Cleveland defectors.[32] He also vowed to strengthen the weakest positions on his nine and sign another first-class battery. The club also offered a contract to the reigning National League batting champion, outfielder Jim O'Rourke from Buffalo.[33] A budget of $10,000 was allotted to improve the club's grounds, which were already among the finest in the nation.[34] Thorner's ambition knew no bounds.

The Union's two Northwestern League additions in Milwaukee and St. Paul both displayed interest in remaining in the circuit for 1885. Milwaukee manager Tom Loftus reported the club had made a profit of $3,000 in their twelve Union games at home, despite boasting a salary list that ranked only behind St. Louis in extravagance.[35] The immense profitability was driven by the club's strength, excellent attendance, and freedom to play Sunday contests. Loftus fully expected his club to be a key cog in the Union Association, even as his well-crafted roster was being picked apart by talent-hungry rivals. He had signed just two of his players to contracts for the coming season, catcher Anton Falch and pitcher Henry Porter, who had been pursued with great zeal by the Cincinnati Red Stockings since August.[36] Milwaukee's brass had established a policy of not paying out advances since there was too much risk of a player receiving the advance and jumping to a rival club.[37] The policy hindered the ability of Loftus to retain his roster and sign new talent. As a result, his club was weakened almost immediately after the season ended. Al Myers, the 20-year-old prodigy, had paced the team in hitting while in the Union with a .326/.326/.457 line and was signed by the Philadelphia League club.[38] Meanwhile, Ed Cushman, the dominating lefty, was also heavily pursued. He eventually signed with the Athletics for a $3,500 salary, a marked increase over the reported $70 per start he had received in 1884.[39] Loftus also made plans to expand the park from 5,000 seats to 10,000 seats to accommodate the large Sunday crowds his club had drawn.[40]

St. Paul's interest in remaining in the circuit for 1885 was motivated primarily by the belief that playing in larger markets would help cover their travel expenses and make the club profitable.[41] The club had made no money in 1884, blaming this on the extensive geographic spread of the 12-team Northwestern League and its numerous small markets. Despite the lack of profitability, the club had also avoided going into debt. This was thanks to the sensible management of Andrew Thompson. Any iteration of the 1885 club would be absent two of the stronger players. Catcher Charlie Ganzel, who had wowed onlookers with his outstanding receiving skills and brainy play, was wooed by several clubs, including Ted Sullivan's Kansas City squad. He eventually joined his former pitching mate, Elmer Foster, in signing with Philadelphia in the NL.[42] Captain Moxie Hengel also joined the National League by signing with Buffalo.

The Union Association had the full support of all five of its western clubs, while its two remaining eastern nines were noncommittal. Any realistic configuration for 1885 would require eight clubs. There were between one and three spots available in the league. The growing uncertainty surrounding the viability of many American Association and National League clubs created a sense of mystery and intrigue, and no one could predict what the upcoming season would hold. The upcoming league meetings for each of the three major leagues would go a long way to sort out the messy situation and provide some clarity for the coming year.

23

Almost Equivalent
to Actual Dishonesty

Baseball's biggest changes always seemed to happen in hotels. The magnates and moneymen liked to make a great show of gathering together to plot out the next steps for their respective leagues and clubs. The Union Association was formed at the Monongahela House in Pittsburgh on September 12, 1883. That event had turned the 1884 season into a topsy-turvy roller coaster for every magnate, player, and fan. As 1884 came to a close, there were five league meetings scheduled in the coming weeks. Each of the three major leagues had its annual meetings scheduled. In addition, the interested projectors for a revamped Eastern League and a new minor western circuit would be gathering. These meetings would clear up the uncertainty surrounding the viability of various franchises and determine the final configurations of each league in 1885.

The first of these meetings took place on November 17 in Kansas City, where the Western Amateur Base Ball League announced its formation. Despite the name, the league would be a professional minor league located entirely in the western states. Clubs would primarily be located in the states of Kansas and Missouri. Representatives were present from Kansas City, Leavenworth, St. Joseph, Topeka, Atchison, and an unnamed locale in Louisiana.[1] Additional consideration was given to placing clubs in Hannibal, Missouri, Keokuk, Iowa, and Quincy, Illinois. In a historic twist, this new Western League would align itself with the Union Association and follow a similar constitution while also adhering to their playing rules. If it came to fruition, it would be the first league to align itself with the wreckers. The plan put forth in August 1884 by Henry Lucas and Justus Thorner had advocated for the support of other leagues.

Five days later, the National League's annual gathering took place from November 22–23 at the Fifth Avenue Hotel in New York City. Despite the fragility of the Cleveland and Detroit situation, nothing on that matter was formally discussed. Somewhat cryptically, Detroit's disgruntled president, William G. Thompson, did not attend the proceedings.[2] Several blacklisted players, including Dupee Shaw and an unnamed member of the Cleveland trio who defected to Cincinnati, applied for reinstatement.[3] The National League guard made a stern example of these men officially ruling: "The League will never consent to the reinstatement of any player who had deserted or may hereafter desert any club identified with the League."[4] This stance would prove to be a key obstacle for many players heading into the season. Little else of note was discussed at the meeting, aside from a proposal to walk back the previous rule change that allowed pitchers to deliver the ball overhand. The absence of Thompson prevented the vote from being finalized, however.

President Henry Lucas was busy strategizing how their league would look in 1885. In late November and early December, the enterprising leader visited Indianapolis and Columbus to suss out the situation in those cities. He floated the possibility of each club joining the Union Association for 1885.[5] Indianapolis's standing in the American Association was still undecided and would remain so until the AA meeting on December 10 in New York. The club's resourceful manager, Bill Watkins, had remained active in his pursuit of players. He fully expected to be a full-fledged member of the AA in 1885. Despite this confidence, the general belief amongst baseball men was that the AA would drop Indianapolis and reduce to only eight teams. Lucas was so confident that he bet three-to-one odds with the leading baseball men of the city that Indianapolis would be shut out of the Association.[6] He also detailed his plans for the Union's configuration as a western circuit with clubs in Kansas City, St. Louis, Milwaukee, St. Paul, Cincinnati, Indianapolis, Columbus, and potential clubs in Cleveland and Detroit, pending their National League status.[7] Lucas laid out the advantages that Indianapolis would be entitled to by joining his league. First, every city but Detroit and Cleveland would allow lucrative Sunday contests. Second, for the 1885 season, visiting clubs would receive 30 percent of the gate, rather than the $75 guarantee of the prior season, which could prove more lucrative for everyone. He also made a somewhat veiled threat noting that his traveling partner, Kansas City manager Ted Sullivan, had already signed several Indianapolis players to provisional contracts should they remain in the Association.[8] This included the club's top pitcher, Larry McKeon, and starting shortstop Marr Phillips. Neither Lucas nor Ted Sullivan met with the club's directors during their visit. The men chose instead to rely on the city's baseball enthusiasts to spread the message. They passed along assurances that if Indianapolis were dropped, they would have a home in the Union.[9]

Columbus had disbanded abruptly in October, but the club's strong performance and the bitter end to their existence had left the baseball-loving fans of the city with a hankering for another franchise. In early December, Lucas visited the Ohio capital. He met with the club's former manager, Gus Schmelz, and several interested investors to gauge the viability and interest of the city becoming home to a Union nine in 1885.[10] An informal proposal to raise $5,000 in stock for the club's formation yielded $2,300 almost immediately, while Lucas vowed to pitch in another $1,000, leaving $1,700 to be raised.[11] The brief rush of excitement and promise soon came to a crashing halt over a dispute with a local man named Thomas J. Dundon. He was the older brother of Columbus pitcher Edward J. Dundon, the first deaf-mute player in major league history. The elder Dundon had just purchased the remnants of the Columbus franchise, including the ballpark, fixtures, buildings, and uniforms at auction for $525.[12] Lucas left town and entrusted the logistics and finances to Schmelz. The former Columbus manager quickly became engaged in negotiations with Dundon, the new owner of the grounds, to rent the ballpark for the coming season. Dundon sensed an opportunity to make a quick buck and asked for an exorbitant fee of $1,500 to rent the grounds for the coming season.[13] This dispute was not resolved, and the plans for a Union club quickly died.

The Eastern League met on December 3, 1884, to plan their reformation for 1885. The circuit had collapsed in August after the departure of Wilmington to join the Union Association. League president Henry H. Diddlebock had overseen the circuit in 1884. He was either a relentless optimist or a glutton for punishment and took on the role of league president once again. It was hoped an eight-team league concentrated in New York, New Jersey, and Pennsylvania, featuring larger markets like Philadelphia, Newark, and Jersey City, would increase league stability.[14] Some old friends were invited to join the party, including former Altoona manager Edwin R. Curtis, who hoped to place another professional nine in the Mountain City. The primary takeaway from the meeting was the pending status of Mike Scanlon's Washington Nationals and W.C. Seddon's Richmond, Virginia, club. Both were promised slots in the Eastern League. The pair anxiously awaited the upcoming American Association meeting. It would determine if Washington and Virginia would gain AA membership for 1885. Diddlebock and the Eastern League board of directors held off on making a final decision on the status of the two clubs pending the AA's verdict. The directors of the Nationals, including Scanlon, Henry Bennett, and a local banker named R.E. Drinkard, were actively lobbying with the big wigs of the AA for official entry.[15] Meanwhile, the Virginia directors prepared to file a claim if denied membership in the American Association at the hands of the Washington club because they were members in good standing in the AA.[16]

The tension came to a head at the annual meeting of the Association on December 10–11 at the Fifth Avenue Hotel in New York City. The fate of three franchises, Indianapolis, Virginia, and Washington, would be decided during these two days. It was presumed that the blowback would set forth a chain of dominoes that would define the coming season. The first order of business for the AA's directorship was the resolution of the Tony Mullane case.[17] As in the previous winter, Mullane was the center of a legal dispute after signing contracts with multiple teams. In this case, he had signed with St. Louis after Toledo folded in late October but soon after that signed a contract with the Cincinnati Red Stockings. Since both clubs claimed his rights, the AA's directors were tasked with determining Mullane's fate for the coming season. The decision would significantly impact both the league and the on-field performance of the St. Louis and Cincinnati clubs.

For all his warts, Mullane was a tremendous hurler. He was very popular with the fans because of his dashing appearance, which earned him the nickname "the Apollo of the Box." Mullane had won 30 games in each of his first three full seasons, including 36 for Toledo. His time in Toledo was marred by his ongoing legal battle with Henry Lucas, who had sued the pitcher to prevent him from appearing. His season was also defined by his racist treatment of his catcher, Moses Walker, whom he actively tried to embarrass. Mullane would later recount:

> He [Walker] was the best catcher I ever worked with, but I disliked a Negro and whenever I had to pitch to him, I used to pitch anything I wanted without looking at his signals. One day he signaled me for a curve and I shot a fast ball at him. He caught it and came down to

me. … He said, "I'll catch you without signals, but I won't catch you if you are going to cross me when I give you signals." And all the rest of that season, he caught me and caught anything I pitched without knowing what was coming.[18]

The incident demonstrates the reprehensible figure Mullane often was, as he actively sabotaged the performance of himself and his team to defend his racist ideology.

The case was brought before the AA directors. Missouri State Representative J.J. O'Neill prosecuted the case on behalf of the Brown Stockings. O.P. Caylor was the defense on behalf of the Red Stockings.[19] Mullane was called as a witness in the proceedings but failed to appear. Caylor made a forceful defense, but in the end, the directors sided with St. Louis. They cited the fact that making an example of Mullane might hurt Cincinnati in the short term but would be of benefit to the other clubs in the long run. Mullane was found "guilty of conduct tending to bring discredit on the base ball profession, causing discontent and insubordination among all professional players and setting an example of sharp practice almost equivalent to actual dishonesty."[20] Mullane was suspended for the 1885 season and ordered to pay back the $1,000 advance he had received from Cincinnati. His contract was determined to be valid, however, and it would commence in 1886 after the suspension's conclusion. The aftermath of the decision saw Caylor and the Cincinnati directors threaten to leave the AA and join the National League. This dispute would be resolved shortly thereafter but foreshadowed the Red Stockings' eventual departure from the AA in 1889. Mullane's suspension likely cost the Irishman a 30-win season right in his prime. When his major league career ended in 1894, he had 284 career victories, just 16 short of the magical 300 win barrier. It seems very likely that his banishment in 1885 cost him a Hall of Fame induction. To date, every pitcher with at least 300 major league victories is in the Hall.

On the subject of the Washington Nationals' application, the matter was set aside for future consideration. Scanlon remained optimistic about his club's chances of joining the AA, still confident that the New York Metropolitans would move to Brooklyn, creating another opening in the league.[21] As expected by baseball insiders, both Indianapolis and Virginia were dropped from the circuit. The reason given was that a 10-team league would make scheduling impossible, while a 12-team league would result in too many weak clubs being propped up by the stronger organizations.[22] Since both Indianapolis and Virginia had been members in good standing and had already signed players to valid contracts, the AA directors insisted that none of the other Association clubs poach any players from the two clubs. A telegraph was sent to the National League's president A.G. Mills, asking the NL clubs to respect these contracts as well. For Virginia and Washington, the Eastern League was their next option. Both clubs were formally accepted on December 12 at the EL meeting.[23] Indianapolis's status remained uncertain, though President Lucas was still courting the club for entry into the Union Association.[24]

On December 11, 1884, the second day of the AA meeting, a bombshell was dropped in the form of a letter sent to *Sporting Life* by A.L. Bird, a purportedly close friend of Henry Lucas. The letter described the Union Association president's plan to desert the Union Association and put a National League club in St. Louis:

I have some news for you and it is startling, if not sensational.... I know Mr. Lucas-the head and front of the Union Association-very well, and I know that from the very beginning he had had the welfare of the professional ball players at heart in what he has undertaken within the past year. I freely acknowledge that he has, at times, been wrong in his premises, and also made mistakes in his estimates, but they have been errors of judgment and not of the heart. In fact, he has taken up the cause of the alleged oppressed class of ball players with a knightly feeling, only to realize, however, that his battle in their cause has not been prolific of a grateful reward. Be that as it may ... he has come to the conclusion that a change of base would be desirable, and he proposes to bring it about in this way. Being desirous of seeing St. Louis second to no other city in the West in the base ball field, he thought he could present a model team through the medium of the Union Association, and at the same time resent what he regarded as an oppressive attack upon the players, made by the League through their reserve rule. Experience has taught him that the only way to attain his object is through the medium of the League, and with the characteristic energy which has led him through the past season's Union campaign he proposes to accomplish the present object he has in view, which is neither more nor less than *to have St. Louis represented in the League in 1885!*[25]

The letter further outlined that St. Louis was the best paying baseball town in the west and that a Lucas-led club would accomplish what the city's previous league club in 1876–1877 had not. For the National League and the rival Brown Stockings, letting Lucas into the league would "disappear all vestiges of the Union Association."[26] It was intimated that Lucas could put together a League nine in St. Louis that would put forth a better effort than either Cleveland or Detroit. A promise was made that the new nine would not contain a player who had broken an AA or NL contract or jumped the reserve rule. On its face, this claim was patently absurd since Lucas's Union nine contained seven regular players who had jumped their contracts. Without Fred Dunlap, Orator Shafer, Jack Gleason, Charlie Sweeney, Dave Rowe, Tom Dolan, and Henry Boyle, his mighty roster would be rendered entirely impotent.

Another telegram from an interested party outlined the conditions of Lucas's acceptance into the National League and suggested that Lucas had done a 180 on the reserve rule.[27] It was thought that Lucas had been disgusted by the ingratitude of contract jumpers, namely Billy Taylor and Buttercup Dickerson. The duo had deserted Lucas in July for spots in the American Association. Adding smoke to the fire, Lucas's lawyer, Newton Crane, reportedly met with Chris von der Ahe to discuss the conditions that needed to be met by Lucas. Five conditions were laid out at this point for Lucas's Unions to be accepted to the league. First, the club would take the place of the Cleveland franchise. Second, Lucas would withdraw all opposition to the reserve rule. Third, he would sell no beer at games. Fourth, the club would play no Sunday games. Fifth, he would cast all of his blacklisted players adrift.[28] These reports were treated with utmost seriousness, at least amongst his players, who were now put in the stressful position of worrying about whether they would ever play professional baseball again.[29]

The fascinating component of these letters is how much they reveal about Henry Lucas's motivations. Notably, the Bird letter mentioned his desire to put a club in St. Louis and atone for the failures of the city's previous National League club that his older brother had helmed. Lucas's rivalry with Chris von der Ahe was indirectly mentioned under the guise that a National League nine would cause fewer problems than his Union club had. It would also provide a more legitimate alternative to the Brown Stockings than his Union squad. Lucas's opposition to the reserve rule and desire to improve the lot of players was also mentioned, though in the same breath seemingly, he was willing to cast those ideals aside for the chance to own a League club.

From the perspective of the National League, taking in Lucas would serve two primary functions. First, it would almost certainly put an end to the Union Association. The rival league had not threatened the existence of the NL or the AA, but it had proved to be a great nuisance. The haggling over players, constant threats of blacklist, and increased competition for fan interest had done a disservice to the established leagues. It had cost significant time and money and had also undermined the strength of the reserve rule. Second, it would allow the NL to replace their weakest market in Cleveland with one of baseball's strongest markets in St. Louis. Accepting Lucas's club would provide a pathway into St. Louis and possibly weaken Chris von der Ahe and the American Association. If Lucas's club could replicate their 1884 success in the NL on the field and at the gate, they would be poised to overtake the Brown Stockings as the city's premier club. If the plan worked accordingly, Lucas would join the NL, the UA would be out of the picture, and the NL would get stronger while the AA would be weakened.

The Union Association's meeting took place exactly one week later, on December 18, at Laclede Hotel in St. Louis. The revelations about President Lucas had to have been on the mind of everyone in attendance. Representatives from Cincinnati, St. Louis, Milwaukee, and Kansas City were present, while Lucas represented Indianapolis by proxy.[30] St. Paul was also reportedly represented.[31] Another five clubs made applications to the league while the Iowa State League reportedly applied for an alliance.[32] In a somewhat surprising move, given his extracurricular activities, Henry Lucas was elected league president once again while William Warren White was re-elected as secretary.[33] St. Louis was awarded the pennant, and Secretary Warren White was given a budget of $100 to purchase a championship banner for the nine. The Baltimore club officially withdrew. A hearty thank you was extended to Albert H. Henderson for all of his "endeavors to advance the interests of the Association."[34] As expected, no one from the Boston or Washington clubs appeared, and those clubs were formally dropped from the circuit. It was noted that a $787.71 deficit existed in the overall receipts for the season. The disbandment of Altoona and Chicago caused this deficit, and the owing amount would be split across the five clubs present at the meeting.[35] Milwaukee president Charles M. Kipp put forth a plan that would see each club in the association put forth a $500 guarantee upon admission to ensure compliance with circuit guidelines and completion of the schedule.[36] The proposed changes to payouts to visiting clubs were adopted, with 30 percent of gate receipts going to the visitors rather than the current guarantee of $75.[37] Lucas and Thorner also made plans to visit the locales of interested applicants.[38] The official meeting minutes did not mention the rumors about Lucas and his abandonment of the Union Association. In the days to follow, the ambitious owner was inundated with questions from reporters trying to determine his intentions. Lucas acknowledged the reports were accurate about the National League's offer to join but that he had not reached out to the league; rather, they had come to him.[39] The reported conditions of no Sunday games, no liquor sold on the grounds, 50-cent admission, and the release of his star players were too much for Lucas to agree to. For the present, he resumed his duties as Union Association president with his "customary zeal and energy."[40]

Lucas and Thorner remained in hot pursuit of the Indianapolis market, hoping they could secure the city. After the American Association had passed the resolution vowing to respect the contracts of the Indianapolis players, the National League was notified, with a request to cooperate with this motion. Providence president Henry Root did not agree to the request. He cited that since Indianapolis was no longer in the American Association, they were no longer under the protection of the National Agreement; thus, his club was under no obligation to respect their contracts.[41] If Providence or another National League club attempted to sign their players, the Indianapolis directors might have sufficient motivation to join the rival Union circuit. This motivation would add to the extant bitterness regarding what they perceived as their unjust removal from the Association.

The uncertainty surrounding the two weaklings of the National League, Detroit and Cleveland, remained through the end of the year. Until that was answered, Henry Lucas and the Union Association were in a state of flux. Another Union Association meeting was scheduled in Milwaukee for January 18, 1885, which would shed light on the situation. If Lucas remained with the circuit, another UA season would likely take place. However, if Lucas were to take his club to the National League, there would not be enough juice left in the orange to continue onwards. It was also expected that if Lucas bolted, he would be followed by his right-hand man, Thorner. The Cincinnati Unions were expected to make their own application to the National League pending Lucas's decision.

As the year 1884 ended, there was a strong possibility that both Cleveland and Detroit would be booted from the National League. Lucas had continually floated the possibility of the two clubs joining the Union Association. The *Cleveland Herald* offered a vociferous denial of the rumors noting, "Lucas could not buy a man from Cleveland, and the Unions could not purchase our franchise for $20,000."[42] One report by a National League insider had both Cleveland and Detroit being dumped, with Lucas's club and the Cincinnati American Association team joining in their stead.[43] Lucas gave an interview to a Cincinnati scribe on Christmas eve that outlined his plans for 1885, which were pretty much business as usual: "Yes, we will try and secure as strong a circuit as possible and one that meets with the most favor. Ah, yes, it will embrace Cincinnati, Indianapolis, Kansas City, St. Louis, Milwaukee, St. Paul, Detroit, Cleveland, and it is possible that we will be represented in Columbus with a strong club."[44] Lucas also disavowed any notion of his club jumping to the National League: "We are perfectly satisfied to remain where we are at present, and you can just say for me that the St. Louis Club will be a member of the Union Association next season."[45] Despite the certainty of Lucas's proclamations, as 1884 concluded, there were still just as many questions as answers.

24

The Double Cross

"Now anybody who knows me should know that I never go back on anybody that sticks to me."—Henry V. Lucas, *St. Louis Republican*, December 18, 1884

As the year 1885 began, Henry Lucas had a choice to make. He could continue onwards with the Union Association, fighting tooth and nail for respectability and waging a long-term war against Chris von der Ahe and the St. Louis Brown Stockings, the reserve rule, and the National Agreement. Alternatively, he could bring his pennant-winning St. Louis Unions to the National League and continue the battle with von der Ahe without having to spend thousands to keep the Union Association afloat. Joining the National League would require him to embrace the very things he had sought to undermine when he threw his hat in the proverbial baseball ring 15 months before. Lucas's decision would have huge ramifications for the Union Association, the National League, and the American Association.

Meanwhile, the directors of the Cleveland franchise were standing at the edge of a precipice. Under President C.H. Bulkeley, the club nearly copped the 1883 National League pennant, but the Union raids had sent the squad into disarray. With five of their top performers now in the rival league, the nine sleepwalked to an abysmal seventh-place finish in 1884. Given the poor on-field product and general lack of interest amongst the locals, there seemed little appetite for the directors to continue onwards in 1885. As a result, Bulkeley and the club stockholders were looking for a way out of the precarious situation. They also hoped to recoup some of their investment. As the days passed in the build-up to the National League meeting on January 10, 1885, it seemed increasingly likely that Cleveland would no longer be a member of the league.

As recently as the Union Association meeting on December 18, 1884, President Lucas was still angling for the Cleveland franchise to join his circuit. The main obstacle was the well-earned resentment that the Cleveland directors and even the local fan base had towards Lucas and his circuit. Despite repeated overtures to have the Ohioans join, Lucas and Thorner were rebuffed, and Cleveland remained in the NL for the time being. With that avenue shut off, Lucas pursued his other plan. He would purchase the Cleveland club for pennies on the dollar, dissolve it, and formally enter his St. Louis nine into the National League.

On January 4, a report surfaced that Lucas had bought out the Cleveland club and would join the National League along with Justus Thorner's Cincinnati Unions.[1] Lucas's purchase of the bereft franchise came at a price of $2,500, which he believed would grant him rights to the remnants of the franchise, including all club property and rights to the players on the Cleveland roster.[2] Much to his dismay, the formal written agreement provided by Cleveland's directors withheld from Lucas with any club property or player rights.[3] It simply gave him the rights to the club as an entity, which would clear the way to join the National League. If he wanted a crack at the Cleveland players, he would have to put forth more cash.

Before Lucas could furnish a suitable offer, another vulture had swooped in to complicate the matter. Charles Byrne, the president of the Brooklyn Base Ball Club in the American Association, had beaten Lucas to the punch. The clever Byrne hammered out an arrangement with the Cleveland directors to sign manager Charles Brackett and acquire the rights to seven players on the Cleveland roster for the sum of $4,000.[4] The players were Bill Phillips, Germany Smith, George Pinkney, Pete Hotaling, Bill Krieg, and John Harkins. Notably, Smith and Krieg had starred in the Union Association for Altoona and Chicago, respectively. For Cleveland's C.H. Bulkeley, the move garnered a large amount of cash and had the added benefit of freezing Lucas out of the acquisition of the club's talent, limited as it may be.

Less than a week later, the National League held a meeting on January 10, 1885, in New York City at the Fifth Avenue Hotel. At this gathering, the National League directors officially accepted the resignation of the Cleveland club and awarded their spot to Henry Lucas and his Union nine.[5] The addition of Justus Thorner's Cincinnati franchise was also being considered, most likely to replace the unstable Detroit club.[6] All members of the National League universally accepted the motion to accept St. Louis. When the matter was posed to the directors of the American Association clubs, there was far less agreement. As expected, Chris von der Ahe was deeply opposed, while Cincinnati's O.P. Caylor also expressed his annoyance. Von der Ahe would reportedly not give consent unless Lucas paid out the $10,000 in damages he claimed to have suffered due to Lucas's rival club.[7] For Caylor, the acceptance of the Union club in St. Louis would pave the way for his rival Thorner to join the NL as well.[8] The dispute over Lucas would rage for several weeks, with National League honchos threatening to tear up the National Agreement if the American Association heads did not accept their terms. Lucas's membership in the National League was believed to be dependent upon his willingness to meet the same conditions that had been broached the prior month, with the added catch that von der Ahe was asking for full payment of damages.

The acceptance of St. Louis into the National League came as a great surprise to the Union Association directors in Kansas City and Milwaukee. They had expected Lucas's continued involvement in the circuit. The UA had another meeting scheduled for January 15, 1885, at which point the organization's fate would be determined. In light of the recent news, President Lucas was expected to attend the meeting and provide an explanation. Even without St. Louis in the circuit or the feisty leadership of Lucas, there were still enough interested parties to continue on with the league in 1885. Justus Thorner was committed to joining the National League along with Lucas, but his entry depended on forces outside his control. He was entirely reliant on Detroit's directors and the approval of his bitter rival O.P. Caylor. Without a clear opening in the NL, Thorner would almost certainly have to hedge his bets through his continued involvement in the Union circuit. In the days leading up to the Union meeting, Thorner had sent a telegraph to the Milwaukee directors confirming this notion and his plans to attend the conference.[9]

The first Union Association meeting of 1885 would also be the last in the circuit's history. The conference was marked by the absence of its three most influential members. President Lucas failed to show and explain his decision to jump to the National League. Justus Thorner was also absent despite his recent claims of loyalty to the upstart league. Albert H. Henderson had withdrawn his support for the circuit at the previous Union meeting in December when he announced the disbandment of his Baltimore nine. Secretary Warren White also no-showed, perhaps sensing that the lack of an eastern presence in the league would spell the end of his influence. The only attendees were the representatives for Kansas City and Milwaukee. The representatives waited all morning for the duo of Lucas and Thorner to appear or give word of their intentions. By the afternoon, the glaring absence of two of the circuit's driving figures and financial backers for the 1884 season spelled certain doom for the rebel league. With only two members left, the league in its current form was officially dead.

The meeting continued despite the betrayal of Lucas and Thorner, and a new plan for an 1885 circuit was hatched. Kansas City president A.V. McKim was elected as the temporary president while one of the Milwaukee representatives, George Ziegler, was named secretary.[10] The first order of business at the meeting was to officially disband the Union Association and form a new league. The new circuit would be called the Western League and would apply for entrance into the National Agreement. A conflicting report in Cincinnati claimed that Milwaukee and Kansas City also telegraphed the American Association directors asking for admission, with the request ignored.[11]

Emboldened by the plans for the new circuit, the resourceful Ted Sullivan instantly got to work recruiting potential clubs with the same fervor he recruited ballplayers. He sent a telegram to the Toledo directors asking if they would be able to put together a ball club. The request received a resounding "yes." The directors of the Indianapolis team, who had been courted by Lucas and Thorner the past few months, also confirmed their intentions to join the league in 1885.[12] At the close of the meeting, the new league now had four participants, Kansas City, Milwaukee, Toledo, and Indianapolis. Sullivan made plans to visit Cleveland, Toledo, and Columbus to arrange clubs. Milwaukee president Charles M. Kipp would undertake similar visits to St. Paul and Minneapolis.[13] The final Union meeting had turned into the first meeting of the Western League. If all went as planned, the western league that Lucas had envisioned before his departure to the NL would come to fruition. It would be a Union Association 2.0, as it were, sans Lucas and Thorner.

The collapse of the Union Association was met with a mixture of scorn and lament. *Sporting Life* called the final meeting "the funeral of the Union Association."[14] The lack of regard demonstrated by Lucas and Thorner in abandoning the Union Association was met with criticism. In Milwaukee, the duo's actions were villainized since both men had confirmed their desire to remain with the Union Association at the December meeting.[15] Manager Tom Loftus reportedly engaged in a heated conversation with Lucas in Chicago after the January meeting.[16] In Kansas City, there was similar disdain for the duo, now christened "Judas Iscariot Lucas" and his "man Friday" Thorner.[17] The league's most vociferous critiques had always come from the *Cincinnati Commercial*, and their parting words for the circuit were sufficiently harsh:

> One matter is decided. The Union Association is dead. It was rotten before it gave up the ghost. It goes down into the mud unwept and unregretted. Its inception was dishonest. Its existence was a fraud. Its end is annihilation. The only monuments to keep its memory in min are the poor fool players who allowed themselves to be made monkey paws for Lucas & Co. to rake out the chestnuts.[18]

From a player's perspective, the demise of the circuit was a significant loss, as *Sporting Life* noted: "Nine out of ten base ball players view the collapse of the Union Association with regret. While it did base ball players more harm than good, yet it was undoubtedly a means to deter the rival clubs and managers from exerting their power for tyranny and injustice too far."[19]

For the players who signed with the Unions and now faced permanent blacklisting, the league's demise was a source of great concern. The National League and the American Association had remained steadfast in their commitment to preventing the Union defectors from ever playing again for a club in the National Agreement. What this stance meant for Lucas was clear. He may have gained entrance into the National League but, in doing so, risked losing the vast majority of his roster. If this happened, his club would be a lame duck in the vastly more competitive National League. What does it profit a man to gain the world but lose his starting lineup in the process?

For star players like Fred Dunlap, Jack Glasscock, and Jim McCormick, their banishment would prematurely end their careers at the height of their powers. For younger players like Charlie Sweeney and Henry Boyle, the blacklist would cut off their burgeoning talents at the knees. The reinstatement of the jumpers was of the utmost importance to Lucas, who saw it as his only chance at competing. He needed to keep the likes of Dunlap and Sweeney on his club. For all his faults and disloyalty to his fellow owners in the Union Association, Lucas remained steadfast in his fight for the players who had trusted in him and his circuit.

While Lucas had been accepted into the National League, there remained one final obstacle for the feisty mogul. Chris von der Ahe and the St. Louis Brown Stockings remained steadfastly opposed to Lucas's admission into the National League. Either Lucas would need to obtain his approval, or the National Agreement would have to be dissolved. The dissolution of the National Agreement would almost certainly mean another baseball war between the NL and the AA. Over the final two weeks of January, the directors of the National League threatened to blow up the National Agreement in order to allow Lucas in.[20] For von der Ahe, he simply wanted Lucas to pay damages, and certain conditions met, namely no Sunday games, 50-cent admission fees, and no beer sold at games.[21] The NL's staunch support for Lucas was almost certainly motivated by their desire to feature a franchise in St. Louis, which had proven itself one of the most lucrative baseball markets in the country.

Lucas remained cagey and antagonistic towards von der Ahe. He threatened to propose a bill to the Missouri state government outlawing Sunday baseball.[22] This bill, if passed, would make a significant dent to von der Ahe's considerable profits. Lucas offered to withhold his bill if von der Ahe would consent to allow him into the National League. Other rumors had Lucas jumping back to the newly formed Western League, wielding his power there, and continuing his war against the baseball establishment.

A special meeting of the American Association was scheduled for January 27, 1885. This meeting would determine the fate of Lucas's National League bid and the National Agreement. In a strange serendipity, the meeting would occur at the Monongahela House in Pittsburgh, the same building that witnessed the Union Association's birth back in September 1883. The meeting turned out to be anticlimactic. Von der Ahe and Lucas had met in St. Louis two days before, on January 25. The men made amends at the behest of J.J. O'Neill, a Missouri congressional representative, who was also von der Ahe's regular legal consult.[23] The pair of rival magnates made an agreement by which Lucas would repay an estimated $2,500 in damages to von der Ahe.[24] In exchange, Lucas would receive the Brown Stockings' consent and approval to join the National League.

While Lucas got what he wanted at the NL meeting, his friend Justus Thorner was stuck in limbo. To the best of anyone's knowledge, Detroit had not disbanded and would take the field in 1885 in the NL. Thorner had burned his bridges with the new Western League, owing to his absence at their inaugural meeting. If he wanted his club to take the field in 1885, he would either need to persuade the NL to drop Detroit, or he would have to come crawling back to the directors of the Western League. As January ended, it seemed that either outcome was unlikely.

This agreement between Lucas and von der Ahe ended the impasse between the National League and the American Association heads, restored peace and kept the National Agreement in place for the coming season. The reconciliation was formally announced at the January 27 meeting. The mighty St. Louis Unions were now the Mound City's National League representatives. Henry V. Lucas, the determined and unrelenting younger brother of John B.C. Lucas, had gotten St. Louis back into the National League.

It was at Monongahela House on September 12, 1883, that the Union Association was born. And it was at Monongahela House on January 27, 1885, with the official confirmation of Lucas's acceptance into the National League, that the Union Association was given its final burial.

25

◇◇◇◇◇◇◇◇◇◇◇◇◇◇◇◇

What Killed
the Union Association?

The Union Association was officially dead once Henry V. Lucas reached an agreement with Chris von der Ahe, allowing the St. Louis Unions to join the National League. Until that moment, there was a slim chance that Lucas might try to align with the newly formed Western League that formed out of the ashes of the Union or possibly pursue another path for his club. Once the deal was done, however, Lucas was gung-ho on joining the National League. This raises a fundamental question: why did Lucas choose to jump ship?

The primary reason is money. Lucas was reported to have lost anywhere from $30,000 to $40,000 during the inaugural Union Association season.[1] Where did Lucas's $40,000 in losses come from? The cost of starting up a new team was high and included signing players, park construction, uniforms, equipment, legal fees, administrative costs, marketing, and promotion. A breakdown of the Milwaukee directors' financial expenses in 1884 found that $53,500 was spent to get the club up and running, and that was in the lower-salaried Northwestern League:

24 players and manager	$19,200
Printing and advertising	2,000
Suits, bats, balls, etc.	650
Janitor and help on grounds	900
Grandstand, seats and diamond	3,500
Estimated pay to visiting clubs	9,000
Tax, interest, repairs, etc., on grounds	900
Charter, plans, seal, etc.	150
Cost of grounds	11,500
Traveling expense of two nines and managers	5,000
Special expenses not yet accounted for	700
TOTAL	$53,500[2]

Lucas would have taken on the same expenses and likely spent even more on getting his team up and running. The salary list for Lucas's 1884 club was estimated at $21,000, which made his club this highest paid in the circuit. Lucas and his backers had also spent $15,000 on building the club's ballpark. The club played 55 home games and, at $75 per contest, would have paid out at least $4125 in road guarantees to visiting clubs. Given Lucas's tendencies towards lavishness, it seems probable that he spent large sums on uniforms, equipment, advertising, and other expenses.

Lucas bore the costs of his own club and also put money into the league. Each club demonstrated vastly different levels of financial stability, and Lucas was known to have invested money into several clubs. A deep dive into the finances of the circuit reveals that the Union Association was on exceedingly shaky ground after its first season. Even though Lucas lost money, his St. Louis was reportedly the most profitable in the league. They drew exceptionally well on the season, bringing over 160,000 fans to the Union Base Ball Park.[3] Washington was reportedly the second most profitable club in the league, with a $12,000 profit reported at the end of August.[4] No published figure of St. Louis's profits for the 1884 season exists, but using Washington's profits as a reference point, it can be inferred that Lucas's club likely cleared over $12,000 on the season. The Kansas City Unions made $6,000 while Milwaukee made $3,000. St. Paul did not make any money on the season but reportedly covered all of their expenses during their brief stint in the league. As a standalone entity, Baltimore was thought to have broken even or come close to doing so. However, the failure of the Chicago/Pittsburgh Unions lost $12,000. That means that the Henderson syndicate was at least down $12,000. Boston reportedly lost $10,000 on the season. The Keystones were also $10,000 to $12,000 in the red at the time of their disbandment. Justus Thorner's Cincinnati club lost $11,000. Wilmington lost $1,500 during their month in the Union. Altoona's losses were never reported, but it can be assumed they were behind at least a few thousand dollars on their season.

These figures indicate that four out of 12 teams turned significant profits, St. Louis, Washington, Kansas City, and Milwaukee. Two clubs were in the realm of breaking even, Baltimore and St. Paul. The other six clubs were big money losers; four clubs lost at least $10,000 while Altoona and Wilmington lost thousands in abbreviated seasons.

The key factor in determining a team's profitability was drawing fans to the ballpark. The most profitable teams in the Union Association were the best drawing ones. St. Louis, Washington, Kansas City, and Milwaukee drew crowds that averaged between 1500 and 3000 per game. All but Washington had the luxury of playing Sunday contests. Baltimore had stretches of excellent attendance in the summer, and the club came close to breaking even. The clubs that lost money drew between 100 to 500 fans for the majority of their games. This poor attendance was not sustainable, no matter how low the salary list was. Just ask Altoona.

As the league's primary financial backer, Lucas was paying for his own nine and also assuming the costs of running the league. While his own club may have turned a profit, the costs incurred in helping the UA survive the season put him deep in the hole. He put money into the formation of other clubs in the league, who each bore similar startup costs to the ones provided by Milwaukee. Existing reports suggest that the majority of Lucas's losses came from trying to build up the league and support its lesser franchises. Lucas was known to have contributed money to help the Boston Unions get up and running. At midseason, he had worked out a deal alongside fellow directors Justus Thorner and Albert H. Henderson to take on Boston's losses for the season to keep them from disbanding. It seems likely that Lucas did the same with other clubs in the circuit, though with Altoona and Wilmington, he pulled the plug rather than digging deep into his pockets to keep the doormats afloat.

Having endured a tumultuous inaugural season, it seems likely that Lucas was reticent to continue the venture knowing full well the vast uncertainty of the league going forward. In the National League, he would not have to worry about keeping the Altoonas and Wilmingtons of the world alive. He could focus his energy, money, and attention entirely on making his own club a success. There was a greater chance of profitability in the National League, particularly if he could harness the interest in his Union club into fans who would now pay double the price for the privilege of watching his club. The one downside to joining the NL would be the loss of the right to play Sunday contests.

It is worth considering the alternate scenario where Henry Lucas remains in the Union Association in 1885. Since he had lost tens of thousands of dollars and only four of the league's franchises were profitable, it meant that the configuration of the league in the 1885 season would need to focus on building a solid foundation. St. Louis, Kansas City, and Milwaukee would be the strongest clubs financially in the coming season, while Cincinnati, despite their losses, was also committed to taking the field. That still meant that four more teams needed to be found to make an eight-team league. The league's second most profitable team, the Nationals, under Mike Scanlon had expressed no interest in remaining in the league owing to a dispute with Lucas. Boston and Baltimore also withdrew. The withdrawals meant that the league now had only three teams who had made money in 1884. It also meant that the league would have had to be based entirely in the west since there were no viable eastern markets expressing interest.

A number of western cities were speculated to be potential members of the Union Association, including Columbus, Indianapolis, St. Paul, Detroit, Dayton, and Cleveland. St. Paul and Indianapolis were likely inclusions for 1885, as each city was represented at the December 1884 Union meeting. The Columbus directors were profitable in 1884, thanks to the sale of their team. With the Columbus park under new ownership, there were doubts a deal could be worked out for 1885. Dayton had fielded an independent club in 1884 and expressed interest in joining the Union, but the market was likely too small to be considered. Detroit and Cleveland both had National League teams in flux. Their respective situations would need to be resolved, and neither locale had established that they could draw enough fans to cover costs.

The most likely configuration of the Union Association in 1885 would have seen teams in St. Louis, Cincinnati, Kansas City, Milwaukee, Indianapolis, St. Paul, with the remaining two spots going to Columbus, Detroit, or Cleveland. This theoretical league would have stood a better chance at profitability since there were no tiny markets, and travel costs would have been reduced by ignoring the east coast. There were still major red flags, though. If fans in Detroit and Cleveland were wary of supporting a National League team, why would they support a Union team? Cleveland, in particular, had a particular hatred for all things Lucas and would likely reject any team with Union connections. Cincinnati had Thorner's determined leadership and willingness to spend, but they were still likely to lose money in 1885. They boasted a high salary list and were competing against the city's more popular American Association club. Indianapolis was a smaller market, and questions about their ability to support a pro team abounded. They had failed to support their National League club in 1878 and their AA entrant in 1884.

These potential outcomes do not even address the fact that the entire crux of Henry Lucas and Justus Thorner's plan to gain entry into the National League involved the disbandment of the Cleveland and Detroit clubs. If those two cities joined the Union Association, that would have created openings in the NL. This would have meant the almost certain departure of Lucas and Thorner, which would have sunk the league anyway. Assuming the best-case scenario, that Cleveland and Detroit join the Union while both St. Louis and Cincinnati stay put, there was a potentially viable western circuit.

The Union Association both came into existence and failed because of Henry Lucas. His vision, leadership, and bankroll enabled the league to see play in April 1884. The league likely would not have made it past the meeting stage without his financing and relentless hustle. He built relationships, sought out members, and had the money to turn the idea into reality. Albert H. Henderson lacked the chutzpah that Lucas had, even if he possessed more sound business acumen. Lucas's willingness to spend money freely also helped keep clubs afloat and ensured that the season was completed in some form or fashion.

That being said, Lucas made several tactical mistakes that put the league in a precarious position almost from its inception. Lucas's aggressive pursuit of star players and big-spending forced others like Henderson, Thorner, and Tom Pratt to open their wallets and try to obtain stars. This approach antagonized the National Agreement clubs while also yielding relatively little in terms of quality players. Of the pre-season defectors who were on opening day rosters, only Fred Dunlap, Orator Shafer, and George Bradley were what could be considered star players. The rest of the experienced major leaguers signed by the Union Association were mid-tier to lower-tier talents, often with significant question marks attached to them.

Even when players signed Union contracts, there was no guarantee they would honor them, as the cases of Tony Mullane and Larry Corcoran demonstrated. The Union Association offered little advantage to players over the National Agreement clubs, particularly once the Day resolution was in place. A player jumping his contract to join the Unions risked his entire future. He might receive a higher salary in 1884, but there was little guarantee the league would survive the season. This is the very reason Lucas was handing out wads of cash to players; he wanted them to see that the money was real. In response, the National Agreement clubs wielded the threat of blacklist aggressively, attempting to ensure that every reserved player who had signed a Union contract was back in the fold before the season. The Union had no recourse in those cases, and the tactic kept players from jumping ship.

The Henderson strategy of focusing on lower costed Northwestern League talent presented an alternate path of team construction that was likely more sustainable and would probably have drawn less animosity. Despite being signatories in the National Agreement, the Northwestern League wielded little power and received little support from the NL or the AA. The league viewed the agreement as a means of enabling the protection of their players under the reserve rule. When Henderson was poaching players from the league in October 1883, his actions received little attention or comment from either the NL or the AA directorship. Conversely, when Lucas signed Tony Mullane and other major-league players, the pearl-clutching and hand wringing about the sanctity of contracts began. Lucas made the Union Association into a threat to the establishment for better or for worse. Had Lucas followed the Henderson path, it seems likely that the Union would not have drawn nearly the negativity from the media or major league magnates.

The eight original Union teams demonstrated a variety of approaches in spending and roster construction, and no one approach guaranteed success at the box office or on the field. St. Louis and Cincinnati spent big and won big on the field. St. Louis was a moneymaker, while Thorner's club lost thousands. Philadelphia and Boston each tried to field heavily local teams composed of old names from the past and young upstarts from the sandlots, but both lost big financially, despite modest salary lists. Henderson's Baltimore nine finished in third place and broke even financially with a roster made up almost entirely of Northwestern League alumni. Conversely, his Chicago team was a loser at the gate and on the field, despite following much the same approach. Washington and Altoona both went cheap and performed poorly on the field. Washington was exceptionally profitable, while Altoona lasted six weeks and collapsed. A cohesive and consistent strategy for spending and roster construction might have mitigated the extreme competitive and financial imbalance that came to mark the league.

Perhaps the most critical factor in the league's failure was timing. The Union Association came along a year or two too late. By the time the league formed, the American Association was just wrapping up its second season. The National Agreement was in place, which ensured roster stability while most AA and NL markets did not overlap. The ones that did, New York and Philadelphia, were each large enough to sustain two teams. The majority of viable western and eastern markets were home to teams by the end of 1883. When the Union formed, few open markets remained, which caused tiny Altoona to be added in February. Of the original eight clubs, seven were playing in opposition to AA or NL clubs. The arrival of the Union Association caused the AA and the NL to double down and fight the new league while also strengthening the power of the reserve rule. Had Lucas and company started up in 1882 or even in the offseason of 1883 when the National Agreement was still being worked out, there would have been a higher chance of success.

Eighteen eighty-four was also a year with too much baseball, to be frank. An all-time record of 33 major league teams took the field, appearing in 34 cities. In addition to the three major leagues, there were 14 more recognized minor leagues, numerous reserve teams, and a multitude of semi-pro, independent, and amateur clubs. Every one of these leagues saw some level of turmoil, with countless teams disbanding and circuits folding. There simply were not enough good baseball players in the country to sustain that many teams, and the competition for players was fierce. Without the protection of the National Agreement and with every club in the country in search of ballplayers, the Union Association was incredibly vulnerable to deserters. With no allies in the baseball world, the circuit was left to fend for itself. Sure, they could blacklist players, as they did at the July 1884 meeting, but that really meant nothing. The legal system had little interest in haggling over baseball contracts, as the Tony Mullane case showed. The Union had no recourse against the power of the National Agreement. While they successfully induced many players to join, they also had many desert them in return. For every Fred Dunlap, Dupee Shaw, or Charlie Sweeney, there was a Tony Mullane, Billy Taylor, or Buttercup Dickerson.

There was a road to profitability for the Union Association, but it required a cohesive vision. If Lucas had sought to use his resources to bolster the rosters of other clubs in the league as well as his own, the issue of gross competitive imbalance would have been mitigated. In theory, this could have improved attendance in certain markets that had tuned out on the league. Alternatively, a fusion of the Baltimore, Washington, and Boston approaches could also have led to success on the field and saved money. Keeping costs low was a pivotal factor to sustainability, but drawing fans to the park was equally important. Balancing these two factors was the problem that needed to be solved. An eight-team league whose rosters were both evenly balanced and low costed would have stood a better chance at seeing play in 1885. Achieving such a circuit would have required an exceptional unity amongst the directors and incredibly skillful scouting and roster construction. This combination may have proven impossible to achieve.

In reality, even though the Union Association was dead, the men who made it were still alive. The 1885 season would see these men and the ghosts of the organization continue to influence every facet of the baseball world.

26

The Ghosts of the Union

Henry V. Lucas, the millionaire scion of the Lucas dynasty, one of the wealthiest and renowned families in St. Louis, was now a magnate in the National League. Through a mixture of unrelenting gall and hubris, and seemingly unlimited financial resources, Lucas had forged his identity upon the baseball world. The question remained, could he make good in the National League? History shows that the definitive answer to the question was a resounding no.

Lucas's NL tenure got off to a rocky start in the months leading up to the beginning of the 1885 season. The status of the Union Association's blacklisted players was the source of heated contention throughout the offseason. Lucas's insistence that contract jumpers be reinstated drew the ire of his National League associates. Both the AA and the NL were determined to make an example of the players and flex their considerable power to show what would happen to a player who challenged the reserve rule or broke a contract.[1] To his credit, Lucas refused to roll over on the matter. He was steadfast in his fight to reinstate the players who had trusted in his dream:

> I was the means of making these men break their contracts. I offered them larger salaries than they were receiving. I induced them to desert, and if they committed any crime, surely I was a party to it. Now the League has taken me into its fold and it refuses to reinstate them. I don't know exactly what I can do just yet as to forming a nine. I will organize a team, the best I can get, and make strenuous efforts to impress on the minds of the League officials that they are acting unwisely in refusing to allow my men to play.[2]

Lucas's intentions were not entirely out of benevolence, as he recognized how difficult his club's chances would be without the blacklisted stars. Still, every public quote he gave on the subject voiced support for the players and their reinstatement.

In the months leading up the season, there remained uncertainty about whether Lucas would stay in the League without the blacklisted players. One report from the *Cincinnati Commercial* inferred Lucas was "privately at work in an effort to betray the National League," intending to infiltrate the leadership of the Western League, the same one that had formed out of the ashes of the Union Association.[3] The Western League directors in Indianapolis, Cleveland, and Milwaukee were reportedly wary of such a plot.[4] It is not clear if Lucas had floated the rumor to force the NL's hand or if it was invented by O.P. Caylor, Lucas's most unabashed critic. Regardless of the veracity of the rumor, by early April, Lucas had committed to playing his league dates. The *St. Louis Post-Dispatch* implied that Lucas's official committal resulted from his belief that the "reserve rule jumpers would be placed on good footing again."[5]

With or without his reinstated stars, Lucas's club, now dubbed the Maroons or the Leagues, was slated to play an eight-game exhibition series with the rival Browns (formerly the Brown Stockings) that would last through April. The series began on April 11, with Lucas's club a shadow of its former self because of the absence of the blacklisted players. In a strange irony, Lucas had signed the battery of Fleury Sullivan and Billy Colgan out of East St. Louis, Illinois. This pair had deserted the Union Association in spring 1884 for the Pittsburgh Alleghenys after signing contracts with the Chicago Unions, eventually earning a Union blacklist that July. The duo may have been better off sticking with the Union, as Sullivan went 16–35 with a 4.20 ERA while Colgan hit just .155/.171/.193 in the stronger AA. The pair was the battery in the first contest, which saw over 2,000 fans turn out to Sportsman's Park despite the brutally cold weather.[6] Sullivan and Colgan faced off against the Brown Stockings duo of Dave Foutz and Doc Bushong. Foutz was dominant for the Browns, allowing just one hit as his club took the contest, 7–0. Lucas's nine featured several members of his Union squad, notably Fred Lewis, Henry Boyle, Joe Quinn, George Baker, and Jack Brennan. Still, they lacked the star power that Dunlap, Shafer, and Sweeney had provided. The duo of Sullivan and Colgan proved to be a bust for Lucas and were soon released into the baseball hinterlands. Neither man would make it out his thirties alive, with Colgan perishing on August 8, 1895, after being crushed by a coal car while working as a switchman in Montana.[7] Sullivan was shot to death less than two years later in 1897 after a heated political argument in an East St. Louis saloon.[8]

The teams met again on April 13 in front of 2,000 fans at Lucas's grounds. The home team, colloquially referred to as the Preserves by some observers, took a come from behind 6–4 victory, thanks to a solid pitching performance by Handsome Henry Boyle. The pitcher had been reinstated from his blacklist in February by the Eastern League. It was found that he was owed money by Reading in July 1884 and had been encouraged by the team directors to find a better situation for himself.[9] He was a free man when he signed with the Unions the previous summer and should not have been blacklisted. Game three took place on April 16 in front of 1,000 fans at the Browns home grounds and resulted in another thrashing of Fleury Sullivan's deliveries, with Dave Foutz again winning by shutout, 8–0.[10] Game four on April 17 was postponed because of inclement weather. The series would soon be ground to a halt by the events of the following day.

The National League held a special meeting on April 18, 1885, less than two weeks before opening day. After months of haggling, Lucas finally got what he wanted. The National League players blacklisted for jumping their contracts or breaking the reserve rule to join the Union Association were finally re-admitted. Each banned player could receive reinstatement if they paid a fine for the various offenses related to their jump. Fred Dunlap, Orator Shafer, Hugh Daily, and Emil Gross were given $500 fines for jumping the reserve rule.[11] More severe fines of $1,000 each were assessed to Jack Glasscock, Charles Briody, Jim McCormick, and Dupee Shaw since each man had broken their playing contracts mid-season. Charlie Sweeney was also fined the amount of $1,000, with his charge being the insubordination that had caused his departure from Providence the previous July. Every player reportedly paid their fines, though the enigmatic Gross never played profession- ally again and later claimed to have refused to pay the fine.[12] The reinstated men were now free to sign with any club in the National League. Lucas was expected to re-sign Dunlap, Shafer, and Sweeney. He also planned to snap up the Cincinnati Union trio. The addition of these six men would give Lucas's National League nine a much-needed boost and a fighting chance in their new league. Shaw planned to sign with Boston while the status of Daily and Gross was uncertain.

Lucas cast the reinstatements as good for his players, good for St. Louis, and good for the National League:

> I am proud of the fact that I didn't desert the black-listed men who trusted in me and signed with me last year. They kept faith with me, and I guess the public will concede that I have kept faith with them. Of course, I am happy to have a good team to present against other League teams. As for viewing the final result in the light of a personal triumph, I will not do anything of the kind. I will leave others to say what they please on that score while I will feel grateful to the other members of the League for the spirit they have shown toward me, and I hope that when they visit St. Louis, they will be convinced that their action ... was only what the city deserved in return for its patronage of the game.[13]

Justus Thorner sent Lucas a telegraph congratulating him on his victory and for standing up for their former players.[14]

The American Association remained staunchly opposed to the reinstatement of the players it viewed as guilty of jumping AA contracts. Cincinnati's George Bradley, Philadelphia's Sam Weaver, Baltimore's Al Atkinson, and Gid Gardner were black- listed. Tony Mullane also earned a blacklist for signing with both the Cincinnati and St. Louis Association clubs. Three members of Lucas's Union Association champi- ons, Jack Gleason, Tom Dolan, and Dave Rowe, would also be ineligible in 1885.[15] Chris von der Ahe painted the National League's decision to reinstate the jumpers as a bald-faced assault on the American Association, which he believed was now the premier league in baseball.[16] He vowed to cancel pending exhibition games against National League clubs, including the fledgling city series against Lucas's Maroons.

In the following days, Lucas officially signed Dunlap, Sweeney, and Shafer to NL contracts. He also signed Jack Glasscock and Charles Briody. Despite rumors that McCormick would also sign and give St. Louis a dynamic 1–2 punch with Sweeney, the pitcher signed with Providence for $2,500.[17] He would join forces with Old Hoss Radbourn in their fight to repeat as world champions. This failure to sign the work- horse from Paterson, New Jersey, was a big blow to the club's pitching staff. St. Lou- is's fate would depend on Sweeney and Boyle replicating their results from the Union Association.

While Lucas was readying his club for the coming National League season, his old friend Justus Thorner was fighting for his club's survival. Detroit was staying put in the NL, closing off the only avenue for his club to join the NL. That left Thorner to try to apply to the Western League. The other directors viewed his application with suspicion due to his past betrayal and alliance with Lucas.[18] Thorner sent word that he would attend the February meeting of the league, hoping to gain entrance. As he had in January, he failed to show for the gathering, "doubtless realizing the fact that

[his] club would not be admitted to membership," since it might cost the league a spot in the National Agreement.[19] Cincinnati was an outlaw club with no league to play in, and Thorner had no options to take the field in 1885. The Cincinnati Unions were officially dead, and Thorner's career in baseball came to an abrupt end.

While Cincinnati went bust, several other former Union organizations were also preparing for the 1885 season. Milwaukee and Kansas City were both expected to field strong clubs in the Western League. At the same time, Mike Scanlon had more or less brought back the final iteration of his 1884 Nationals squad for competition in the Eastern League. Unexpectedly, two of the disbanded Union clubs would also take the field in some form that spring. A revamped semi-professional nine called the Boston Unions formed in March 1885. They would feature six members of the 1884 squad in John Irwin, Tommy McCarthy, Frank "Kid" Butler, Mike Slattery, Henry Mullin, and Jim McKeever. The club's time in Boston proved short-lived as they relocated to Biddeford, Maine, after an April tour of New England.[20] The club began play in the Eastern New England League but relocated once again to Newburyport, Massachusetts, and finished in last place with a 25–55 record. In Wilmington, John T. West took another crack at making professional baseball work in his hometown, hastily constructing a team for entry in the Eastern League.

Opening day in the National League arrived on April 30, with the Maroons welcoming the visiting Chicago White Stockings to the Union Grounds. Lucas could not have been more thrilled with the result. Seven thousand fans turned out to welcome him to the National League, and the mercurial Charlie Sweeney was on his best behavior. The moody hurler pitched a beautiful contest allowing just three hits to a star-studded White Stockings lineup while outdueling the diminutive Larry Corcoran for a 3–2 victory. Hard-hitting Fred Lewis won the day for the Maroons with three hits, including a home run. This thrilling victory was arguably the club's high point on the season. After starting the season 6–4, the club lost nine straight games to fall to 6–13. The streak cemented the club in the second division and was the first of five different losing streaks of five games or longer.

The Maroons came to be disparagingly referred to as the Black Diamonds. This was thanks to the presence of so many formerly blacklisted players in their lineup. A brutal stretch from July 10 to September 15 saw the club go just 2–20–1. The club posted a miserable 36–72–3 record, good for last place. The club met a similar fate at the gate. Interest in the club fell after their opening series, and the club reportedly drew just 62,000 fans across 58 home games.[21] This figure was a considerable drop from the 160,000 plus fans who attended the 55 St. Louis Union home games the previous year.

Henry Lucas blamed the club's struggles on factionalism, with a clique led by Fred Dunlap supposedly responsible for the club's collapse in the standings.[22] The absolute lack of hitting depth in the lineup and the steep decline in Charlie Sweeney's performance were the more likely culprits. The Maroons finished last in the National League in virtually every hitting category. They scored just 390 runs, 52 fewer than Providence, the next lowest scoring club. Dunlap, for his part, hit respectably but nowhere near his 1884 levels. He also failed to match his previous National League numbers. "Sure Shot" posted a .270/.334/.333 batting line and a career-low 119

OPS+. Only Fred Lewis, newcomer Alex McKinnon at first base, Dunlap, and Glass-cock posted an OPS+ north of 100 in regular action. "Pebbly Jack" was the club's best player, posting a .280/.324/.341 batting line and a 118 OPS+ while playing his customary excellent defense at shortstop. He posted a 5.1 WAR on the season, which marked his highest total to date. Glasscock's excellence would continue for many years, peaking with an outstanding 1890 campaign for the New York Giants that saw him hit .336 to win the National League batting title while posting a career-high 7.1 WAR. He had the dual misfortune to labor for generally weak teams while never being identified with a specific club. He appeared for Cleveland, St. Louis, Indianapolis, New York, Pittsburgh, Louisville, and Washington at various points, along with his stint in the Union Association. The hallmarks of his career were his solid hitting ability and outstanding defense. Despite finishing with over 2,000 career hits, 61.6 career WAR, and a reputation as one of the best defensive shortstops of the era, to date, he has not been elected to the Baseball Hall of Fame.

The Maroons' other Union Association stars, Orator Shafer, Charles Briody, and Joe Quinn, performed dreadfully. The trio posted OPS+ of 65, 62, and 57, respectively. Despite Quinn's awful hitting as a first sacker, he had already developed a reputation as an intelligent and honest player in the mold of his mentor Charlie Comiskey. The brainy Quinn parlayed his abilities into a lengthy major league career that would see him play until 1901 when he finished up with the American League's Washington Senators. Although he never hit much, with a career batting line of .262/.303/.328 and 76 OPS+, he was revered for his intangibles and steady leadership. Quinn later starred for the Boston Beaneaters in the 1890s, and at one point, he was voted "America's Most Popular Player" in a *Sporting Life* poll.[23] In a strange irony befitting a Union Association alumnus, Quinn had the peculiar fortune to play for the team with the best winning record in major league history (St. Louis Unions) and the worst, when he served as captain of the fabled 1899 Cleveland Spiders, who went 20–134.

Other key contributors to the Unions also struggled mightily in the stronger National League. George Baker, the Union club's defensive wizard behind the plate, hit an

Dave Rowe was one of Henry Lucas's first signees in November 1883. He was blacklisted by the American Association for defecting to the Union Association. He led the Union Association in at-bats and hit .293. He was refused reinstatement by the AA after 1884 and became embroiled in a legal dispute with Chris von der Ahe that forced him to miss much of the 1885 season (courtesy Southern Illinois University Press).

astonishingly poor .122/.179/.122, good for an OPS+ of precisely 0. Charlie Sweeney struggled to an 11–21 record with a 3.93 ERA, both of which were massive declines from his performance with Providence, the prior season when he posted a 17–8 record with a 1.55 ERA. The club's pitching staff allowed 593 runs, which was the second-worst total in the league. The only area that saw the Maroons appear respectable was their defense, posting the league's second-highest fielding percentage with .916 and the fourth-best defensive efficiency with .661.

The season was also marred by the ongoing blacklist of Dave Rowe, Jack Gleason, and Tom Dolan. The trio, while not stars, were capable major-league players, and their absence hurt the Maroons. The legal proceedings involving Rowe, in particular, would drag out nearly the entire season. Rowe had filed a lawsuit against Chris von der Ahe for $25,000 due to the blacklist, claiming that he had not signed a contract with the Brown Stockings after his 1883 Baltimore contract expired.[24] Rowe acknowledged in his deposition that he had entered into negotiations with the Brown Stockings but had chosen to sign with Lucas after being contacted by Ted Sullivan. Rowe reportedly won a $500 injunction against St. Louis for unjust expulsion.[25]

At an American Association meeting on June 7 in Philadelphia, the proposed reinstatement of the reserve list jumpers was put towards the directors. The motion was expected to pass easily, but the Mullane and Rowe cases proved too contentious, and the ban continued.[26] Gid Gardner was reinstated as he hadn't broken his AA contract and had jumped to the Union Association only after being expelled for bad behavior.[27] In light of the negative result, Lucas held a benefit game for his trio of blacklisted stars on June 28, which drew nearly 6,000 fans.[28] The trio also played for semi-pro clubs in the area to bide their time.[29] Rowe's case would finally be heard in the St. Louis courts in late August. President Lucas was one of the witnesses asked to provide a deposition, and he noted that he had not signed a contract with Rowe for the 1885 season, but there was a verbal understanding that he would sign Rowe if he were eligible to play.[30] On September 8, Rowe withdrew his suit against von der Ahe in exchange for his reinstatement by the American Association.[31] In October, Gleason and Dolan were

Tom Dolan was a hard-nosed catcher who defected to the Union Association late in the season after a dispute with Chris von der Ahe. Like teammates Dave Rowe and Jack Gleason, he was refused reinstatement by the AA and missed almost the entire 1885 season (courtesy Southern Illinois University Press).

reinstated, and the pair joined the Maroons for the final few contests of the season.[32]

The one that got away, Jim McCormick, had his own tumultuous 1885 season. McCormick had eschewed Lucas's offer to sign with Providence, the defending world champions. His time with the club was very brief. He made only four appearances with the club in two and half months before being traded to Chicago for outfielder/pitcher George Van Haltren and $2,000. It seems likely his $2,500 salary was too much for the cash-strapped Rhode Islanders. McCormick pitched wonderfully down the stretch for the White Stockings, helping them clinch the pennant with a 20–4 record supporting the otherworldly performance of Northwestern League alumnus John Clarkson who won 53 games that year. Had McCormick signed with the Maroons, it would have gone a long way towards pushing the club towards respectability, though a pennant was likely out of reach. McCormick spent two more seasons with Chicago and closed out his career in Pittsburgh in 1887. Like his old teammate Jack Glasscock, he has not been elected to the Hall of Fame, despite

Jack Gleason was a talented infielder who had starred alongside his brother Bill for the St. Louis Brown Stockings. Gleason defected to Henry Lucas's nine in November 1883, after he was offered a lowly $1,000 salary by Louisville. He had a career high .324 in 92 games in the Union Association (courtesy Southern Illinois University Press).

a strong case. His career marks of 265–214, 2.43 ERA, 118 ERA+, 4275.2 innings, and 76.2 WAR align favorably with previous candidates. It appears that his early career spent laboring for mediocre Cleveland clubs prevented him from reaching 300 wins. His reputation as one of the great pitchers of the 1880s has generally been forgotten.

The remaining trio of blacklisted players, George Bradley, Al Atkinson, and Sam Weaver, were all reinstated at the American Association meeting on October 16, 1885.[33] The meeting also saw the signing of a new National Agreement. The new accord saw its members put a maximum salary of $2,000 per player in place for 1886, no doubt a lingering after-effect of the tumultuous 1884 campaign. Each of the three reinstated pitchers signed with the Athletics for the coming season. Bradley had spent 1885 embroiled in a lawsuit of his own with Justus Thorner and his Cincinnati club, arguing that the club had breached his contract by not paying him for the 1885 season. He eventually settled for $636.[34] Despite a year of rest, Bradley's arm was shot. He appeared in just 13 games at shortstop for the Athletics in 1886 before being released. He spent several more years as a minor league infielder. When he died of liver cancer at age 79 in 1931, his legacy as one of the National League's first stars and author of its first no-hitter remained intact.[35]

Atkinson spent 1885 pitching for a semipro club in St. Joseph, Missouri, and re-signed with the Athletics. He won 25 games in 1886 for the A's and threw his second career no-hitter, a 3–2 win on May 1, 1886, against New York. Despite his win total, he was essentially a mediocre pitcher, leading the league in home runs allowed and hit batsmen while posting a 3.95 ERA and 87 ERA+. His major league career ended in 1887, and he became a farmer in Missouri, where he lived until the ripe old age of 91. Upon his death in 1952, he was one of the last surviving UA players.[36]

Weaver pitched poorly for the Athletics. He was released in May after making two dreadful appearances, posting a 14.73 ERA and allowing 29 runs and 30 hits in 11 innings of work. His struggles ended his professional career at age 30. Like Bradley, he also became a Philadelphia police officer after his career. When he passed at age 59 in 1914, his obituaries were sure to note that he was baseball's original "Buck" Weaver.[37]

As bad as Lucas's inaugural NL season was, the struggles of the Western League were even worse. The six-team circuit comprised Kansas City, Milwaukee, Indianapolis, Toledo, Cleveland, and Omaha. Indianapolis, Kansas City, and Milwaukee were ostensibly versions of the clubs that had played in the major leagues the prior season, with the Toledo and Cleveland nines unrelated to their 1884 predecessors. St. Paul, guided by 1884 manager Andrew M. Thompson, dropped out in late March after the club failed to secure a ballpark for the coming season.[38] Irony of ironies, the team that played all its games on the road, was still without a home. Omaha was quickly enlisted to replace them. The new Nebraska nine were unconnected to the Union Pacifics nine that had almost gained entry into the Union Association the previous September. Interest continued unabated from the previous year in Milwaukee, with the club drawing an average of "1,000 for Tuesdays, Wednesdays, and Thursdays, 1,000 for Saturdays, and 5,000 for Sundays in cold weather."[39] In Kansas City, attendance was similarly impressive. Their Sunday contests drew 5,000 or more and weekday contests often drew over 1,000 fans despite the cold and rainy weather that marred the early season.

Indianapolis proved to be the class of the league, with every single member of the roster eventually boasting major league experience. Future Hall of Famer Sam Thompson and four Union Association alumni: Sam Crane, Mox McQuery, Cyclone Miller, and Dan Casey starred for the club. The club was so dominant that local interest was diminished by their one-sided victories.[40]

The league's other squads proved as fragile as the weaklings that marred the Union Association. The hastily built Omaha nine struggled on the field, posting a 4–22 record before relocating to Keokuk, Iowa, on June 6. The franchise's singular historical contribution is a famous team photograph that features nineteenth-century Black baseball legend Bud Fowler, who made eight appearances for the Midwestern club. The Toledo Avengers failed to avenge much of anything and disbanded on June 7 with an 8–21 record after reportedly "dying a financial death."[41]

The Cleveland Forest Citys had also disbanded on June 6, $2,500 in debt, after posting a mediocre 13–17 record.[42] The club's roster featured two more Black players in the famed Walker brothers, Moses and Welday, who had integrated the major leagues the previous season with Toledo. Bill Sweeney, the star pitcher of the Baltimore Unions, was the purported ace of the nine. He struggled to replicate his success of the prior year and posted a 2–5 record. Due to arm troubles, he was no longer capable of pitching regularly, no doubt thanks to the 538 innings he pitched the year before.

With the league in shambles, first-place Indianapolis sold out of the circuit holding a 27–4 record. The club directors sold the franchise to the owners of the Detroit club for a reported $5,000.[43] Thanks to this influx of talent and the astute acquisition of Indianapolis manager Bill Watkins, the moribund Detroits were turned into a competitive squad, going 34–36 down the stretch after an abysmal 7–31 start. The Indianapolis purchase, which included future superstar Sam Thompson, was the first of many moves Detroit would make over the next few seasons, culminating in a National League pennant in 1887 and a legacy as one of the most famous clubs of the 19th century. With Indianapolis's departure, Milwaukee and Kansas City were left with no one else to play. Despite strong crowds in some markets and a number of quality players, the Western League was dead on June 15, 1885. At least they lasted longer than Altoona.

By contrast, Mike Scanlon was having a ball in the Eastern League. His Washington Nationals, fielding much the same roster as he had in the Union Association, were the class of the circuit. Like the Western League, the reconstituted eight-team circuit faced its own uncertainties as the season progressed. Another former Union Association city was the first club to falter. John T. West, apparently not put off by the dreadful experience of his Wilmington club in 1884, had put together another nine to represent the state of Delaware. The club was an unmitigated disaster on and off the field. They relocated to Atlantic City on June 20 before folding for good on June 25 with a pathetic 2–22 record. Several other clubs folded, including Jersey City, Trenton, Lancaster, Norfolk, and eventually the Virginia franchise that had played in the American Association in 1884. By the season's close, the Nationals had won the pennant with a 70–25 record.

Scanlon's nine had continued to draw well even in the minor circuit, often topping 1,000 fans, with a season-high 6200 attending an exhibition game against the eventual American Association champion St. Louis Brown Stockings on September 14.[44] The Nationals played a hard-fought contest against the champs, losing by a respectable 4–1 score. On October 16, the Nationals played perhaps the most remarkable game in their history. Facing off against New York, who was fresh off a second-place finish in the National League, the Washington nine took home a remarkable 2–1 victory.[45] Hometown hero Bob Barr out-dueled future Hall of Famer "Smiling" Mickey Welch in a game called by darkness after seven innings. This win added to a string of victories the club had scored over the AA clubs from Philadelphia, Louisville, and Baltimore. The strength of Scanlon's nine on the field and at the box office meant they were a prime contender to join either the American

Association or the National League in 1886. There is an excellent case to be made that by the close of the 1885 season, the Nationals were the best Union Association alumni in existence, besting Lucas's once-prized nine. In a manner befitting the Union Association that feels right somehow. The last shall be first, and the first shall be last.

27

◇◇◇◇◇◇◇◇◇◇◇◇◇◇

Henry Lucas Opts Out

February 8, 1889

Henry V. Lucas arrived in his hometown to visit his wife and son. He was once the talk of the baseball world, as the driving force of the Union Association, and the man who brought League baseball back to St. Louis. But now, the man formerly known as Millionaire Lucas was a railroad clerk. He was living in St. Paul, Minnesota, working out of the Wisconsin Central office. The former magnate still had friends in the city where he had made such an impact, though. He may have left baseball behind, but when he walked into the lobby of the Laclede Hotel, it all came rushing back to him. For there stood Fred Dunlap, the King of Second Basemen, now a bit heavier and starting to show his age. The man they called "Dunnie" was on his way to Hot Springs, Arkansas, to undergo a rigorous training regimen to prepare for the coming season. The two men exchanged pleasantries and expressed their joy upon seeing one another for the first time in several years. His star had shone so brightly during that magical year of 1884, turning the St. Louis Unions into the prized club in all of baseball. The two men then sat down for several hours, chatting about the prospects for Dunlap's Pittsburgh club in 1889, who both men felt had a chance at the pennant. Dunlap was still the undisputed King, the highest paid man in baseball, continuing the trend started by Lucas all those years ago. The men commiserated about the unfortunate fate of the St. Louis National League club and how it all unraveled in the summer of 1886.

Eighteen eighty-six saw the final stake driven in the heart of Henry V. Lucas's aspirations as a baseball magnate. In September 1885, Lucas announced his resignation as the managing director of the St. Louis Athletic Association, the parent organization of the St. Louis National League club.[1] Benjamin J. Fine, an agent for the Chesapeake and Ohio Railroad, was hired to fill the vacancy. Lucas's departure meant he would no longer manage the day-to-day operations of his ball club. It was speculated that Lucas was stepping aside to focus more time on his business affairs outside the baseball world. The passionate leader was also dismayed by the ups and downs of running a baseball club, particularly a losing one. He had lost at least $30,000 on the inaugural Union Association season and had lost another $10,000 on his first season in the NL. The combination of high salaries and diminished attendance meant he was running his own nine at a loss. The St. Louis Maroons had surprised the world by finishing in last place in 1885, and Fred Dunlap had even vowed late in the season that he would never play for the club again.[2] Lucas was able to talk his frustrated star off the ledge, and Dunlap was once again the club's everyday second baseman and highest-paid player in 1886.

The 1885 season was equally tumultuous for the National League as a whole. In mid–September 1885, amidst rumors of their pending dismissal from the NL, Buffalo sold off their four best players to Detroit for $7,000, essentially throwing the towel on the franchise.[3] The so-called "Big Four" comprised two Hall of Famers in third baseman James "Deacon" White and first baseman Dan Brouthers, along with outfielder Hardy Richardson and shortstop Jack Rowe, the brother of Dave Rowe. The once-moribund Michigan club was shaping up to be one of the strongest clubs in the league, though their improvement had come from cannibalizing a rival.

In Providence, the 1884 world champions endured a mediocre 1885 season that saw the club struggling to make money once again. In July, President Henry Root stepped down, and many observers thought the club would soon be dropped from the NL.[4] The market had simply proven too small, and the National League was aggressively replacing its weaker markets. In November, the contracts of Providence's players were sold to Boston owner Arthur Soden for $6,600.[5] This deal was primarily made so Boston could acquire the rights to their long-time nemesis, Old Hoss Radbourn, who would now pitch for his hated rivals in the Hub.

The departure of the Buffalo and Providence clubs created openings for two clubs. Mike Scanlon's Nationals had been a prime candidate to join the National League thanks to their sterling performance in the Eastern League, along with their consistently strong attendance. At the National League meeting on November 20, 1885, it was reported that the Nationals would take the place of Providence.[6] Scanlon worked out a deal to sign a number of the Providence players that had not gone to Boston. Paul Hines, an outstanding outfielder and Washington native, was the key player in the transaction. He was joined by outfielder Cliff Carroll, catcher Barney Gilligan, and second baseman Jack Farrell. Two key figures from the old Boston Unions, Dupee Shaw and Ed Crane, also joined the nine. Scanlon's successful bid to join the National League had proven that there was more than one way to skin a cat. Henry Lucas had lost tens of thousands of dollars and antagonized the baseball establishment in order to gain a National League franchise. Conversely, Mike Scanlon had run a threadbare and frugal operation and achieved the same goal while making a solid profit.

In place of Buffalo, the NL directors sought a western franchise. The competition for the spot was fierce and came down to the three strongest clubs in the failed Western League: Indianapolis, Milwaukee, and Kansas City. The Milwaukee club was represented by Tom Loftus and Charles M. Kipp, who had run the city's Union nine. Americus V. McKim, Joseph Heim, and E.E. Menges headed the Kansas City group. Milwaukee and Kansas City had engaged in a somewhat pathetic war of words in the months after the demise of the Western League, over which city was the better market for baseball. Both markets had proven capable of supporting a ball club, and there was little to pick from between the two.

The decision on which city would join the National League was made at the league meeting on February 10, 1886, in Chicago. Indianapolis was dismissed outright as too small a market, and the club's directors reportedly made little effort to present a viable case.[7] Milwaukee had expressed concern over the National League's ban on Sunday contests and reported that their financial situation was uncertain due to the collapse of the local streetcar company.[8] These factors eliminated Cream City from the running, and just like that, Kansas City was selected as the NL's eighth franchise for the season.[9] Like Scanlon in Washington, A.V. McKim had also obtained a National League team without any of the strife or massive expenditures that Lucas had endured.

The new Kansas City franchise would lack the services of Ted Sullivan. After the failure of the Western League in summer 1885, Sullivan had traveled down to Memphis and managed the club there. Sullivan remained ever the organizer in the off-season. After Milwaukee's failed National League bid, he joined forces with Charles M. Kipp and began work on forming a new Northwestern League. The new circuit would include Milwaukee, Minneapolis, St. Paul, Duluth, Eau Claire, and Oshkosh. Sullivan would take the reins of the new Milwaukee nine.

Thus, the 1886 season commenced with four former Union Association clubs still extant in some form. St. Louis, Kansas City, Washington, would each be represented in the National League, and the Northwestern League would be home to Milwaukee. Though the Kansas City and Milwaukee clubs had technically folded with the collapse of the Western League, the 1886 version featured the same ownership groups and some of the same players. The Northwestern League, now in its third iteration, would also feature a new St. Paul franchise, which bore some connection to the Union Association nine. The club's 1884 manager Andrew M. Thompson would be involved with the financing of the new squad.[10]

If there was any consolation for Henry Lucas during the 1886 season, it was that Kansas City and Washington performed so poorly that his Maroons no longer had a stranglehold on last place. The season was another slog for Lucas's nine, riddled once again by dissension. Charlie Sweeney completed his metamorphosis from the most prized young pitcher in baseball to full-fledged cancer. Late in the 1885 season, Sweeney had sucker-punched his teammate, the genial outfielder Emmett Seery. The attack alienated the bulk of his teammates who sided with the innocent party.[11] Often intoxicated and increasingly embittered, Sweeney continued to torment Seery throughout the 1886 season. Sweeney formed a clique with his drinking buddies, including fellow Californian Jerry Denny and catcher Tom Dolan. In mid–May, Sweeney was attacked by five men as he walked home from the Lucas grounds after a game. There was speculation that the attack was made by some friends of Seery, who were seeking revenge for their pal.[12] Sweeney's on-field performance did nothing to mitigate his off-field antics or justify his presence on the club. On June 12, three years and five days after he set the National League record for strikeouts in a game with 19, he set a far more ignominious record by allowing seven home runs during a 14–7 loss to newly ascendant Detroit. Shortly after the contest, Sweeney, Denny, and Dolan were fined and suspended. Both Sweeney and Dolan were released the following week.

For Sweeney, that was the end of his relevance in the baseball world. His arm was dead. After a 36 game stint with Cleveland of the American Association in 1887, he returned to his native California. He partnered with ex-major leaguer James

McDonald in a drinking hole called "The Battery" in San Francisco, but the business soon failed.[13] Sweeney married McDonald's sister and had a child. He became a police officer, but that did not last long for reasons that should be glaringly obvious. He soon found work as a bodyguard for a San Francisco gangster named "King" McManus. On July 15, 1894, Sweeney got into a drunken altercation with McManus's brother Con.[14] Sweeney pulled out a pistol and shot and killed the man. Despite claims of self-defense, Sweeney was sentenced to eight years in San Quentin Prison. Due to improprieties during his trial, the sentence was commuted, and he was released in 1898.[15] Around this time, he became ill with consumption, and he passed away in 1902 at the age of 39. Sweeney's story tells that most tragic of all tales, that of wasted potential.

By July of 1886, Henry Lucas had started to recognize that the Maroons were a losing proposition on the field and an even bigger loser off it. Running a ball club was fun if you were winning and he could handle sinking money into that, but the bloom had come off the rose after a season and a half of losing. His beloved nine stood no chance of competing in the National League standings or matching the success of his rival Chris von der Ahe's burgeoning dynasty. Lucas had given an interview in February 1886 that hinted at his growing dismay with the business of

The 1886 St. Louis Maroons were Henry Lucas's final club. The team was riddled by dissension and was saved from a last place finish in the National League only by the presence of the newly-admitted Kansas City and Washington clubs. Top row, left to right: Al Bauer, pitcher; Charlie Sweeney, pitcher; Jerry Denny, third baseman; Emmett Seery, left fielder; John Cahill, right fielder; and Jack Glasscock, shortstop. Middle row, from left: Henry Boyle, pitcher; Jack McGeachey, center fielder; Egyptian Healy, pitcher; Gus Schmelz, manager; Tom Dolan, catcher; John Kirby, pitcher; and Alex McKinnon, first baseman. Bottom row, from left: Joe Quinn, center fielder; Fred Dunlap, second baseman; and George Myers, catcher (Wikimedia Commons).

baseball: "I think that base ball business is the meanest profession on the face of the earth. I don't mean the players, but the running and management of a club. It is an awful pull on a man, and is enough to turn his hair gray after he has been a year at the business."[16]

Lucas's financial stability was also coming under scrutiny. In May 1886, Lucas was sued by a St. Louis lawyer named Valle Reyburn over the payment of a promissory note regarding stock in the St. Louis Union Association baseball club for the amount of $3,000.[17] The suit was sided in Reyburn's favor, with the plaintiff awarded $4,066.66.[18] The Reyburn case demonstrated the fragile state of Lucas's finances, as he was using other people's money to fund his baseball venture. After the suit, there was the further threat of more lawsuits by other holders of the promissory notes. These notes totaled over $100,000 and formed the bulk of the funding for Lucas's ball club.[19] As his losses mounted, his financial situation had become increasingly precarious. Amidst this financial strain, Lucas expressed his desire to get out of baseball, with rumors that Chris von der Ahe would purchase the club.[20] Proof of Lucas's weakened financial state was given in July 1886, when Lucas sold off almost all of his real estate property for the sum of $250,000. The transactions were remarkable considering the standing of the Lucas family as one of the leading families in the city, with significant real estate holdings dating back generations.[21]

In the following weeks, Lucas took the first step towards the dismantling of his once prized nine, authorizing the sale of Fred Dunlap to Detroit for the sum of $5,000. One observer commented dramatically that "the Maroons without Dunlap would be worse than 'Hamlet' with the melancholy Dane left out."[22] The severing of the relationship with Dunlap signaled Lucas's increasing dismay with the financial toll of running the club. It also gave his friend a chance to play for a quality nine, as Detroit was holding down first place. The sale of Dunlap would be Henry Lucas's final move as the head of the St. Louis Maroons.

On August 17, 1886, Lucas and his partner, Fred Espenschied, sold the Maroons to a broker named L.A. Coquard. The broker had been loaning money to the duo to cover the team's costs and agreed to a convoluted scheme by which he would obtain the mortgage and all rights to the St. Louis National League club.[23] As part of the agreement, the Maroons would play out the schedule under the guidance of the National League, and then the club would be put up for sale in the offseason.

Henry Lucas offered up his explanation of his decision to sell in an interview with the *St. Louis Post-Dispatch* on August 18, 1886:

> Well, I'm out of the base ball business now, once and forever, lock, stock and barrel. I've tried my best to make it a success and I've sunk my money like a little man, and I don't propose to sink any more of it. I've lost on base ball business up to date the sum of $61,000, and before the affairs of the club are all wound up and settled, I shall have lost $70,000 and that's the last the base ball business will ever get out of me.[24]

He laid out his belief that the club's failure was caused by negative coverage in the local newspapers:

> Personally, I lay the blame of the Maroons' failure on the *Post-Dispatch*, and by the other papers following in the wake of it. The newspapers have killed the club, and I hope they're

satisfied. I'm out of base ball now, and if the citizens of St. Louis came to me with $100,000 and gave it to me to run a base ball club with, I would give it back to them and respectfully decline.[25]

Despite the harsh critique of the newspaper, the article concluded with a generous appreciation of Lucas's time in baseball: "To do Mr. Lucas justice, he deserves more credit for his energy, push and liberality than any other base ball man in America, and his failure is his misfortune, not his fault. Indeed it has been his liberality and his loyalty to his friends and associates in the League that has helped more to cause a failure than anything." Thus ended Henry V. Lucas's life in baseball.

The inaugural National League seasons in Kansas City and Washington were proving to be equally challenging, as neither club fielded a competitive configuration. This was despite possessing rosters that on paper appeared to have some modicum of experience and ability. Kansas City was managed by former St. Louis Union Dave Rowe, who also started in centerfield. Rowe compiled an impressive-looking pitching staff that included "Grasshopper" Jim Whitney, who had been the ace of the 1883 pennant-winning Boston aggregate, and former 20-game winners in George "Stump" Weidman and Larry McKeon. The staff would also feature appearances by a future 30-game winner in Pete Conway and future St. Louis Brown Stockings ace, 18-year-old Charles "Silver" King. Starting in 1887, King would start a four-year stretch that saw him win 162 contests and pace the league in ERA, ERA+, and shutouts on two occasions. But in 1886, he went just 1–3 with a 4.85 ERA across five late-season starts for Rowe's club. The problem for Kansas City was that their pitchers were either has-beens or future stars but of little use in the present. Whitney, Weidman, and McKeon failed to replicate their past successes, and Conway and King were too green to contribute. On offense, Rowe enlisted former Union players Al Myers, Charles Briody, and Mox McQuery in his starting lineup while former St. Louis Unions catcher George Baker made one token appearance for the club. Myers and McQuery performed respectably, while Briody and Rowe struggled at-bat. The team posted the league's second-worst offense, the second-worst pitching staff, and fielded the league's worst defense. At the gate, the club drew reasonably well early in the season, as the novelty of National League baseball was still fresh. The lack of Sunday games, which had been such a spectacle and moneymaker for the previous iterations of the club, affected team revenue significantly. Season attendance for their 57 home games was estimated at 55,000.

In Washington, Mike Scanlon's Eastern League champions were even worse than Kansas City. Washington's lineup represented a fusion of the Eastern League roster headed by Phil Baker, Buck Gladmon, Bill Wise, Bob Barr, and Hank O'Day and the acquisitions from Providence. Hometown boy Paul Hines was excellent, batting .312/.358/.462 for a 157 OPS+, but the team was surprisingly dismal. Dupee Shaw was a workhorse but failed to rise above the club's weaknesses. He posted a 13–31 record and 3.34 ERA for a 96 ERA+ in 385.2 innings. The club used 15 different pitchers on the season, each seemingly worse than the last. The trio of Union Association vets, Hugh Daily, Bill Wise, and Ed Crane, compiled a dreadful 1–14 record and a combined ERA over 7. Crane's abysmal play carried over to his hitting, as he batted just .171/.207/.229 for an OPS+ of 37 across 80 contests. Any semblance of the ability he showed at the plate back in 1884 seemed to have vanished entirely. Other Union alumni who made appearances for the club included Bill Krieg and Harry Decker. The once sought-after Larry Corcoran, just two years removed from a 35-win season with Chicago, was on his last legs and was hit hard in two appearances for the Nationals. The club's primary historical legacy remains the discovery of the legendary Connie Mack, who made his major league debut with the club on September 11, 1886. Manager Scanlon's failure to make his club even remotely competitive resulted in his resignation with a 13–67 record, though he remained a stockholder. He was replaced by John Gaffney, who guided the club to a more respectable 15–25 over the season's final 40 contests.

Scanlon's managerial career was over, but he remained a fixture in Washington's baseball community for the following decades. His anecdotes and stories often appeared in Washington newspapers and helped to keep the legacy of the 1885 Eastern League champions alive. Several of his former charges, including Phil Baker and Bill Wise, also remained in the nation's capital after their careers were over and often spoke glowingly about Scanlon and their days on the old Nationals. When Scanlon passed away in 1929 at age 83, he took with him a well-deserved reputation as a pioneer of professional baseball in Washington, D.C.

For those keeping score in 1886, St. Louis finished in sixth with a 43–79–4 record, Kansas City was seventh at 30–91–5, while Washington brought up the rear with a pathetic 28–92–5 mark. The Chicago White Stockings took home the pennant with a 90–34–2 record, led in part by Jim McCormick, who won 31 games in his penultimate major league season. His nine would lose the World Series to the St. Louis Brown Stockings in six games. The struggles of the three former Union delegations give credence to the National League's strength in 1886. In the big scheme of things, the former Union Association clubs were demonstrably second class.

Ted Sullivan's Northwestern League was surprisingly stable. His Milwaukee club finished with a disappointing 35–42 record and ended up in last place. More importantly, all six teams in the circuit completed the season, a nice improvement over the Western League or the Union Association. The venture proved fruitful enough for a second league season in 1887, though Sullivan sold his Milwaukee interests to become an umpire in the International League.[26]

The 1886 offseason saw another wave of change in the major league organizational structure. The National League dropped Kansas City to make room for the Pittsburgh Alleghenys, who had fled the American Association. Kansas City, with continued involvement from Americus V. McKim, entered the ten-team Western League in 1887. The club successfully gained entry into the American Association as the Cowboys in 1888. The club played two more dismal seasons posting a combined 98–171 record before folding for good. The Cowboys were dumped from the AA, and McKim's career in professional baseball ceased. When he died in 1910, few people remembered his legacy in professional baseball. Thanks to the Society of American Baseball Research's Kansas City Chapter, McKim was given a fitting piece of recognition, with a new grave marker that reads the "Father of Kansas City Baseball."[27]

Their counterparts in Washington fared somewhat better. The club remained in the National League for three more seasons from 1887 to 1889 but endured a losing record in each of them. Ted Sullivan managed the 1888 club for part of the season, posting a 38–57 record in what would be his final major league managerial position. He continued his nomadic existence and was actively involved in forming new leagues and teams into the 1910s. Sullivan also acted as a scout for his old friend Charles Comiskey and the Chicago White Sox. He helped organize the famed 1913 World Tour by the White Sox and the New York Giants and later wrote a book about the trip.[28] He eventually met his final resting place when he died in Washington, D.C., on June 22, 1929, at age 78.

Henry Lucas's former club, the St. Louis Maroons, was officially sold to a group of Indianapolis investors in February 1887. The club and its assets were moved there for the coming season. Now rebranded as the Hoosiers, the team played three uneventful seasons in Indiana, failing to improve their lot on the field or financially. After the 1889 season, both Washington and Indianapolis were dropped from the National League to make room for two more American Association clubs, the Brooklyn Bridegrooms and the Cincinnati Reds. The disbandment of the Hoosiers formally ended the tumultuous existence of the franchise that Henry Lucas had started with such high hopes back in October 1883. The ghosts of the Union Association had finally given up.

A Final Scene

October 3, 1889

Henry Boyle stepped into the batter's box for the Indianapolis Hoosiers in the top of the seventh inning. He had entered the bottom of the sixth, facing a 2–1 deficit to the visiting Philadelphia Phillies. Whatever spark he had left in his right arm was quickly extinguished by a string of hard hits. By the time the inning was done, the score stood 10–1. Boyle was tired and weary. It had been another losing year, his club mired in seventh place. There were only a few more days left in the season. Then he could go back home to Philadelphia and recuperate. He had logged over 370 innings on the year, and he could use a break.

He was the last man left on the club who could claim to have played for the famed Lucas nine way back in '84. But that was ages ago, and it might as well have never happened. Fred Dunlap had left in '86, as did President Lucas. Charlie Sweeney, Jack Gleason, Tom Dolan, and George Baker were gone too. Heck, he was the only one from those glory days who ended up in Indianapolis when the club was sold by in '87. He had endured five straight losing seasons, two in St. Louis and now three in Hoosierville, and he was ready for it to all be over.

As the beleaguered and exhausted hurler walked to the plate, one of the tiny crowd of 500 dismayed Hoosier rooters shouted to him, "Here he is," in mock appreciation for his struggles in the previous half-inning. Back in '84, he was the idol of the crowds, "Handsome Henry," they called him. But now, he was a loser and just a joke to these fans. His pain, sacrifice, and ability all meant nothing to the fans when the club was down.

In response to the ridicule from the entitled rooter, Boyle mockingly tipped his cap to the fan in question and took a robust bow. With that, Henry Boyle, the last of the famed St. Louis Unions, promptly walked off the field, never to appear in the majors again.

Epilogue

My favorite Union Association moment took place on August 16, 1884. The Baltimore Unions were in Boston to play the hometown nine in a battle of two of the stronger clubs in the circuit. Boston catcher Lew Brown failed to show up to the park for his scheduled appearance behind the plate. Unexplained absences were not unusual for Brown, whose career had been derailed by his fondness for alcohol. Like Rube Waddell years later, he was an often good-natured person with a carefree approach to life. Brown was as likely to have stopped by a sandlot to play with some local kids as he was to have stopped off at the bar to get drunk. Whatever the reason, he was not at the park, which meant that Ed Crane would have to catch "the Wizard" Dupee Shaw.

Shaw was famous for his dazzling curves, but needed a skilled and experienced catcher to keep him under control. In the second inning of the contest, he was holding on to a 3–0 lead. With a man on first base and no one out, Shaw delivered a fastball that nearly ripped his catcher's finger off. With Brown absent and Crane now debilitated, the Boston Unions had no catchers left. If they could not find someone to fill the spot behind the plate, the club would have to forfeit the game and refund the modest gate receipts. Boston manager and first baseman Tim Murnane did not want to do this, and so he petitioned the members of the crowd for a replacement. "Is there a catcher in the house?" he asked.

At this point, a young man yelled out from the crowd, claiming to be a backstop. Murnane looked the youngster over and said, "What's your name, kid?" The young man answered, "Murphy." Without another option, Murnane took his word for it. The kid dressed in street clothes walked to the field and took his position behind the plate. The umpire barked, "Murphy, now catching for Boston." Murnane sensed the risks inherent in catching a pitcher such as Shaw and summoned the less intimidating and softer throwing James Burke in from right field to switch places with the Wizard. Once the men were all set in their new positions, play resumed.

This was the era before catchers wore gloves, when any pitch could spell catastrophe in terms of a wild pitch, passed ball, or more worrying, a gruesome injury. If you thought this was a story of a young unknown plucked from obscurity and thrust into stardom against all odds, you are looking in the wrong place. Young Murphy, the purported catcher, proved woefully incapable of the task. Within just a few minutes, Murphy had made three errors, and Baltimore was rallying back.

Murnane was now fearful of losing. The inning would never end if Murphy remained behind the plate. The disgusted manager had enough and summoned Tom O'Brien in from second base to replace Murphy. O'Brien was an inexperienced catcher, but at least a professional ballplayer. Murphy was exiled to left field since Boston had no one left on the bench and the previous left fielder, Kid Butler, had taken O'Brien's place at second base.

O'Brien proved more than capable of handling Burke, and they escaped the inning with just two runs allowed and remained in the lead. Murphy would spend the rest of the contest in left, where he did no further damage, and he even drew a base on balls in one of his four at-bats. The Boston Unions added another three runs and held off a late Baltimore rally to take the contest by a score of 6–4. Murphy would disappear from history, his identity remaining undiscovered to this day. An ignominious defensive line and a few whimsical game accounts in the local Boston papers remain the only evidence of his existence.

This event is emblematic of so much of what the Union Association represents. For one strange season, it became the home to men of all stripes. For men like Lew Brown, a noted ne'er-do-well, it was another chance to prove he could make good. For men like Baltimore's Ned Cuthbert and Boston's Tim Murnane, it was another chance for two of baseball's veteran gladiators to prove they still had something left to give and perhaps inspire the next generation with the fruits of their baseball wisdom. For men like Dupee Shaw and Bill Sweeney, it was a chance to escape the grasps of tyrannical club owners and break the power of the reserve rule. For youngsters like Ed Crane and William "Yank" Robinson, it was an opportunity to establish their reputations. And for men like Murphy, it was simply a moment when anything was possible, no matter how absurd or unexpected.

What Does the Union Association Mean?

If the Union Association is discussed at all these days, it is primarily a conversation focused on its merits as a major league. Fred Dunlap's superlative statistical profile is used as evidence of the inferiority of the circuit, alongside the fact that so few of the league's purported stars enjoyed any sustained major league success either before or after the 1884 season.

This discussion is something of a moot point since it ignores the simple fact that in 1884, the Union Association set up shop and tried to compete directly with the National League and American Association. Henry Lucas, Justus Thorner, Albert Henderson, Tom Pratt, and the rest of the league's owners brought the Union Association venture to fruition as a direct competitor. They went into the season fully convinced of their ability to match wits and abilities with the best clubs of the National League and the American Association. They recruited the best players available and sought out major league talent to fill their rosters.

Media coverage at the time was certainly skeptical of the quality of the league, particularly the lesser lights in Washington and Altoona. Still, the league was given ample coverage alongside the National League and the American Association. The league presented itself and was covered as if it were a rival league, with the caveat being that they were operating outside of the National Agreement.

When the Union Association collapsed in early 1885, the league's champion, St. Louis Unions were accepted into the National League. In 1886, the Washington Nationals and Kansas City Cowboys, both under the same ownership and with similar rosters to their Union seasons, entered the National League, having spent the 1885 season in the Eastern League and Western League, respectively. While none of these clubs ended up contending in the National League, the simple fact that three Union Association clubs would eventually gain entry into baseball's premier league speaks to the validity of the UA's status as a major league.

The UA's marginal reputation in the eyes of baseball history has been exacerbated by the fact that there is no singular legacy for the league. The National Association was in existence from 1871 to 1875. While not recognized as a major league by some parties, it did give birth to the nucleus of the National League and proved that professional baseball was a viable business. The National League, which has been in operation since 1876, is the oldest sports league in North America and needs no further explanation of its import. The American Association existed from 1882 to 1891 and opened up baseball to the working-class fan through the innovations of Sunday ball, 25-cent tickets, and the sale of alcohol at games. Furthermore, the league gave birth to four of baseball's most iconic franchises, the St. Louis Cardinals, the Brooklyn Dodgers, the Cincinnati Reds, and the Pittsburgh Pirates. The Players' League lasted just the 1890 season. The league was an attempt by the players to wrest control of baseball away from greedy magnates. Despite its failure, it was an early step towards true agency for players, one of the defining themes throughout baseball history. The American League came about in 1901 and forged its place as the one true rival to the National League. The final upstart major league to date, the Federal League of 1914–15, left its legacy through the famed 1922 Supreme Court judgment *Federal Baseball Club vs. National League* that gave major league baseball an antitrust exemption.

Unlike these other major leagues, the Union Association offers no easily definable legacy. On its surface, the leagues' clubs challenged the relatively new reserve rule and fought for players' rights. Indeed, Henry Lucas was consistent in his desire to sign reserved and contracted players. He remained constant in his fight for his players even after they were blacklisted and he had joined the National League. Other Union members did not universally share this vision. Notably, the Washington Nationals and the Altoona Unions eschewed the pursuit of reserved players. Albert H. Henderson's Baltimore and Chicago syndicate challenged the reserve rule but focused almost exclusively on signing players from the Northwestern League. While Lucas had a clear vision, his fellow directors took their own approaches with wildly varying results. This hodgepodge of ideas in direction and execution contributed to the league's failure.

Perhaps the closest analog is the Federal League, whose clubs sought to acquire elite major league talent but were generally unsuccessful in this endeavor. The result was a circuit that was clearly a distant third in talent level behind the American and National Leagues and whose top performers failed to replicate their successes upon the folding of the league in 1915. Not unlike the Union Association.

A few men would try to tell the Union Association story over the years. Al Spink, the fabled founder of the *Sporting News*, claimed to have worked as a secretary for Henry Lucas's Union club. His sympathies towards the league were on display in his essential 1910 history of baseball, *The National Game*, which provided one of the first accounts of the league's history. He dedicated several pages to the league's history, providing a succinct and favorable summary of the league's history, as well as lineups and rosters. His work was not without faults, as he failed to mention the involvement of the Wilmington, Milwaukee, or St. Paul franchises. Henry Lucas was painted as a benevolent but naïve patron of the players' cause.

Two of the league's player-managers, Tim Murnane and Sam Crane, became leading sportswriters in the country. Both men would occasionally sprinkle their columns with Union Association anecdotes. Occasionally, an alumnus like Tommy McCarthy or Henry Boyle would give an account of their experiences in the league. Still, very little was said by anyone that contextualized the league or discussed its historical significance. Once the league collapsed, it seemed like almost everyone involved tried to forget that it happened.

The same year that Spink's book was published, Henry Lucas died in St. Louis. He had spent the previous decade in financial ruin. After departing baseball, he worked as a railroad clerk for several years into the 1890s. In 1902, he filed for bankruptcy, erasing $40,000 in personal debt. In 1903, his wife Louise divorced him, citing non-support and desertion. By 1907, he was earning $75 a month as a city street inspector. While the popular story posited that Lucas had lost his million-dollar fortune on baseball, it was more complicated than that. He claimed to have lost $70,000 combined on his Union Association and National League ventures. That figure was far less than his reported wealth. He had also lost an estimated $300,000 through the failure of a barge line he had started between St. Louis and New Orleans. His mass liquidation of real estate in 1886 suggested that he had significant debts owing from a variety of ventures. Lucas would often describe his baseball experience as a failure but seemed to bear no grudges or regrets about the path his life had taken.

Cincinnati Unions founder Justus Thorner left baseball behind after the 1884 season and his failed attempt to jump to the National League alongside Henry Lucas. He returned to the brewery industry in Cincinnati, acting as a traveling salesman for the George Gerke brewery until the 1890s. By 1900, Thorner had become a manager for the Cincinnati branch of the Anheuser-Busch brewery. He shifted careers, and in 1905, he was named vice president of the S. Obermayer Company, a Cincinnati-based foundry. He remained a prominent member of Cincinnati's Jewish community until his death at age 81 in 1928.

The Chicago and Baltimore Unions founder, Albert H. Henderson, also left the baseball world after 1884 and forged ahead in business in his hometown of Baltimore. He made a name as an inventor and medical practitioner. He served as an advisor in creating America's first electric street railway in Baltimore in 1885. Henderson is not known to have commented publicly about his Union Association investment in the remaining years of his life, and he also passed away at age 81 in 1928.

The King of Second Basemen, Fred Dunlap, passed away on December 1, 1902, in his hometown of Philadelphia at age 43. His career was cut short prematurely by a fractured ankle in 1891, and he spent the next decade in relative obscurity, reportedly spending his considerable savings in secret before dying penniless. In the tributes about his career, most write-ups focused on his role on the 1887 Detroit club, which had won the National League pennant and the World Series over the St. Louis Brown Stockings. The club had become universally regarded as one of the greatest teams of the 19th century. Dunlap's time in the Union Association was generally overlooked.

Without photos or accurate records readily available, the Union Association story became codified into a brief narrative. It went something like this: Millionaire Henry Lucas and the St. Louis Maroons dominated the Union Association in its one year of existence, starting the season 20–0 and setting the record for winning percentage in a season, but the cost was his fortune. There is no talk of its impact on baseball or what it meant to the men who lived it.

The record books tell one story: cartoonish batting lines, absurd mismatches, and remarkable success and futility. The history books have told another, one of a reckless, naïve, and generous millionaire, loyal to his players to a fault, who bought a winning team but bankrupted himself in the process.

The real story is much richer and a whole lot more fun. There are new conversations to be had about the Union Association. New names waiting to be discovered in the digitized box scores that now permeate the internet, and old names waiting to be brought back to life (Jack Glasscock and Jim McCormick for the Hall of Fame!). There are new questions to be asked. Were the Cincinnati Unions as good as the Lucas nine? Could the league have succeeded if Lucas stuck by it? What is the true identity of Baltimore's outfielder, Scott? And most important: Where is left field, Mr. Baker?

Notes

Preface

1. John Thorn, "Why Is the National Association Not a Major League ... and Other Records Issues," *Our Game*, May 4, 2015, https://ourgame.mlblogs.com/why-is-the-national-association-not-a-major-league-and-other-records-issues-7507e1683b66.

2. Joseph L. Reichler, ed., *The Baseball Encyclopedia: The Complete and Official Record of Major League Baseball* (New York: Macmillan, 1969), 2327–28.

3. Baseball Reference, "Negro Leagues Are Major Leagues," last modified October 12, 2021, https://www.baseball-reference.com/negro-leagues-are-major-leagues.shtml.

Chapter 1

1. Richard Hershberger, "The First Baseball War: The American Association and the National League," *SABR Baseball Research Journal*, Fall 2020, https://sabr.org/journal/article/the-first-baseball-war-the-american-association-and-the-national-league/.

2. Baseball Reference, "Reserve Rule," last modified November 30, 2012, https://www.baseball-reference.com/bullpen/Reserve_clause.

3. "The League," *New York Clipper*, September 30, 1882.

4. Hershberger, "The First Baseball War."

5. *Ibid.*

6. "They Win a Game," *Pittsburgh Daily Post,* August 31, 1883.

7. Brian McKenna, "Ed Swartwood," *SABR Baseball Biography Project,* https://sabr.org/bioproj/person/ed-swartwood/.

8. "The New Pitcher's Debut," *Pittsburgh Daily Post,* June 25, 1883.

9. *Ibid.*

10. "Base Ball," *Pittsburgh Daily Post,* July 23, 1883.

11. "Notes," *Cincinnati Enquirer*, September 2, 1883.

12. "The New Base Ball League," *Indianapolis News*, September 3, 1883.

13. "The American Association Meeting," *New York Clipper*, March 24, 1883.

14. "Baseball News," *New York Daily Tribune*, September 4, 1883.

15. "Another New Association—On Paper," *Sporting Life*, September 10, 1883.

16. "Our National Game," *National Police Gazette*, September 29, 1883.

17. "Baseball News," *New York Daily Tribune*, September 4, 1883.

18. "Our National Game," *National Police Gazette*, June 20, 1885.

19. "Stolen Bases," *Rochester Democrat and Chronicle* (New York), April 22, 1887.

20. "New Associations," *Sporting Life*, September 17, 1883.

21. "A New Ball Club in St. Louis," *Philadelphia Times*, October 25, 1883.

22. "New Associations," *Sporting Life*, September 17, 1883.

23. "The Union Base-Ball Association-Base-Ball Notes," *Baltimore Sun*, October 22, 1883.

24. Brian McKenna, "Baltimore Baseball: The Beginnings, 1858–1872," *Baltimore Baseball History*, 167, https://bmorebbhistory.files.wordpress.com/2018/07/baltimore-baseball.pdf.

25. "Local Notes," *Chicago Daily Inter Ocean*, June 7, 1883.

26. *Ibid.*

27. "As to New Members," *Sporting Life*, July 29, 1883.

28. Letter from E.S. Hengel to William Robinson, 1883 August 30, BL-2733-81-24, Box 12, Folder 1, BL02733-81, William Robinson correspondence, the National Baseball Hall of Fame and Museum, Cooperstown, New York, https://collection.baseballhall.org/PASTIME/letter-e-s-heugle-yank-robinson-1883-august-30.

29. Letter from A.H. Henderson to William Robinson, 1883 August 04, BL-2733-81-24, Box 12, Folder 1, BL02733-81, William Robinson correspondence, the National Baseball Hall of Fame and Museum, Cooperstown, New York, https://collection.baseballhall.org/PASTIME/letter-a-h-henderson-yank-robinson-1883-august-04.

30. "A Friendly View," *Sporting Life*, September 17, 1883.

31. "New Associations," *Sporting Life*, September 17, 1883.

32. "As to New Members," *Sporting Life*, July 29, 1883.

Chapter 2

1. Joan M. Thomas, "Henry V. Lucas," *SABR Baseball Biography Project*, https://sabr.org/bioproj/person/henry-v-lucas/.
2. Jeff Kittel, e-mail message to author, June 4, 2019.
3. Jon David Cash, *Before They Were Cardinals* (Columbia: University of Missouri, 2002), 40.
4. *Ibid., 41*
5. *Ibid., 44.*
6. *Ibid., 39.*
7. Richard Egenriether, "Chris von der Ahe: Baseball's Pioneering Huckster," *SABR Baseball Research Journal*, 1989, http://research.sabr.org/journals/chris-von-der-ahe-baseballs-pioneering-huckster.
8. Edward Achorn, *The Summer of Beer and Whiskey* (New York: Public Affairs, 2013).
9. *Ibid.*
10. "The Lucas-Wainwright Club," *St. Louis Republican*, October 25, 1883.
11. "Our National Game," *National Police Gazette*, October 20, 1883.
12. "Cleveland's Troubles," *Sporting Life*, October 29, 1883.
13. "Regarding the New Club," *St. Louis Republican*, October 28, 1883.
14. Thomas, "Henry V. Lucas."
15. "The New Base Ball Association," *St. Louis Republican*, November 3, 1883.
16. "Baseball," *Encyclopedia Dubuque*, last modified July 3, 2020, http://www.encyclopediadubuque.org/index.php?title=BASEBALL.
17. Frank Vaccaro, "Ted Sullivan," *SABR Baseball Biography Project*, https://sabr.org/bioproj/person/ted-sullivan/.
18. T.P. Sullivan, *Humorous Stories of the Ball Field* (Chicago: M.A. Donohue & Company, 1903), https://summerofjeff.wordpress.com/2011/08/08/ted-sullivan-humorous-stories-of-the-ball-field/.
19. "The Sullivan Game at Sportsman's Park a Farce," *St. Louis Republican*, November 5, 1883.
20. "Notes," *Cleveland Leader*, October 12, 1883.
21. "Notes and Comments," *Sporting Life*, October 15, 1883.
22. "Base Ball News," *Port Huron Daily Times* (Michigan), September 22, 1883.
23. "Notes and Comments," *Sporting Life*, October 22, 1883.
24. "1884 Union Association Base Ball Contract—Only Example Known!," 2011 November 10–11, Vintage Sports Collectibles Signature Auction—Dallas #7041, *Heritage Auctions*, https://sports.ha.com/itm/baseball-collectibles/others/1884-union-association-base-ball-contract-only-example-known-/a/7041-81202.s.
25. "The Union Association," *Sporting Life*, October 22, 1883.

26. "Sporting Notes," *Pittsburgh Daily Post*, February 17, 1890.
27. "The Allegheny Club," *Sporting Life*, October 29, 1883.
28. "The New Ball Club Makes Six Sensational Contracts," *St. Louis Daily Globe-Democrat*, November 9, 1883.
29. Rochelle Llewelyn Nicholls, *Joe Quinn Among the Rowdies* (Jefferson, NC: McFarland, 2014), 55.
30. *Ibid.*
31. "Notes and Comments," *Sporting Life*, September 10, 1883.
32. "Those Already Engaged for Next Season," *Cleveland Plain Dealer*, November 3, 1883.
33. "The New St. Louis Club," *Buffalo Express*, December 3, 1883.
34. James J. Corbett, "Henry Lucas Was First Man to Pay Modern Salaries," *St. Louis Star*, January 28, 1919.
35. "Sporting Notes," *Boston Daily Globe*, November 22, 1883.

Chapter 3

1. "The New Union Association Making Inroads Into the League," *Philadelphia Times*, November 11, 1883.
2. Dick Farrington, "Half a Century Through Joe Quinn's Eyes: Union Star Recalls Birth of 'the Sporting News,'" *The Sporting News* (St. Louis, Missouri), May 21, 1936.
3. Rochelle Nichols, "Joe Quinn," *SABR Baseball Biography Project*, https://sabr.org/bioproj/person/joe-quinn/.
4. *Ibid.*
5. "Breaking the Reserve Rule," *Philadelphia Times*, December 10, 1883.
6. "Sporting Sundries," *St. Louis Post-Dispatch*, December 4, 1883.
7. "Local Briefs," *Pittsburgh Daily Post*, December 13, 1883.
8. David Nemec, "Thorner, Justus," *Major League Baseball Profiles, 1871–1900, Volume 2* (Lincoln: University of Nebraska Press, 2011), 187.
9. "Mr. Lucas in the City," *Cincinnati Enquirer*, December 14, 1883.
10. "The Phoenix Club," *Cincinnati Daily Star*, September 11, 1878.
11. "Thorner's Tale," *Cleveland Leader*, February 10, 1881.
12. Nemec, *Major League Baseball Profiles*, 187.
13. "Thorner vs. The Cincinnati Base Ball Club," *Cincinnati Enquirer*, December 31, 1882.
14. Nemec, *Major League Baseball Profiles*, 187.
15. *Ibid.*
16. "Base Ball," *Cleveland Leader*, December 11, 1879.
17. Nemec, *Major League Baseball Profiles*, 187.
18. "Echoes of the Convention," *Sporting Life*, December 26, 1883.
19. *Ibid.*

20. "A Poor Policy," *St. Louis Post-Dispatch*, January 1, 1884.

Chapter 4

1. "As to New Members," *Sporting Life*, July 29, 1883.
2. "1884 Register League Encyclopedia," *Baseball Reference*, https://www.baseball-reference.com/register/league.cgi?year=1884.
3. "1883 Register League Encyclopedia," *Baseball Reference*, https://www.baseball-reference.com/register/league.cgi?year=1883.
4. Harold Seymour and Dorothy Seymour Mills, *Baseball: The Early Years* (New York: Oxford University Press, 1989), 152.
5. *Ibid.*
6. *Ibid.*, 153.
7. "The Situation," *Sporting Life*, January 2, 1884.
8. "Manager Spalding on the Situation," *St. Louis Post-Dispatch*, January 7, 1884.
9. "Corcoran's Backdown," *Sporting Life*, January 16, 1884.
10. Bob Lemoine, "Larry Corcoran," *SABR Baseball Biography Project*, https://sabr.org/bioproj/person/larry-corcoran/.
11. Frank Vaccaro, "Hugh Daily," *SABR Baseball Biography Project*, https://sabr.org/bioproj/person/hugh-daily/.
12. "Out and In-Door Sports," *Cleveland Plain Dealer*, September 3, 1883.
13. "Baseball Notes," *Buffalo Daily Times*, March 12, 1884.
14. "Tony Mullane Claimed by Toledo," *St. Louis Daily Globe-Democrat*, February 2, 1884.
15. "New Contracts," *Philadelphia Times*, February 17, 1884.
16. "The Northwestern League," *Wheeling Register* (West Virginia), January 11, 1884.
17. "The Northwestern League," *Sporting Life*, January 23, 1884.
18. "Easter Goose Eggs," *Cincinnati Enquirer*, May 13, 1883.
19. "1880 United States Census," *Wikipedia*, last modified May 24, 2020, https://en.wikipedia.org/wiki/1880_United_States_Census.
20. "Notes and Comments," *Sporting Life*, October 22, 1883.
21. "The Inter-State Meeting," *Sporting Life*, January 9, 1884.
22. "Altoona's Players," *Altoona Times* (Pennsylvania), February 7, 1884.
23. *Ibid.*
24. *Sporting Life*, January 2, 1884.
25. "Diamond Dust," *St. Louis Daily Globe-Democrat*, February 25, 1884.
26. "Base-Ball in Boston," *Baltimore Sun*, April 24, 1884.
27. "Base Ball," *Fall River Daily Evening News* (Massachusetts), March 3, 1884.
28. *Ibid.*
29. "Base-Ball in Boston," *Baltimore Sun*, April 24, 1884.

30. Charles Bevis, "Frank Winslow," *SABR Baseball Biography Project*, https://sabr.org/bioproj/person/frank-winslow/.
31. Charles Bevis, "Dartmouth Street Grounds (Boston)," *SABR Baseball Biography Project*, https://sabr.org/bioproj/park/dartmouth-street-grounds-boston/.

Chapter 5

1. "George Gerke Dies," *Cincinnati Enquirer*, July 23, 1923.
2. "League Park (Cincinnati)," *Wikipedia*, last modified October 23, 2019, https://en.wikipedia.org/wiki/League_Park_(Cincinnati).
3. *Ibid.*
4. "New York Clipper," *Wikipedia*, last modified April 21, 2021, https://en.wikipedia.org/wiki/New_York_Clipper.
5. "Henry Chadwick (writer)," *Wikipedia*, last modified August 20, 2021, https://en.wikipedia.org/wiki/Henry_Chadwick_(writer).
6. Bill Burgess III, "Sports Writer Register," *The Baseball Guru*, 2011, http://baseballguru.com/bburgess/analysisbburgess20.html.
7. "Base-Ball," *Cincinnati Enquirer*, April 18, 1884.
8. *Ibid.*
9. *Ibid.*
10. *Ibid.*
11. "Bradley and the Athletic Club," *St. Louis Daily Globe-Democrat*, January 17, 1884.
12. "Base-Ball," *Cincinnati Enquirer*, April 18, 1884.
13. *Ibid.*
14. "Base Ball," *Cincinnati Commercial*, April 18, 1884.
15. *Ibid.*
16. "Nationals, 7; Unions 3," *Boston Daily Globe*, April 18, 1884.
17. "1880 United States Census," *Wikipedia*.
18. Sam Gazdziak, "Grave Story: Billy Barnie (1853–1900)," *RIP Baseball*, December 6, 2018, https://ripbaseball.com/2018/12/06/grave-story-billy-barnie-1853-1900/.
19. *Ibid.*
20. John Thorn, "Baseball's Bans and Blacklists," *Our Game*, February 8, 2016, https://ourgame.mlblogs.com/baseballs-bans-and-blacklists-5182f08d43ff.
21. "New Public Bath Open," *New York Tribune*, January 21, 1908.
22. "From Baltimore," *Sporting Life*, March 5, 1884.
23. "Opening Game at Baltimore," *Cincinnati Enquirer*, April 18, 1884.
24. "Base Ball at the Capital," *Boston Herald*, April 5, 1884.
25. "Base Ball," *Washington Evening Star*, March 29, 1884.
26. "Base Ball Notes," *Boston Daily Globe*, April 13, 1884.
27. "Base Ball at the Capital," *Boston Herald*, April 5, 1884.

28. "Notes and Comments," *Sporting Life*, June 4, 1884.

29. "The Union Association Meeting," *Cincinnati Enquirer*, March 18, 1884.

30. "Notes and Comments," *Sporting Life*, June 4, 1884.

31. "Base-Ball Gossip," *Philadelphia Times*, January 27, 1884.

32. "Opening Game at Baltimore," *Cincinnati Enquirer*, April 18, 1884.

33. "Notes and Comments," *Sporting Life*, April 16, 1884.

34. "Notes and Comments," *Sporting Life*, January 2, 1884.

35. David Nemec, *The Great Encyclopedia of Nineteenth-Century Major League Baseball* (Tuscaloosa: University of Alabama Press, 2006), 266.

36. *Ibid.*, 254.

37. "The Keystones Beaten," *Philadelphia Times,* April 18, 1884.

38. "Base Ball," *Philadelphia Inquirer*, April 18, 1884.

39. "The Keystones Beaten," *Philadelphia Times*, April 18, 1884.

Chapter 6

1. Joan M. Thomas, "Union Base Ball Park (St. Louis)," *SABR Baseball Biography Project*, https://sabr.org/bioproj/park/union-base-ball-park-st-louis/.

2. Achorn, *Beer and Whiskey League.*

3. "Gussie Busch," *Wikipedia*, last modified July 31, 2020, https://en.wikipedia.org/wiki/Gussie_Busch.

4. "Diamond Dust," *St. Louis Daily Globe-Democrat*, April 11, 1884.

5. Thomas, "Union Base Ball Park (St. Louis)."

6. *Ibid.*

7. *Ibid.*

8. *Ibid.*

9. *Ibid.*

10. "Base Hits," *St. Louis Republican*, April 18, 1884.

11. "Well Patronized Opening," *Cincinnati Enquirer*, April 19, 1884.

12. "St. Thomas, Ontario," *Wikipedia*, last modified June 12, 2020, https://en.wikipedia.org/wiki/St._Thomas,_Ontario.

13. "At the Union Park," *Cincinnati Enquirer,* April 19, 1884.

14. "The Union Game," *Cincinnati Enquirer,* April 20, 1884.

15. "They Turn the Tables," *Cincinnati Enquirer,* April 19, 1884.

16. "Base Ball Notes," *Franklin Repository* (Chambersburg, Pennsylvania), April 22, 1884.

17. "Signing Two Contracts," *Sporting Life*, April 30, 1884.

18. "Tom Pratt's Team," *Sporting Life*, March 26, 1884.

19. "Diamond Chips," *St. Louis Republican*, April 20, 1884.

20. "The Finest! The Nearest! The Prettiest!" *St. Louis Republican*, April 20, 1884.

21. "Just Think of It!" *St. Louis Republican*, April 21, 1884.

22. "The Overture," *St. Louis Post-Dispatch*, April 26, 1884.

23. *Ibid.*

24. "Just Think of It!" *St. Louis Republican*, April 21, 1884.

25. "Base Ball Notes," *St. Louis Republican*, April 19, 1884.

26. "Base Ball Notes," *St. Louis Republican*, April 24, 1884.

27. *Ibid.*

28. "The Altoonas," *St. Louis Republican*, April 23, 1884.

29. *Ibid.*

30. *Ibid.*

31. "Over the Fence," *St. Louis Republican*, April 25, 1884.

32. "In the Lead," *St. Louis Republican*, April 28, 1884.

33. "Shaeffer's Latest Oration," *Philadelphia Evening Item*, May 5, 1884.

34. Chris Rainey, "Tommy Bond," *SABR Baseball Biography Project*, https://sabr.org/bioproj/person/tommy-bond/.

35. "Their First Defeat," *Cincinnati Enquirer*, April 28, 1884.

36. "The Unions as Batters (?)," *Cincinnati Commercial*, April 27, 1884.

Chapter 7

1. "Diamond Chips," *St. Louis Republican*, April 28, 1884.

2. "Notes and Comments," *Sporting Life*, May 28, 1884.

3. "A Great St. Louis Victory," *St. Louis Republican*, May 1, 1884.

4. "St. Louis Unions, 15; Altoona, 2," *St. Louis Daily Globe-Democrat*, May 1, 1884.

5. "Sluggers Slugged," *Pittsburgh Commercial Gazette*, July 23, 1883.

6. "St. Louis Unions, 15; Altoona, 2," *St. Louis Daily Globe-Democrat*, May 1, 1884.

7. "Leary Expelled from the Manchesters," *Boston Daily Globe*, May 31, 1878.

8. "Mike Kelly," *Boston Sunday Globe*, February 19, 1878.

9. "Muscle and Speed," *Rochester Democrat and Chronicle*, July 11, 1879.

10. "Speed, Skill and Science," *Rochester Democrat and Chronicle*, April 11, 1880.

11. "Sporting Matters," *Detroit Free Press*, June 23, 1881.

12. "Diamond Dust," *St. Louis Daily Globe-Democrat*, May 21, 1882.

13. "Notes and Comments," *Sporting Life*, July 29, 1883.

14. "Notes and Comments," *Sporting Life*, October 15, 1883.

15. "From Altoona," *Sporting Life*, May 14, 1884.

16. "Notes and Comments," *Sporting Life*, May 14, 1884.

17. "Fair Balls," *Minneapolis Tribune*, June 2, 1884.

18. "Diamond Chips," *St. Louis Post-Dispatch*, July 8, 1884.

19. "Notes," *Nashville Banner*, September 5, 1885.

20. "Ball Notes," *Nashville Banner*, June 3, 1886.

21. "Leary Release for Drinking," *New Haven Register*, July 9, 1887.

22. Letter to Dr. Marguerite E. Lerner from Lee Allen, May 13, 1960, John J. Leary Player File, National Baseball Hall of Fame Player File.

23. "Special to the Republican," *St. Louis Republican*, May 4, 1884.

24. "Sunday Sporting Events," *Wikipedia*, last modified July 19, 2021, https://en.wikipedia.org/wiki/Sunday_sporting_events.

25. "From Altoona," *Sporting Life*, May 14, 1884.

26. "Altoona Wins," *Cincinnati Enquirer*, May 11, 1884.

27. "Union Association," *Sporting Life*, May 21, 1884.

28. *Ibid.*

29. "Keystones 9; Altoonas, 8," *Boston Sunday Herald*, May 18, 1884.

30. "Notes and Comments," *Sporting Life*, May 28, 1884.

31. *Ibid.*

32. "Notes and Comments," *Sporting Life*, May 14, 1884.

33. "Notes and Comments," *Sporting Life*, June 4, 1884.

34. *Ibid.*

35. "Notes and Comments," *Sporting Life*, June 4, 1884.

36. "A Great Game," *Cincinnati Enquirer*, May 28, 1884.

37. "A Bum Game," *Altoona Times*, May 30, 1884.

38. "Don't You Play, Tony," Don't Play," *St. Louis Republican*, May 6, 1884.

39. "Mullane Whips Lucas," *Cincinnati Commercial*, May 14, 1884.

40. Seymour, 156.

41. "Mullane's Case," *Sporting Life*, May 28, 1884.

42. Seymour, 156.

43. *Wright & Ditson's Base Ball Guide* (Boston: Wright & Ditson, 1884), 16.

44. Samantha Grossman, "7 Things You Didn't Know About Memorial Day," *Time,* May 25, 2012, https://newsfeed.time.com/2012/05/28/7-things-you-didnt-know-about-memorial-day/slide/it-was-originally-called-decoration-day/.

45. "Boston Unions 12; Chicago Unions 4," *Boston Daily Globe*, May 31, 1884.

46. "The National Game," *Chicago Daily Tribune,* May 31, 1884.

47. "A Coincidence," *Cincinnati Enquirer,* May 31, 1884.

48. "Only a Little Pastime," *Cincinnati Enquirer,* May 31, 1884.

49. "Beaten Again," *Altoona Times*, May 31, 1884.

50. *Ibid.*

51. "The Last Game," *Altoona Times*, June 2, 1884.

52. *Ibid.*

53. *Ibid.*

54. "Union Association," *Sporting Life*, June 11, 1884.

55. "The Last Game," *Altoona Times*, June 2, 1884.

56. "From Altoona," *Sporting Life,* June 11, 1884.

57. "The Club Drops out of the Union Association-Minor Notes," *Sporting Life,* June 11, 1884.

Chapter 8

1. "Altoona's Retirement," *Sporting Life*, July 9, 1884.

2. "Base Ball," *Washington Evening Star*, March 15, 1884.

3. "Altoona's Retirement," *Sporting Life*, July 9, 1884.

4. "The Union Association Meeting," *Cincinnati Enquirer*, March 18, 1884.

5. "Notes and Comments," *Sporting Life*, May 28, 1884.

6. "Notes and Comments," *Sporting Life*, March 26, 1884.

7. "Kansas City in the Union," *Kansas City Daily Times* (Missouri), June 3, 1884.

8. "Diamond Chips," *St. Louis Republican*, June 7, 1884.

9. "The Altoona Successors," *Sporting Life*, June 11, 1884.

10. "From Altoona," *Sporting Life*, June 11, 1884.

11. "Disbanded for Good," *Sporting Life*, June 25, 1884.

12. "Diamond Chips," *St. Louis Republican*, June 4, 1884.

13. *Ibid.*

14. "The Altoona Successors," *Sporting Life*, June 11, 1884.

15. "Diamond Dust," *St. Louis Republican*, June 6, 1884.

16. "Diamond Dust," *St. Louis Republican*, May 31, 1884.

17. "Notes and Comments," *Sporting Life*, June 18, 1884.

18. "Diamond Dust," *St. Louis Republican*, June 7, 1884.

19. "Opening Game at Kansas City," *Cincinnati Enquirer*, June 8, 1884.

20. "First Blood for the Strangers," *Kansas City Daily Times*, June 8, 1884.

21. *Ibid.*

22. *Ibid.*

23. "Cut Short by the Rain," *Kansas City Daily Times*, June 9, 1884.

24. "Without an Error," *Cincinnati Enquirer*, June 10, 1884.

25. "Caught on the Fly," *Kansas City Daily Times*, June 10, 1884.

26. Gregory H. Wolf, "Bill Hutchison," *SABR Baseball Biography Project*, https://sabr.org/bioproj/person/bill-hutchison/.

27. *Ibid.*

28. "Not a Very Good Game," *Cincinnati Enquirer*, June 12, 1884.

29. "Sporting Notes," *Buffalo Commercial Advertiser*, June 17, 1884.

30. "2015–16 Golden State Warriors season," *Wikipedia*, last modified July 10, 2020, https://en.wikipedia.org/wiki/2015%E2%80%9316_Golden_State_Warriors_season.

31. "Notes," *Cincinnati Commercial*, May 18, 1884.

32. "Notes and Announcements," *Cincinnati Commercial*, June 22, 1884.

Chapter 9

1. "Notes and Comments," *Sporting Life*, July 9, 1884.

2. "The Union Association Meeting," *Cincinnati Enquirer*, July 3, 1884.

3. *Ibid.*

4. "Lucas and the Hub Unions," *Boston Herald*, February 2, 1886.

5. *Ibid.*

6. "Base Ball Notes," *Camden Post* (New Jersey), May 10, 1884.

7. "The Union Meeting," *Sporting Life*, July 9, 1884.

8. "Sporting," *Buffalo Commercial Advertiser*, June 21, 1884.

9. *Ibid.*

10. "Notes and Comments," *Sporting Life*, July 9, 1884.

11. *Ibid.*

12. Erik Miklich, "1867 Washington Nationals Tour," *19C Baseball*, 2016, http://www.19cbaseball.com/tours-1867-washington-nationals-tour.html.

13. "The Nationals' Prospects," *Cincinnati Enquirer*, August 10, 1884.

14. "Our National Game," *National Police Gazette*, May 10, 1884.

15. "Left in Disgust," *Cincinnati Enquirer*, May 11, 1884.

16. "A Very Fine Game," *Cincinnati Enquirer*, June 17, 1884.

17. "An Exciting Game," *Cincinnati Enquirer*, June 25, 1884.

18. "The Sulky Player got Even," *Kansas City Star* (Missouri), August 10, 1906.

19. *Ibid.*

20. John Thorn, "Henry Moore, Mystery Man of Baseball," *Our Game*, July 21, 2015, https://ourgame.mlblogs.com/henry-moore-mystery-man-of-baseball-80d9265bded4.

21. *Ibid.*

22. "From Washington," *Sporting Life*, July 16, 1884.

23. "Twice Victorious," *Washington National Republican*, July 5, 1884.

24. *Ibid.*

25. *Ibid.*

26. "From Washington," *Sporting Life*, July 16, 1884.

27. "Sporting," *St. Louis Republican*, July 15, 1884.

28. "Current Sporting," *Washington National Republican*, July 28, 1884.

29. *Ibid.*

30. "From Washington," *Sporting Life*, August 13, 1884.

31. "Vultures Hovering Over the Dying," *Cincinnati Enquirer*, August 3, 1884.

32. *Ibid.*

33. *Ibid.*

34. "Sporting Variety," *Washington National Republican*, August 7, 1884.

Chapter 10

1. Nemec, *Nineteenth-Century Major League Baseball*, 238.

2. *Ibid.*

3. David Nemec, "The Union Association: An Unexpected Last Stop," *Base Ball* 3.1 (Spring 2009): 46.

4. *Ibid.*

5. "Many Games of Ball," *Baltimore American*, July 5, 1884.

6. *Ibid.*

7. *Ibid.*

8. "Baltimore Unions 12, St. Louis Unions, 10," *Baltimore Sun*, July 5, 1884.

9. "Our National Game," *National Police Gazette*, December 1, 1883.

10. "Many Games of Ball," *Baltimore American*, July 5, 1884.

11. "Baltimore Unions 12, St. Louis Unions, 10," *Baltimore Sun*, July 5, 1884.

12. "A Wrangle in Baltimore," *Cincinnati Enquirer*, July 6, 1884.

13. "Around the Bases," *Boston Herald*, July 12, 1884.

Chapter 11

1. "Notes and Comments," *Sporting Life*, July 9, 1884.

2. "Gossipy Gleanings," *Boston Daily Globe*, July 6, 1884.

3. "Notes and Comments," *Sporting Life*, July 16, 1884.

4. Connie Nisinger, "Charlie Hodnett," *Find A Grave*, last modified October 24, 2001, https://www.findagrave.com/memorial/5885950/charles-hodnett.

5. "Taylor and Baker," *Sporting Life*, July 9, 1884.

6. "Released on Bail," *Pittsburgh Daily Post*, October 18, 1883.

7. "She Married the Umpire," *Lincoln Daily State Journal* (Nebraska), November 8, 1883.

8. "The Allegheny Club," *Sporting Life*, November 14, 1883.

9. "Joined the Contract Breakers," *St. Louis Republican*, July 10, 1884.

10. Thorn, "Baseball's Bans and Blacklists."

11. "Diamond Dust," *St. Louis Daily-Globe Democrat*, July 25, 1884.

12. "The National Game," *Baltimore Sun*, July 17, 1884.

13. "Diamond Dust," *St. Louis Republican*, July 31, 1884.

14. "Diamond Dust," *St. Louis Daily Globe-Democrat*, July 12, 1884.

15. "Base Ball," *Detroit Free Press*, July 11, 1884.

16. *Ibid.*

17. *Ibid.*

18. "Fair Ball," *Detroit Free Press*, July 12, 1884.

19. "Bond and Brown," *Sporting Life*, July 16, 1884.

20. "The Union Nine Releases Bond and Brown," *Boston Daily Globe*, July 5, 1884.

21. Rainey, "Tommy Bond."

22. "Lucas and the Hub Unions," *Boston Herald*, February 2, 1886.

23. "Notes and Comments," *Sporting Life*, October 8, 1884.

24. Al Spink, "Puzzle-Pitches Often Amusing," *Reno Evening Gazette* (Nevada), October 23, 1920.

25. "It Was the Gray's Turn," *Boston Journal*, July 18, 1884.

26. "St. Louis Unions, 1; Boston Unions, 0," *Boston Daily Globe*, July 20, 1884.

Chapter 12

1. Edward Achorn, "June 7, 1884: Charlie Sweeney Strikes Out 19 for Providence," *SABR Baseball Games Project*, https://sabr.org/gamesproj/game/june-7-1884-sweeney-strikes-out-nineteen.

2. *Providence Journal*, June 7, 1884.

3. "Nineteen Struck Out," *Boston Daily Globe*, June 8, 1884.

4. Achorn, "June 7, 1884."

5. *Ibid.*

6. Brian McKenna, "Old Hoss Radbourn," *SABR Baseball Biography Project*, https://sabr.org/bioproj/person/old-hoss-radbourn/.

7. *Ibid.*

8. *Ibid.*

9. "A Good Clean Lead," *Boston Daily Globe*, July 17, 1884.

10. *Ibid.*

11. "Base Ball," *Fall River Daily Evening News*, July 19, 1884.

12. "Is Radbourne Going to St. Louis," *Boston Herald*, July 20, 1884.

13. "Sporting Matters," *Providence Morning Star*, July 23, 1884.

14. *Ibid.*

15. *Ibid.*

16. "Providence in Doubt," *Trenton Evening Times*, July 31, 1884.

17. "Sporting Matters," *Providence Morning Star*, July 23, 1884.

18. *Ibid.*

19. *Ibid.*

20. McKenna, "Old Hoss Radbourn."

21. "Base Ball Notes," *Providence Evening Press*, July 24, 1884.

22. "Sweeny to Come to St. Louis," *St. Louis Republican*, July 25, 1884.

23. "Sporting," *St. Louis Daily Globe-Democrat*, August 2, 1884.

24. "Sporting Budget," *St. Louis Post-Dispatch*, August 2, 1884.

Chapter 13

1. "Catchers and Pitches," *Boston Daily Globe*, August 7, 1883.

2. "Luff Falls," *Sporting Life*, June 4, 1884.

3. Bill Carle, "Billy Geer," *SABR Baseball Biography Project*, https://sabr.org/bioproj/person/billy-geer/.

4. *Ibid.*

5. *Ibid.*

6. David Nemec, "Jack Clements," *SABR Baseball Biography Project*, https://sabr.org/bioproj/person/jack-clements/.

7. "Freezing Them Out," *Rocky Mountain News* (Denver), April 7, 1884.

8. "The Union Association," *Sporting Life*, August 13, 1884.

9. *Ibid.*

10. *Ibid.*

11. "Base Ball Gossip," *Philadelphia City Item*, August 8, 1884.

12. *Ibid.*

13. "One Ball Club Less," *Wilmington Morning News* (Delaware), September 16, 1884.

14. "Base Ball Notes," April 19, 1884.

15. "Balls and Strikes," *Boston Daily Globe*, August 2, 1884.

16. "Notes," *Quincy Daily Journal* (Illinois), August 11, 1884.

17. *Ibid.*

18. "Sporting," *St. Louis Republican*, August 15, 1884.

19. *Ibid.*

20. "St. Louis Unions," *St. Louis Post-Dispatch*, August 15, 1884.

21. "Base Ball," *Quincy Daily Journal*, August 16, 1884.

22. "Base Ball," *Quincy Daily Journal*, August 18, 1884.

23. "Notes,' *Quincy Daily Journal*, August 15, 1884.

24. "Gone to the Unions," *Wilmington Morning News*, August 19, 1884.

25. *Ibid.*

26. *Ibid.*

Chapter 14

1. "The Cleveland Club," *Louisville Courier-Journal*, August 8, 1884.

2. *Ibid.*

3. "Base Ball Players Desert," *Sporting Life*, August 13, 1884.

4. *Ibid.*

5. "The Cause of the Delay," *Grand Rapids Evening Leader* (Michigan), August 16, 1884.

6. "The Grand Rapids Club Disbands," *Cleveland Leader*, August 12, 1884.

7. "In and Out-Door Sports," *Cleveland Plain Dealer*, August 8, 1884.

8. "A Terrific Shock," *Cleveland Leader*, August 9, 1884.

9. *Ibid.*

10. *Ibid.*

11. "What Induced It—a Foolish Charge—What Welfeld Says," *Wheeling Register*, August 17, 1884.

12. *Ibid.*

13. "In and Out-Door Sports," *Cleveland Plain Dealer*, August 13, 1884.

14. "A Terrific Shock," *Cleveland Leader*, August 9, 1884.

15. *Ibid.*

16. "Notes," *Louisville Courier-Journal*, August 15, 1884.

17. "Diamond Dust," *St. Louis Daily Globe-Democrat*, August 10, 1884.

18. "The End of the Scheming," *Sporting Life*, August 20, 1884.

19. "A Beautiful Game Yesterday," *Cincinnati Enquirer*, August 11, 1884.

20. "Base Hits Everywhere," *New York Clipper*, August 23, 1884.

21. "Foul Tips," *Boston Daily Globe*, July 17, 1884.

22. Dan Brown, "Screwballs populate early baseball team," *London Free Press* (Ontario), December 22, 2017, https://lfpress.com/2017/12/22/screwballs-populate-early-baseball-team/wcm/c4df2b96-576c-d869-4a20-b4014051f4c6/.

23. "Notes," *Cincinnati Enquirer*, April 13, 1884.

24. "Notes," *Cincinnati Enquirer*, August 11, 1884.

25. "A Base-Ball Player Sues for Salary," *Cincinnati Enquirer*, August 26, 1884.

13. *Ibid.*

14. "A Disgraceful Performance," *Baltimore Sun*, July 3, 1884.

15. Bevis, "Gid Gardner."

16. "Notes and Comments," *Sporting Life*, October 8, 1884.

17. "Union Club at Pittsburg Next Year," *Cincinnati Enquirer*, August 16, 1884.

18. "Diamond Dust," *St. Louis Daily Globe-Democrat*, January 8, 1884.

19. "Next Year's Nine," *Pittsburgh Press*, July 15, 1884.

20. "No Money in it," *Pittsburgh Press*, September 13, 1884.

21. "Will We Get the Providence Club?" *Pittsburgh Press*, August 9, 1884.

22. "They Promised Price," *Pittsburgh Daily Post*, August 11, 1884.

23. *Ibid.*

24. "The Chicago Unions to Be Transferred to Pittsburg," *Chicago Daily Tribune*, August 20, 1884.

25. "The New Club," *Pittsburgh Post-Gazette*, August 20, 1884.

26. *Ibid.*

27. *Ibid.*

28. "Reorganization of the Union," *St. Louis Daily Globe-Democrat*, August 20, 1884.

29. "Dissatisfaction Over Battin's Release," *St. Louis Daily Globe-Democrat*, August 7, 1884.

30. "Base Ball Notes," *Chester Times* (Pennsylvania), August 14, 1884.

31. "Price's Boys," *Pittsburgh Post-Gazette*, August 26, 1884.

32. *Ibid.*

33. *Ibid.*

34. *Ibid.*

35. "Bill Krieg," *Wikipedia*, June 19, 2020, https://en.wikipedia.org/wiki/Bill_Krieg.

36. "Price's Boys," *Pittsburgh Post-Gazette*, August 26, 1884.

Chapter 15

1. "Base Hits," *Boston Herald*, August 5, 1884.

2. "Base Ball," *Fall River Daily Evening News*, August 13, 1884.

3. "Minor Games," *Chicago Daily Inter Ocean*, August 2, 1884.

4. Charlie Bevis, "Dan Cronin," *SABR Baseball Biography Project*, https://sabr.org/bioproj/person/dan-cronin/.

5. Vaccaro, "Hugh Daily."

6. *Ibid.*

7. *Ibid.*

8. *Ibid.*

9. "Money in Base Ball," *Ottawa Daily Republic* (Kansas), July 18, 1884.

10. "Diamond Dust," *Winfield Daily Courier* (Kansas), March 26, 1887.

11. "Baseball Gossip," *National Police Gazette*, August 18, 1888.

12. Charlie Bevis, "Gid Gardner," *SABR Baseball Biography Project,* https://sabr.org/bioproj/person/gid-gardner/.

Chapter 16

1. "Gone to the Unions," *Wilmington Morning News*, August 19, 1884.

2. *Washington National Republican*, August 19, 1884.

3. "Notes," *Wilmington News Journal* (Delaware), August 20, 1884.

4. "Union Association," *Sporting Life*, August 27, 1884.

5. "Notes," *Wilmington News Journal*, August 20, 1884.

6. *Ibid.*

7. "Notes and Comments," *Sporting Life*, September 3, 1884.

8. "Dennis Casey," *BR Bullpen*, May 3, 2020, https://www.baseball-reference.com/bullpen/Dennis_Casey.

9. "Notes and Comments," *Sporting Life*, September 3, 1884.

10. John Thorn, "The Only Nolan," *Our Game*, May 18, 2015, https://ourgame.mlblogs.com/the-only-nolan-bc7474dae960.

11. *Ibid.*

12. *Ibid.*

13. "One Ball Club Less," *Wilmington Morning News.*

14. "In Boston," *Wilmington News Journal*, August 26, 1884.

15. "Superintendent of Schools Resigns," *Fall River Evening News*, June 9, 1919.

16. "Fell Down an Elevator Well," *Wilmington Morning News*, September 5, 1884.

17. *Ibid.*

18. "An Umpire's Accident," *Wilmington Morning News*, September 5, 1884.

19. "Brought to a Sudden Close," *Wilmington Daily Republican* (Delaware), September 5, 1884.

20. "Some Good Playing," *Wilmington Morning News*, September 6, 1884.

21. "Notes," *Wilmington Daily Republican*, September 15, 1884.

22. "Bad for Wilmington," *Sporting Life*, September 17, 1884.

23. "One Club Less," *Wilmington Morning News*, September 16, 1884.

24. *Ibid.*

25. *Ibid.*

26. *Ibid.*

27. "Mr. Lucas Righted," *Sporting Life*, October 1, 1884.

Chapter 17

1. "Atkisson's Act," *Sporting Life*, July 30, 1884.

2. "The Pittsburgh Unions," *Pittsburgh Post-Gazette*, August 29, 1884.

3. "Drawn on Account of Darkness," *Cincinnati Enquirer*, September 12, 1884.

4. "No Money in It," *Pittsburgh Press*, September 13, 1884.

5. "They Will Not Disband," *Pittsburgh Press*, September 15, 1884.

6. "Notes and Comments," *Sporting Life*, September 17, 1884.

7. "Sporting Summary," *Washington National Republican*, September 20, 1884.

8. "The Pittsburg Unions Disband," *Baltimore American*, September 20, 1884.

9. *Ibid.*

10. "Pick-ups," *Minneapolis Tribune*, September 29, 1884.

11. "The Pittsburg Unions Disband," *Baltimore American*, September 20, 1884.

12. "The U.P.'s Tour," *Omaha Daily Bee*, September 15, 1884.

13. *Ibid.*

14. "Future Dates," *Omaha Daily Bee*, September 17, 1884.

15. "President Lucas Home Again," *St. Louis Republican*, September 23, 1884.

16. "The Union Schedule," *St. Louis Daily Globe-Democrat*, September 25, 1884.

17. "Notes," *St. Paul Daily Globe*, September 16, 1884.

18. "Balls and Strikes," *Boston Daily Globe*, August 2, 1884.

19. "Bat and Bridle," *St. Paul Daily Globe*, September 18, 1884.

20. "The St. Paul Team," *St. Paul Daily Globe*, September 25, 1884.

Chapter 18

1. "A Pleasing Finish," *Washington National Republican*, September 26, 1884.

2. "The Latest Acquisition," *Pittsburgh Press*, September 22, 1884.

3. "Current Sporting," *Washington National Republican*, September 22, 1884.

4. Gene Gomes, "Abner Powell," *SABR Biography Project*, https://sabr.org/bioproj/person/abner-powell/.

5. *Ibid.*

6. *Ibid.*

7. *Ibid.*

8. *Ibid.*

9. "Notes and Comments," *Sporting Life*, September 10, 1884.

10. Denis Pajot, *The Rise of Milwaukee Baseball* (Jefferson, NC: McFarland, 2009), 103.

11. *Ibid.*, 105.

12. *Ibid.*

13. *Ibid.*

14. *Ibid.*, 101.

15. "Lady Baldwin," *Wikipedia*, Last modified July 12, 2020, https://en.wikipedia.org/wiki/Lady_Baldwin.

16. Dennis Pajot, "Anton Falch," *SABR Baseball Biography Project*, https://sabr.org/bioproj/person/anton-falch/.

17. Pajot, *The Rise of Milwaukee Baseball*, 107.

18. "Notes and Comments," *Sporting Life*, October 8, 1884.

19. "Base Ball," *Washington National Republican*, September 30, 1884.

20. "Notes and Comments," *Sporting Life*, October 8, 1884.

21. *Ibid.*

22. Charlie Bevis, "George Bignell," *SABR Baseball Biography Project*, https://sabr.org/bioproj/person/george-bignell/.

23. Pajot, 108.

24. Bevis, "George Bignell."

25. Pajot, 109.

26. *Ibid.*

Chapter 19

1. "Base Ball," *New Orleans Times-Picayune*, September 8, 1883.

2. "A Change of Management," *St. Paul Daily Globe*, July 28, 1884.

3. *Ibid.*

4. "Andrew Thompson (Manager)," *Wikipedia*, last modified August 1, 2020, https://en.wikipedia.org/wiki/Andrew_Thompson_(manager).

5. "Diamond Chips," *St. Louis Post-Dispatch*, October 8, 1884.

6. *Ibid.*

7. "Monumental Inscription," *St. Paul Daily Globe*, September 22, 1884.

8. "Sporting," *St. Louis Republican*, October 5, 1884.

9. Peter Morris, e-mail message to author, July 7, 2020.

10. "Notes," *Cincinnati Enquirer*, September 26, 1884.

11. "Notes," *Cincinnati Enquirer*, September 27, 1884.

12. "The Opening Union Game Yesterday," *Cincinnati Enquirer*, September 28, 1884.

13. "Notes," *Cincinnati Enquirer*, September 29, 1884.

14. "Notes," *Cincinnati Enquirer*, October 1, 1884.

15. "Fifth Day and No Response," *Cincinnati Enquirer*, October 10, 1884.

16. "Off for Nashville," *Cincinnati Enquirer*, October 10, 1884.

17. "A Direct Benefit to the 'Common Enemy,'" *St. Louis Daily Globe-Democrat*, October 6, 1884.

18. "Mr. Mill's Decision," *Sporting Life*, October 15, 1884.

19. "Sporting," *St. Louis Republican*, October 4, 1884.

20. "Sporting," *St. Louis Republican*, October 7, 1884.

21. "Lewis Released," *St. Louis Post-Dispatch*, September 20, 1884.

22. "Affairs in the Mound City," *Sporting Life*, September 3, 1884.

Chapter 20

1. "Our Luckless Ball Team," *Kansas City Daily Times*, July 23, 1884.

2. "Base Ball," *Bay City Evening Press* (Michigan), July 26, 1884.

3. "Short Stops," *Kansas Daily City Times*, August 10, 1884.

4. David Ball, "Kid Baldwin," *SABR Baseball Biography Project*, https://sabr.org/bioproj/person/kid-baldwin/.

5. *Ibid.*

6. *Ibid.*

7. *Ibid.*

8. "Peek-A-Boo Veach," *Wikipedia*, last modified July 23, 2020, https://en.wikipedia.org/wiki/Peek-A-Boo_Veach.

9. Peter Morris, *Catcher: How the Man Behind the Plate Became an American Folk Hero* (Chicago: Ivan R. Dee, 2009), 195–196.

10. *Ibid.*, 196.

11. "Notes of the Diamond Field," *Philadelphia Inquirer*, October 1, 1890.

12. Adam Bunch, "The Con Artist Harry Decker—Toronto's First Star Baseball Catcher," *The Toronto Dreams Project*, March 29, 2018, http://torontodreamsproject.blogspot.com/2018/03/the-con-artist-harry-decker-torontos.html.

13. *Ibid.*

14. "Lew Brown's Last Sleep," *Boston Daily Globe*, January 19, 1889.

15. "St. Paul's Club," *Sporting Life*, October 29, 1884.

16. "Diamond Chips," *St. Louis Post-Dispatch*, September 10, 1884.

17. "Ed Crane Beats the Record for Long Throwing," *Cincinnati Enquirer*, October 13, 1884.

18. "Crane's Thrown Surveyed by Civil Engineers," *Cincinnati Enquirer*, October 14, 1884.

19. "Crane's Throwing," *Sporting Life*, October 29, 1884.

20. Bill Lamb, "Tommy McCarthy," *SABR Baseball Biography Project*, https://sabr.org/bioproj/person/tommy-mccarthy/.

21. "Notes and Comments," *Sporting Life*, November 5, 1884.

22. *Ibid.*

23. "To Mark 40th Anniversary of First Trolley," *Baltimore Sun*, August 10, 1925.

24. "Shut Out," *St. Louis Republican*, October 20, 1884.

25. *Ibid.*

26. *Ibid.*

Chapter 21

1. Philip Von Borries, "Pete Browning," *SABR Baseball Biography Project*, https://sabr.org/bioproj/person/pete-browning/.

2. "Base Ball Notes," *Cincinnati Enquirer*, April 6, 1884.

3. "The Keystone Unions," *Philadelphia Times*, April 6, 1884.

4. "The Keystones defeat the Richmonds," *Richmond Dispatch*, June 6, 1884.

5. "Nearly Shut Out," *Chester Times*, June 18, 1884.

6. "Around the Canvas Bags," *Chester Times*, September 15, 1884.

7. "Notes and Comments," *Sporting Life*, November 5, 1884.

8. "The Portsmouths Entitled to the Game," *The Norfolk Virginian* (Virginia), August 13, 1884.

9. "Sports Sphere," *Kansas Daily City Times*, October 27, 1884.

10. "Hecker's Hurrah," *Cincinnati Enquirer*, October 19, 1884.

11. *Ibid.*

12. "Hammering Hecker," *Cincinnati Enquirer*, October 20, 1884.

13. "Base Ball," *Cincinnati Commercial*, October 20, 1884.

14. "Entertaining the Union Players," *Cincinnati Enquirer*, October 21, 1884.

15. *Ibid.*

16. Paul Browne, "Dan O'Leary," *SABR Baseball Biography Project*, https://sabr.org/bioproj/person/dan-oleary/.

17. *Ibid.*

18. "Notes," *Cincinnati Enquirer*, June 22, 1884.

19. "Story of 'Carnation Dan,'" *Chicago Daily Tribune*, June 29, 1922.

20. "Sam Crane Arrested," *Semi-Weekly Standard* (Hazleton, Pennsylvania), August 21, 1889.

21. "Sam Crane (Second Baseman)," *Wikipedia*,

Last modified July 24, 2020, https://en.wikipedia.org/wiki/Sam_Crane_(second_baseman).

22. "The Maroons Downed," *St. Louis Republican*, October 25, 1884.

23. "Sporting," *St. Louis Republican*, October 26, 1884.

Chapter 22

1. Letter from W.C. Henderson to Friend Robby, 1884 December 02, BL-2733-81-24, Box 12, Folder 1, BL02733-81, William Robinson correspondence, the National Baseball Hall of Fame and Museum, Cooperstown, New York, https://collection.baseballhall.org/PASTIME/letter-w-c-henderson-friend-robby-1884-december-02.

2. "William Edward White," *Wikipedia*, last modified July 24, 2020, https://en.wikipedia.org/wiki/William_Edward_White.

3. "Sold Out. Columbus Sells Its Players Like Slaves to Pittsburg," *Cincinnati Enquirer*, October 31, 1884.

4. *Ibid.*

5. *Ibid.*

6. *Ibid.*

7. *Ibid.*

8. "Washington's Club," *Sporting Life*, December 3, 1884.

9. "From Detroit," *Sporting Life*, October 22, 1884.

10. *Ibid.*

11. Nemec, *Nineteenth-Century Major League Baseball*, 286.

12. "A Disgusted President," *Sporting Life*, October 22, 1884.

13. "St. Paul's Club," *Sporting Life*, October 29, 1884.

14. "A Base Ball War," *Philadelphia Times*, January 18, 1885.

15. "Notes and Comments," *Sporting Life*, December 3, 1884.

16. "Washington's Club," *Sporting Life*, December 3, 1884.

17. *Ibid.*

18. *Ibid.*

19. "Base Ball Notes," *Pittsburgh Post*, October 21, 1884.

20. "St. Paul's Club," *Sporting Life*, October 29, 1884.

21. "Notes and Comments," *Sporting Life*, November 19, 1884.

22. "Notes and Comments," *Sporting Life*, November 5, 1884.

23. Frank Jackson, "Lessons from Lakefront Park, 1884," *The Hardball Times*, July 5, 2012, https://tht.fangraphs.com/lessons-from-lakefront-park-1884/.

24. *Ibid.*

25. "Notes and Comments," *Sporting Life*, November 19, 1884.

26. "Base Ball," *Kansas City Daily Times*, December 9, 1884.

27. "Future Prospects for Base Ballists," *Wilmington Daily Republican*, November 20, 1884.

28. "Notes and Comments," *Sporting Life*, November 5, 1884.

29. *Ibid.*

30. "The Outlook for Next Season-Notes About Players, Etc., Etc.," *Sporting Life*, November 5, 1884.

31. *Ibid.*

32. *Ibid.*

33. *Ibid.*

34. *Ibid.*

35. Pajot, 109.

36. *Ibid.*

37. *Ibid.*

38. *Ibid.*

39. *Ibid.*

40. "Milwaukee's Club," *Sporting Life*, December 31, 1884.

41. "St. Paul's Club," *Sporting Life*, October 29, 1884.

42. "A New Catcher for the Phillies," *Sporting Life*, November 5, 1884.

Chapter 23

1. "The New Western League," *Sporting Life,* December 3, 1884.

2. "The League Meeting," *Sporting Life*, November 26, 1884.

3. *Ibid.*

4. *Ibid.*

5. "Matters at the Hoosier Capital-Lucas Laying Lines," *Sporting Life*, December 3, 1884.

6. *Ibid.*

7. *Ibid.*

8. *Ibid.*

9. *Ibid.*

10. "Columbus Matters," *Sporting Life*, December 10, 1884.

11. *Ibid.*

12. *Ibid.*

13. *Ibid.*

14. "Plenty of Clubs, But How Shall the Circuit be Formed," *Sporting Life*, December 10, 1884.

15. "Election of National Club Officers-The Outlook for Next Season," *Sporting Life*, December 10, 1884.

16. *Ibid.*

17. "A Great Gathering," *Sporting Life*, December 17, 1884.

18. Ray Birch, "Tony Mullane," *SABR Baseball Biography Project*, https://sabr.org/bioproj/person/tony-mullane/.

19. "A Great Gathering," *Sporting Life,* December 17, 1884.

20. *Ibid.*

21. "What Does It Mean?" *Sporting Life*, December 24, 1884.

22. "A Great Gathering," *Sporting Life*, December 17, 1884.

23. "Getting Ready for Another Campaign-Details of the Meeting," *Sporting Life*, December 17, 1884.

24. "Uncertain Clubs," *Sporting Life*, December 24, 1884.

25. "A Startling Story," *Sporting Life*, December 17, 1884.

26. *Ibid.*

27. "A Seeming Confirmation," *Sporting Life*, December 17, 1884.

28. *Ibid.*

29. "Further Developments," *Sporting Life*, December 17, 1884.

30. "Sporting," *St. Louis Daily Globe-Democrat*, December 19, 1884.

31. "The Union Association," *Sporting Life*, December 24, 1884.

32. *Ibid.*

33. *Ibid.*

34. "The Union Association," *Sporting Life*, December 24, 1884.

35. *Ibid.*

36. *Ibid.*

37. *Ibid.*

38. *Ibid.*

39. "Uncertain Clubs," *Sporting Life*, December 24, 1884.

40. *Ibid.*

41. *Ibid.*

42. "Cleveland's Position," *Sporting Life*, December 31, 1884.

43. "More Rumors of Changes," *Sporting Life*, December 31, 1884.

44. "From Cincinnati," *Sporting Life*, December 31, 1884.

45. *Ibid.*

Chapter 24

1. "Excitement in the Ball World," *St. Louis Republican*, January 4, 1885.

2. "Some Base Ball Secrets," *Philadelphia Times*, January 13, 1885.

3. *Ibid.*

4. "On the Ragged Edge," *Sporting Life*, January 28, 1885.

5. "The League Meeting," *Sporting Life*, January 14, 1885.

6. *Ibid.*

7. "Later-A Hitch," *Sporting Life*, January 14, 1885.

8. "From Porkopolis," *Sporting Life*, January 14, 1885.

9. "Milwaukee Mad," *Sporting Life*, January 28, 1885.

10. "Gone Up," *Sporting Life*, January 21, 1885.

11. "Base Ball," *Cincinnati Commercial*, January 18, 1885.

12. "Gone Up," *Sporting Life*, January 21, 1885.

13. *Ibid.*

14. "Notes and Comments," *Sporting Life*, January 21, 1885.

15. "Milwaukee Mad," *Sporting Life*, January 28, 1885.

16. *Ibid.*

17. "The Plot Thickens," *Kansas City Daily Times*, January 17, 1885.

18. "Base Ball," *Cincinnati Commercial*, January 18, 1885.

19. "Notes and Comments," *Sporting Life*, January 21, 1885.

20. "On the Ragged Edge," *Sporting Life*, January 28, 1885.

21. *Ibid.*

22. "Another Shot From Lucas," *Sporting Life*, January 28, 1885.

23. "Peace Once More," *Sporting Life*, February 4, 1885.

24. *Ibid.*

Chapter 25

1. "Mr. Lucas's Club Admitted," *Philadelphia Times*, January 11, 1885.

2. Pajot, *The Rise of Milwaukee Baseball*, 96–97.

3. Justin Mckinney, "Season on the Brink," *Base Ball* 11 (2019), 184.

4. "Notes," *Cincinnati Enquirer*, August 31, 1884.

Chapter 26

1. "Base Ball News," *Philadelphia Times*, February 1, 1885.

2. "Diamond Chips," *St. Louis Post-Dispatch*, March 14, 1885.

3. "Is Lucas Trying to Capture the Western League," *Kansas City Star* (Missouri), March 19, 1885.

4. *Ibid.*

5. "Reinstatement," *St. Louis Post-Dispatch*, April 7, 1885.

6. "Sporting," *St. Louis Daily Globe-Democrat*, April 12, 1885.

7. Jeremy Watterson, "Billy Colgan," *SABR Baseball Biography Project*, https://sabr.org/bioproj/person/billy-colgan/.

8. *Ibid.*

9. "Base Ball Notes," *Philadelphia Times*, January 11, 1885.

10. "Sporting," *St. Louis Daily Globe-Democrat*, April 17, 1885.

11. "Fined and Reinstated," *St. Louis Daily Globe-Democrat*, April 19, 1885.

12. "Diamond Dust," *Winfield Daily Courier*, March 26, 1887.

13. "Fined and Reinstated," *St. Louis Daily Globe-Democrat,* April 19, 1885.

14. "Congratulations," *St. Louis Republican*, April 20, 1885.

15. Brian Flaspohler, "Jack Gleason," *SABR Baseball Biography Project*, https://sabr.org/bioproj/person/jack-gleason/.

16. "Fined and Reinstated," *St. Louis Daily Globe-Democrat* ,April 19, 1885.

17. "Diamond Chat," *St. Louis Republican*, May 5, 1885.

18. "City News," *Indianapolis News*, February 7, 1885.

19. "Pastime Pointers," *Chicago Daily Inter Ocean*, February 13, 1885.

20. "Base Ball," *Fall River Daily Evening News*, May 6, 1885.

21. Nemec, *Nineteenth-Century Major League Baseball*, 46.

22. "Dunlap's Defi," *St. Louis Post-Dispatch*, September 21, 1885.

23. Rochelle Nicholls, "Joe Quinn," SABR Biography Project.

24. "Rowe vs. von der Ahe," *St. Louis Post-Dispatch*, August 27, 1885.

25. "Sporting," *Decatur Saturday Herald* (Illinois), June 13, 1885.

26. "The American Rules Changed," *Sporting Life*, June 17, 1885.

27. *Ibid.*

28. Flaspholer, "Jack Gleason."

29. *Ibid.*

30. "Rowe vs. von der Ahe," *St. Louis Post-Dispatch,* August 27, 1885.

31. "Diamond Dust," *St. Louis Daily Globe-Democrat*, September 8, 1885.

32. "Reinstatement of Gleason and Dolan," *St. Louis Daily Globe-Democrat*, October 7, 1885.

33. "The Great Meeting," *Sporting Life,* October 21, 1885.

34. "Diamond Drift," *Boston Daily Globe*, November 10, 1885.

35. Brian Engelhardt, "George Bradley," *SABR Baseball Biography Project*, https://sabr.org/bioproj/person/george-bradley/.

36. "Al Atkinson (Baseball)," *Wikipedia*, Last modified June 11, 2020, https://en.wikipedia.org/wiki/Al_Atkinson_(baseball).

37. "Famous Baseball Player Dies; Was Original Buck Weaver," *Wichita Beacon* (Kansas), February 2, 1914.

38. "The Base Ball Grounds," *St. Paul Daily Globe*, March 21, 1885.

39. "From the Cream City," *Sporting Life*, June 10, 1885.

40. "The Hoosiers," *Sporting Life*, June 10, 1885.

41. "The Toledo Club in Trouble," *Sporting Life*, August 6, 1885.

42. "The Western League," *Sporting Life*, June 17, 1885.

43. "The New Detroit Club," *St. Louis Post-Dispatch*, June 16, 1885.

44. "Open-Air Sports," *Washington National Republican*, September 15, 1885.

45. "Open Air Diversions," *Washington National Republican*, October 17, 1885.

Chapter 27

1. "Lucas's Loss," *St. Louis Daily Globe-Democrat*, September 7, 1885.

2. "Dunlap's Defi," *St. Louis Post-Dispatch*, September 21, 1885.

3. "Big Four Coming," *Detroit Free Press*, September 18, 1885.

4. Charlie Bevis, "Providence Grays Team Ownership History," *SABR Team Ownership Histories Project*, https://sabr.org/bioproj/topic/providence-grays-team-ownership-history/.

5. *Ibid.*

6. "Baseball in Washington," *Paterson Morning Call* (New Jersey), November 22, 1885.

7. "The Eighth Club," *Sporting Life*, February 17, 1886.

8. *Ibid.*

9. *Ibid.*

10. "St. Paul Matters," *St. Paul Daily Globe*, March 1, 1886.

11. Chris Rainey, "Charlie Sweeney," *SABR Baseball Biography Project*, https://sabr.org/bioproj/person/charlie-sweeney/.

12. *Ibid.*

13. *Ibid.*

14. *Ibid.*

15. *Ibid.*

16. "Base Ball Management," *New Orleans Times-Democrat*, February 8, 1886.

17. "Court Notes," *St. Louis Post-Dispatch*, March 19, 1886.

18. "A Verdict Against Lucas," *St. Louis Post-Dispatch*, May 29, 1886.

19. "Reyburn vs. Lucas," *St. Louis Post-Dispatch*, July 6, 1886.

20. "Rumors of Changes," *New York Times*, July 10, 1886.

21. "A Big Transaction," *St. Louis Post-Dispatch*, July 10, 1886.

22. "The Maroons to Disband," *Philadelphia Times*, August 8, 1886.

23. "Done at Last," *St. Louis Post-Dispatch*, August 18, 1886.

24. *Ibid.*

25. *Ibid.*

26. Vaccaro, "Ted Sullivan."

27. Tom Denardo, "Americus McKim," *Find a Grave*, last modified August 1, 2006, https://www.findagrave.com/memorial/15113654/americus-mckim.

28. Vaccaro, "Ted Sullivan."

Bibliography

Archival Material

John J. Leary Player File. National Baseball Hall of Fame Player File. The National Baseball Hall of Fame and Museum. Cooperstown, New York.

William Robinson Correspondence. 1883–1884. BL-2733-81-24, Box 12, Folder 1, BL02733-81. The National Baseball Hall of Fame and Museum. Cooperstown, New York.

Book and Journal Articles

Egenriether, Richard. "Chris von der Ahe: Baseball's Pioneering Huckster." *SABR Baseball Research Journal* (1989). Accessed August 10, 2021. http://research.sabr.org/journals/chris-von-der-ahe-baseballs-pioneering-huckster.

Hershberger, Richard. "The First Baseball War: The American Association and the National League." *SABR Baseball Research Journal* (Fall 2020). Accessed August 13, 2021. https://sabr.org/journal/article/the-first-baseball-war-the-american-association-and-the-national-league/.

Mckinney, Justin. "Season on the Brink." In *Base Ball 11: New Research on the Early Game*, edited by Don Jensen, 167–192. Jefferson, NC: McFarland, 2019.

Nemec, David. "The Union Association: An Unexpected Last Stop." *Base Ball: A Journal of the Early Game* 3, no. 1 (Spring 2009): 44–52.

Newspapers

Altoona Times (Pennsylvania)
Baltimore American
Baltimore Sun
Bay City Evening Press (Michigan)
Boston Daily Globe
Boston Herald
Boston Sunday Globe
Boston Sunday Herald
Buffalo Commercial Advertiser
Buffalo Daily Times
Buffalo Express
Camden Post (New Jersey)
Chester Times (Pennsylvania)
Chicago Daily Inter Ocean
Chicago Daily Tribune
Cincinnati Commercial
Cincinnati Daily Star
Cincinnati Enquirer
Cleveland Leader
Cleveland Plain Dealer
Decatur Saturday Herald (Illinois)
Detroit Free Press
Fall River Daily Evening News (Massachusetts)
Franklin Repository (Chambersburg, Pennsylvania)
Grand Rapids Evening Leader (Michigan)
Indianapolis News
Kansas City Daily Times (Missouri)
Kansas City Star (Missouri)
Lincoln Daily State Journal (Nebraska)
Louisville Courier-Journal
Minneapolis Tribune
Nashville Banner
National Police Gazette
New Haven Register
New Orleans Times-Picayune
New York Clipper
New York Daily Tribune
New York Tribune
Norfolk Virginian
Omaha Daily Bee
Ottawa Daily Republic (Kansas)
Paterson Morning Call (New Jersey)
Philadelphia Evening Item
Philadelphia Inquirer
Philadelphia Times
Pittsburgh Commercial Gazette
Pittsburgh Daily Post
Pittsburgh Post-Gazette
Pittsburgh Press
Port Huron Daily Times (Michigan)
Providence Evening Press
Providence Morning Star
Quincy Daily Journal (Illinois)
Reno Evening Gazette (Nevada)
Richmond Dispatch
Rochester Democrat and Chronicle
Rocky Mountain News (Denver, Colorado)
St. Louis Daily Globe-Democrat
St. Louis Post-Dispatch
St. Louis Republican
St. Louis Star
St. Paul Daily Globe

Semi-Weekly Standard (Hazleton, Pennsylvania)
Sporting Life
Sporting News
Trenton Evening Times
Washington Evening Star
Washington National Republican
Wheeling Register (West Virginia)
Wichita Beacon (Kansas)
Wilmington Daily Republican (Delaware)
Wilmington Morning News (Delaware)
Wilmington News Journal (Delaware)
Winfield Daily Courier (Kansas)

Online Content

Achorn, Edward. "June 7, 1884: Charlie Sweeney strikes out 19 for Providence." *SABR Baseball Games Project*. Accessed August 21, 2021. https://sabr.org/gamesproj/game/june-7-1884-sweeney-strikes-out-nineteen.

"Al Atkinson (Baseball)." *Wikipedia*. Last modified June 11, 2020. https://en.wikipedia.org/wiki/Al_Atkinson_(baseball).

"Andrew Thompson (Manager)." *Wikipedia*. Last modified August 1, 2020. https://en.wikipedia.org/wiki/Andrew_Thompson_(manager).

Ball, David. "Kid Baldwin." *SABR Baseball Biography Project*. Accessed August 21, 2021. https://sabr.org/bioproj/person/kid-baldwin/.

"Baseball." *Encyclopedia Dubuque*. Last modified July 3, 2020. http://www.encyclopediadubuque.org/index.php?title=BASEBALL.

Bevis, Charlie. "Dan Cronin." *SABR Baseball Biography Project*. Accessed August 21, 2021. https://sabr.org/bioproj/person/dan-cronin/.

———. "Dartmouth Street Grounds (Boston)." *SABR Baseball Biography Project*. Accessed August 21, 2021. https://sabr.org/bioproj/park/dartmouth-street-grounds-boston/.

———. "Frank Winslow." *SABR Baseball Biography Project*. Accessed August 21, 2021. https://sabr.org/bioproj/person/frank-winslow/.

———. "George Bignell." *SABR Baseball Biography Project*. Accessed August 21, 2021. https://sabr.org/bioproj/person/george-bignell/.

———. "Gid Gardner." *SABR Baseball Biography Project*. Accessed August 21, 2021. https://sabr.org/bioproj/person/gid-gardner/.

———. "Providence Grays Team Ownership History." *SABR Team Ownership Histories Project*. Accessed August 21, 2021. https://sabr.org/bioproj/topic/providence-grays-team-ownership-history/.

"Bill Krieg." *Wikipedia*. Last modified June 19, 2020. https://en.wikipedia.org/wiki/Bill_Krieg.

Birch, Ray. "Tony Mullane." *SABR Baseball Biography Project*. Accessed August 21, 2021. https://sabr.org/bioproj/person/tony-mullane/.

Brown, Dan. "Screwballs Populate Early Baseball Team." *London Free Press* (Ontario). December 22, 2017. https://lfpress.com/2017/12/22/screwballs-populate-early-baseball-team/wcm/c4df2b96-576c-d869-4a20-b4014051f4c6/.

Browne, Paul. "Dan O'Leary." *SABR Baseball Biography Project*. Accessed August 21, 2021. https://sabr.org/bioproj/person/dan-oleary/.

Bunch, Adam. "The Con Artist Harry Decker—Toronto's First Star Baseball Catcher." *The Toronto Dreams Project*. March 29, 2018. http://torontodreamsproject.blogspot.com/2018/03/the-con-artist-harry-decker-torontos.html.

Burgess, Bill, III. "Sports Writer Register." *The Baseball Guru*. 2011. http://baseballguru.com/bburgess/analysisbburgess20.html.

Carle, Bill. "Billy Geer." *SABR Baseball Biography Project*. Accessed August 21, 2021. https://sabr.org/bioproj/person/billy-geer/.

Denardo, Tom. "Americus McKim." *Find A Grave*. August 1, 2006. https://www.findagrave.com/memorial/15113654/americus-mckim.

"Dennis Casey." *BR Bullpen*. Last modified May 3, 2020. https://www.baseball-reference.com/bullpen/Dennis_Casey.

"1880 United States Census." *Wikipedia*. Last modified May 24, 2020. https://en.wikipedia.org/wiki/1880_United_States_Census.

"1884 Register League Encylcopedia." *Baseball Reference*. Accessed August 21, 2021. https://www.baseball-reference.com/register/league.cgi?year=1884.

"1883 Register League Encylcopedia." *Baseball Reference*. Accessed August 21, 2021. https://www.baseball-reference.com/register/league.cgi?year=1883.

Engelhardt, Brian. "George Bradley." *SABR Baseball Biography Project*. Accessed August 21, 2021. https://sabr.org/bioproj/person/george-bradley/.

Flaspohler, Brian. "Jack Gleason." *SABR Baseball Biography Project*. Accessed August 21, 2021. https://sabr.org/bioproj/person/jack-gleason/.

Gazdziak, Sam. "Grave Story: Billy Barnie (1853–1900)." *RIP Baseball*. December 6, 2018. https://ripbaseball.com/2018/12/06/grave-story-billy-barnie-1853-1900/.

Gomes, Gene. "Abner Powell." *SABR Baseball Biography Project*. Accessed August 21, 2021. https://sabr.org/bioproj/person/abner-powell/.

Grossman, Samantha. "7 Things You Didn't Know About Memorial Day." *Time*. May 25, 2012. https://newsfeed.time.com/2012/05/28/7-things-you-didnt-know-about-memorial-day/slide/it-was-originally-called-decoration-day/.

"Gussie Busch." *Wikipedia*. Last modified July 31, 2020. https://en.wikipedia.org/wiki/Gussie_Busch.

"Henry Chadwick (Writer)." *Wikipedia*. Last modified August 20, 2021. https://en.wikipedia.org/wiki/Henry_Chadwick_(writer).

Heritage Auctions. "1884 Union Association Base Ball Contract—Only Example Known!" 2011 November 10–11 Vintage Sports Collectibles Signature Auction—Dallas #7041. 2011. https://sports.ha.com/itm/baseball-collectibles/others/1884-union-association-base-ball-contract-only-example-known-/a/7041-81202.s.

Jackson, Frank. "Lessons from Lakefront Park, 1884." *The Hardball Times*. July 5, 2012.

https://tht.fangraphs.com/lessons-from-lakefront-park-1884/.

Kittel, Jeffrey. *This Game of Games*. Accessed October 17, 2021. http://thisgameofgames.com/.

"Lady Baldwin." *Wikipedia*. Last modified July 12, 2020. https://en.wikipedia.org/wiki/Lady_Baldwin.

Lamb, Bill. "Tommy McCarthy." *SABR Baseball Biography Project*. Accessed August 21, 2021. https://sabr.org/bioproj/person/tommy-mccarthy/.

"League Park (Cincinnati)." *Wikipedia*. Last modified October 23, 2019. https://en.wikipedia.org/wiki/League_Park_(Cincinnati).

Lemoine, Bob. "Larry Corcoran." *SABR Baseball Biography Project*. Accessed August 21, 2021. https://sabr.org/bioproj/person/larry-corcoran/.

McKenna, Brian. "Baltimore Baseball: The Beginnings, 1858–1872." *Baltimore Baseball History*. 2018. https://bmorebbhistory.files.wordpress.com/2018/07/baltimore-baseball.pdf.

———. "Ed Swartwood." *SABR Baseball Biography Project*. Accessed August 21, 2021. https://sabr.org/bioproj/person/ed-swartwood/.

———. "Old Hoss Radbourn." *SABR Baseball Biography Project*. Accessed August 21, 2021. https://sabr.org/bioproj/person/old-hoss-radbourn/.

Miklich, Erik. "1867 Washington Nationals Tour." *19C Baseball*. 2016. http://www.19cbaseball.com/tours-1867-washington-nationals-tour.html.

"Negro Leagues Are Major Leagues." *Baseball Reference*. Last modified October 12, 2021. https://www.baseball-reference.com/negro-leagues-are-major-leagues.shtml.

Nemec, David. "Jack Clements." *SABR Baseball Biography Project*. Accessed August 21, 2021. https://sabr.org/bioproj/person/jack-clements/.

"New York Clipper." *Wikipedia*. Last modified April 21, 2021. https://en.wikipedia.org/wiki/New_York_Clipper.

Nicholls, Rochelle. "Joe Quinn." *SABR Baseball Biography Project*. Accessed August 21, 2021. https://sabr.org/bioproj/person/joe-quinn/.

Nisinger, Connie. "Charlie Hodnett." *Find A Grave*. October 24, 2011. https://www.findagrave.com/memorial/5885950/charles-hodnett.

Pajot, Dennis. "Anton Falch." *SABR Baseball Biography Project*. Accessed August 21, 2021. https://sabr.org/bioproj/person/anton-falch/.

"Peek-A-Boo Veach." *Wikipedia*. Last modified July 23, 2020. https://en.wikipedia.org/wiki/Peek-A-Boo_Veach.

Rainey, Chris. "Charlie Sweeney." *SABR Baseball Biography Project*. Accessed August 21, 2021. https://sabr.org/bioproj/person/charlie-sweeney/.

———. "Tommy Bond." *SABR Baseball Biography Project*. Accessed August 21, 2021. https://sabr.org/bioproj/person/tommy-bond/.

"Reserve rule." *Baseball Reference*. Last modified November 30, 2012. https://www.baseball-reference.com/bullpen/Reserve_clause.

"St. Thomas, Ontario." *Wikipedia*. Last modified June 12, 2020. https://en.wikipedia.org/wiki/St._Thomas,_Ontario.

"Sam Crane (Second Baseman)." *Wikipedia*. Last modified July 24, 2020. https://en.wikipedia.org/wiki/Sam_Crane_(second_baseman).

"Sunday Sporting Events." *Wikipedia*. Last modified July 19, 2021. https://en.wikipedia.org/wiki/Sunday_sporting_events.

Thomas, Joan M. "Henry V. Lucas." *SABR Baseball Biography Project*. Accessed August 21, 2021. https://sabr.org/bioproj/person/henry-v-lucas/.

———. "Union Base Ball Park (St. Louis)." *SABR Baseball Biography Project*. Accessed August 21, 2021. https://sabr.org/bioproj/park/union-base-ball-park-st-louis/.

Thorn, John. "Baseball's Bans and Blacklists." *Our Game*. February 8, 2016. https://ourgame.mlblogs.com/baseballs-bans-and-blacklists-5182f08d43ff.

———. "Henry Moore, Mystery Man of Baseball." *Our Game*. July 21, 2015. https://ourgame.mlblogs.com/henry-moore-mystery-man-of-baseball-80d9265bded4.

———. "The Only Nolan." *Our Game*. May 18, 2015. https://ourgame.mlblogs.com/the-only-nolan-bc7474dae960.

———. "Why Is the National Association Not a Major League ... and Other Records Issues." *Our Game*. May 4, 2015. https://ourgame.mlblogs.com/why-is-the-national-association-not-a-major-league-and-other-records-issues-7507e1683b66.

"2015–16 Golden State Warriors season." *Wikipedia*. Last modified July 10, 2020. https://en.wikipedia.org/wiki/2015%E2%80%9316_Golden_State_Warriors_season.

Vaccaro, Frank. "Hugh Daily." *SABR Baseball Biography Project*. Accessed August 21, 2021. https://sabr.org/bioproj/person/hugh-daily/.

———. "Ted Sullivan." *SABR Baseball Biography Project*. Accessed August 21, 2021. https://sabr.org/bioproj/person/ted-sullivan/.

Von Borries, Philip. "Pete Browning." *SABR Baseball Biography Project*. Accessed August 21, 2021. https://sabr.org/bioproj/person/pete-browning/.

Watterson, Jeremy. "Billy Colgan." *SABR Baseball Biography Project*. Accessed August 21, 2021. https://sabr.org/bioproj/person/billy-colgan/.

"William Edward White." *Wikipedia*. Last modified July 24, 2020. https://en.wikipedia.org/wiki/William_Edward_White.

Wolf, Gregory H. "Bill Hutchison." *SABR Baseball Biography Project*. Accessed August 21, 2021. https://sabr.org/bioproj/person/bill-hutchison/.

Books

Achorn, Edward. *Fifty-nine in '84*. New York: HarperCollins Plisher, 2011.

———. *The Summer of Beer and Whiskey*. New York: Public Affairs, 2013.

Cash, Jon David. *Before They Were Cardinals*. Columbia: University of Missouri Press, 2002.

Morris, Peter. *Catcher: How the Man Behind the*

Plate Became an American Folk Hero. Chicago: Ivan R. Dee, 2009.

Nemec, David. *The Great Encyclopedia of Nineteenth-Century Major League Baseball.* Tuscaloosa: University of Alabama Press, 2006.

_____. *Major League Baseball Profiles, 1871–1900, Volume 2.* Lincoln: University of Nebraska Press, 2011.

Nicholls, Rochelle Llewelyn. *Joe Quinn Among the Rowdies.* Jefferson, NC: McFarland, 2014.

Pajot, Denis. *The Rise of Milwaukee Baseball.* Jefferson, NC: McFarland, 2009.

Reichler, Joseph L., ed. *The Baseball Encyclopedia: The Complete and Official Record of Major League Baseball.* New York: Macmillan, 1969.

Seymour, Harold, and Dorothy Seymour Mills. *Baseball: The Early Years.* New York: Oxford University Press, 1989.

Spink, Alfred H. *The National Game.* 2nd edition. Carbondale: Southern Illinois University Press, [1911] 2000.

Sullivan, T.P. *Humorous Stories of the Ball Field.* Chicago: M.A. Donohue & Company, 1903.

Wright & Ditson's Base Ball Guide. Boston: Wright & Ditson, 1884.

Index

Numbers in *bold italics* indicate pages with illustrations